MISSION COLLEGE
LEARNING RESOURCE SERVICE
WITHDRAWN

D0481271

FOR REFERENCE
Do Not Take
From This Room

3 1215 00061 8501

MISSION COLLEGE
LEARNING RESOURCE SERVICE

Twentieth-Century

Short Story Explication

Supplement II to Third Edition

With Checklists of Books and Journals Used

WARREN S. WALKER
Horn Professor of English
Texas Tech University

THE SHOE STRING PRESS, INC.
1984

MISSION COLLEGE
LEARNING RESOURCE SERVICE

First edition published 1961
Supplement I to first edition published 1963
Supplement II to first edition published 1965
Second edition published 1967
Supplement I to second edition published 1970
Supplement II to second edition published 1973
Third edition published 1977
Supplement I to third edition published 1980
Supplement II to third edition published 1984

Third Edition, Supplement II
© The Shoe String Press, Inc., 1984
Hamden, Connecticut 06514

All rights reserved

Library of Congress Cataloging in Publication Data (Revised for vol. 2)

Walker, Warren S.
    Twentieth-century short story explication.

    Includes indexes.
    1. Short stories—Indexes. I. Title.
Z5917.S5W33   1977, Suppl [PN3373] v.   016.8093'1   80-16175
ISBN 0-208-02005-5 (3rd Ed., S.II)
ISBN 0-208-01813-1 (V. 1)

Printed in the United States of America

The paper in this book meets the guidelines for permanence
and durability of the Committee on Production Guidelines
for Book Longevity of the Council on Library Resources.

CONTENTS

PREFACE

Twentieth-Century Short Story Explication is a bibliography of interpretations which have appeared since 1900 of short stories published after 1800. In the Third Edition (1977) were materials on the works of 866 short story authors; Supplement I (1980) extended the number of authors by 186; this Second Supplement adds another 246, bringing the total number of short story writers cited to 1,298. The Third Edition carried the coverage through 31 December 1975; Supplement I moved the coverage forward through 1978; and the present volume includes primarily studies published during 1979, 1980, and 1981. Also included, however, are items previously overlooked or unavailable, as well as recent reprintings of earlier works. Reprintings of explications that appeared in the Third Edition are here preceded by an asterisk.

The term *short story* has the same meaning it carries in the Wilson Company's *Short Story Index*: ". . . a brief narrative of not more than 150 average-sized pages." By *explication* I suggest simply interpretation or explanation of the meaning of a story, including observations on theme, symbol, and sometimes structure. This excludes from the bibliography what are essentially studies of sources, biographical data, and background materials. Occasionally there are explicatory passages cited in works otherwise devoted to one of these external considerations. Page numbers refer strictly to interpretive passages, not to the longer works in which they occur.

Although the entries refer predominantly to studies written in English, the reader will also find citations of key materials in several other major languages of Western Europe. Attention is called to many important books published abroad as well as to articles in such readily available foreign-language journals as *Hispamerica, Monatshefte, French Review*, and *Slavic & East European Journal*.

The profusion of interpretations generated in the "knowledge explosion" required that, beginning with the Third Edition, we adopt a system of coding and consequently a format different from that used in the first two editions. Each book is cited by author or editor and a short title; the full title and publication data are provided in a Checklist of Books Used (533). For an article in a journal or an essay in a critical collection, the full publication information is provided the first time the study is cited. In subsequent entries only the critic's or scholar's name and a short title are used as long as these entries appear under the name of the same short story author; if an article or essay explicates stories by two or more authors, a complete initial entry is made for each author. As in Supplement I, we have again included a Checklist of Journals Used (386). This should be especially helpful to students who may not be familiar with the titles of professional journals, much less the abbreviations for such titles.

Again I am indebted to the editors of such journals as *PMLA, Modern Fiction Studies*, and *Journal of Modern Literature*. I wish to extend personal thanks to the Interlibrary Loan Department of Texas Tech University Library, particularly to Oleta Armstrong, Gloria Lyerla, and Jackie Underwood. As usual, my greatest debt is to my wife, Barbara K. Walker, for her untiring assistance.

Warren S. Walker
Texas Tech University

PARK ABBOTT

"Last Laugh"
Chu, Limin. *The Image of China*..., 191-193.

PETER ABRAHAMS

"The Virgin"
Ogungbesan, Kolawole. ...*Peter Abrahams*, 20-23.

CHINUA ACHEBE

"Akueke"
Carroll, David. *Chinua Achebe*, 2nd ed., 159-160.

"Civil Peace"
Carroll, David. *Chinua Achebe*, 2nd ed., 166-167.

"Dead Man's Path"
Carroll, David. *Chinua Achebe*, 2nd ed., 155-156.
Nandakumar, Prema. "The Theme of Religion in the Fiction of Chinua Achebe,"
   J Karnatak Univ, 20 (1970), 263.
Wren, Robert M. *Achebe's World*..., 15.

"Girls at War"
Carroll, David. *Chinua Achebe*, 2nd ed., 164-165.
Nandakumar, Prema. "The Theme of Religion...," 263-264.

"The Madman"
Carroll, David. *Chinua Achebe*, 2nd ed., 160-161.

"Marriage Is a Private Affair"
Carroll, David. *Chinua Achebe*, 2nd ed., 155.
Wren, Robert M. *Achebe's World*..., 14-15.

"The Sacrificial Egg"
Carroll, David. *Chinua Achebe*, 2nd ed., 156-158.

"Uncle Ben's Choice"
Carroll, David. *Chinua Achebe*, 2nd ed., 158-159.

"Vengeful Creditors"
Carroll, David. *Chinua Achebe*, 2nd ed., 162-164.

JAMES AGEE

"Dream Sequence"
Doty, Mark A. *Tell Me Who I Am*..., 104-116.

"The Morning Watch"
Doty, Mark A. *Tell Me Who I Am*..., 75-86.

"The Waiting"
*Mizener, Arthur. *A Handbook*..., 4th ed., 115-117.

SHMUEL YOSEF AGNON [SHMUEL YOSEF CZACZKES]

"Another Face"
Winchell, Mark R. "Fear of Falling: Point of View in Agnon's 'Another Face,'"
    So Central Bull, 41 (1981), 124-126.

"Edo and Enam"
Ben-Amos, Dan. "Nationalism and Nihilism: The Attitudes of Two Hebrew
    Authors Toward Folklore," *Int'l Folklore R*, 1 (1981), 15-16.

Schaked, G. "S. Y. Agnon –'Ido und Enam': Versuch einer Interpretation," *Colloquia
    Germanica*, 1 (1970), 84-99.

"The Face and the Image"
Baumgarten, Murray. "Mirror of Words: Language in Agnon and Borges," *Comp
    Lit*, 31 (1979), 360-363.

AGYEYA [whole name]

"Gangrene"
Karn, Chandreshwar. "The Short Stories of Agyeya," *Indian Lit*, 22, v (1979), 32.

ILSE AICHINGER

"Wo ich wohne"
Nicolai, Ralf R. "'Wo ich wohne': Ilse Aichingers Kritik des modernen Bewusst-
    seins," *Literatur und Kritik*, 153 (1981), 175-179.

AMA ATA AIDOO

"Certain Winds from the South"
Brown, Lloyd W. *Women Writers in Black Africa*, 108-110.

"Everything Counts"
Brown, Lloyd W. *Women Writers in Black Africa*, 118-119.

"For Whom Things Did Not Change"
Brown, Lloyd W. *Women Writers in Black Africa*, 114-116.

"A Gift from Somewhere"
*Brown, Lloyd W. *Women Writers in Black Africa*, 104-108.

"In the Cutting of a Drink"
*Brown, Lloyd W. *Women Writers in Black Africa*, 101-104.

"Last of the Proud Ones"
Brown, Lloyd W. *Women Writers in Black Africa*, 100-101.

"The Late Bud"
Little, Kenneth. ...*Urban Women's Image*..., 74-75.

"The Message"
Brown, Lloyd W. *Women Writers in Black Africa*, 112-114.

"No Sweetness Here"
*Brown, Lloyd W. *Women Writers in Black Africa*, 116-118.

"Something to Talk About on the Way to the Funeral"
*Brown, Lloyd W. *Women Writers in Black Africa*, 110-112.

"The Two Sisters"
Brown, Lloyd W. *Women Writers in Black Africa*, 119-121.
Little, Kenneth. ...*Urban Women's Image*..., 13-14.

CONRAD AIKEN

"The Dark City"
Waterman, Arthur. "The Short Stories of Conrad Aiken," *Stud Short Fiction*, 16
    (1979), 26-27.

"The Last Visit"
Waterman, Arthur. "The Short Stories...," 22-23.

"Life Isn't a Short Story"
Waterman, Arthur. "The Short Stories...," 27-28.

"Round by Round"
Allen, Walter. *The Short Story*..., 136-138.

"Silent Snow, Secret Snow"
Altenbernd, Lynn, and Leslie L. Lewis. *Instructor's Manual*..., 3rd ed., 1-2.
Slap, Laura A. "Conrad Aiken's 'Silent Snow, Secret Snow': Defense Against the
    Primal Scene," *Am Imago*, 37 (1980), 1-11.
Waterman, Arthur. "The Short Stories...," 24-25.

"Spider, Spider"
Waterman, Arthur. "The Short Stories . . .," 29–30.

"Strange Moonlight"
Waterman, Arthur. "The Short Stories . . .," 28–29.

"Thistledown"
Waterman, Arthur. "The Short Stories . . .," 24.

"Your Obituary, Well Written"
Waterman, Arthur. "The Short Stories . . .," 23.

CHINGIZ AITMATOV

"Farewell, Gul'sary!"
Shneidman, N. N. *Soviet Literature* . . . , 35–36.

"Spotted Dog by the Sea's Edge"
Shneidman, N. N. *Soviet Literature* . . . , 41–43.

VASILY AKSENOV

"Halfway to the Moon"
Johnson, John J. "Introduction: The Life and Works of Aksenov," in Aksenov, Varsily. *"The Steel Bird" and Other Stories*, xiii–xiv.
Meyer, Priscilla. "Aksenov and the Soviet Literature of the 1960s," *Russian Lit Tri-Q*, 6 (Spring, 1973), 451–452.

"Local Troublemaker Abramashvili"
Johnson, John J. "Introduction . . .," xvii–xviii.

"The Odd-Ball"
Johnson, John J. "Introduction . . .," xvii.

"Oranges from Morocco"
Johnson, John J. "Introduction . . .," xiv–xv.
Meyer, Priscilla. "Aksenov . . .," 452–453.

"The Overloaded Packing-Barrels" [same as "The Overstocked Tare of Barrels"]
Brown, Deming. . . . *Literature Since Stalin*, 202–203.
Johnson, John J. "Introduction . . .," xxiii–xxv.

"Papa, What Does It Spell?"
Johnson, John J. "Introduction . . .," xii–xiii.
Meyer, Priscilla. "Aksenov . . .," 452.

"Paved Roads"
Johnson, John J. "Introduction . . .," x.

"Rendezvous"
Brown, Deming. . . . *Literature Since Stalin*, 203.

"The Steel Bird"
Johnson, John J. "Introduction...," xix–xxii.

"The Strange One"
Brown, Deming. ...*Literature Since Stalin*, 201–202.

"A Ticket to the Stars"
Meyer, Priscilla, "Aksenov...," 451.

"Victory"
Meyer, Priscilla. "Aksenov...," 455.

AKUTAGAWA RYŪNOSUKE

"Cogwheels"
Yamanouchi, Hisaaki. *The Search for Authenticity*..., 101–103.

"The Handkerchief"
Yamanouchi, Hisaaki. *The Search for Authenticity*..., 96–97.

"The Hell Screen"
Yamanouchi, Hisaaki. *The Search for Authenticity*..., 92–93.

"In a Grove"
Yamanouchi, Hisaaki. *The Search for Authenticity*..., 93–94.

"Kappa"
Yamanouchi, Hisaaki. *The Search for Authenticity*..., 99–100.

"Tobacco and the Devil"
Yamanouchi, Hisaaki. *The Search for Authenticity*..., 94.

PEDRO ANTONIO DE ALARCÓN

"The Comendadora"
DeCoster, Cyrus. *Pedro Antonio de Alarcón*, 40–41.

"Death's Friend"
DeCoster, Cyrus. *Pedro Antonio de Alarcón*, 45–46.

"The Foreigner"
DeCoster, Cyrus. *Pedro Antonio de Alarcón*, 36.

"The French Sympathizer"
DeCoster, Cyrus. *Pedro Antonio de Alarcón*, 35–36.

"Moors and Christians"
DeCoster, Cyrus. *Pedro Antonio de Alarcón*, 47–48.

"The Nail"
DeCoster, Cyrus. *Pedro Antonio de Alarcón*, 38–40.

"The Six Veils"
DeCoster, Cyrus. *Pedro Antonio de Alarcón*, 45.

"The Tall Woman"
DeCoster, Cyrus. *Pedro Antonio de Alarcón*, 46–47.

"The Wooden Cross"
DeCoster, Cyrus. *Pedro Antonio de Alarcón*, 43.

IGNACIO ALDECOA

"Amadis"
Fiddian, Robin. *Ignacio Aldecoa*, 134–135.

"The Apprentice Conductor"
Fiddian, Robin. *Ignacio Aldecoa*, 94–95.

"An Artist Called Pheasant"
Fiddian, Robin. *Ignacio Aldecoa*, 122–123.

"At the 400 Kilometer Mark"
Fiddian, Robin. *Ignacio Aldecoa*, 109–110.

"Ballad of the River Manzanares"
Fiddian, Robin. *Ignacio Aldecoa*, 116–117.

"Benito the Libelist"
Fiddian, Robin. *Ignacio Aldecoa*, 124–125.

"Bird of Paradise"
Fiddian, Robin. *Ignacio Aldecoa*, 130–132.

"The Birds of Baden Baden"
Fiddian, Robin. *Ignacio Aldecoa*, 132–134.

"The Bus at 7:40"
Fiddian, Robin. *Ignacio Aldecoa*, 105–106.

"A Buzzard Has Made Its Nest in the Café"
Fiddian, Robin. *Ignacio Aldecoa*, 127–129.

"The Eye of Silence"
Fiddian, Robin. *Ignacio Aldecoa*, 99–100.

"The Folk from Andin Lane"
Fiddian, Robin. *Ignacio Aldecoa*, 101–103.

"The Heart and Other Bitter Fruits"
Fiddian, Robin. *Ignacio Aldecoa*, 113–114.

"The Humble Life of Sebastián Zafra"
Fiddian, Robin. *Ignacio Aldecoa*, 92–94.

"The Market"
Fiddian, Robin. *Ignacio Aldecoa*, 103-105.

"The Owl's Hoot"
Fiddian, Robin. *Ignacio Aldecoa*, 129-130.

"The Picador's Mount"
Fiddian, Robin. *Ignacio Aldecoa*, 114-115.

"Saint Eulalia of Steel"
Fiddian, Robin. *Ignacio Aldecoa*, 100-101.

"The Stones in the Wilderness"
Fiddian, Robin. *Ignacio Aldecoa*, 118.

"Young Sánchez"
Fiddian, Robin. *Ignacio Aldecoa*, 110-111.

BRIAN W. ALDISS

"The Saliva Tree"
Wendell, Carolyn. "The Alien Species: A Study of Women Characters in the
Nebula Award Winners, 1965-1973," *Extrapolation*, 20 (1979), 349-350.

THOMAS BAILEY ALDRICH

"Marjorie Daw"
Smith, Elliott L., and Andrew W. Hart, Eds. *The Short Story*..., 236-238.

SHOLOM ALEICHEM [SHOLOM RABINOWITZ]

"Dreyfus in Kasrilevke"
Alexander, Edward. *The Resonance of Dust*..., 7-8.

SABAHATTIN ALI

"Geese"
Soucek, Svat. "Sabahattin Ali," *Turkish Stud Assoc Bull*, 5, i (1981), 13.

"Hasanboğuldu"
Soucek, Svat. "Sabahattin Ali," 14-15.

"The Ox Cart"
Soucek, Svat. "Sabahattin Ali," 13-14.

"Voice"
Soucek, Svat. "Sabahattin Ali," 14.

MARIAN ALLEN

"Ah Foo, the Fortune Teller"
Chu, Limin. *The Image of China* . . . , 185-186.

JOÃO ALPHONSUS

"Skyrockets in the Distance"
Sadlier, Darlene J. "The Pattern of Contradiction As Narrative Technique in João
  Alphonsus's 'Foguetes ao longe,'" *Stud Short Fiction*, 18 (1981), 171-177.

GUSTAVO ALVAREZ GARDEAZÁBAL

"La boba y el Buda"
Gyurko, Lanin A. "The Phantasmagoric World of Gardeazábal," *Hispanic J*, 2, i
  (1980), 27-40.

KINGSLEY AMIS

"All the Blood Within Me"
Gardner, Philip. *Kingsley Amis*, 138-141.

"Dear Illusion"
Gardner, Philip. *Kingsley Amis*, 141-143.

"I Spy Strangers"
Gardner, Philip. *Kingsley Amis*, 136-138.

"Moral Fibre"
Gardner, Philip. *Kingsley Amis*, 134-135.

POUL ANDERSON

"Sam Hall"
Warrick, Patricia S. *The Cybernetic Imagination* . . . , 141-142.

SHERWOOD ANDERSON

"Adventure"
Atlas, Marilyn J. "Sherwood Anderson and the Women of Winesburg," in
  Anderson, David D., Ed. *Critical Essays* . . . , 259-260.
Rigsbee, Sally A. "The Feminine in *Winesburg, Ohio*," *Stud Am Fiction*, 9 (1981),
  235-236.

"The Book of the Grotesque"
Stouck, David. "*Winesburg, Ohio* As a Dance of Death," *Am Lit*, 48 (1977), 532-533;
  rpt. Anderson, David D., Ed. *Critical Essays* . . . , 186-187.

"Death"
Rigsbee, Sally A. "The Feminine...," 240–241.

"Death in the Woods"
Barker, Gerard A. *Instructor's Manual*..., 18–20.
Brooks, Cleanth, and Robert P. Warren. *Instructor's Manual*..., 3rd ed., 37–39.
Ferguson, Mary A. "Sherwood Anderson's 'Death in the Woods': Toward a New Reading," *Midamerica*, 7 (1980), 73–95; rpt. Anderson, David D., Ed. *Critical Essays*..., 217–234.
Rohrberger, Mary. *Instructor's Manual*..., 17–18.

"Departure"
*Gold, Herbert. "The Purity and Cunning of Sherwood Anderson," in Anderson, David D., Ed. *Critical Essays*..., 142.

"Drink"
Stouck, David. "...Dance of Death," 534; rpt. Anderson, David D., Ed. *Critical Essays*..., 187–188.

"The Egg"
Bassett, Patrick and Barbara. "Anderson's 'The Egg,'" *Explicator*, 40, i (1981), 53–54.
Mesher, David R. "A Triumph of the Ego in Anderson's 'The Egg,'" *Stud Short Fiction*, 17 (1980), 180–183.
*Mizener, Arthur. *A Handbook*..., 4th ed., 142–144.
Savin, Mark. "Coming Full Circle: Sherwood Anderson's 'The Egg,'" *Stud Short Fiction*, 18 (1981), 454–457.
Scott, Virgil, and David Madden. *Instructor's Manual*..., 4th ed., 12–14; Madden, David. *Instructor's Manual*..., 5th ed., 71–73.

"Godliness"
Atlas, Marilyn J. "...Women of Winesburg," 258–259.

"Hands"
Stouck, David. "...Dance of Death," 533; rpt. Anderson, David D., Ed. *Critical Essays*..., 187.

"I Want to Know Why"
Bischoff, Peter. "Zur Genese der modernen amerikanischen Short Story: Sherwood Andersons 'I Want to Know Why,'" *Arbeiten aus Anglistik und Amerikanistik*, 6 (1981), 261–271.
Fetterley, Judith. *The Resisting Reader*..., 12–22.

"I'm a Fool"
Altenbernd, Lynn, and Leslie L. Lewis. *Instructor's Manual*..., 3rd ed., 3.
Pecile, Jordon. "On Sherwood Anderson and 'I'm a Fool,'" in Skaggs, Calvin, Ed. *The American Short Story*, I, 148–149.

"Loneliness"
*Gold, Herbert. "The Purity...," 141–142.

"A Man of Ideas"
Atlas, Marilyn J. "...Women of Winesburg," 259.

"The Man Who Became a Woman"
*Gold, Herbert. "The Purity...," 141.
Malmsheimer, Lonna M. "Sexual Metaphor and Social Criticism in Anderson's
'The Man Who Became a Woman,'" *Stud Am Fiction*, 7, i (1979), 17-26.

"Mother"
Rigsbee, Sally A. "The Feminine...," 237-239.

"The New Englander"
*Weber, Brom. "Anderson and 'The Essence of Things,'" in Anderson, David D.,
Ed. *Critical Essays...*, 132-134.

"Paper Pills"
Atlas, Marilyn J. "...Women of Winesburg," 256-257.

"Queer"
Stouck, David. "...Dance of Death," 534; rpt. Anderson, David D., Ed. *Critical
Essays...*, 188.

"Respectability"
Atlas, Marilyn J. "...Women of Winesburg," 260-261.

"Sophistication"
Stouck, David. "...Dance of Death," 537-538; rpt. Anderson, David D., Ed. *Critical
Essays...*, 190-191.

"Surrender"
Rigsbee, Sally A. "The Feminine...," 234.

"Unlighted Lamps"
Ahrends, Günter. *...Kurzgeschichte*, 141-143.

"The Untold Lie"
*Gold, Herbert. "The Purity...," 140-141.

ENRIQUE ANDERSON IMBERT

"Blackout in New York"
Lusky, Mary H. "The Function of Fantasy: Creativity and Isolation as Related
Themes in the Fiction of Enrique Anderson Imbert," *Latin Am Lit R*, 7
(1979), 32-33.

"The Determinist Goblins"
Lusky, Mary H. "The Function of Fantasy...," 36.

"The General Makes a Fine Corpse"
Lusky, Mary H. "The Function of Fantasy...," 36-37.

"The Ghost"
Lusky, Mary H. "The Function of Fantasy...," 29-30.

"My Cousin May"
Lusky, Mary H. "The Function of Fantasy...," 37.

"The Queen of the Forest"
Lusky, Mary H. "The Function of Fantasy...," 30.

IVO ANDRIC

"Alipasha"
Johnson, Vida T. "Ivo Andric's *Kuca na Osami* (*The House in a Secluded Place*): Memories and Ghosts of the Writer's Past," in Birnbaum, Henrik, and Thomas Eekman, Eds. *Fiction and Drama*..., 243-244.

"Baron Dorn"
Johnson, Vida T. "...Writer's Past," 244.

"Bonvalpasha"
Johnson, Vida T. "...Writer's Past," 243.

"Lives"
Johnson, Vida T. "...Writer's Past," 246-247.

"Loves"
Johnson, Vida T. "...Writer's Past," 247.

"The Slave Girl"
Johnson, Vida T. "...Writer's Past," 245-246.

"A Story"
Johnson, Vida T. "...Writer's Past," 245.

RAFAEL ARÉVALO MARTÍNEZ

"Bewitched"
Salgado, María A. *Rafael Arévalo Martínez*, 112-113.

"The Colombian Troubadour"
Salgado, María A. *Rafael Arévalo Martínez*, 105-106.

"La Farnecina"
Salgado, María A. *Rafael Arévalo Martínez*, 114-115.

"The Man Who Looked Like a Horse"
Salgado, María A. *Rafael Arévalo Martínez*, 99-105.

"Sexual Complexity"
Salgado, María A. *Rafael Arévalo Martínez*, 113-114.

"The Sign of the Sphynx"
Salgado, María A. *Rafael Arévalo Martínez*, 108-111.

"The Wild Beasts of the Tropics"
Salgado, María A. *Rafael Arévalo Martínez*, 106-108.

JOSÉ MARÍA ARGUEDAS

"Los escoleros"
Muñoz, Silverio. "El juego como propedéutica social en 'Los escoleros,'" *Revista de Crítica*, 6, xii (1980), 41-53.

"Warma Kuyay"
Muñoz, Silverio. "Exilio y lirismo en 'Warma Kuyay,'" *Romance Notes*, 22 (1981), 20-26.

"Water"
Escobar, Alberto. "La utopía de la lengua en el primer Arguedas," *Revista de Crítica*, 6, xii (1980), 7-40.

JUAN JOSÉ ARREOLA

"The Switchman"
Cheever, Leonard A. "The Little Girl and the Cat: 'Kafkaesque' Elements in Arreola's 'The Switchman,'" *Am Hispanist*, 7, xxxiv-xxxv (1979), 3-4.

SHOLEM ASCH
"Kola Street"
Gittleman, Sol. *From Shtetl to Suburbia...*, 98-100.

"A Quiet Garden Spot"
Gittleman, Sol. *From Shtetl to Suburbia...*, 135-136.

"Sanctification of the Name"
Gittleman, Sol. *From Shtetl to Suburbia...*, 96-98.

ISAAC ASIMOV

"The Bicentennial Man"
Warrick, Patricia S. *The Cybernetic Imagination...*, 71-74.
———. "The Contrapuntal Design of Artificial Evolution in Asimov's 'The Bicentennial Man,'" *Extrapolation*, 22 (1981), 231-241.

"Feminine Intuition"
Warrick, Patricia S. *The Cybernetic Imagination...*, 69-70.

"The Life and Times of Multivac"
Warrick, Patricia S. *The Cybernetic Imagination...*, 68-69.

"Nightfall"
Rose, Mark. *Alien Encounter...*, 41–43.

VIKTOR ASTAF'EV

"The King of the Fish"
Shneidman, N. N. *Soviet Literature...*, 21.

EDWIN V. ATKINSON

"A Study in Ochre"
Chu, Limin. *The Image of China...*, 188.

MARGARET ATWOOD

"Dancing Girls"
Davidson, Arnold E. and Cathy N., Eds. *The Art...*, 112–113.

"Giving Birth"
Davidson, Arnold E. and Cathy N., Eds. *The Art...*, 117–119.

"The Hair Jewellery"
Davidson, Arnold E. and Cathy N., Eds. *The Art...*, 113–114.

"The Lives of the Poets"
Davidson, Arnold E. and Cathy N., Eds. *The Art...*, 115.

"The Man from Mars"
Davidson, Arnold E. and Cathy N., Eds. *The Art...*, 111–112.

"Polarities"
Davidson, Arnold E. and Cathy N., Eds. *The Art...*, 121–122.
Houghton, Gregory. "Margaret Atwood: Some Observations and Textual Considerations," *World Lit Written Engl*, 20 (1981), 85–92.

"Rape Fantasies"
Davidson, Arnold E. and Cathy N., Eds. *The Art...*, 115–116.

"The Resplendent Quetzal"
Davidson, Arnold E. and Cathy N., Eds. *The Art...*, 114–115.

"A Travel Piece"
Davidson, Arnold E. and Cathy N., Eds. *The Art...*, 116–117.

"Under Glass"
Davidson, Arnold E. and Cathy N., Eds. *The Art...*, 119–120.

"The War in the Bathroom"
Davidson, Arnold E. and Cathy N., Eds. *The Art...*, 110–111.

STACY AUMONIER

"The Two Friends"
Allen, Walter. *The Short Story*..., 162-164.

MARY HUNTER AUSTIN

"The Bandit's Prayer"
*Robinson, Cecil. *Mexico*..., 244-245.

"The Conversion of Ah Lew Sing"
Chu, Limin. *The Image of China*..., 198-199.

"The Politeness of Cuesta La Plata"
Robinson, Cecil. *Mexico*..., 207-208.

WILLIAM AUSTIN

"Peter Rugg, the Missing Man"
Doubleday, Neal F. *Variety of Attempt*..., 117-123.

MARCEL AYMÉ

"Les Bottes de sept lieues"
Lord, Graham. *The Short Stories*..., 81-82, 124-125.

"La Canne"
Lord, Graham. *The Short Stories*..., 113-114.

"La Carte"
Lord, Graham. *The Short Stories*..., 103-104.

"La Clé sous le paillasson"
Lord, Graham. *The Short Stories*..., 80-81.

"Les Clochards"
Lord, Graham. *The Short Stories*..., 115-116.

"Dermuche"
Lord, Graham. *The Short Stories*..., 38-39.

"Deux victimes"
Lord, Graham. *The Short Stories*..., 119-120.

"En arriète"
Lord, Graham. *The Short Stories*..., 137-138.

"En attendant"
Lord, Graham. *The Short Stories*..., 131-133.

"La Fabrique"
Lord, Graham. *The Short Stories...*, 41–42.

"Fiançailles"
Lord, Graham. *The Short Stories...*, 23–24.

"L'Huissier"
Lord, Graham. *The Short Stories...*, 27–29.

"L'Individu"
Lord, Graham. *The Short Stories...*, 107–108.

"Josse"
Lord, Graham. *The Short Stories...*, 139–140.

"Legénde poldève"
Lord, Graham. *The Short Stories...*, 25–26.
Lorian, Al. "Les Noms aimés de Marcel Aymé," *Studii şi Cercetàri Lingvistice*, 31 (1980), 571–575.

"Le Loup"
Lord, Graham. *The Short Stories...*, 70–72.

"Le Passe-muraille"
Lord, Graham. *The Short Stories...*, 52–53.

"Rechute"
Lord, Graham. *The Short Stories...*, 52–53.

"Samson"
Lord, Graham. *The Short Stories...*, 44–45.

"Traversée de Paris"
Lord, Graham. *The Short Stories...*, 146–148.

"La Vamp et le Normalien"
Lord, Graham. *The Short Stories...*, 154–155.

"Le Vin de Paris"
Lord, Graham. *The Short Stories...*, 108–109.

AZORÍN [JOSÉ MARTÍNEZ RUIZ]

"The Closed House"
Sieburth, Renée. "Commentary on Azorín's 'La casa cerrada,'" *Revista Danadiense de Estudios Hispánicos*, 3 (1979), 291–296.

"The Clouds"
Glenn, Kathleen M. *Azorín...*, 23–24.

"Don Quixote, Vanquished"
Glenn, Kathleen M. *Azorín*..., 125–126.

"The Good Judge"
Glenn, Kathleen M. *Azorín*..., 68–69.

ISAAC EMMANUILOVICH BABEL

"Di Grasso"
Freiden, Gregory. "Fat Tuesday in Odessa: Isaac Babel's 'Di Grasso' as Testament and Manifesto," *Russian R*, 40 (1981), 101–121.

"My First Goose"
Altenbernd, Lynn, and Leslie L. Lewis. *Instructor's Manual*..., 3rd ed., 4.

INGEBORG BACHMANN

"Ein Schritt nach Gomorrha"
Dodds, Dinah. "The Lesbian Relationship in Bachmann's 'Ein Schritt nach Gomorrha,'" *Monatshefte*, 72 (1980), 431–438.

JAMES BALDWIN

"Come Out the Wilderness"
Sylvander, Carolyn W. *James Baldwin*, 119–121.

"Exodus"
Altenbernd, Lynn, and Leslie L. Lewis. *Instructor's Manual*..., 3rd ed., 5.

"Going to Meet the Man"
Ahrends, Günter. ...*Kurzgeschichte*, 187–189.
Barker, Gerard A. *Instructor's Manual*..., 61–63.
Sylvander, Carolyn W. *James Baldwin*, 121–123.
Whitlock, Roger. "Baldwin's 'Going to Meet the Man': Racial Brutality and Sexual Gratification," *Am Imago*, 34 (1977), 351–356.

"Man Child"
Sylvander, Carolyn W. *James Baldwin*, 112–114.

"The Outing"
Sylvander, Carolyn W. *James Baldwin*, 111–112.

"The Rockpile"
Altenbernd, Lynn, and Leslie L. Lewis. *Instructor's Manual*..., 3rd ed., 5–6.
Sylvander, Carolyn W. *James Baldwin*, 110–111.

"Sonny's Blues"
Franzbecker, Rolf. "Music versus Language? James Baldwin's 'Sonny's Blues' als Paradigma zwischenmenschlicher Kommunikationsproblematik," *Anglistik & Englischunterricht*, 9 (December, 1979), 107–129.

Lobb, Edward. "James Baldwin's Blues and the Function of Art," *Int'l Fiction R*,
6, ii (1979), 143–148.
Sylvander, Carolyn W. *James Baldwin*, 116–117.

"This Morning, This Evening, So Soon"
Scott, Virgil, and David Madden. *Instructor's Manual...*, 4th ed., 97–99.
Sylvander, Carolyn W. *James Baldwin*, 116–119.

J. G. BALLARD

"The Overloaded Man"
Franklin, H. Bruce. "What Are We to Make of J. G. Ballard's Apocalypse?" in
Clareson, Thomas D., Ed. *Voices for the Future...*, II, 87–88.

"The Subliminal Man"
Franklin, H. Bruce. "What Are We...," 99–100.

JOSÉ BALZA

"Un libro de Rodolfo Iliackwood"
Miranda, Julio E. "Balza, Mata, Britto: Un intertexto," *Escritura*, 4, vii (1979),
117–127.

HONORÉ DE BALZAC

"The Abandoned Woman"
Festa-McCormick, Diana. *Honoré de Balzac*, 130–131.

"Christ in Flanders"
Vandegans, André. "'Jésus-Christ en Flandres,' Erasme et Ghelderode," *L'Année
Balzacienne*, [n.v.] (1978), 27–48.

"Gobseck"
Pasco, Allan H. "Descriptive Narration in Balzac's 'Gobseck,'" *Virginia Q R*,
56 (1980), 99–108.

"The House of the Cat and the Racket"
Festa-McCormick, Diana. *Honoré de Balzac*, 124–125.

"Louis Lambert"
Festa-McCormick, Diana. *Honoré de Balzac*, 36–40.

"A Passion in the Desert"
Madden, David. *Instructor's Manual...*, 5th ed., 44–45.
Smith, Elliott L. and Wanda V. *Instructor's Manual...*, 3–4.

"The Secrets of the Princess Cadignan"
Festa-McCormick, Diana. *Honoré de Balzac*, 126–129.

TONI CADE BAMBARA

"My Man Bovanne"
Rosinsky, Natalie M. "Mothers and Daughters: Another Minority Group," in
Davidson, Cathy N., and E. M. Broner, Eds. *The Lost Tradition...*, 283–284.

IMAMU AMIRI BARAKA [formerly LE ROI JONES]

"The Alternative"
Brown, Lloyd W. *Amiri Baraka*, 90–91.
Lacey, Henry C. *To Raise, Destroy, and Create...*, 182–186.

"Answers in Progress"
Lacey, Henry C. *To Raise, Destroy, and Create...*, 193–194.

"A Chase (Alighieri's Dream)"
Brown, Lloyd W. *Amiri Baraka*, 89–90.
Lacey, Henry C. *To Raise, Destroy, and Create...*, 181–182.

"The Death of Horatio Alger"
Brown, Lloyd W. *Amiri Baraka*, 91–93.
Lacey, Henry C. *To Raise, Destroy, and Create...*, 177–179.

"Going Down Slow"
Brown, Lloyd W. *Amiri Baraka*, 95–96.
Lacey, Henry C. *To Raise, Destroy, and Create...*, 187–188.

"Heroes Are Gang Leaders"
Brown, Lloyd W. *Amiri Baraka*, 95–96.
Lacey, Henry C. *To Raise, Destroy, and Create...*, 186–187.

"The Largest Ocean in the World"
Brown, Lloyd W. *Amiri Baraka*, 93–94.

"No Body No Place"
Brown, Lloyd W. *Amiri Baraka*, 100–101.

"Salute"
Brown, Lloyd W. *Amiri Baraka*, 96–97.

"The Screamers"
Brown, Lloyd W. *Amiri Baraka*, 100.
Lacey, Henry C. *To Raise, Destroy, and Create...*, 178–180.

"Uncle Tom's Cabin: Alternate Ending"
Brown, Lloyd W. *Amiri Baraka*, 87–88.
Lacey, Henry C. *To Raise, Destroy, and Create...*, 174–177.

"Unfinished"
Lacey, Henry C. *To Raise, Destroy, and Create...*, 190–192.

N. BARANSKAYA

"Just Another Week"
Gasiorowska, Xenia. "On Happiness in Recent Soviet Fiction," *Russian Lit Tri-Q*, 9 (Spring, 1974), 475–477.

JULES AMÉDÉE BARBEY D'AUREVILLY

"A un dîner d'athées"
Tranouez, Pierre. "Un Récit révocatoire: 'A un dîner d'athées,'" *Littérature*, 38 (1980), 27–42.

DJUNA BARNES

"Cassation"
Fuchs, Miriam. "Djuna Barnes: 'Spillway' into Nightmare," *Hollins Critic*, 18, iii (1981), 4.

"Go Down, Matthews"
Fuchs, Miriam. "Djuna Barnes...," 6.

PIO BAROJA

"The Bakers"
Landeira, Ricardo L., and Janet W. Díaz. "Irony and Death in Pio Baroja's 'Los panaderos,'" in Bowman, Sylvia, *et al.*, Eds. *Studies... Gerald E. Wade*, 121–132.

RAYMOND BARRIO

"The Campesinos"
Scott, Virgil, and David Madden. *Instructor's Manual...*, 4th ed., 106–108.

JOHN BARTH

"Ambrose His Mark"
Hinden, Michael. "*Lost in the Funhouse*: Barth's Use of the Recent Past," *Twentieth Century Lit*, 19 (1973), 110; rpt. Waldmeir, Joseph J., Ed. *Critical Essays on John Barth*, 193.

"Bellerophoniad"
Davis, Cynthia. "'The Key to the Treasure': Narrative Movements and Effects in *Chimera*," *J Narrative Technique*, 5 (1975), 109–110; rpt. Waldmeir, Joseph J., Ed. *Critical Essays on John Barth*, 221–222.
Powell, Jerry. "John Barth's *Chimera*: A Creative Response to the Literature of Exhaustion," *Critique*, 18, ii (1976), 63–65; rpt. Waldmeir, Joseph J., Ed. *Critical Essays on John Barth*, 232–234.

"Chimera"
Davis, Cynthia. "Heroes, Earth Mothers, and Muses: Gender Identity in Barth's Fiction," *Centennial R*, 24 (1980), 315-319.

"Dunyazadiad"
Davis, Cynthia. "'The Key to the Treasure'. . .," 105-107; rpt. Waldmeir, Joseph J., Ed. *Critical Essays on John Barth*, 217-220.
Powell, Jerry. "John Barth's *Chimera*. . .," 60-61; rpt. Waldmeir, Joseph J., Ed. *Critical Essays on John Barth*, 229-230.

"Echo"
Bienstock, Beverly G. "Lingering on the Autognostic Verge: John Barth's *Lost in the Funhouse*," *Mod Fiction Stud*, 19 (1973), 70-71; rpt. Waldmeir, Joseph J., Ed. *Critical Essays on John Barth*, 202.
Ziegler, Heide. "John Barth's 'Echo': The Story in Love with Its Author," *Int'l Fiction R*, 7 (1980), 90-93.

"Life-Story"
Bienstock, Beverly G. "Lingering. . .," 71-72; rpt. Waldmeir, Joseph J., Ed. *Critical Essays on John Barth*, 202-203.
Gardner, John. *On Moral Fiction*, 95-96.
Howard, Daniel F., and John Ribar. *Instructor's Manual*. . ., 4th ed., 77.

"Lost in the Funhouse"
Ahrends, Günter. . . . *Kurzgeschichte*, 218-221.
Baker, Sheridan, and George Perkins. *Instructor's Manual*. . ., 32.
Bienstock, Beverly G. "Lingering. . .," 74-77; rpt. Waldmeir, Joseph J., Ed. *Critical Essays on John Barth*, 206-208.
Hinden, Michael. "*Lost in the Funhouse*. . .," 112-113; rpt. Waldmeir, Joseph J., Ed. *Critical Essays on John Barth*, 195-196.
Howard, Daniel F., and William Plummer. *Instructor's Manual*. . ., 3rd ed., 76; rpt. Howard, Daniel F., and John Ribar. *Instructor's Manual*. . ., 4th ed., 76.
Knapp, Edgar H. "Found in the Barthhouse: Novelist as Savior," *Mod Fiction Stud*, 14 (1969), 446-451; rpt. Waldmeir, Joseph J., Ed. *Critical Essays on John Barth*, 183-189.
Mizener, Arthur. *A Handbook*. . ., 4th ed., 165-168.
Seymour, Thom. "One Small Joke and a Packed Paragraph in John Barth's 'Lost in the Funhouse,'" *Stud Short Fiction*, 16 (1979), 189-194.

"Menelaiad"
Bienstock, Beverly G. "Lingering. . .," 71-74; rpt. Waldmeir, Joseph J., Ed. *Critical Essays on John Barth*, 203-206.
Hinden, Michael. "*Lost in the Funhouse*. . .," 114-115; rpt. Waldmeir, Joseph J., Ed. *Critical Essays on John Barth*, 197-198.

"Night-Sea Journey"
Hinden, Michael. "*Lost in the Funhouse*. . .," 111-112; rpt. Waldmeir, Joseph J., Ed. *Critical Essays on John Barth*, 194-195.

"Perseid"
Davis, Cynthia. "'The Key to the Treasure'. . .," 107-109; rpt. Waldmeir, Joseph J., Ed. *Critical Essays on John Barth*, 220-221.

Powell, Jerry. "John Barth's *Chimera*...," 61-63; rpt. Waldmeir, Joseph J., Ed. *Critical Essays on John Barth*, 230-232.

"Title"
Scott, Virgil, and David Madden. *Instructor's Manual*..., 4th ed., 63-65; Madden, David. *Instructor's Manual*..., 5th ed., 65-67.

"Water Message"
Hinden, Michael. "*Lost in the Funhouse*...," 112; rpt. Waldmeir, Joseph J., Ed. *Critical Essays on John Barth*, 195.

DONALD BARTHELME

"The Abduction from the Seraglio"
Gordon, Lois. *Donald Barthelme*, 205-207.

"Alice"
Gordon, Lois. *Donald Barthelme*, 98-99.

"And Now Let's Hear It for the Ed Sullivan Show!"
Gordon, Lois. *Donald Barthelme*, 155-156.

"The Apology"
Gordon, Lois. *Donald Barthelme*, 197-199.

"At the End of the Mechanical Age"
Ahrends, Günter. ...*Kurzgeschichte*, 223-224.
Gordon, Lois. *Donald Barthelme*, 192-193.

"At the Tolstoy Museum"
Ahrends, Günter. ...*Kurzgeschichte*, 225-227.
Gordon, Lois. *Donald Barthelme*, 109-110.

"The Balloon"
Brooks, Cleanth, and Robert P. Warren. *Understanding Fiction*, 3rd ed., 289-292.
Couturier, Maurice. "Barthelme's Uppity Bubble: 'The Balloon,'" *Revue Français d'Études Américaines*, 8 (1979), 183-201.
Gordon, Lois. *Donald Barthelme*, 88-91.
Kreutzer, Eberhard. "City Spectacles as Artistic Acts: Donald Barthelme's 'The Balloon' and 'The Glass Mountain,'" *Anglistik & Englischunterricht*, 13 (April, 1981), 43-55.

"Belief"
Gordon, Lois. *Donald Barthelme*, 205.

"The Big Broadcast of 1938"
Gordon, Lois. *Donald Barthelme*, 44-47.

"Bone Bubbles"
Gordon, Lois. *Donald Barthelme*, 118.

"Bunny Image, Loss of: The Case of Bitsy S."
Gordon, Lois. *Donald Barthelme*, 156–157.

"The Catechist"
Gordon, Lois. *Donald Barthelme*, 134–135.
Robinson, Fred M. "Nonsense and Sadness in Donald Barthelme and Edward
Lear," *So Atlantic Q,* 80 (1981), 172–173.

"City Life"
Gordon, Lois. *Donald Barthelme*, 120–121.

"A City of Churches"
Gordon, Lois. *Donald Barthelme*, 126–127.
Rohrberger, Mary. *Instructor's Manual.* . . , 43–44.

"Concerning the Body Guard"
Gordon, Lois. *Donald Barthelme*, 208–209.

"Cortés and Montezuma"
Gordon, Lois. *Donald Barthelme*, 200–203.

"The Crisis"
Gordon, Lois. *Donald Barthelme*, 196–197.

"Daumier"
Gordon, Lois. *Donald Barthelme*, 137–142.

"The Death of Edward Lear"
Gordon, Lois. *Donald Barthelme*, 208.
Robinson, Fred M. "Nonsense and Sadness. . .," 164–167.

"The Dolt"
Gordon, Lois. *Donald Barthelme*, 95.

"Down the Line with the Annual"
Gordon, Lois. *Donald Barthelme*, 144–145.

"The Dragon"
Gordon, Lois. *Donald Barthelme*, 153.

"The Educational Experience"
Gordon, Lois. *Donald Barthelme*, 188–189.

"Engineer-Private Paul Klee Misplaces an Aircraft Between Milbertshofen and
Cambrain, March 1916"
Gordon, Lois. *Donald Barthelme*, 129–131.

"The Explanation"
Gordon, Lois. *Donald Barthelme*, 113–116.

"A Film"
Gordon, Lois. *Donald Barthelme*, 131–132.

"The Flight of Pigeons from the Palace"
Gordon, Lois. *Donald Barthelme*, 135-136.
Robinson, Fred M. "Nonsense and Sadness...," 169.

"Florence Green in 81"
Gordon, Lois. *Donald Barthelme*, 35-40.

"For I'm the Boy Whose Only Joy Is Loving You"
Gordon, Lois. *Donald Barthelme*, 41-44.

"Game"
Gordon, Lois. *Donald Barthelme*, 97-98.

"The Genius"
Gordon, Lois. *Donald Barthelme*, 124-126.
Robinson, Fred M. "Nonsense and Sadness...," 168-169.

"The Glass Mountain"
Gordon, Lois. *Donald Barthelme*, 111-113.
Kreutzer, Eberhard. "City Spectacles...," 43-55.

"Heliotrope"
Gordon, Lois. *Donald Barthelme*, 155.

"An Hesitation on the Bank of the Delaware"
Gordon, Lois. *Donald Barthelme*, 153-154.

"I Bought a Little City"
Gordon, Lois. *Donald Barthelme*, 184.

"The Indian Uprising"
Ahrends, Günter. *...Kurzgeschichte*, 221-223.
Bocock, Maclin. "'The Indian Uprising' or Donald Barthelme's Strange Object
    Covered with Fur: Maclin Bocock on Donald Barthelme," *Fiction International*,
    4/5 (1975), 134-146.
Gordon, Lois. *Donald Barthelme*, 85-88.
Howard, Daniel F., and John Ribar. *Instructor's Manual...*, 4th ed., 85.

"Kierkegaard Unfair to Schlegel"
Gordon, Lois. *Donald Barthelme*, 113-116.

"The King of Jazz"
Gordon, Lois. *Donald Barthelme*, 203-204.

"L'Lapse"
Gordon, Lois. *Donald Barthelme*, 148-149.

"The Leap"
Gordon, Lois. *Donald Barthelme*, 210-211.

"Marie, Marie, Hold on Tight"
Gordon, Lois. *Donald Barthelme*, 53-55.

"Me and Miss Mandible"
Gordon, Lois. *Donald Barthelme*, 48–52.
Howard, Daniel F., and John Ribar. *Instructor's Manual...*, 4th ed., 84.

"A Nation of Wheels"
Gordon, Lois. *Donald Barthelme*, 157–158.

"The New Member"
Gordon, Lois. *Donald Barthelme*, 191–192.

"The New Music"
Gordon, Lois. *Donald Barthelme*, 199–200.

"On Angels"
Gordon, Lois. *Donald Barthelme*, 118–120.

"Our Work and Why We Do It"
Gordon, Lois. *Donald Barthelme*, 179–180.

"The Palace"
Gordon, Lois. *Donald Barthelme*, 152–153.

"Paraguay"
Gordon, Lois. *Donald Barthelme*, 108.

"The Party"
Gordon, Lois. *Donald Barthelme*, 127–129.
Robinson, Fred M. "Nonsense and Sadness...," 172.

"Perpetua"
Gordon, Lois. *Donald Barthelme*, 126.

"The Phantom of the Opera's Friend"
Gordon, Lois. *Donald Barthelme*, 116–117.

"The Photographs"
Gordon, Lois. *Donald Barthelme*, 158–159.

"The Piano Player"
Gordon, Lois. *Donald Barthelme*, 40–41.
Warde, William B. "Barthelme's 'The Piano Player': Surreal and Mock Tragic,"
    Xavier R, 1, i–ii (1980–1981), 58–64.

"A Picture History of the War"
Gordon, Lois. *Donald Barthelme*, 99–101.

"The Police Band"
Gordon, Lois. *Donald Barthelme*, 95–96.

"The Policemen's Ball"
Gordon, Lois. *Donald Barthelme*, 110–111.

"Porcupines at the University"
Gordon, Lois. *Donald Barthelme*, 187–188.
Klinkowitz, Jerome. *The Practice of Fiction . . .*, 108–110.
Shelton, Frank W. "Barthelme's Western Tall Tale: 'Porcupines at the University,'"
   Notes Contemp Lit, 9, i (1979), 2–3.

"The President"
Gordon, Lois. *Donald Barthelme*, 101–102.

"The Question Party"
Gordon, Lois. *Donald Barthelme*, 204.

"Rebecca"
Gordon, Lois. *Donald Barthelme*, 189–190.

"The Reference"
Gordon, Lois. *Donald Barthelme*, 190–191.

"Report"
Altenbernd, Lynn, and Leslie L. Lewis. *Instructor's Manual . . .*, 3rd ed., 6.
Gordon, Lois. *Donald Barthelme*, 93–95.
Scott, Virgil, and David Madden. *Instructor's Manual . . .*, 4th ed., 41–43; Madden,
   David. *Instructor's Manual . . .*, 5th ed., 42–44.

"Robert Kennedy Saved from Drowning"
Gordon, Lois. *Donald Barthelme*, 92–93.

"The Royal Treatment"
Gordon, Lois. *Donald Barthelme*, 154–155.

"The Sandman"
Gordon, Lois. *Donald Barthelme*, 132–133.

"The School"
Gordon, Lois. *Donald Barthelme*, 182–183.

"See the Moon?"
Gordon, Lois. *Donald Barthelme*, 102–103.

"Sentence"
Gordon, Lois. *Donald Barthelme*, 117–118.

"The Sergeant"
Gordon, Lois. *Donald Barthelme*, 185–186.

"A Shower of Gold"
Gordon, Lois. *Donald Barthelme*, 58–61.

"Snap Snap"
Gordon, Lois. *Donald Barthelme*, 146–147.

"Some of Us Had Been Threatening Our Friend Colby"
Gordon, Lois. *Donald Barthelme*, 181–182.

"Subpoena"
Gordon, Lois. *Donald Barthelme*, 133–134.

"Swallowing"
Gordon, Lois. *Donald Barthelme*, 150–152.

"The Teaching of Don B.: A Yankee Way of Knowing"
Gordon, Lois. *Donald Barthelme*, 149–150.

"The Temptation of St. Anthony"
Gordon, Lois. *Donald Barthelme*, 136–137.

"That Cosmopolitan Girl"
Gordon, Lois. *Donald Barthelme*, 145–146.

"This Newspaper Here"
Gordon, Lois. *Donald Barthelme*, 91–92.

"To London and Rome"
Gordon, Lois. *Donald Barthelme*, 57–58.

"Up, Aloft in the Air"
Gordon, Lois. *Donald Barthelme*, 55–57.

"The Viennese Opera Ball"
Gordon, Lois. *Donald Barthelme*, 47–48.

"Views of My Father Weeping"
Gordon, Lois. *Donald Barthelme*, 107–108.

"What to Do Next"
Gordon, Lois. *Donald Barthelme*, 186.

"The Wound"
Gordon, Lois. *Donald Barthelme*, 180–181.

"The Young Visitors"
Gordon, Lois. *Donald Barthelme*, 152.

"The Zombies"
Gordon, Lois. *Donald Barthelme*, 209–210.

HAMILTON BASSO

"The Age of Fable"
Millichap, Joseph R. *Hamilton Basso*, 133–135.

"The Broken Horn"
Millichap, Joseph R. *Hamilton Basso*, 138-140.

"The Edge of the Wilderness"
Millichap, Joseph R. *Hamilton Basso*, 135-136.

"Fabulous Man"
Millichap, Joseph R. *Hamilton Basso*, 129-130.

"I Can't Dance"
Millichap, Joseph R. *Hamilton Basso*, 124-125.

"A Kind of a Special Gift"
Millichap, Joseph R. *Hamilton Basso*, 136-138.

"King Rail"
Millichap, Joseph R. *Hamilton Basso*, 132-133.

"Me and the Babe"
Millichap, Joseph R. *Hamilton Basso*, 128-129.

"Rain on Aspidistra"
Millichap, Joseph R. *Hamilton Basso*, 125-128.

"The Wild Turkey"
Millichap, Joseph R. *Hamilton Basso*, 130-132.

ADAH F. BATELLE

"The Sacking of Grubbville"
Chu, Limin. *The Image of China*. . ., 168-169.

H. E. BATES

"The Cruise of *The Breadwinner*"
Allen, Walter. *The Short Story*. . ., 265-267.

"Death of a Huntsman"
Allen, Walter. *The Short Story*. . ., 263-265.

"The Gleaner"
Allen, Walter. *The Short Story*, 262-263.

HARRY BATES

"Farewell to the Master"
Warrick, Patricia S. *The Cybernetic Imagination*. . ., 108-109.

ANN BEATTIE

"Shifting"
Rohrberger, Mary. *Instructor's Manual*. . ., 32–33.

"Through the Octascope"
Gerlach, John. "Through 'The Octascope': A View of Ann Beattie," *Stud Short Fiction*, 17 (1980), 489–494.

SAMUEL BECKETT

"The Calmative"
Hamilton, Alice and Kenneth. *Condemned to Life*. . ., 139–140.
Levy, Eric. "The Beckettian Narrator in Six Stories and *Nouvelles*," *Canadian J Irish Stud*, 4, i (1978), 27–28.
Megged, Matti. "Exile into Silence in Beckett's First French Writings," *Centerpoint*, 4 (1980), 138–140.

"Dante and the Lobster"
Hamilton, Alice and Kenneth. *Condemned to Life*. . ., 110–112.

"Ding Dong"
Hamilton, Alice and Kenneth. *Condemned to Life*. . ., 109–110.

"The End"
Hamilton, Alice and Kenneth. *Condemned to Life*. . ., 136–137.

"Enough"
Levy, Eric. "The Beckettian Narrator. . .," 31–33.
————. *Beckett*. . ., 113–115.

"The Expelled"
Hamilton, Alice and Kenneth. *Condemned to Life*. . ., 138–139.
Megged, Matti. "Exile into Silence. . .," 138–140.

"Fingal"
Power, Mary. "Samuel Beckett's 'Fingal' and the Irish Tradition," *J Mod Lit*, 9 (1981), 151–156.

"First Love"
Levy, Eric. "The Beckettian Narrator. . .," 30–31.
————. *Beckett*. . ., 111–113.
Megged, Matti. "Exile into Silence. . .," 138–140.

"For to End Yet Again"
Levy, Eric. *Beckett*. . ., 119–121.

"From an Abandoned Work"
Levy, Eric. "The Beckettian Narrator. . .," 33–34.
————. *Beckett*. . ., 115–117.

"Horn Came Always"
Levy, Eric. *Beckett...*, 122–123.

MAX BEERBOHM

"Enoch Soames"
Briggs, Julia. *Night Visitors...*, 94–95.

MARY BELL

"Sing Kee's China-Lily"
Chu, Limin. *The Image of China...*, 211–212.

SAUL BELLOW

"A Father-to-Be"
Dietrich, R. F. "The Biological Draft-Dodger in Bellow's 'A Father-to-Be,'" *Stud Hum*, 9, i (1981), 45–51.
Madden, David. *Instructor's Manual...*, 5th ed., 95–96.

"Leaving the Yellow House"
Altenbernd, Lynn, and Leslie L. Lewis. *Instructor's Manual...*, 3rd ed., 7–8.
Rodrigues, Eusebio L. "A Rough-Hewn Heroine of Our Time: Saul Bellow's 'Leaving the Yellow House,'" *Saul Bellow J*, 1, i (1981), 11–17.

"Looking for Mr. Green"
Ahrends, Günter. *...Kurzgeschichte*, 195–196.
Mizener, Arthur. *A Handbook...*, 4th ed., 50–52.

"The Mexican General"
Gunn, Drewey W. *American and British Writers...*, 205–206.
Newman, Judie. "Saul Bellow and Trotsky: 'The Mexican General,'" *Saul Bellow J*, 1, i (1981), 26–31.

"Mosby's Memoirs"
Gunn, Drewey W. *American and British Writers...*, 207–208.

"Seize the Day"
*Galloway, David. *The Absurd Hero...*, 2nd rev. ed., 147–151.
Kulshrestha, Chirantan. *Saul Bellow...*, 77–94.
Morahg, Gilead. "The Art of Dr. Tamkin: Matter and Manner in 'Seize the Day,'" *Mod Fiction Stud*, 25 (1979), 103–116.
Rovit, Earl. "Saul Bellow and the Concept of the Survivor," in Schraepen, Edmond, Ed. *Saul Bellow...*, 97–98.
Shear, Walter. "*Steppenwolf* and 'Seize the Day,'" *Saul Bellow J*, 1, i (1981), 32–34.
Stock, Irvin. *Fiction as Wisdom...*, 201–204.

ANDREI BELY [BORIS NIKOLAEVICH]

"Adam"
Peterson, Ronald E., Ed. *Andrei Bely...*, 19–21.

"The Bush"
Peterson, Ronald E., Ed. *Andrei Bely...*, 17–18.

"A Luminous Fairy Tale"
Peterson, Ronald E., Ed. *Andrei Bely...*, 15–16.

"A Man"
Peterson, Ronald E., Ed. *Andrei Bely...*, 22–23.

"The Mountain Princess"
Peterson, Ronald E., Ed. *Andrei Bely...*, 18–19.

"We Await His Return"
Peterson, Ronald E., Ed. *Andrei Bely...*, 16–17.

"The Yogi"
Peterson, Ronald E., Ed. *Andrei Bely...*, 21–22.

MARIO BENEDETTI

"El cambiazo"
Foster, David W. *...Spanish-American Short Story*, 102–109.

JUAN BENET

"Baalbec"
Díaz, Janet. "Variations on the Theme of Death in the Short Fiction of Juan Benet," *Am Hispanist*, 4, xxxvi (1979), 8.

"Catálisis"
Díaz, Janet. "Variations...," 10.

"De legos"
Díaz, Janet. "Variations...," 9.

"Después"
Díaz, Janet. "Variations...," 7–8.

"Duelo"
Díaz, Janet. "Variations...," 7.

"Reichenau"
Díaz, Janet. "Variations...," 9–10.

"Syllabus"
Díaz, Janet. "Variations...," 10.

"TLB"
Díaz, Janet. "Variations...," 9.

M. J. BERDYCZEWSKI

"The Lonely"
Ewen, Josef. "The Contrast Pair as a Thematic Phenomenon and as a Literary
    Device in the Stories of M. J. Berdyczewski," in Heinemann, Joseph, and
    Shmuel Werses, Eds. *Studies in Hebrew Narrative Art...*, 147-148.

"My Enemy"
Ewen, Josef. "The Contrast Pair...," 148-149.

"Partners"
Ewen, Josef. "The Contrast Pair...," 142.

"The Qaddish and Two Far Away"
Ewen, Josef. "The Contrast Pair...," 140-141, 146-147.

"The Two"
Ewen, Josef. "The Contrast Pair...," 140, 141, 144.

"Two Josephs"
Ewen, Josef. "The Contrast Pair...," 150.

GINA BERRIAULT

"The Stone Boy"
Smith, Elliott L., and Andrew W. Hart, Eds. *The Short Story...*, 248-249.
Smith, Elliott L. and Wanda V. *Instructor's Manual...*, 10-11.

DORIS BETTS

"The Dead Mule"
Evans, Elizabeth. "Another Mule in the Yard: Doris Betts' Durable Humor," *Notes
    Contemp Lit*, 11, ii (1981), 5-6.

AMBROSE BIERCE

"The Boarded Window"
Baker, Sheridan, and George Perkins. *Instructor's Manual...*, 17-18.

"The Haunted Valley"
Chu, Limin. *The Image of China...*, 205.

"An Occurrence at Owl Creek Bridge"
Ahrends, Günter. . . . *Kurzgeschichte*, 119–121.
Barker, Gerard A. *Instructor's Manual*. . . , 43–45.
*Brooks, Cleanth, and Robert P. Warren. *Understanding Fiction*, 3rd ed., 64–65.

"One of the Missing"
Allen, Walter. *The Short Story*. . . , 52–54.
Hartwell, Ronald. "Fallen Timbers—a Death Trap: A Comparison of Bierce and
  Munro," *Research Stud*, 49 (1981), 61–66.

"Parker Adderson, Philosopher"
Kazin, Alfred. "On Ambrose Bierce and 'Parker Adderson, Philosopher,'" in
  Skaggs, Calvin, Ed. *The American Short Story*, I, 79–81.

ANDREI BITUV

"Country Place"
Brown, Deming. . . . *Literature Since Stalin*, 196–197.

"Journey to a Childhood Friend"
Bakich, Olga H. "A New Type of Character in the Literature of the 1960s: The
  Early Works of Andrei Bituv," *Canadian Slavonic Papers*, 23 (1981), 132–133.

"Penelopa"
Bakich, Olga H. "A New Type of Character. . . ," 128–132.

ALGERNON BLACKWOOD

"The Listener"
Sullivan, Jack. *Elegant Nightmares*. . . , 125–127.

"A Psychical Invasion"
Briggs, Julia. *Night Visitors*. . . , 62–63.

"Secret Worship"
Briggs, Julia. *Night Visitors*. . . , 61–62.

"The Transfer"
Sullivan, Jack. *Elegant Nightmares*. . . , 112–113.

"The Willows"
Sullivan, Jack. *Elegant Nightmares*. . . , 120–123.

HEINRICH BÖLL

"The Bread of Spring"
Plüddemann, Ulrich. "Heinrich Böll, 'Das Brot der frühen Jahre': Lehrpraktische
  Analyse," *Deutschunterricht in Südafrika*, 10, ii (1979), 4–31.

"Epilogue to Stifter's *Nachsommer*"
Conrad, Robert C. "Heinrich Böll's Political Reevaluation of Adalbert Stifter:
An Interpretation of Böll's 'Epilogue to Stifter's *Nachsommer*,'" *Michigan
Academician*, 14 (1981), 31–39.

"Traveler, If You Go to the Spa--"
Kegel, Rudolf. "Heinrich Böll's 'Wanderer, kommst du nach Spa,'" *J School Lang*,
5, i–ii (1977–1978), 152–161.

ARNA BONTEMPS

"A Summer Tragedy"
Smith, Elliott L. and Wanda V. *Instructor's Manual*..., 9.

WOLFGANG BORCHERT

"At Night Rats Go to Sleep, After All"
Fickert, Kurt J. *Signs and Portents*..., 25–26.

"Billbrook"
Fickert, Kurt J. *Signs and Portents*..., 17–19.
Klarmann, Adolf. "Wolfgang Borchert: The Lost Voice of a New Germany," *Germ
R*, 27 (1952), 116–117.

"Bread"
Fickert, Kurt J. *Signs and Portents*..., 27–28.

"Coffee Is Indefinable"
Fickert, Kurt J. *Signs and Portents*..., 23.

"The Crow Flies Home at Night"
Klarmann, Adolf. "Wolfgang Borchert...," 114–115.

"The Dandelion"
Fickert, Kurt J. *Signs and Portents*..., 14–17.
Klarmann, Adolf. "Wolfgang Borchert...," 113–114.

"Down the Long, Long Street"
Fickert, Kurt J. *Signs and Portents*..., 26–27.

"The Giraffe"
Fickert, Kurt J. *Signs and Portents*..., 17.

"Jesus Won't Do His Part Any More"
Fickert, Kurt J. *Signs and Portents*..., 21.

"The Kitchen Clock"
Fickert, Kurt J. *Signs and Portents*..., 23–24.

"Maybe She Has a Pink Blouse"
Fickert, Kurt J. *Signs and Portents...*, 24-25.

"My Pale Brother"
Fickert, Kurt J. *Signs and Portents...*, 20-21.

"Stay a While, Giraffe"
Fickert, Kurt J. *Signs and Portents...*, 17.

"A Sunday Morning"
Fickert, Kurt J. *Signs and Portents...*, 30-31.

"The Three Dark Kings"
Fickert, Kurt J. *Signs and Portents...*, 21-22.

"Voices Are There—in the Air, in the Night"
Fickert, Kurt J. *Signs and Portents...*, 16-17.

JORGE LUIS BORGES

"The Aleph"
Arroyo, Anita. *Narrativa...*, 210-213.
Bell-Villada, Gene H. *Borges and His Fiction...*, 219-229.
Foster, David W. *...Spanish-American Short Story*, 21-25.
López Morales, Berta. "El modelo de la literatura fantástica aplicado en 'El Aleph,'"
    Estudios Filológicos, 15 (1980), 73-80.
McMurray, George R. *Jorge Luis Borges*, 29-31, 170-173.

"The Approach to Almotásim"
Bell-Villada, Gene H. *Borges and His Fiction...*, 65-68.
Holloway, James E. "Anatomy of Borges' 'El acercamiento a Almotásim,'" *Revista
    Canadiense de Estudios Hispánicos*, 5, i (1980), 37-59.
McMurray, George R. *Jorge Luis Borges*, 117-119.

"Averroes' Search"
Bell-Villada, Gene H. *Borges and His Fiction...*, 166-174.
Hulme, Peter. "The Face in the Mirror: Borges's 'La busca de Averroes,'" *Forum
    Mod Lang Stud*, 15 (1979), 292-297.
McMurray, George R. *Jorge Luis Borges*, 32-35.
Mahin, Linda R. "Jorge Luis Borges: An Archeology of Wonder," *Gypsy Scholar*,
    4 (1977), 139-140.

"The Babylonian Lottery"
Bell-Villada, Gene H. *Borges and His Fiction...*, 108-111.
Dyson, A. E. "'You, fiction reader..': Jorge Luis Borges," *Critical Q*, 21, iv
    (1979), 12-14.
McMurray, George R. *Jorge Luis Borges*, 41-43.

"Biography of Tadeo Isidoro Cruz (1829-1874)"
McMurray, George R. *Jorge Luis Borges*, 95-97.

"The Book of Sand"
Dyson, A. E. "'You, fiction reader...,'" 24-25.

"Borges and I"
Foster, David W. ...Spanish-American Short Story, 8-12.
Lydenberg, Robin. "Borges as a Writer of Parables: Reversal and Infinite
Regression," *Int'l Fiction R*, 6, i (1979), 38-39.

"The Bribe"
McMurray, George R. *Jorge Luis Borges*, 227-228.

"The Challenge"
McMurray, George R. *Jorge Luis Borges*, 141-143.

"The Circular Ruins"
Bell-Villada, Gene H. *Borges and His Fiction*..., 85-89.
Howard, David C. "Mind as Reality: Borges' 'Circular Ruins' and Garcia Marquez'
One Hundred Years of Solitude," *Coll Lang Assoc J*, 23 (1980), 409-415.
Lydenberg, Robin. "...Infinite Regression," 35-36.
McMurray, George R. *Jorge Luis Borges*, 67-69, 166-167.

"The Dead Man"
Bell-Villada, Gene H. *Borges and His Fiction*..., 179-183.
McMurray, George R. *Jorge Luis Borges*, 19-21.

"Death and the Compass"
Adelstein, Miriam. "Visión de la vida en dos cuentos de Jorge Luis Borges," in
Gutiérrez de la Solana, Alberto, and Elio Alba-Buffill, Eds. *Festschrift José Cid
Pérez*, 261-266.
Arroyo, Anita. *Narrativa*..., 196-198.
Baumgarten, Murray. "Mirror of Words: Language in Agnon and Borges," *Comp
Lit*, 31 (1979), 363-366.
Bell-Villada, Gene H. *Borges and His Fiction*..., 89-92.
Carroll, Robert C. "Borges and Bruno: The Geometry of Infinity in 'La muerte
y la brújula,'" *Mod Lang Notes*, 94 (1979), 321-342.
Grossvogel, David I. *Mystery*..., 140-146.
McMurray, George R. *Jorge Luis Borges*, 14-19.
Mahin, Linda R. "...Archeology of Wonder," 144.
Porter, Dennis. *The Pursuit of Crime*..., 254-257.
Sanchis Bañús, José. "Decurso narrativo y planos de realidad en dos cuentos de
Jorge Luis Borges: 'Tlön, Uqbar, Orbis Tertius' y 'La muerte y la brújula,'"
in *Mélanges à la mémoire d'André Joucla-Ruau*, 1181-1197.

"Deutsches Requiem"
Bell-Villada, Gene H. *Borges and His Fiction*..., 190-195.
McMurray, George R. *Jorge Luis Borges*, 37-38.

"Dr. Brodie's Report"
McMurray, George R. *Jorge Luis Borges*, 46-50.

"The Duel"
McMurray, George R. *Jorge Luis Borges*, 92-93.

"Emma Zunz"
Bell-Villada, Gene H. *Borges and His Fiction...*, 183-188.
McMurray, George R. *Jorge Luis Borges*, 35-37.

"The End"
Bell-Villada, Gene H. *Borges and His Fiction...*, 75-78.
McMurray, George R. *Jorge Luis Borges*, 89-92.

"The End of the Duel"
McMurray, George R. *Jorge Luis Borges*, 21-23.

"Everything and Nothing"
Bell-Villada, Gene H. *Borges and His Fiction...*, 245-246.

"An Examination of the Work of Herbert Quain"
Bell-Villada, Gene H. *Borges and His Fiction...*, 115-118.
McMurray, George R. *Jorge Luis Borges*, 226-227.

"The Form of the Sword"
McMurray, George R. *Jorge Luis Borges*, 93-95.

"Funes the Memorious"
Bell-Villada, Gene H. *Borges and His Fiction...*, 96-101.
*Howard, Daniel F., and John Ribar. *Instructor's Manual...*, 4th ed., 48.
Irwin, John T. *American Hieroglyphics...*, 175-178.
McMurray, George R. *Jorge Luis Borges*, 10-12.
Mahin, Linda R. "...Archeology of Wonder," 143-144.

"The Garden of Forking Paths"
Arroyo, Anita. *Narrativa...*, 207-210.
Bell-Villada, Gene H. *Borges and His Fiction...*, 93-96.
McMurray, George R. *Jorge Luis Borges*, 102-106.
Rohrberger, Mary. *Instructor's Manual...*, 36.
Rudy, Stephen. "The Garden *of* and *in* Borges' 'Garden of Forking Paths,'" in
    Kodjak, Andrej, Michael J. Connolly, and Krystyna Pomorska, Eds. ...
    Narrative Texts, 132-144.
Scott, Virgil, and David Madden. *Instructor's Manual...*, 4th ed., 60-62.

"The God's Script"
Alvarez, Nicolas E. "Aristoteles y Platon en 'La escritura de Dios' (Borges),"
    Explicación de Textos Literarios, 9, ii (1981), 99-102.
Bell-Villada, Gene H. *Borges and His Fiction...*, 203-212.
Foster, David W. ...*Spanish-American Short Story*, 16-17.
Lydenberg, Robin. "...Infinite Regression," 36-38.

"The Gospel According to Mark"
Baker, Sheridan, and George Perkins. *Instructor's Manual...*, 37-38.
McMurray, George R. *Jorge Luis Borges*, 108-110.

"Guayaquil"
Foster, David W. ...*Spanish-American Short Story*, 25-26.
McMurray, George R. *Jorge Luis Borges*, 12-14.

"Horse"
Doxey, William S. "Borges's 'Caballo' Labyrinth: The Intricacy of Beauty," *J Mod Lit*, 7 (1979), 548-552.

"The House of Asterión"
Bell-Villada, Gene H. *Borges and His Fiction*..., 141-145.
McMurray, George R. *Jorge Luis Borges*, 23-24.
Ruscalleda Bercedóniz, Jorge María. "Acercamiento estructural a 'La casa de Asterión' y 'La otra muerte' de Jorge Luis Borges," *Sin Nombre*, 11, i (1980), 69-75.

"Ibn-Hakkan al-Bokhari, Dead in His Labyrinth"
Bell-Villada, Gene H. *Borges and His Fiction*..., 138-141.
McMurray, George R. *Jorge Luis Borges*, 25-28.

"The Immortal"
Arrimondi Pieri, Emilio. "La rección verbal en 'El immortal' de *El Aleph* de Jorge Luis Borges," in Várvaro, Alberto, Ed. *XIV Congresso internazionale*..., 163-180.
Arroyo, Anita. *Narrativa*..., 201-204.
Bell-Villada, Gene H. *Borges and His Fiction*..., 229-237.
McMurray, George R. *Jorge Luis Borges*, 81-84.

"The Intruder"
McMurray, George R. *Jorge Luis Borges*, 143-145.

"The Library of Babel"
Arroyo, Anita. *Narrativa*..., 204-206.
Bell-Villada, Gene H. *Borges and His Fiction*..., 111-115.
McMurray, George R. *Jorge Luis Borges*, 6-10.
Nouhaud, Dorita and Jean-Pierre. "Examen de la bibliothèque de Jorges Luis Ménard," *Imprévue*, 1 (1981), 67-93.

"The Life of Tadeo Isidoro Cruz"
Bell-Villada, Gene H. *Borges and His Fiction*..., 145-151.
Mahin, Linda R. "...Archeology of Wonder," 140.

"The Man at the Pink Corner"
Omil, Alba. "A medio siglo de 'Hombre de la esquina rosada,'" *Sur*, 348 (1981), 63-67.

"The Man on the Threshold"
Bell-Villada, Gene H. *Borges and His Fiction*..., 189-190.
McMurray, George R. *Jorge Luis Borges*, 106-108.

"The Meeting"
Brooks, Cleanth, and Robert P. Warren. *Instructor's Manual*..., 3rd ed., 48-50.
McMurray, George R. *Jorge Luis Borges*, 145-148.

"The Mirror and the Mask"
McMurray, George R. *Jorge Luis Borges*, 156.

"The Other"
McMurray, George R. *Jorge Luis Borges*, 126-129.

"The Other Death"
Bell-Villada, Gene H. *Borges and His Fiction*..., 195-201.
McMurray, George R. *Jorge Luis Borges*, 75-77.
Ruscalleda Bercedóniz, Jorge María. "Acercamiento estructural...," 69-75.

"Pierre Menard, Author of *Quixote*"
Bell-Villada, Gene H. *Borges and His Fiction*..., 122-128.
Borinsky, Alicia. "Repetitions, Museums, Libraries: Jorge Luis Borges," *Glyph*, 2 (1977), 91-96.
Grossvogel, David I. *Mystery*..., 136-138.
McMurray, George R. *Jorge Luis Borges*, 124-126.
Marval de McNair, Nora de. "'Pierre Menard, autor del *Quijote*': Huellas y sentido," in *Homenaje a Humberto Piñera*..., 159-165.
Nouhaud, Dorita and Jean-Pierre. "Examen de la bibliothèque...," 67-93.

"The Secret Miracle"
Adelstein, Miriam. "Visión de la vida...," 261-266.
Barker, Gerard A. *Instructor's Manual*..., 46-48.
Bell-Villada, Gene H. *Borges and His Fiction*..., 81-85.
McMurray, George R. *Jorge Luis Borges*, 64-67, 204-205.
————. "Borges' 'The Secret Miracle': A Self-Conscious, Self-Begetting *Ficción*," in Vera, Catherine, and George R. McMurray, Eds. *In Honor of Boyd G. Carter*..., 43-48.
Mahin, Linda R. "...Archeology of Wonder," 145.

"The Sect of the Phoenix"
Bell-Villada, Gene H. *Borges and His Fiction*..., 102-108.
McMurray, George R. *Jorge Luis Borges*, 43-44.

"The Sect of Thirty"
Dyson, A. E. "'You, fiction reader...,'" 22-24.

"The Shape of the Sword"
Bell-Villada, Gene H. *Borges and His Fiction*..., 72-73.

"The South"
Bell-Villada, Gene H. *Borges and His Fiction*..., 78-81.
McMurray, George R. *Jorge Luis Borges*, 131-136.

"The Story of Rosendo Juárez"
McMurray, George R. *Jorge Luis Borges*, 140-141.

"Story of the Warrior and the Captive"
Bell-Villada, Gene H. *Borges and His Fiction*..., 152-158.
Echavarría Ferrari, Arturo. "'Historia del guerrero y de la cautiva' de Borges: Tentativa de codificacion de un lenguaje 'americano,'" in Gordon, Alan M., and Evelyn Rugg, Eds. *Actas del Sexto Congreso Internacional*..., 222-224.
McMurray, George R. *Jorge Luis Borges*, 122-124.

"Streetcorner Man"
Bell-Villada, Gene H. *Borges and His Fiction...*, 62-65.
McMurray, George R. *Jorge Luis Borges*, 136-139.

"Theme of the Traitor and the Hero"
Bell-Villada, Gene H. *Borges and His Fiction...*, 73-75.
McMurray, George R. *Jorge Luis Borges*, 69-72.
*Scholes, Robert. *Elements of Fiction*, 2nd ed., 76-79.

"The Theologians"
Bell-Villada, Gene H. *Borges and His Fiction...*, 158-166.
McMurray, George R. *Jorge Luis Borges*, 120-122.

"Three Versions of Judas"
Bell-Villada, Gene H. *Borges and His Fiction...*, 118-122.
Dyson, A. E. "'You, fiction reader...,'" 19-22.
McMurray, George R. *Jorge Luis Borges*, 38-41.

"Tlön, Uqbar, Orbis Tertius"
Bell-Villada, Gene H. *Borges and His Fiction...*, 128-137.
Dyson, A. E. "'You, fiction reader...,'" 14-16.
Grossvogel, David I. *Mystery...*, 130-131.
McMurray, George R. *Jorge Luis Borges*, 56-61.
Sanchis Bañús, José. "Decurso narrativo...," 1181-1197.
Sosnowski, Saúl. "'Tlön, Uqbar, Orbis Tertius': Histórica y desplazamentos," in
    Minc, Rose S., Ed. ...*Latin American Short Story*, 35-43.

"The Two Kings and Their Two Labyrinths"
McMurray, George R. *Jorge Luis Borges*, 24-25.

"Utopia of a Tired Man"
McMurray, George R. *Jorge Luis Borges*, 44-46.

"The Waiting"
McMurray, George R. *Jorge Luis Borges*, 72-74.

"The Watcher"
Mahin, Linda R. "...Archeology of Wonder," 137.

"The Zahir"
Bell-Villada, Gene H. *Borges and His Fiction...*, 212-219.
Lydenberg, Robin. "...Infinite Regression," 33-35.
McMurray, George R. *Jorge Luis Borges*, 62-64.

JEAN LOUIS BOUQUET

"Assirata, or The Enchanted Mirror"
Ziolkowski, Theodore. *Disenchanted Images...*, 224–225.

ELIZABETH BOWEN

"The Demon Lover"
Barker, Gerard A. *Instructor's Manual...*, 53–55.
Fraustino, Daniel V. "Elizabeth Bowen's 'The Demon Lover': Psychosis or
    Seduction?" *Stud Short Fiction*, 17 (1980), 483–487.

"The Happy Autumn Fields"
Lee, Hermione. *Elizabeth Bowen...*, 158–159.

"Her Table Spread"
Church, Margaret. "The Irish Writer, Elizabeth Bowen, 'Her Table Spread':
    Allusion and 'Anti-Roman,'" *Folio*, 11 (1978), 17–20.
Lee, Hermione. *Elizabeth Bowen...*, 141–143.

"Ivy Gripped the Steps"
Allen, Walter. *The Short Story...*, 259–261.
Lee, Hermione. *Elizabeth Bowen...*, 161–163.

"Look at All Those Roses"
Altenbernd, Lynn, and Leslie L. Lewis. *Instructor's Manual...*, 3rd ed., 8–10.

"Mysterious Kor"
Allen, Walter. *The Short Story...*, 258–259.

"The Tommy Crans"
Lee, Hermione. *Elizabeth Bowen...*, 145–146.

JANE BOWLES

"Camp Cataract"
Bernikow, Louise. *Among Women*, 90–92.

"Plain Pleasures"
Dillon, Millicent. *A Little Original Sin...*, 128–129.

"A Stick of Green Candy"
Dillon, Millicent. *A Little Original Sin...*, 183–184.

PAUL BOWLES

"The Delicate Prey"
Pounds, Wayne. "Paul Bowles and 'The Delicate Prey': The Psychology of
    Predation," *Revue Belge*, 59 (1981), 620–633.

HJALMAR HJORTH BOYESEN

"Asathor's Vengeance"
Fredrickson, Robert S. *Hjalmar Hjorth Boyesen*, 47–48.

"A Dangerous Virtue"
Fredrickson, Robert S. *Hjalmar Hjorth Boyesen*, 70–71.

"A Disastrous Partnership"
Fredrickson, Robert S. *Hjalmar Hjorth Boyesen*, 71.

"The Horns of a Dilemma"
Fredrickson, Robert S. *Hjalmar Hjorth Boyesen*, 71.

"A Norse Emigrant"
Fredrickson, Robert S. *Hjalmar Hjorth Boyesen*, 66–67.

"Queen Titania"
Fredrickson, Robert S. *Hjalmar Hjorth Boyesen*, 94–95.

"A Story of a Blue Vein"
Fredrickson, Robert S. *Hjalmar Hjorth Boyesen*, 95–96.

"The Story of an Outcast"
Fredrickson, Robert S. *Hjalmar Hjorth Boyesen*, 46–47.

"Swart Among the Buckeyes"
Fredrickson, Robert S. *Hjalmar Hjorth Boyesen*, 93–94.

"Truls, the Nameless"
Fredrickson, Robert S. *Hjalmar Hjorth Boyesen*, 45–46.

RAY BRADBURY

"And the Moon Be Still As Bright"
Gallagher, Edward J. "The Thematic Structure of 'The Martian Chronicle,'" in
    Greenberg, Martin H., and Joseph D. Olander, Eds. *Ray Bradbury*, 63–65.

"And the Rock Cried Out"
Scott, Virgil, and David Madden. *Instructor's Manual . . .*, 4th ed., 1–2.

"Dark They Were and Golden Eyed"
Wolfe, Gary K. "The Frontier Myth in Ray Bradbury," in Greenberg, Martin
    H., and Joseph D. Olander, Eds. *Ray Bradbury*, 47–48.

"The Earth Men"
Gallagher, Edward J. "The Thematic Structure . . .," 59–61.

"The Fire Balloons"
*Dimeo, Steven. "Man and Apollo: Religion in Bradbury's Science Fantasies," in
    Greenberg, Martin H., and Joseph D. Olander, Eds. *Ray Bradbury*, 163–164.

Woodman, Tom. "Science Fiction, Religion and Transcendence," in Parrinder, Patrick, Ed. *Science Fiction...*, 113-114.

"The Fireman"
McNelly, Willis E. "Ray Bradbury—Past, Present, and Future," in Greenberg, Martin H., and Joseph D. Olander, Eds. *Ray Bradbury*, 21-23.

"G. B. S.—Mark V"
Mengeling, Marvin E. "The Machineries of Joy and Despair: Bradbury's Attitudes Toward Science and Technology," in Greenberg, Martin H., and Joseph D. Olander, Eds. *Ray Bradbury*, 106-107.

"Jack-in-the-Box"
Diskin, Lahna. "Bradbury on Children," in Greenberg, Martin H., and Joseph D. Olander, Eds. *Ray Bradbury*, 150-151.

"The Long Years"
Gallagher, Edward J. "The Thematic Structure...," 78-79.

"The Lost City of Mars"
Mengeling, Marvin E. "The Machineries of Joy...," 107-108.

"The Man Upstairs"
Diskin, Lahna. "Bradbury on Children," 142-144.

"The Martian"
Gallagher, Edward J. "The Thematic Structure...," 72-74.

"The Miracles of Jamie"
*Dimeo, Steven. "Man and Apollo...," 159-160.

"The Musicians"
Gallagher, Edward J. "The Thematic Structure...," 69-70.

"The Next in Line"
Pierce, Hazel. "Ray Bradbury and the Gothic Tradition," in Greenberg, Martin H., and Joseph D. Olander, Eds. *Ray Bradbury*, 172-173.

"The Night Meeting"
Gallagher, Edward J. "The Thematic Structure...," 67-69.

"The Off Season"
Gallagher, Edward J. "The Thematic Structure...," 75-76.

"The Other Foot"
Rabkin, Eric S. "To Fairyland by Rocket: Bradbury's 'The Martian Chronicles,'" in Greenberg, Martin H., and Joseph D. Olander, Eds. *Ray Bradbury*, 124-125.

"Rocket Summer"
Gallagher, Edward J. "The Thematic Structure...," 57-58.

"The Settlers"
Gallagher, Edward J. "The Thematic Structure...," 65–66.

"Skeleton"
Pierce, Hazel. "...Gothic Tradition," 175–176.

"The Small Assassin"
Diskin, Lahna. "Bradbury on Children," 152–154.

"The Strawberry Window"
Mengeling, Marvin E. "The Machineries of Joy...," 102–103.

"The Summer Night"
Gallagher, Edward J. "The Thematic Structure...," 57–59.

"There Will Come Soft Rains"
Gallagher, Edward J. "The Thematic Structure...," 79–80.

"The Third Expedition"
Gallagher, Edward J. "The Thematic Structure...," 61–63.

"Usher II"
Wolfe, Gary K. "The Frontier Myth...," 51–52.

"Way in the Middle of the Air"
Gallagher, Edward J. "The Thematic Structure...," 70–72.

"The Wilderness"
Wolfe, Gary K. "The Frontier Myth...," 49–50.

RICHARD BRAUTIGAN

"The Kool-Aid Wino"
Kennedy, X. J. *Instructor's Manual...*, 2nd ed., 15–16.

"The World War I Los Angeles Airplane"
Madden, David. *Instructor's Manual...*, 5th ed., 62–64.

BERTOLT BRECHT

"Das Experiment"
Ley, Ralph. *Brecht as Thinker*, 218–220.

"Der Soldat von La Ciotat"
Ley, Ralph. *Brecht as Thinker*, 123–126.

CLEMENS BRENTANO

"Brave Kasperl and Beautiful Annerl" [same as "Brave Casper and Beautiful Annie"]
Fetzer, John F. *Clemens Brentano*, 103–106.
Swales, Martin. "Narrative Sleight-of-Hand: Some Notes on Two German
    Romantic Tales," *New Germ Stud*, 6 (1978), 1–4.

"The Chronicle of the Traveling Student"
Fetzer, John F. *Clemens Brentano*, 93–96.

"Gockel and Hinkel" [revised as "Gockel, Hinkel, and Gacheleia"]
Fetzer, John F. *Clemens Brentano*, 127–130.

ALICE BROWN

"At Sudleigh Fair"
Walker, Dorothea. "Freeman's Nun and Brown's Witch: A New Look at the New
    England Spinster," *Nassau R*, 3, i (1975), 6–8.

"A Last Assembling"
Walker, Dorothea. "...New England Spinster," 4–6.

"The Way of Peace"
Pearson, Carol, and Katherine Pope. *The Female Hero...*, 195–196.

CHARLES BROCKDEN BROWN

"Jessica"
Grabo, Norman. *The Coincidental Art...*, 49–50.

JOHN ROSS BROWNE

"A Dangerous Journey"
Scheick, William J. *The Half-Breed...*, 19–20.

JOHN BRUNNER

"Host Age"
De Bolt, Joe. "The Development of John Brunner," in Clareson, Thomas D., Ed.
    Voices for the Future..., II, 110–111.

"Thou Good and Faithful"
De Bolt, Joe. "The Development...," 107–108.

"Web of Everywhere"
De Bolt, Joe. "The Development...," 126–127.

KATHARINE BRUSH

"Night Club"
Smith, Elliott L. and Wanda V. *Instructor's Manual*..., 3.

ERNEST BUCKLER

"Last Delivery Before Christmas"
Chambers, Robert D. *Sinclair Ross and Ernest Buckler*, 62–63.

"A Present for Miss Merriam"
Chambers, Robert D. *Sinclair Ross and Ernest Buckler*, 61–62.

"The Quarrel"
Chambers, Robert D. *Sinclair Ross and Ernest Buckler*, 59–61.

IVAN BUNIN

"Aglaya"
Kryzytski, Serge. *The Works*..., 112–113.

"Aleksey Alekseevich"
Kryzytski, Serge. *The Works*..., 192–193.

"Antonov Apples"
Kryzytski, Serge. *The Works*..., 51–52.

"The Archives"
Kryzytski, Serge. *The Works*..., 128–129.

"Ash Wednesday"
Kryzytski, Serge. *The Works*..., 208–209.

"A Ballad"
Kryzytski, Serge. *The Works*..., 210–211.

"Brethren" [originally titled "A Christmas Story"]
Connolly, Julian W. "Desire and Renunciation: Buddhist Elements in the Prose
    of Ivan Bunin," *Canadian Slavonic Papers*, 23 (1981), 13–16.
Kryzytski, Serge. *The Works*..., 130–134.
Woodward, James B. *Ivan Bunin*..., 109–115.

"By the Road"
Kryzytski, Serge. *The Works*..., 121–125.
Woodward, James B. *Ivan Bunin*..., 143–146.

"The Caucasus"
Woodward, James B. *Ivan Bunin*..., 217–218.

"Celestial Bird" [originally titled "Poor Is the Devil"]
Kryzytski, Serge. *The Works...*, 61–62.

"The Chapel"
Kryzytski, Serge. *The Works...*, 210.

"Cold Autumn"
Kryzytski, Serge. *The Works...*, 207–208.

"A Compatriot"
Kryzytski, Serge. *The Works...*, 134–135.

"Comrade Dozornyj"
Kryzytski, Serge. *The Works...*, 164–165.

"The Cricket"
Kryzytski, Serge. *The Works...*, 87–88.

"The Cup of Life"
Kryzytski, Serge. *The Works...*, 125–128.
Woodward, James B. *Ivan Bunin...*, 115–118.

"Dark Alleys"
Kryzytski, Serge. *The Works...*, 211–212.
Woodward, James B. *Ivan Bunin...*, 131–133.

"The Devouring Fire"
Kryzytski, Serge. *The Works...*, 192–193.

"The Dreams of Chang"
Kryzytski, Serge. *The Works...*, 135–139.
Woodward, James B. *Ivan Bunin...*, 118–121.

"The Elagin Affair"
Connolly, Julian W. "Desire and Renunciation...," 18–19.

"Elijah the Prophet"
Kryzytski, Serge. *The Works...*, 110–111.

"Ermil" [originally titled "Crime"]
Kryzytski, Serge. *The Works...*, 139–141.

"The Eternal Spring"
Woodward, James B. *Ivan Bunin...*, 163–165.

"The Eve"
Woodward, James B. *Ivan Bunin...*, 207–208.

"Fedosevna"
Woodward, James B. *Ivan Bunin...*, 50–51.

"The Fog"
Woodward, James B. *Ivan Bunin...*, 71–74.

"A Gay Farmhouse"
Kryzytski, Serge. *The Works...*, 89-91.
Woodward, James B. *Ivan Bunin...*, 51-54.

"The Gentleman from San Francisco"
Kryzytski, Serge. *The Works...*, 154-161.
Woodward, James B. *Ivan Bunin...*, 126-133.

"The Goddess of Reason"
Woodward, James B. *Ivan Bunin...*, 162-164.

"God's Tree"
Kryzytski, Serge. *The Works...*, 188-190.

"The Grammar of Love"
Kryzytski, Serge. *The Works...*, 114-117.
Woodward, James B. *Ivan Bunin...*, 146-149.

"Holy Mountains"
Woodward, James B. *Ivan Bunin...*, 77-78.

"I Say Nothing"
Kryzytski, Serge. *The Works...*, 107-109.

"Ida"
Kryzytski, Serge. *The Works...*, 182-184.
Woodward, James B. *Ivan Bunin...*, 195-197.

"Ignat"
Kryzytski, Serge. *The Works...*, 94-96.
Woodward, James B. *Ivan Bunin...*, 137-145.

"In an Alien Land" [same as "Away from Home"]
Kryzytski, Serge. *The Works...*, 44-45.

"In Autumn"
Woodward, James B. *Ivan Bunin...*, 72-74.

"In the Field" [originally titled "Lazy Bones"]
Kryzytski, Serge. *The Works...*, 53-55.

"In the Fruit Orchard"
Kryzytski, Serge. *The Works...*, 186-188.

"In the Summer House" [same as "At the Dacha"]
Kryzytski, Serge. *The Works...*, 56-57.

"Ioann the Weeper"
Kryzytski, Serge. *The Works...*, 109-110.
Woodward, James B. *Ivan Bunin...*, 100-103.

"Kastryuk"
Kryzytski, Serge. *The Works...*, 41-42.

"Kazimir Stanislavovich"
Kryzytski, Serge. *The Works...*, 120–121.

"The Last Day"
Kryzytski, Serge. *The Works...*, 105–106.
Woodward, James B. *Ivan Bunin...*, 58–59.

"The Last Rendezvous" [same as "The Last Meeting"]
Kryzytski, Serge. *The Works...*, 117–120.

"Light Breathing"
Kryzytski, Serge. *The Works...*, 145–148.
Woodward, James B. *Ivan Bunin...*, 149–154.

"Looped Ears" [same as "Knotted Ears" or "Thieves' Ears"]
Kryzytski, Serge. *The Works...*, 148–149.
Marullo, Thomas G. "Crime Without Punishment: Ivan Bunin's 'Loopy Ears,'"
    Slavic R, 40 (1981), 614–624.
Wehrle, Albert J. "Bunin's Story 'Petlistye Ushi,'" *Russian Lit Tri-Q*, 11 (Winter,
    1975), 443–454.
Woodward, James B. *Ivan Bunin...*, 121–126.

"Mitya's Love"
Kryzytski, Serge. *The Works...*, 169–178.

"The Mordvinian Sarafan"
Kryzytski, Serge. *The Works...*, 184–185.
Woodward, James B. *Ivan Bunin...*, 197–199.

"Muza"
Woodward, James B. *Ivan Bunin...*, 218–225.

"The New Growths"
Kryzytski, Serge. *The Works...*, 113–114.

"News from Home"
Kryzytski, Serge. *The Works...*, 42–44.

"Night"
Connolly, Julian W. "Desire and Renunciation...," 17–18.

"The Night of Denial"
Connolly, Julian W. "Desire and Renunciation...," 16–17.

"A Nocturnal Conversation"
Kryzytski, Serge. *The Works...*, 85–87.

"An Old Man" [same as "An Ancient Man," but originally titled "One Hundred Eight"]
Kryzytski, Serge. *The Works...*, 92.

"The Pines"
Kryzytski, Serge. *The Works...*, 60–61.

"A Premature Spring"
Kryzytski, Serge. *The Works*..., 163–164.

"The Prince Among Princes"
Kryzytski, Serge. *The Works*..., 103–105.

"Rusya"
Woodward, James B. *Ivan Bunin*..., 215–217.

"The Sacrifice"
Kryzytski, Serge. *The Works*..., 111–112.

"The School Master" [same as "The Teacher"]
Kryzytski, Serge. *The Works*..., 55–56.

"The Seekers"
Kryzytski, Serge. *The Works*..., 144–145.

"The Son"
Kryzytski, Serge. *The Works*..., 143–144.
Woodward, James B. *Ivan Bunin*..., 154–159.

"A Spring Evening"
Kryzytski, Serge. *The Works*..., 141–142.
Woodward, James B. *Ivan Bunin*..., 97–100.

"Sunstroke"
Kryzytski, Serge. *The Works*..., 181–182.
Woodward, James B. *Ivan Bunin*..., 182–188.

"Tan'ka"
Kryzytski, Serge. *The Works*..., 40–41.

"Tanya"
Kryzytski, Serge. *The Works*..., 212–213.
Woodward, James B. *Ivan Bunin*..., 214–215.

"To One's Forefathers' Kin"
Kryzytski, Serge. *The Works*..., 195–196.

"To the Edge of the World"
Kryzytski, Serge. *The Works*..., 45–47.

"The Tree of God"
Woodward, James B. *Ivan Bunin*..., 165–166.

"Visiting Cards"
Kryzytski, Serge. *The Works*..., 209–210.

"The Weed"
Kryzytski, Serge. *The Works*..., 150–154.

"The Yelagin Affair"
Kryzytski, Serge. *The Works...*, 178–181.

"Zakhar Vorobyov" [same as "Zaxar Vorob'ev"]
Kryzytski, Serge. *The Works...*, 92–94.
Woodward, James B. *Ivan Bunin...*, 103–105.

VASIL BYKOV

"His Battalion"
Shneidman, N. N. *Soviet Literature...*, 52–54.

"Obelisk"
Shneidman, N. N. *Soviet Literature...*, 51–52.

C. E. B. [unidentified]

"A Celestial Tragedy"
Chu, Limin. *The Image of China...*, 174–177.

ERSKINE CALDWELL

"Knife to Cut the Cornbread With"
Allen, Walter. *The Short Story...*, 197–198.

MORLEY CALLAGHAN

"A Cap for Steve"
Allen, Walter. *The Short Story...*, 207–209.

"A Sick Call"
Allen, Walter. *The Short Story...*, 205–206.
Smith, Elliott L., and Andrew W. Hart, Eds. *The Short Story...*, 68–70.

"The Young Priest"
Allen, Walter. *The Short Story...*, 204–205.

JOHN W. CAMPBELL

"The Last Evolution"
Warrick, Patricia S. *The Cybernetic Imagination...*, 103–104.

MEG CAMPBELL

"Just Saying You Love Me Doesn't Make It So"
Scott, Virgil, and David Madden. *Instructor's Manual...*, 4th ed., 46–49; Madden, David. *Instructor's Manual...*, 5th ed., 5–7.

ALBERT CAMUS

"The Adulterous Woman"
Lazere, Donald. *The Unique Creation*..., 200–202.
Miller, Owen J. "'L'exil et la royaume': Cohérence du recueil," *La Revue des Lettres Modernes*, Nos. 360–365 (1973), 28–33.
Noyer-Weidner, Alfred. "Albert Camus im Stadium der Novelle," *Zeitschrift für französiche Sprache und Literatur*, 70 (1960), 25; rpt. Suther, Judith D., Ed. *Essays*..., trans. Ernest Allen, 72.
Onimus, Jean. "Camus, 'The Adulterous Woman,' and the Starry Sky," trans. Earle D. Clowney, *Cahiers Universitaires Catholiques*, 10 (1960), 561–570; rpt. Suther, Judith D., Ed. *Essays*..., 121–131.

"The Fall"
*Bartfeld, Fernande. "Two Exiles of Camus: Clamence and the Renegade," trans. Patricia M. Hopkins, in Suther, Judith D., Ed. *Essays*..., 279–299.
Boll-Johansen, Hans. "L'Idéologie cachée de 'La Chute' d'Albert Camus," *Revue Romane*, 14 (1979), 174–184.
Cohn, Lionel. "Signification du sacre dans 'La Chute,'" in Gay-Crosier, Raymond, Ed. *Albert Camus 1980*..., 110–117.
Duncan, Robert L. "Judgment without Redemption: Camus' Version of the Fall," *Christianity & Lit*, 30, ii (1981), 43–50.
Gifford, P. "Socrates in Amsterdam: The Uses of Irony in 'La chute,'" *Mod Lang R*, 73 (1978), 499–512.
Keefe, Terry. "Clamence and Women in Albert Camus' 'La Chute,'" *Mod Fiction Stud*, 25 (1980), 646–651.
Lottman, Herbert R. *Albert Camus*..., 561–563.
Meagher, Robert E., Ed. *Albert Camus*..., 239–247.
Rizzuto, Anthony. *Camus' Imperial Vision*, 108–136.
Theis, Raimund. "Albert Camus's Return to Sisyphus," trans. William E. Pohl, in Suther, Judith D., Ed. *Essays*..., 35–37.

"The Growing Stone"
Lazere, Donald. *The Unique Creation*..., 207–209.
Miller, Owen J. "...Coherence du recueil," 40.
Noyer-Weidner, Alfred. "Albert Camus im Stadium...," 31; rpt. Suther, Judith D., Ed. *Essays*..., trans. Ernest Allen, 78.
Schwarz, Martin. "La valeur symbolique du decor dans 'La Pierre qui pousse' d'Albert Camus," *So Central Bull*, 3 (1970), 114.
Segovia, Jaime Castro. "Reflections of the Afro-Brazilian World in 'The Growing Stone,'" trans. Cynthia C. Cornelius, *Présence Francophone*, 7 (Autumn, 1970), 105–120; rpt. Suther, Judith D., Ed. *Essays*..., 171–188.
Theis, Raimund. "Albert Camus's Return...," 40–42.

"The Guest"
*Fortier, Paul A. "The Symbolic Decor of 'The Guest,'" trans. Joseph G. Morello, in Suther, Judith D., Ed. *Essays*..., 203–215.
Greenlee, James W. "Camus' 'Guest': The Inadmissible Complicity," *Stud Twentieth Century Lit*, 2 (1978), 127–139.
Guers-Villate, Yvonne. "Rieux and Daru or the Deliberate Refusal to Influence Others," trans. Joseph G. Morello, *Papers Lang & Lit*, 3 (1967), 229–236; rpt. Suther, Judith D., Ed. *Essays*..., 143–151.

Harth, Erica. "The Creative Alienation of the Writer: Sartre, Camus, and Simone de Beauvoir," *Mosaic*, 8, iii (1975), 182.
Lazere, Donald. *The Unique Creation*..., 205–206.
Madden, David. *Instructor's Manual*..., 5th ed., 96–98.
Noyer-Weidner, Alfred. "Albert Camus im Stadium...," 27–29; rpt. Suther, Judith D., Ed. *Essays*..., trans. Ernest Allen, 75–77.
Sterling, Elwyn F. "A Story of Cain: Another Look at 'L'Hôte,'" *French R*, 54 (1981), 524–529.
Theis, Raimund. "Albert Camus's Return...," 29–31.
Womack, William R., and Francis S. Heck. "A Note on Camus's 'The Guest,'" *Int'l Fiction R*, 2 (1975), 163–165.

"Jonas, or The Artist at Work"
Cryle, Peter. "The Written Painting and the Painted Word in 'Jonas,' in Gay-Crosier, Raymond, Ed. *Albert Camus 1980*..., 123–129.
Fitch, Brian. "'Jonas' ou la Production d'une étoile," *La Revue des lettres modernes*, Nos. 360–365, vi (1973), 51–65.
Godenne, René. "La Nouvelle selon Albert Camus," *Orbis Litterarum*, 31 (1976), 308–315.
Lazere, Donald. *The Unique Creation*..., 206–207.
Noyer-Weidner, Alfred. "Albert Camus im Stadium...," 30; rpt. Suther, Judith D., Ed. *Essays*..., trans. Ernest Allen, 77–78.

"The Renegade"
Bartfeld, Fernande. "Deux Exilés...," 89–112; rpt., trans. Patricia M. Hopkins, in Suther, Judith D., Ed. *Essays*..., 279–299.
Cryle, Peter. "Diversité et symbole dans 'L'exil et le royaume,'" *La Revue des Lettres Modernes*, Nos. 360–365 (1973), 14–15.
————. "Sur 'Le Renégat' et 'El Hadj, ou Le Traité du Faux Prophète' de André Gide," *La Revue des Lettres Modernes*, Nos. 360–365 (1973), 113–118; rpt. Suther, Judith D., Ed. *Essays*..., 301–306.
Douglas, Kenneth, and Sarah N. Lawall. "Masterpieces of the Modern World," in Mack, Maynard, *et al.*, Eds. ... *World Masterpieces*, II, 4th ed., 1289–1290.
*Fortier, Paul A. "The Creation and Function of Atmosphere in 'The Renegade,'" in Suther, Judith D., Ed. *Essays*..., 217–245.
Godenne, René. "La Nouvelle...," 308–315.
Harth, Erica. "The Creative Alienation...," 182–183.
*Hutcheon, Linda. "'The Renegade' as *Nouveau Récit*," trans. Patricia M. Hopkins, in Suther, Judith D., Ed. *Essays*..., 259–278.
Joiner, Lawrence D. "Camus's 'The Renegade': A Quest for Sexual Identity," *Research Stud*, 45 (1977), 171–176.
Lazere, Donald. *The Unique Creation*..., 202–203.
Lekehal, Ali. "Aspects of the Algerian Landscape: The Fantastic in 'The Renegade,'" trans. Judith D. Suther, *Cahiers Algériens de Littérature Comparée*, 3 (1968), 15–32; rpt. Suther, Judith D., Ed. *Essays*..., 153–170.
Nicod-Saraiva, Marguerite. "Une Lecture du 'Renégat,'" *Études de Lettres*, 6, ii (1973), 75–80.
Noyer-Weidner, Alfred. "Albert Camus im Stadium...," 25–26; rpt. Suther, Judith D., Ed. *Essays*..., trans. Ernest Allen, 73–74.

Pelz, Manfred. "The Function of Interior Monologue in 'The Renegade,'" trans. Stephen K. Wright, *Die Neueren Sprachen*, 9 (1970), 462–472; rpt. Suther, Judith D., Ed. *Essays*..., 189–202.

Peters, Renate. "L'Art, la révolte et l'histoire: 'Le Renégat' et *L'Homme révolté*," *French R*, 54 (1981), 517–523.

"The Silent Men"

Lazere, Donald. *The Unique Creation*..., 203–205.

Petrey, Sandy. "Speech, Society and Nature in Camus's 'Les Muets,'" *Romance Notes*, 22 (1981), 161–166.

Rothmund, Alfons. "Albert Camus: 'The Silent Men,'" trans. Jill P. McDonald, *Die Neueren Sprachen*, 11 (1959), 522–528; rpt. Suther, Judith D., Ed. *Essays*..., 111–119.

"The Stranger"

Bartfeld, Fernande. "Aspects du destin dans 'L'Étranger,'" *Hebrew Univ Stud Lit*, 9 (1981), 291–315.

Conroy, William T. "Meursault's Repression: Maman and Murder," *Coll Lit*, 7 (1980), 41–46.

Crumbine, Nancy J. "On Faith," in Perkins, Robert L., Ed. *Kierkegaard's "Fear and Trembling"*..., 189–203.

Doležel, Lumbomír. "Motif Analysis and the System of Sensitivity in 'L'Étranger,'" in Léon, Pierre R., Henri Mitterand, Peter Nesselroth, and Pierre Robert, Eds. *Problèmes*..., 165–175.

Langer, Lawrence L. *The Age of Atrocity*..., 141–148.

Leov, Nola M. "'L'Étranger': The Case for the Defense," *Essays French Lit*, 15 (1978), 82–115.

Michot-Dietrich, Hela. "Symbolische Reflexionen über den 'Étranger' und 'Homo faber,'" *Germanisch-Romanische Monatsschrift*, 30 (1980), 423–437.

Noyer-Weidner, Alfred. "Structure et sens de 'L'Étranger,'" in Gay-Crosier, Raymond, Ed. *Albert Camus 1980*..., 72–85.

O'Hanlon, Redmond. "The Life-Death Nexus in 'L'Étranger,'" *Nottingham French Stud*, 19, ii (1980), 31–48.

Rizzuto, Anthony. *Camus' Imperial Vision*, 11–28.

Sellin, Eric. "Camus' 'L'Étranger,'" *Explicator*, 40, i (1981), 55–57.

Shahbaz, Caterina. "Diversity and Unity in the Naming Technique of Camus' 'L'Étranger,'" *Lit Onomastics Stud*, 7 (1980), 177–188.

Solomon, Robert C. "'L'Étranger' and the Truth," *Philosophy & Lit*, 2 (1978), 141–159.

Tacca, Oscar. "'L'Étranger' comme récit d'auter-transcripteur," in Gay-Crosier, Raymond, Ed. *Albert Camus 1980*..., 87–98.

Thody, Philip. "Camus's 'L'Étranger' Revisited," *Critical Q*, 21, ii (1979), 61–69.

Thomas, P. Aloysius. "The Positive Aspect of Violence in 'L'Étranger,' Part II," *Lang Q*, 16, iii–iv (1978), 15–18.

Vilhena, Maria da Conceição. "'L'Étranger' de Camus: Parole et silence," *Arquipélago*, 2 (1980), 297–315.

Wagner, Monique. "Physical Malaise and Subconscious Death-Wish in 'L'Étranger,'" *Michigan Academician*, 11 (1979), 331–341.

Warde, William B. "Contrapuntal Images in Camus' 'The Stranger,'" *Ball State Univ Forum*, 20, iii (1979), 60–67.

Welsh, Alexander. ...*Hero as Quixote*, 215–216.

Witt, Mary A. "Rage and Racism in 'The Stranger' and *Native Son*," *Comparatist*, 1 (1977), 35–47.

TRUMAN CAPOTE

"Among the Paths of Eden"
Garson, Helen S. *Truman Capote*, 106–110.
Reed, Kenneth T. *Truman Capote*, 46–47.

"Brooklyn"
Garson, Helen S. *Truman Capote*, 115–116.

"Children on Their Birthdays"
Garson, Helen S. *Truman Capote*, 55–59.
Reed, Kenneth T. *Truman Capote*, 59–62.

"A Christmas Memory"
Garson, Helen S. *Truman Capote*, 97–103.

"La Côte Basque"
Garson, Helen S. *Truman Capote*, 170–172.

"Dazzle"
Garson, Helen S. *Truman Capote*, 183–185.

"A Diamond Guitar"
Garson, Helen S. *Truman Capote*, 91–94.
Reed, Kenneth T. *Truman Capote*, 62–64.

"The Headless Hawk"
Garson, Helen S. *Truman Capote*, 44–50.
Reed, Kenneth T. *Truman Capote*, 39–43.

"House of Flowers"
Garson, Helen S. *Truman Capote*, 94–97.
Reed, Kenneth T. *Truman Capote*, 68–70.

"Jug of Silver"
Garson, Helen S. *Truman Capote*, 59–61.

"Kate McCloud"
Garson, Helen S. *Truman Capote*, 178–180.

"Master Misery"
Garson, Helen S. *Truman Capote*, 28–33.

"A Mink of One's Own"
Reed, Kenneth T. *Truman Capote*, 36–38.

"Miriam"
Barker, Gerard A. *Instructor's Manual...*, 49–50.
Garson, Helen S. *Truman Capote*, 39–44.
Kennedy, X. J. *Instructor's Manual...*, 2nd ed., 31–32.
Larsen, Michael J. "Capote's 'Miriam' and the Literature of the Double," *Int'l
    Fiction R*, 7, i (1980), 53–54.

Madden, David. *Instructor's Manual...*, 5th ed., 92-93.
Reed, Kenneth T. *Truman Capote*, 37-40.

"Mojave"
Garson, Helen S. *Truman Capote*, 168-170.
Reed, Kenneth T. *Truman Capote*, 47-49.

"My Side of the Matter"
Reed, Kenneth T. *Truman Capote*, 55-57.

"Preacher's Legend"
Reed, Kenneth T. *Truman Capote*, 53-55.

"Shut a Final Door"
Garson, Helen S. *Truman Capote*, 33-39.
Reed, Kenneth T. *Truman Capote*, 41-43.

"A Tree of Night"
Reed, Kenneth T. *Truman Capote*, 50-54.
Smith, Elliott L., and Andrew W. Hart, Eds. *The Short Story...*, 126-127.

"Unspoiled Monsters"
Garson, Helen S. *Truman Capote*, 172-178.

"The Walls Are Cold"
Reed, Kenneth T. *Truman Capote*, 35-37.

EMILIO CARBALLIDO

"La caja vacía"
Peden, Margaret S. *Emilio Carballido*, 58-60.

"El cubilete"
Peden, Margaret S. *Emilio Carballido*, 56-57.

"Danza antigua"
Peden, Margaret S. *Emilio Carballido*, 64-65.

"La desterrada"
Peden, Margaret S. *Emilio Carballido*, 63-64.

"Las flores blancas"
Peden, Margaret S. *Emilio Carballido*, 61-63.

"A Half-Dozen Sheets"
Peden, Margaret S. *Emilio Carballido*, 57-58.

"Los huéspedes"
Peden, Margaret S. *Emilio Carballido*, 66-68.

"La paz después del combate"
Peden, Margaret S. *Emilio Carballido*, 60–61.

"Los prodijios"
Peden, Margaret S. *Emilio Carballido*, 65–66.

WILLIAM CARLETON

"The Broken Oath"
Wolff, Robert L. *William Carleton...*, 29–31.

"The Brothers"
Wolff, Robert L. *William Carleton...*, 43–44.

"The Death of a Devotee"
Wolff, Robert L. *William Carleton...*, 41–42.

"Denis O'Shaughnessy Going to Maynooth"
Wolff, Robert L. *William Carleton...*, 49–52.

"The Donagh, or the Horse-Stealers"
Wolff, Robert L. *William Carleton...*, 66.

"Father Butler"
Wolff, Robert L. *William Carleton...*, 31–34.

"The Hedge School and the Abduction of Mat Kavanagh"
Wolff, Robert L. *William Carleton...*, 58–60.

"The History of a Chimney Sweep"
Wolff, Robert L. *William Carleton...*, 48.

"The Illicit Distiller or the Force of Conscience"
Wolff, Robert L. *William Carleton...*, 47–48.

"An Irish Wedding"
Wolff, Robert L. *William Carleton...*, 55–57.

"Lachlin Murray and the Blessed Candle"
Wolff, Robert L. *William Carleton...*, 44–45.

"The Lianhan Shee, An Irish Superstition"
Wolff, Robert L. *William Carleton...*, 46–47.

"The Lough Dearg Pilgrim"
Wolff, Robert L. *William Carleton...*, 28–29.

"The Materialist"
Wolff, Robert L. *William Carleton...*, 48–50.

"The Midnight Mass"
Wolff, Robert L. *William Carleton*..., 65-66.

"Party Fight"
Wolff, Robert L. *William Carleton*..., 60-62.

"Phelim O'Toole's Courtship"
Wolff, Robert L. *William Carleton*..., 70.

"Phil Purcel, the Pig-Driver"
Wolff, Robert L. *William Carleton*..., 66-67.

"The Poor Scholar"
Wolff, Robert L. *William Carleton*..., 62-64.

"The Priest's Funeral"
Wolff, Robert L. *William Carleton*..., 42-43.

"A Station"
Wolff, Robert L. *William Carleton*..., 34-41.

ALEJO CARPENTIER

"El camino de Santiago"
Hidalgo, Jorge. "Utopía y frustración en 'El camino de Santiago' de Alejo Carpentier," in Gordon, Alan M., and Evelyn Rugg, Eds. *Actas del Sexto Congreso Internacional*..., 386-390.

"Los fugitivos"
Arrom, José Juan. "*Congrí*: Apostilla lexicográfica a un cuento de Carpentier," *Boletín de la Academia Norteamericana*, 2-3 (1977-1978), 85-87.

"Viaje a la semilla"
Alonso, Carlos. "'Viaje a la semilla': Historia de una entelequía," *Mod Lang Notes*, 94 (1979), 386-393.

RAYMOND CARVER

"Are You a Doctor?"
Boxer, David, and Cassandra Phillips. "Will You Please Be Quiet, Please?: Voyeurism, Dissociation, and the Art of Raymond Carver," *Iowa R*, 10, iii (1979), 84-85.

"Collectors"
Boxer, David, and Cassandra Phillips. "Will You Please...," 86-87.

"The Father"
Boxer, David, and Cassandra Phillips. "Will You Please...," 83-84.

"The Idea"
Boxer, David, and Cassandra Phillips. "Will You Please...," 77-78.

"Neighbors"
Boxer, David, and Cassandra Phillips. "Will You Please...," 76-77.

"Put Yourself in My Shoes"
Boxer, David, and Cassandra Phillips. "Will You Please...," 81-83.

"What's in Alaska?"
Boxer, David, and Cassandra Phillips. "Will You Please...," 80-81.

"'Will You Please Be Quiet, Please?'"
Boxer, David, and Cassandra Phillips. "Will You Please...," 87-90.

WILLA CATHER

"The Clemency of the Court"
Albertini, Virgil. "Willa Cather's Early Short Stories: A Link to the Agrarian Realists," *Markham R*, 8 (1979), 70-71.

"Eleanor's House"
Arnold, Marilyn. "Willa Cather's Nostalgia: A Study in Ambivalence," *Research Stud*, 49 (1981), 23-34.

"Lou, the Prophet"
Albertini, Virgil. "...Agrarian Realists," 70.

"Neighbour Rosicky"
Piacentino, Edward J. "The Agrarian Mode in Cather's 'Neighbour Rosicky,'" *Markham R*, 8 (1979), 52-54.

"On the Divide"
Albertini, Virgil. "...Agrarian Realists," 71-72.

"Paul's Case"
Allen, Walter. *The Short Story...*, 123-125.
Brown, Rosellen. "On Willa Cather and 'Paul's Case,'" in Skaggs, Calvin, Ed. *The American Short Story*, II, 189-194.
Howard, Daniel F., and John Ribar. *Instructor's Manual...*, 4th ed., 22.

"Peter"
Albertini, Virgil. "...Agrarian Realists," 69-70.

"Tom Outland's Story"
Murphy, John J. "The Mesa Verde Story and Cather's 'Tom Outland's Story,'" *Notes Mod Am Lit*, 5, ii (1981), Item 9.

"A Wagner Matinée"
Altenbernd, Lynn, and Leslie L. Lewis. *Instructor's Manual...*, 3rd ed., 10-11.

BLAISE CENDRARS [FRÉDÉRIC SAUSER]

"Le cercle du diamant"
Chefdor, Monique. *Blaise Cendrars*, 120.

"Morganni Nameh"
Chefdor, Monique. *Blaise Cendrars*, 33–35.

"Paris, Port-de-Mer"
Bochner, Jay. "A Geography of Reading in 'Paris, Port-de-Mer,'" *Stud Twentieth Century Lit*, 3 (1979), 187–202.

"La Tour Eiffel sidérale"
Chefdor, Monique. *Blaise Cendrars*, 121–122.

ROBERT W. CHAMBERS

"The Demoiselle d'Ys"
Punter, David. *The Literature of Terror* . . . , 278–279.

"The Repairer of Reputations"
Punter, David. *The Literature of Terror* . . . , 276–278.

RAYMOND CHANDLER

"I'll Be Waiting"
Kennedy, X. J. *Instructor's Manual* . . . , 2nd ed., 35–37.

CHANG HSI-KUO

"The Leader"
Lau, Joseph S. M. "Obsession with Taiwan: The Fiction of Chang Hsi-kuo," in Faurot, Jeannette L., Ed. *Chinese Fiction from Taiwan* . . . , 159–163.

"Red Boy"
Lau, Joseph S. M. "Obsession with Taiwan . . . ," 150–151.

FRANÇOIS-RENÉ de CHATEAUBRIAND

"Atala"
MacAndrew, Elizabeth. *The Gothic Tradition* . . . , 62–65.
Racault, J. M. "D' 'Atala' à 'René' ou la fin de l'utopie des Lumières," *Travaux de Linguistique et de Littérature*, 17, ii (1979), 85–103.

"René"
Benrekassa, Georges. "Le Dit du moi: Du roman personnel à l'autobiographie: 'René'/ *Werther, Poésie et vérité/Mémoires d'outre-tombe*," in Decottignies, Jean, Ed. *Les Sujets* . . . , 85–140.

Kurrik, Maire J. *Literature and Negation*, 71-73.
Racault, J. M. "D' 'Atala' à 'René'...," 85-103.
Stecca, Luciano. "Chateaubriand, 'René': Un caso di autocensura," *Rivista di Letterature*, 32 (1979), 32-44.

JOHN CHEEVER

"The Angel of the Bridge"
Waldeland, Lynne. *John Cheever*, 95-96.

"Artemis, the Honest Well Digger"
Waldeland, Lynne. *John Cheever*, 121-122.

"Boy in Rome"
Waldeland, Lynne. *John Cheever*, 87-88.

"The Brigadier and the Golf Widow"
Waldeland, Lynne. *John Cheever*, 92-94.

"Brimmer"
Waldeland, Lynne. *John Cheever*, 81-83.

"The Brothers"
Waldeland, Lynne. *John Cheever*, 22-23.

"Clementina"
Waldeland, Lynne. *John Cheever*, 100-101.

"The Country Husband"
Waldeland, Lynne. *John Cheever*, 66-68.

"The Cure"
Waldeland, Lynne. *John Cheever*, 35.

"The Death of Justina"
Waldeland, Lynne. *John Cheever*, 79-81.

"An Educated American Woman"
Waldeland, Lynne. *John Cheever*, 97-98.

"The Enormous Radio"
Ahrends, Günter. ...*Kurzgeschichte*, 206-208.
Allen, Walter. *The Short Story*..., 367-369.
Waldeland, Lynne. *John Cheever*, 31-33.

"Expelled"
Waldeland, Lynne. *John Cheever*, 18-19.

"The Five-Forty-Eight"
Waldeland, Lynne. *John Cheever*, 70-71.

"The Fourth Alarm"
Madden, David. *Instructor's Manual...*, 5th ed., 20–21.
Waldeland, Lynne. *John Cheever*, 118–119.

"Gee-Gee"
Higgs, Robert J. *Laurel & Thorn...*, 146–148.

"Goodbye, My Brother"
Scott, Virgil, and David Madden. *Instructor's Manual...*, 4th ed., 85–88.
Waldeland, Lynne. *John Cheever*, 28–30.

"The Hartleys"
Reilly, Edward C. "Cheever's 'The Hartleys' and Its Major Image," *Notes Contemp Lit*, 10, v (1980), 10.

"The Housebreaker of Shady Hill"
Waldeland, Lynne. *John Cheever*, 65–66.

"The Jewels of the Cabots"
Waldeland, Lynne. *John Cheever*, 124–125.

"Just Tell Me Who It Was"
Waldeland, Lynne. *John Cheever*, 68.

"The Lowboy"
Waldeland, Lynne. *John Cheever*, 83–84.

"Metamorphoses"
Waldeland, Lynne. *John Cheever*, 98–99.

"Miscellany of Characters That Will Not Appear"
Waldeland, Lynne. *John Cheever*, 88–89.

"The Music Teacher"
Waldeland, Lynne. *John Cheever*, 95–97.

"O Youth and Beauty!"
Higgs, Robert J. *Laurel & Thorn...*, 144–146.
Waldeland, Lynne. *John Cheever*, 68–70.

"Percy"
Waldeland, Lynne. *John Cheever*, 119–121.

"Publick House"
Waldeland, Lynne. *John Cheever*, 23–24.

"The Scarlet Moving Van"
Waldeland, Lynne. *John Cheever*, 84–85.

"The Seaside House"
Waldeland, Lynne. *John Cheever*, 101–102.

"The Summer Farmer"
Waldeland, Lynne. *John Cheever*, 34.

"The Survivor"
Waldeland, Lynne. *John Cheever*, 94–95.

"The Swimmer"
Reilly, Edward C. "Autumnal Images in John Cheever's 'The Swimmer,'" *Notes Contemp Lit*, 10, i (1980), 12.

"Torch Song"
Pawlowski, Robert S. "Myth as Metaphor: Cheever's 'Torch Song,'" *Research Stud*, 47 (1979), 118–121.
Waldeland, Lynne. *John Cheever*, 30–31.

"The Trouble of Marcie Flint"
Waldeland, Lynne. *John Cheever*, 64–65.

"A Woman Without a Country"
Waldeland, Lynne. *John Cheever*, 99–100.

"The World of Apples"
Allen, Walter. *The Short Story...*, 370–371.
Waldeland, Lynne. *John Cheever*, 122–124.

"The Worm in the Apple"
Waldeland, Lynne. *John Cheever*, 71–72.

"The Wrysons"
Waldeland, Lynne. *John Cheever*, 85–87.

ANTON CHEKHOV

"About Love"
Kirk, Irina. *Anton Chekhov*, 110–111.

"An Anonymous Story"
Winner, Anthony. *Characters...*, 182–188.

"Ariadna"
Tulloch, John. *Chekhov...*, 150–151.

"At Home" [same as "The Homecoming"]
Winner, Anthony. *Characters...*, 147–148.

"The Betrothed"
Stowell, H. Peter. *Literary Impressionism...*, 144–150.

"The Bishop"
Stowell, H. Peter. *Literary Impressionism...*, 135–144.

"The Black Monk"
Kirk, Irina. *Anton Chekhov*, 87–90.
MacAndrew, Elizabeth. *The Gothic Tradition...*, 207.

"The Bride"
Kirk, Irina. *Anton Chekhov*, 121–125.

"The Chameleon"
Kirk, Irina. *Anton Chekhov*, 36–37.

"The Darling"
Kirk, Irina. *Anton Chekhov*, 112–114.
Winner, Anthony. *Characters...*, 143–145.

"Dreams"
Rohrberger, Mary. *Instructor's Manual...*, 15.

"A Dreary Story" [same as "A Boring Story," "A Dull Story," or "A Tedious Tale"]
Kirk, Irina. *Anton Chekhov*, 58–70.
Stowell, H. Peter. *Literary Impressionism...*, 106–109.
Winner, Anthony. *Characters...*, 157–161.

"The Duel"
Kirk, Irina. *Anton Chekhov*, 73–82.
Tulloch, John. *Chekhov...*, 118–131.
Winner, Anthony. *Characters...*, 192–193.

"Fat and Thin"
Kirk, Irina. *Anton Chekhov*, 35–36.
Stowell, H. Peter. *Literary Impressionism...*, 69–71.

"A Fragment"
Stowell, H. Peter. *Literary Impressionism...*, 109–110.

"Gooseberries"
Kirk, Irina. *Anton Chekhov*, 107–110.

"The Grasshopper" [same as "La Cigale"]
Freling, Roger. "A New View of Dr. Dymov in Chekhov's 'The Grasshopper,'"
    Stud Short Fiction, 16 (1979), 183–187.
Rohrberger, Mary. *Instructor's Manual...*, 14–15.

"Grisha"
Stowell, H. Peter. *Literary Impressionism...*, 75–76.

"Gusev"
Ehre, Milton. "The Symbolic Structure of Chekhov's 'Gusev,'" *Ulbandus R*, 2, i
    (1979), 76–85.
Kirk, Irina. *Anton Chekhov*, 70–73.

"The House with the Mezzanine"
Kirk, Irina. *Anton Chekhov*, 97–100.

"In the Cart"
Stowell, H. Peter. *Literary Impressionism*..., 113–119.

"In the Ravine"
Barksdale, E. C. *Daggers of the Mind*..., 127–128.

"The Kiss"
Conrad, Joseph L. "Sensuality in Čexov's Prose," *Slavic & East European J*, 24 (1980), 111–113.
Rosen, Nathan. "The Life Force in Chekhov's 'The Kiss,'" *Ulbandus R*, 2, i (1979), 175–185.
Stowell, H. Peter. *Literary Impressionism*..., 81–85.

"The Lady with the Dog" [same as "The Lady with the Lapdog," "The Lady with the Pet Dog," or "The Lady with the Small Dog"]
Barksdale, E. C. *Daggers of the Mind*..., 122–124.
Kirk, Irina. *Anton Chekhov*, 114–117.
Stowell, H. Peter. *Literary Impressionism*..., 120–135.
Winner, Anthony. *Characters*..., 169–170.

"The Lament" [same as "Misery"]
Madden, David. *Instructor's Manual*..., 5th ed., 69–71.
Winslow, Joan D. "Language as Theme in Chekhov's 'Misery,'" *RE: Artes Liberales*, 4, ii (1979), 1–7.

"Lights"
Kirk, Irina. *Anton Chekhov*, 37–38.

"The Man in a Shell" [same as "The Man in a Case"]
Kirk, Irina. *Anton Chekhov*, 105–107.

"Melyuzga"
Kirk, Irina. *Anton Chekhov*, 37–38.

"Mire"
Conrad, Joseph L. "Sensuality...," 108–109.

"A Misfortune"
Conrad, Joseph L. "Sensuality...," 105–107.

"My Life"
Kirk, Irina. *Anton Chekhov*, 90–92.
Tulloch, John. *Chekhov*..., 163–166.
Winner, Anthony. *Characters*..., 161–168.

"The Native Corner"
Kirk, Irina. *Anton Chekhov*, 103–104.

"The New Villa"
Altenbernd, Lynn, and Leslie L. Lewis. *Instructor's Manual*..., 3rd ed., 11–12.

"On the Road"
Senderovich, Savely. "The Poetic Structure of Čexov's Short Story 'On the Road,'"
    in Kodjak, Andrej, Michael J. Connolly, and Krystyna Pomorska, Eds.
    ...*Narrative Texts*, 44-81.

"Oysters"
Stowell, H. Peter. *Literary Impressionism*..., 72-75.

"Peasants"
Kirk, Irina. *Anton Chekhov*, 100-103.
Winner, Anthony. *Characters*..., 189-192.

"Rothschild's Fiddle"
Kirk, Irina. *Anton Chekhov*, 95-97.

"Sleepy"
Kirk, Irina. *Anton Chekhov*, 43-45.
Stowell, H. Peter. "Chekhov's Prose Fugue: 'Sleepy,'" *Russian Lit Tri-Q*, 11 (Winter,
    1975), 435-442.
_____. *Literary Impressionism*..., 91-97.

"The Steppe"
Kirk, Irina. *Anton Chekhov*, 45-52.
Stowell, H. Peter. *Literary Impressionism*..., 97-105.

"The Story of Miss N. N."
Stowell, H. Peter. *Literary Impressionism*..., 67-77.

"A Tale"
O'Bell, Leslie. "Čexov's 'Skazka': The Intellectual's Fairy Tale," *Slavic & East
    European J*, 25, iv (1981), 33-46.

"Thieves"
Conrad, Joseph L. "Sensuality ...," 113-115.

"A Trifle from Real Life"
Rohrberger, Mary. *Instructor's Manual*..., 14.

"Typhus"
Stowell, H. Peter. *Literary Impressionism*..., 76-77.

"Vanka"
Brooks, Cleanth, and Robert P. Warren. *Understanding Fiction*, 3rd ed., 49-50.
Frost, Edgar L. "The Search for Eternity in Čexov's Fiction: The Flight from
    Time as a Source of Tension," *Russian Lang J*, 108 (1977), 113.
Kirk, Irina. *Anton Chekhov*, 42-43.

"Verochka"
Stowell, H. Peter. *Literary Impressionism*..., 78-81.

"Volodya" [originally titled "His First Love"]
Conrad, Joseph L. "Sensuality...," 109-111.

"Ward No. 6"
Durkin, Andrew R. "Chekhov's Response to Dostoevskii: The Case of 'Ward Six,'"
    Slavic R, 40 (1981), 49–59.
Frost, Edgar L. "The Search for Eternity...," 112.
Kirk, Irina. *Anton Chekhov*, 82–87.
Tulloch, John. *Chekhov...*, 65–66.
Winner, Anthony. *Characters...*, 171–182.

"The Witch"
Conrad, Joseph L. "Sensuality...," 107–108.

CHEN JO-HSI

"Big Blue Fish"
Hsu, Kai-yu. "A Sense of History: Reading Chen Jo-hsi's Stories," in Faurot,
    Jeannette L., Ed. *Chinese Fiction from Taiwan...*, 227–228.

"Black Cat with Gray Eyes"
Hsu, Kai-yu. "A Sense of History...," 208–209.

"Ching-ching's Birthday"
Hsu, Kai-yu. "A Sense of History...," 216–219.

"Hsin Chuang"
Hsu, Kai-yu. "A Sense of History...," 212–213.

"Keng Erh in Peking"
Hsu, Kai-yu. "A Sense of History...," 223–225.

"The Last Performance"
Hsu, Kai-yu. "A Sense of History...," 213–214.

"Pa-li's Journey"
Hsu, Kai-yu. "A Sense of History...," 209–210.

"Spring Comes Late"
Hsu, Kai-yu. "A Sense of History...," 230–231.

"Subway"
Hsu, Kai-yu. "A Sense of History...," 229–230.

"Uncle Ch'in-chih"
Hsu, Kai-yu. "A Sense of History...," 207–208.

CH'EN YING-CHEN

"The Country Village Teacher"
Miller, Lucien. "A Break in the Chain: The Short Stories of Ch'en Ying-chen,"
    in Faurot, Jeannette L., Ed. *Chinese Fiction from Taiwan...*, 98–102.

"My Younger Brother K'ang Hsiung"
Miller, Lucien. "A Break in the Chain...," 88–94.

"Poor, Poor Dumb Mouths"
Miller, Lucien. "A Break in the Chain...," 94–98.

"A Race of Generals"
Miller, Lucien. "A Break in the Chain...," 102–107.

CHARLES W. CHESNUTT

"Aunt Mimy's Son"
Andrews, William L. ...*Charles W. Chesnutt*, 87–88.

"Baxter's Procrustes"
Andrews, William L. ...*Charles W. Chesnutt*, 213–214.

"The Bouquet"
Andrews, William L. ...*Charles W. Chesnutt*, 95–97.

"Cicely's Dream"
Andrews, William L. ...*Charles W. Chesnutt*, 105–106.

"Dave's Neckliss"
Andrews, William L. ...*Charles W. Chesnutt*, 65–67.

"The Doll"
Andrews, William L. ...*Charles W. Chesnutt*, 83–85.

"Evelyn's Husband"
Andrews, William L. ...*Charles W. Chesnutt*, 130–131.

"The Goophered Grapevine"
Andrews, William L. ...*Charles W. Chesnutt*, 61–62.
Myers, Karen M. "Mythic Patterns in Charles Waddell Chesnutt's *The Conjure Woman* and Ovid's *Metamorphoses*," *Black Am Lit Forum*, 13 (1979), 13–14.
Webb, Bernice L. "Picking at 'The Goophered Grapevine,'"*Kentucky Folklore Record*, 25 (1979), 64–67.

"The Gray Wolf's Ha'nt"
Andrews, William L. ...*Charles W. Chesnutt*, 60–61.

"Her Virginia Mammy"
Andrews, William L. ...*Charles W. Chesnutt*, 106–109.

"Mandy Oxendine"
Andrews, William L. ...*Charles W. Chesnutt*, 145–148.

"The March of Progress"
Andrews, William L. ...*Charles W. Chesnutt*, 82–83.

"Mars Jeems's Nightmare"
Barthold, Bonnie J. *Black Time...*, 47–48.
MacKethan, Lucinda H. *The Dream of Arcady...*, 92–94.

"A Matter of Principle"
Andrews, William L. *...Charles W. Chesnutt*, 110–113.

"The Partners"
Andrews, William L. *...Charles W. Chesnutt*, 85–86.

"The Passing of Grandison"
Andrews, William L. *...Charles W. Chesnutt*, 93–95.
Delmar, P. Jay. "The Mask as Theme and Structure: Charles W. Chesnutt's 'The
    Sheriff's Children' and 'The Passing of Grandison,'" *Am Lit*, 51 (1979), 371–375.

"Paul Marchand, F.M.C."
Andrews, William L. *...Charles W. Chesnutt*, 265–267.

"Po' Sandy"
Andrews, William L. *...Charles W. Chesnutt*, 63–65.
Barthold, Bonnie J. *Black Time...*, 107–108.

"The Quarry"
Andrews, William L. *...Charles W. Chesnutt*, 269–272.

"The Rainbow Chasers"
Andrews, William L. *...Charles W. Chesnutt*, 121–122.

"The Sheriff's Children"
Andrews, William L. *...Charles W. Chesnutt*, 100–103.
Delmar, P. Jay. "The Mask as Theme and Structure...," 366–371.

"Uncle Wellington's Wives"
Andrews, William L. *...Charles W. Chesnutt*, 88–91.

"The Web of Circumstance"
Andrews, William L. *...Charles W. Chesnutt*, 97–100.
Delmar, P. Jay. "Charles W. Chesnutt's 'The Web of Circumstance' and Richard
    Wright's 'Long Black Song': The Tragedy of Property," *Stud Short Fiction*,17
    (1980), 178–179.

"The Wife of His Youth"
Andrews, William L. *...Charles W. Chesnutt*, 113–116.

CHIANG HUNG-CHIAO

"The Coward"
Link, E. Perry. *Mandarin Ducks...*, 223–224.

CH'IEN CHUNG-SHU

"Cat"
Gunn, Edward M. *Unwelcome Muse...*, 245–246.

"God's Dream"
Gunn, Edward M. *Unwelcome Muse...*, 244–245.

"Souvenir"
Gunn, Edward M. *Unwelcome Muse...*, 246–249.

KATE CHOPIN

"At Cheniere Caminada"
Dyer, Joyce C. "Kate Chopin's Sleeping Bruties," *Markham R*, 10 (Fall–Winter, 1980–1981), 12–13.

"Athénaïse"
Dyer, Joyce C. "Night Images in the Work of Kate Chopin," *Am Lit Realism*, 14 (1981), 223–224.
Jones, Anne G. *Tomorrow Is Another Day...*, 149–150.

"Azelie"
Dyer, Joyce C. "...Sleeping Bruties," 11–12.

"La Belle Zoraïde"
Jones, Anne G. *Tomorrow Is Another Day...*, 151–152.

"Beyond the Bayou"
Rowe, Anne. "A Note on 'Beyond the Bayou,'" *Kate Chopin Newsletter*, 1, ii (1975), 7–9.

"Désirée's Baby"
Altenbernd, Lynn, and Leslie L. Lewis. *Instructor's Manual...*, 3rd ed., 12–13.
Toth, Emily. "Kate Chopin and Literary Convention: 'Désirée's Baby,'" *Southern Stud*, 20 (1981), 201–208.

"Fedora"
Dyer, Joyce. "The Restive Brute: The Symbolic Presentation of Repression and Sublimation in Kate Chopin's 'Fedora,'" *Stud Short Fiction*, 18 (1981), 261–265.

"The Going Away of Liza"
Dyer, Joyce C. "Night Images...," 218–219.

"Lilacs"
Howell, Elmo. "Kate Chopin and the Pull of Faith: A Note on 'Lilacs,'" *Southern Stud*, 18 (1979), 103–109.

"Loka"
Scheick, William J. *The Half-Breed...*, 28–29.

"Love on the Bon-Dieu"
Dyer, Joyce C. "Night Images...," 221-222.

"Ma'ame Pélagie"
Dyer, Joyce C. "Night Images...," 219-220.
Jones, Anne G. *Tomorrow Is Another Day*..., 152-153.

"A Respectable Woman"
Dyer, Joyce. "Gouvernail, Kate Chopin's Sensitive Bachelor," *Southern Lit J*, 14, i (1981), 46-55.
––––––. "Night Images...," 222-223.

"A Sentimental Soul"
Toth, Emily. "The Cult of Domesticity and 'A Sentimental Soul,'" *Kate Chopin Newsletter*, 1, ii (1975), 12-16.

"The Storm"
Baker, Sheridan, and George Perkins. *Instructor's Manual*..., 21-22.
Jones, Anne G. *Tomorrow Is Another Day*..., 141-142.

"The Story of an Hour"
Altenbernd, Lynn, and Leslie L. Lewis. *Instructor's Manual*..., 3rd ed., 12.

"Vagabonds"
Dyer, Joyce C. "Night Images...," 224-225.

"A Vocation and a Voice"
Dyer, Joyce C. "...Sleeping Bruties," 13-15.
Skaggs, Peggy. "The Boy's Quest in Kate Chopin's 'A Vocation and a Voice,'" *Am Lit*, 51 (1979), 270-276.

AGATHA CHRISTIE

"The Capture of Cerberus"
Bargainnier, Earl F. *The Gentle Art*..., 53-54.

"The Under Dog"
Bargainnier, Earl F. *The Gentle Art*..., 124-125.

"Where There's a Will"
Bargainnier, Earl F. *The Gentle Art*..., 110-111.

CHU HSI-NING

"Molten Iron"
Birch, Cyril. "Images of Suffering in Taiwan Fiction," in Faurot, Jeannette L., Ed. *Chinese Fiction from Taiwan*..., 72-74.

CHUNG LI-HO

"Oleander"
Chang, Shi-huo. "Realism in Taiwan Fiction: Two Directions," in Faurot, Jeannette
L., Ed. *Chinese Fiction from Taiwan* . . . , 37-38.

CHARLES-ALBERT CINGRIA

"Le Petit labyrinthe harmonique"
Beaujour, Michel. "Se promener c'est apprendre à mourir," *Swiss-French Stud*,
2, i (1981), 6-23.

WALTER VAN TILBURG CLARK

"The Portable Phonograph"
Scott, Virgil, and David Madden. *Instructor's Manual* . . . , 4th ed., 27-29; Madden,
David. *Instructor's Manual* . . . , 5th ed., 36-38.

"The Watchful Gods"
Milton, John R. . . . *American West*, 223-224.

ARTHUR C. CLARKE

"The Star"
Nedelkovich, Alexander. "The Stellar Parallels: Robert Silverberg, Larry Niven,
and Arthur C. Clarke," *Extrapolation*, 21 (1980), 348-360.

MARCUS CLARKE

"Pretty Dick"
Scheckter, John. "The Lost Child in Australian Fiction," *Mod Fiction Stud*, 27 (1981),
65-68.

LUCILLE CLIFTON

"The Magic Mama"
Maglin, Nan B. "'Don't never forget the bridge that you crossed over on': The
Literature of Matrilineage,'" in Davidson, Cathy N., and E. M. Broner, Eds.
The Lost Tradition . . . , 261.

MATT COHEN

"Johnny Crackle Sings"
Woodcock, George. "Armies Moving in the Night: The Fiction of Matt Cohen,"
Int'l Fiction R, 6, i (1979), 19-20.

"Korsoniloff"
Woodcock, George. "Armies Moving...," 19.

"Vogel"
Woodcock, George. "Armies Moving...," 18-19.

SIDONIE-GABRIELLE COLETTE

"The Patriarch"
Stockinger, Jacob. "Impurity and Sexual Politics in the Provinces: Colette's
Anti-Idyll in 'The Patriarch,'" *Women's Stud*, 8 (1981), 357-366.

"The Tender Shoot"
McCarthy, Mari. "Possessing Female Space: 'The Tender Shoot,'" *Women's Stud*,
8 (1981), 367-374.

JOHN COLLIER

"Bottle Party"
Scott, Virgil, and David Madden. *Instructor's Manual...*, 4th ed., 34-36.

"The Chaser"
Baker, Sheridan, and George Perkins. *Instructor's Manual...*, 6-7.

"De Mortuis"
*Brooks, Cleanth, and Robert P. Warren. *Understanding Fiction*, 3rd ed., 55-56.

"Green Thoughts"
Altenbernd, Lynn, and Leslie L. Lewis. *Instructor's Manual...*, 3rd ed., 15-16.

WILKIE COLLINS

"Blow Up with the Brig!"
Muller, C. H. "Victorian Sensationalism: The Short Stories of Wilkie Collins,"
Unisa Engl Stud, 11, i (1973), 19-20.

"The Double-Bedded Room"
Muller, C. H. "Victorian Sensationalism...," 18-19.

"Mad Monckton"
Muller, C. H. "Victorian Sensationalism...," 20-21.

"A Terribly Strange Bed"
Muller, C. H. "Victorian Sensationalism...," 13-14.

SARAH COMSTOCK

"Ways That Are Dark"
Chu, Limin. *The Image of China...*, 182.

RICHARD CONNELL

"The Most Dangerous Game"
Smith, Elliott L., and Andrew W. Hart, Eds. *The Short Story*..., 31–34.

JOSEPH CONRAD

"Amy Foster"
D'Elia, Gaetano. "Yanko, The Man Who Came from the Sea: A Note on Conrad's 'Amy Foster,'" trans. Dominic Bisignano, *Conradiana*, 11 (1979), 165–176.
Schwarz, Daniel R. *Conrad*..., 103–108.

"An Anarchist"
Bonney, William W. *Thorns & Arabesques*, 63–67.

"Il Conde"
La Bossière, Camille R. *Joseph Conrad*..., 82–83.
Schwarz, Daniel R. *Conrad*..., 188–191.

"The Duel"
Schwarz, Daniel R. *Conrad*..., 191–193.

"The End of the Tether"
Bonney, William W. *Thorns & Arabesques*, 155–157.
Bruss, Paul. *...Novelist as Navigator*, 147–156.
La Bossière, Camille R. *Joseph Conrad*..., 46–48.
Lombard, François. "Technique Littéraire et Thèmes Cosmiques dans 'The End of the Tether,'" *L'Epoque Conradienne*, [n.v.] (May, 1976), 78–97.
―――. "Metaphysical Metamorphoses in 'The End of the Tether,'" *J Joseph Conrad Soc* (U.K.), 5, ii (1980), 8–16; rpt., expanded, *L'Epoque Conradienne*, [n.v.] (May, 1981), 191–208.
Schwarz, Daniel R. *Conrad*..., 119–128.

"Falk"
Bonney, William W. *Thorns & Arabesques*, 19–21.
Bruss, Paul. *...Novelist as Navigator*, 135–146.
O'Hanlon, Redmond. "Knife, 'Falk' and Sexual Selection," *Essays Crit*, 31 (1981), 127–141.
Schwarz, Daniel R. *Conrad*..., 96–103.

"Freya of the Seven Isles"
Bonney, William W. *Thorns & Arabesques*, 77–88.
La Bossière, Camille R. *Joseph Conrad*..., 53–54.

"Heart of Darkness"
Berthoud, Jacques. *Joseph Conrad*..., 41–63.
Bruss, Paul. *...Novelist as Navigator*, 70–86.
Clark, Michael. "Conrad's 'Heart of Darkness,'" *Explicator*, 39, iii (1981), 47–48.
Darras, J. "Chaînes de Dissidence: Voix royales et Voies du Silence," trans. François Lombard, *L'Epoque Conradienne*, [n.v.] (March, 1975), 1–4.
Guetti, James. *Word-Music*..., 109–123.

Harkness, Bruce. "The Young Roman Trader in 'Heart of Darkness,'" *Conradiana*, 12 (1980), 227-229.

Hawkins, Hunt. "Conrad's Critique of Imperialism in 'Heart of Darkness,'" *PMLA*, 94 (1979), 286-299.

Hawthorn, Jeremy. *Joseph Conrad...*, 7-36.

Horner, Patrick J. "'Heart of Darkness' and the Loss of the Golden Age," *Conradiana*, 11 (1979), 190-192.

Kotzin, Michael C. "The Fairy Tale and Fiction: Enchantment in Early Conrad," *Folklore*, 91 (1980), 21-24.

Kulkarni, H. B. "Buddhistic Structure and Significance in Joseph Conrad's 'Heart of Darkness,'" *So Asian R*, [n.v.] (1979), 67-75.

La Bossière, Camille R. *Joseph Conrad...*, 70-73.

Larsen, Michael J. "Conrad's Secret Sharers," *Wascana R*, 15, i (1980), 24-27.

McClure, John A. *Kipling and Conrad...*, 131-154.

Meisel, Perry. "Decentering 'Heart of Darkness,'" *Mod Lang Stud*, 8, iii (1978), 20-28.

*Mizener, Arthur. *A Handbook...*, 4th ed., 1-8.

Moore, A. Luyat. "Conrad's Technique of the 'Secret Sharer,'" *L'Epoque Conradienne*, [n.v.] (May, 1976), 42-46.

Morrissey, L. J. "The Tellers in *Heart of Darkness*: Conrad's Chinese Boxes," *Conradiana*, 13 (1981), 141-148.

Orisabiyi, N. O. "'Heart of Darkness' As an Anatomy of Moral Failure," *Lagos R Engl Stud*, 1, i (1979), 94-103.

Reitz, Bernhard. "The Meaning of the Buddha-Comparisons in Joseph Conrad's 'Heart of Darkness,'" *Fu Jen Stud*, 13 (1980), 41-53.

Schwarz, Daniel R. *Conrad...*, 63-75.

Stewart, Garrett. "Lying as Dying in 'Heart of Darkness,'" *PMLA*, 95 (1980), 319-331.

Tessitore, John. "Freud, Conrad, and 'Heart of Darkness,'" *Coll Lit*, 7 (1980), 30-40.

Thumboo, Edwin. "Some Plain Reading: Marlow's Lie in 'Heart of Darkness,'" *Lit Criterion*, 16, iii (1981), 12-22.

White, Allon. *The Uses of Obscurity...*, 108-122.

Wirth-Nesher, Hans. "The Strange Case of 'The Turn of the Screw' and 'Heart of Darkness,'" *Stud Short Fiction*, 16 (1979), 318-322.

"The Idiots"

D'Elia, Gaetano. "Some Lotharios in a Seminal Conradian Tale," *J Joseph Conrad Soc*, 5, iii (1980), 12-18.

Schwarz, Daniel R. *Conrad...*, 24-25.

"The Informer"

La Bossière, Camille R. *Joseph Conrad...*, 97-98.

Schwarz, Daniel R. *Conrad...*, 185-188.

"Karain"

Bonney, William W. *Thorns & Arabesques*, 22-24.

Bruss, Paul. ...*Novelist as Navigator*, 47-57.

La Bossière, Camille R. *Joseph Conrad...*, 95-97.

Schwarz, Daniel R. *Conrad...*, 29-30.

"The Lagoon"

*Mroczkowski, Przemyslaw. "A Glimpse Back at the Romantic Conrad: 'The Lagoon,'" in Krzyzanowski, Ludwik, Ed. *Joseph Conrad...*, 75-83.

Nelson, Ronald J. "Conrad's 'The Lagoon,'" *Explicator*, 40, i (1981), 39-41.
Schwarz, Daniel R. *Conrad*..., 27-28.

"An Outcast of the Islands"
Kotzin, Michael C. "The Fairy Tale...," 18-19.

"An Outpost of Progress"
Schwarz, Daniel R. *Conrad*..., 25-27.

"The Planter of Malata"
Bonney, William W. *Thorns & Arabesques*, 59-63.

"The Return"
Schwarz, Daniel R. *Conrad*..., 30-32.

"The Secret Sharer"
Allen, Walter. *The Short Story*..., 83-84.
Altenbernd, Lynn, and Leslie L. Lewis. *Instructor's Manual*..., 3rd ed., 13-15.
Baker, Sheridan, and George Perkins. *Instructor's Manual*..., 40-42.
Barker, Gerard A. *Instructor's Manual*..., 72-74.
Eggenschwiler, David. "Narcissus in 'The Secret Sharer': A Secondary Point of
    View," *Conradiana*, 11 (1979), 23-40.
Garrett, Roland. "Leadership and Knowledge in Joseph Conrad's 'The Secret
    Sharer,'" *Liberal & Fine Arts R*, 1, ii (1981), 1-9.
Howard, Daniel F., and William Plummer. *Instructor's Manual*..., 3rd ed., 18;
    rpt. Howard, Daniel F., and John Ribar. *Instructor's Manual*..., 4th ed., 18.
La Bossière, Camille R. *Joseph Conrad*..., 54-56.
Larsen, Michael J. "Conrad's Secret Sharers," 20-24.
Moore, A. Luyat. "Conrad's Technique...," 35-42.
Morina, Gerardo. "The Freedom from the Absolute: 'The Secret Sharer,'" *L'Epoque
    Conradienne*, [n.v.] (March, 1975), 5-7.
Rosenman, John B. "The L-Shaped Room in 'The Secret Sharer,'" *Claflin Coll
    R*, 1, i (1976), 4-8.
Steiner, Joan E. "Conrad's 'The Secret Sharer': Complexities of the Doubling
    Relationship," *Conradiana*, 12 (1980), 173-186.

"The Shadow Line"
Kotzin, Michael C. "The Fairy Tale...," 17-18.
La Bossière, Camille R. *Joseph Conrad*..., 59-61.
Simon, John. "Between the Conception and the Recreation Falls 'The Shadow
    Line,'" *Hudson R*, 32 (1979), 239-244.

"A Smile of Fortune"
Bonney, William W. *Thorns & Arabesques*, 71-77.
La Bossière, Camille R. *Joseph Conrad*..., 52-53.

"The Tale"
Bonney, William W. *Thorns & Arabesques*, 208-215.
Tarinayya, M. "Kipling's 'Sea Constable' and Conrad's 'The Tale,'" *Lit Criterion*,
    16, iii (1981), 33-45.

"Tomorrow"
Schwarz, Daniel R. *Conrad*..., 118-119.

"Typhoon"
Bruss, Paul. . . . *Novelist as Navigator*, 122–134.
La Bossière, Camille. "The Irony of Surfaces: A Note on 'Typhoon,'" *Joseph Conrad Today*, 4 (1979), 108–109; rpt. in her *Joseph Conrad. . .*, 48–50.
Senn, Werner. *Conrad's Narrative Voice*, 62–63.

"Youth"
Bonney, William W. *Thorns & Arabesques*, 24–26.
Bruss, Paul. . . . *Novelist as Navigator*, 58–69.
Kotzin, Michael C. "The Fairy Tale. . . ," 16.
La Bossière, Camille R. *Joseph Conrad. . .*, 45–46.
Rothfork, John. "The Buddha Center in Conrad's 'Youth,'" *Lit East & West*, 21, i–iv (1977), 121–129.
Schwarz, Daniel R. *Conrad. . .*, 54–63.
Thomas, Lloyd S. "Conrad's 'Jury Rig' Use of the Bible in 'Youth,'" *Stud Short Fiction*, 17 (1980), 79–82.

BENJAMIN CONSTANT

"Adolphe"
Hemmings, F. W. J. "Constant's 'Adolphe': Internal and External Chronology," *Nineteenth-Century French Stud*,7 (1979), 153–164.
Jones, Grahame C. "The Devaluation of Action in Constant's 'Adolphe,'" *Australian J French Stud*, 16 (1979), 17–26.
King, Norman. "'Adolphe' fin de siècle: Critique et idéologie," *Studi Francesi*, 68 (1979), 238–252.

ROSE TERRY COOKE

"How Celia Changed Her Mind"
Toth, Susan A. "Character Studies in Rose Terry Cooke: New Faces for the Short Story," *Kate Chopin Newsletter*, 2, i (1976), 22–24.

"Polly Mariner, Tailoress"
Toth, Susan A. "Character Studies. . . ," 21–22.

ROBERT COOVER

"The Babysitter"
Andersen, Richard. *Robert Coover*, 103–105.
Christ, Ronald. "Forking Narrative," *Latin Am Lit R*, 7 (1979), 54–55.
Rohrberger, Mary. *Instructor's Manual. . .*, 45.

"Beginnings"
Andersen, Richard. *Robert Coover*, 98–99.

"The Brother"
Andersen, Richard. *Robert Coover*, 19–22.

"The Cat in the Hat for President"
Andersen, Richard. *Robert Coover*, 133-137.

"The Dead Queen"
Andersen, Richard. *Robert Coover*, 87-88.

"The Elevator"
Andersen, Richard. *Robert Coover*, 99-101.
Christ, Ronald. "Forking Narrative," 55-56.

"The Gingerbread House"
Andersen, Richard. *Robert Coover*, 84-87.

"The Hat Act"
Andersen, Richard. *Robert Coover*, 105-107.
Kissel, Susan. "The Contemporary Artist and His Audience in the Short Stories of Robert Coover," *Stud Short Fiction*, 16 (1979), 51-52.

"In a Train Station"
Andersen, Richard. *Robert Coover*, 27-28.

"J's Marriage"
Andersen, Richard. *Robert Coover*, 20-22.

"The Kid"
Andersen, Richard. *Robert Coover*, 111-112.

"Klee Dead"
Andersen, Richard. *Robert Coover*, 28-30.

"The Leper's Helix"
Andersen, Richard. *Robert Coover*, 34-35.

"Love Scene"
Andersen, Richard. *Robert Coover*, 112-113.

"Lucky Pierre and the Music Lesson"
Andersen, Richard. *Robert Coover*, 139-140.

"McDuff on the Mound"
Andersen, Richard. *Robert Coover*, 74-78.

"The Magic Poker"
Ahrends, Günter. ...*Kurzgeschichte*, 228-231.
Andersen, Richard. *Robert Coover*, 96-98.
Siegle, Robert. "Coover's 'The Magic Poker' and the Techniques of Fiction," *Essays Lit*, 8 (1981), 203-217.

"The Marker"
Andersen, Richard. *Robert Coover*, 25-26.

"The Milkmaid of Samaniego"
Andersen, Richard. *Robert Coover*, 32–34.

"Morris in Chains"
Andersen, Richard. *Robert Coover*, 92–93.
Cooley, John. "The Garden in the Machine: Three Postmodern Pastorals," *Michigan Academician*, 13 (1981), 408 – 410.

"Panel Game"
Andersen, Richard. *Robert Coover*, 24–25.

"The Pedestrian Accident"
Andersen, Richard. *Robert Coover*, 101–103.
Gardner, John. *On Moral Fiction*, 74–76.

"Quenby and Ola, Swede and Carl"
Andersen, Richard. *Robert Coover*, 89–92.

"Rip Awake"
Andersen, Richard. *Robert Coover*, 113–114.

"Romance of the Thin Man and the Fat Lady"
Andersen, Richard. *Robert Coover*, 93–96.

"Scene for 'Winter'"
Andersen, Richard. *Robert Coover*, 31–32.

"The Second Son"
Andersen, Richard. *Robert Coover*, 58–60.

"A Theological Position"
Andersen, Richard. *Robert Coover*, 114–116.

"Whatever Happened to Gloomy Gus of the Chicago Bears?"
Andersen, Richard. *Robert Coover*, 137–139.

A. E. COPPARD

"Adam and Eve and Pinch Me"
Scott, Virgil, and David Madden. *Instructor's Manual...*, 4th ed., 43–46.

"The Higgler"
Allen, Walter. *The Short Story...*, 177–179.

DANIEL CORKERY

"Carrig-an-Afrinn" [same as "The Mass Rock"]
Lucy, Sean. "Place and People in the Short Stories of Daniel Corkery," in Rafroidi, Patrick, and Terence Brown, Eds. *The Irish Short Story*, 166–168.

"The Priest"
Lucy, Sean. "Place and People...," 170.

JULIO CORTÁZAR

"All Fires the Fire"
Benavides, Manuel. "La abolición del tiempo: Análisis de 'Todos los fuegos el fuego,'" *Cuadernos Hispanoamericanos*, 364–366 (1980), 484–494.

"Axolotl"
Bernstein, Jerome S. "In Some Cases Jumps Are Made: 'Axolotl' from an Eastern Point of View," in Pope, Randolph D., Ed. *The Analysis...*, 175–184.
Neyenesch, John. "On This Side of the Glass: An Analysis of Julio Cortázar's 'Axolotl,'" in Minc, Rose S., Ed. *...Latin American Short Story*, 54–60.
Pearson, Lon. "Erotic Symbolism in Julio Cortázar's 'Axolotl,'" *Pubs Missouri Philol Assoc.*, 4 (1979), 50–58.
Planells, Antonio. "Comunicación pro metamorfosis: 'Axolotl' de Julio Cortázar," in Gordon, Alan M., and Evelyn Rugg, Eds. *Actas del Sexto Congreso Internacional...*, 575–578.

"Blow-Up" [same as "Las babas del diablo"]
Chatman, Seymour. "The Rhetoric of Difficult Fiction: Cortázar's 'Blow-Up,'" *Poetics Today*, 1, iv (1980), 23–57.

"Continuity of Parks"
Brooks, Cleanth, and Robert P. Warren. *Understanding Fiction*, 3rd ed., 248–249.

"Cuello de gatito negro"
Sommer, Doris. "Pattern and Predictability in the Stories of Julio Cortázar," in Minc, Rose S., Ed. *...Latin American Short Story*, 74–75.

"End of the Game"
Morell, Hortensia R. "Uso del gato en la construcción artistica de 'Final de juego,'" *Romance Notes*, 21 (1981), 283–286.

"House Taken Over"
Brandt Rojas, José H. "Asedios a 'Casa tomada' de Julio Cortázar," *Revista de Estudios Hispánicos* (Puerto Rico), 7 (1980), 75–84.

"Instructions for John Howell"
Quackenbush, L. H. "'Instrucciones para John Howell' de Julio Cortázar: Un papel en busca de personaje," in Minc, Rose S., Ed. *...Latin American Short Story*, 61–70.

"Manuscripto hallado en un bolsillo"
Sommer, Doris. "Pattern and Predictability...," 74.

"The Night Face Up"
Antolín, Francisco. "'La noche boca arriba' de Cortázar: Oposición de paradigmas," *Explicación de Textos Literarios*, 9, ii (1981), 147–151.

"The Pursuer"
Cifo González, Manuel. "Relativismo espacio-temporal en 'El perseguidor' de
Julio Cortázar," *Cuadernos Hispanoamericanos*, 364-366 (1980), 414-423.
Felkel, Robert W. "The Historical Dimension in Julio Cortázar's 'The Pursuer,'"
Latin Am Lit R, 7 (1979), 20-27.
Gyurko, Lanin A. "Artist and Critic in Cortázar's 'El persiguidor':
Antagonists or Doubles?" *Ibero-Amerikanisches Archiv*, 6, iii (1980), 205-238.
Verani, Hugo J. "Las máscaras de la nada: *Apocalopsis* de Dylan Thomas y 'El
perseguidor' de Julio Cortázar," *Cuadernos Americanos*, 227 (1979), 234-247.

"Secret Weapons"
Foster, David W. . . . *Spanish-American Short Story*, 83-101.

"Verano"
Planells, Antonio. "Repressión sexual, frigidez y maternidad frustrada: 'Verano'
de Julio Cortázar," *Bull Hispanic Stud*, 56 (1979), 233-237.
Sommer, Doris. "Pattern and Predictability. . . ," 76.

JOHN COULTER

"Boy at a Prayer Meeting"
Anthony, Geraldine. *John Coulter*, 139-140.

"The Catholic Walk"
Anthony, Geraldine. *John Coulter*, 140.

"Dinner Hour at the Mill"
Anthony, Geraldine. *John Coulter*, 140.

"Muskoka Respite"
Anthony, Geraldine. *John Coulter*, 141.

STEPHEN CRANE

"The Blue Hotel"
Kent, Thomas L. "The Problem of Knowledge in 'The Open Boat' and 'The Blue
Hotel,'" *Am Lit Realism*, 14 (1981), 264-267.
Kimball, Sue L. "Circles and Squares: The Design of Stephen Crane's 'The Blue
Hotel,'" *Stud Short Fiction*, 17 (1980), 425-430.
McFarland, Ronald E. "The Hospitality Code and Crane's 'The Blue Hotel,'"
Stud Short Fiction, 18 (1981), 447-451.
Vidan, Ivo. "Forms of Fortuity in the Short Fiction of Stephen Crane," *Studia
Romanica et Anglica*, 38 (December, 1974), 39-47.
Wolter, Jürgen. "Drinking, Gambling, Fighting, Paying: Structure and
Determinism in 'The Blue Hotel,'" *Am Lit Realism*, 12 (1979), 295-298.

"The Bride Comes to Yellow Sky"
Allen, Walter. *The Short Story*. . . , 58-59.
French, Warren. "Stephen Crane: Moment of Myth," *Prairie Schooner*, 55, i-ii (1981),
164-165.

Smith, Elliott L. and Wanda V. *Instructor's Manual...*, 13–14.

"The Clan of No-Name"
Nagel, James. ...*Literary Impressionism*, 132–135.

"Death and the Child"
Nagel, James. ...*Literary Impressionism*, 72–77.
Vidan, Ivo. "Forms of Fortuity...," 22–24.

"An Episode of War"
Nagel, James. ...*Literary Impressionism*, 101–102.

"An Experiment in Misery"
Kwiat, Joseph J. "Stephen Crane, Literary Reporter: Commonplace Experience and Artistic Transcendence," *J Mod Lit*, 8 (1980), 134–135.
Nagel, James. ...*Literary Impressionism*, 139–140.
Slotkin, Alan R. "Dialect Manipulation in 'An Experiment in Misery,'" *Am Lit Realism*, 14 (1981), 273–276.

"The Five White Mice"
Vidan, Ivo. "Forms of Fortuity...," 26–27.

"George's Mother"
Nagel, James. ...*Literary Impressionism*, 65–68.
Weinstein, Bernard. "'George's Mother' and the Bowery of Experience," *Markham R*, 9 (1980), 45–49.

"Horses—One Dash"
Gunn, Drewey W. *American and British Writers...*, 48–49.

"An Illusion in Red and White"
Nagel, James. ...*Literary Impressionism*, 40–41.

"Maggie: A Girl of the Streets"
Candela, Joseph L. "The Domestic Orientation of American Novels, 1893–1913," *Am Lit Realism*, 13 (1980), 2–5.
Nagel, James. ...*Literary Impressionism*, 94–100.

"A Man and Some Others"
Robinson, Cecil. *Mexico...*, 202–203.

"The Monster"
Morace, Robert A. "Games, Play, and Entertainments in Crane's 'The Monster,'" *Stud Am Fiction*, 9 (1981), 65–81.

"Moonlight on the Snow"
Robinson, Cecil. *Mexico...*, 191–192.

"The Open Boat"
Allen, Walter. *The Short Story...*, 55–57.
Altenbernd, Lynn, and Leslie L. Lewis. *Instructor's Manual...*, 3rd ed., 16–17.
Kent, Thomas L. "The Problem of Knowledge...," 262–264.

Rohrberger, Mary. *Instructor's Manual...*, 12-13.
Scott, Virgil, and David Madden. *Instructor's Manual...*, 4th ed., 78-81.
Spofford, William K. "Stephen Crane's 'The Open Boat': Fact or Fiction?" *Am Lit Realism*, 12 (1979), 316-321.
Vidan, Ivo. "Forms of Fortuity...," 30-39.

"The Price of the Harness"
Vidan, Ivo. "Forms of Fortuity...," 24-26.

"The Silver Pageant"
Kwiat, Joseph J. "Stephen Crane...," 135-136.

"Three Miraculous Soldiers"
Nagel, James. *...Literary Impressionism*, 44-47.

"Uncle Jake and the Bell-Handle"
Nagel, James. *...Literary Impressionism*, 61-62.

"The Upturned Face"
Vidan, Ivo. "Forms of Fortuity...," 20-22.

GASTÃO CRULS

"Meu Sósia"
Andrade, Ana L. "Uma Leitura Cumplice: A Função do Duplo em 'Meu Sósia' de Gastão Cruls," *Kentucky Romance Q*, 28 (1981), 417-425.

CUBENA [CARLOS GUILLERMO WILSON]

"The Family"
Jackson, Richard L. *Black Writers...*, 188-189.

"The Little African Grandmother"
Jackson, Richard L. *Black Writers...*, 188.

ELIZABETH CULLINAN

"The Voices of the Dead"
Murphy, Maureen. "Elizabeth Cullinan: Yellow and Gold," in Casey, Daniel J., and Robert E. Rhodes, Eds. *Irish-American Fiction...*, 143.

ROBERT BONTINE CUNNINGHAME GRAHAM

"A Hegira"
Gunn, Drewey W. *American and British Writers...*, 42-43.

DANIEL CURLEY

"A Story of Love, Etc."
Altenbernd, Lynn, and Leslie L. Lewis. *Instructor's Manual . . .*, 3rd ed., 17–18.

KISHOREE DAS

"Husband, the Supreme Teacher"
Mohanty, Pratap Chandra. "A Study of Kishoree Das's Short Stories," *Indian Lit*,
    21, i (1978), 68.

"Manihara"
Mohanty, Pratap Chandra. ". . . Kishoree Das's Short Stories," 71.

"Million Birds"
Mohanty, Pratap Chandra. ". . . Kishoree Das's Short Stories," 70.

"Sangeeta's Father"
Mohanty, Pratap Chandra. ". . . Kishoree Das's Short Stories," 71.

"Wild Peacock"
Mohanty, Pratap Chandra. ". . . Kishoree Das's Short Stories," 69–70.

FRANK DALBY DAVIDSON

"Fathers and Sons"
Rorabacher, Louise E. *Frank Dalby Davidson*, 121–123.

"Fields of Cotton"
Rorabacher, Louise E. *Frank Dalby Davidson*, 120–121.

"Further West"
Rorabacher, Louise E. *Frank Dalby Davidson*, 119–120.

"The Good Herdsman"
Rorabacher, Louise E. *Frank Dalby Davidson*, 128.

"Here Comes the Bride"
Rorabacher, Louise E. *Frank Dalby Davidson*, 112–114.

"Lady with a Scar"
Rorabacher, Louise E. *Frank Dalby Davidson*, 123–124.

"A Letter from Colleen"
Rorabacher, Louise E. *Frank Dalby Davidson*, 111–112.

"Meet Darkie Hoskins"
Rorabacher, Louise E. *Frank Dalby Davidson*, 125–126.

"The Night Watch"
Rorabacher, Louise E. *Frank Dalby Davidson*, 117–118.

"Nobody's Kelpie"
Rorabacher, Louise E. *Frank Dalby Davidson*, 114–115.

"Return of the Hunter"
Rorabacher, Louise E. *Frank Dalby Davidson*, 115.

"The Road to Yesterday"
Rorabacher, Louise E. *Frank Dalby Davidson*, 131–133.

"Sojourners"
Rorabacher, Louise E. *Frank Dalby Davidson*, 110–111.

"Soldier of Fortune"
Rorabacher, Louise E. *Frank Dalby Davidson*, 111.

"Tank-sinkers"
Rorabacher, Louise E. *Frank Dalby Davidson*, 128–130.

"Transition"
Rorabacher, Louise E. *Frank Dalby Davidson*, 130–131.

"The Wasteland"
Rorabacher, Louise E. *Frank Dalby Davidson*, 118–119.

"The Woman at the Mill"
Rorabacher, Louise E. *Frank Dalby Davidson*, 115–117.

"The Yarns Men Tell"
Rorabacher, Louise E. *Frank Dalby Davidson*, 124–125.

RHYS DAVIES

"Canute"
Allen, Walter. *The Short Story*. . . , 225–227.

"The Dilemma of Catherine Fuchsias"
Allen, Walter. *The Short Story*. . . , 222–225.

"Nightgown"
Allen, Walter. *The Short Story*. . . , 228–230.

H. L. DAVIS

"World of Little Doves"
Altenbernd, Lynn, and Leslie L. Lewis. *Instructor's Manual*. . . , 3rd ed., 18–19.

RICHARD HARDING DAVIS

"Eleanore Cuyler"
Osborne, Scott C., and Robert L. Phillips. *Richard Harding Davis*, 92-94.

"The Exiles"
Osborne, Scott C., and Robert L. Phillips. *Richard Harding Davis*, 104-105.

"Her First Appearance"
Osborne, Scott C., and Robert L. Phillips. *Richard Harding Davis*, 99-100.

"The Men of Zanzibar"
Osborne, Scott C., and Robert L. Phillips. *Richard Harding Davis*, 131-132.

"My Buried Treasure"
Osborne, Scott C., and Robert L. Phillips. *Richard Harding Davis*, 135-136.

"The Other Woman"
Osborne, Scott C., and Robert L. Phillips. *Richard Harding Davis*, 98-99.

"Ranson's Folly"
Osborne, Scott C., and Robert L. Phillips. *Richard Harding Davis*, 111-112.

"The Reporter Who Made Himself King"
Osborne, Scott C., and Robert L. Phillips. *Richard Harding Davis*, 90-92.

"An Unfinished Story"
Osborne, Scott C., and Robert L. Phillips. *Richard Harding Davis*, 102-103.

"The Vagrant"
Osborne, Scott C., and Robert L. Phillips. *Richard Harding Davis*, 110-111.

"Van Bibber's Burglar"
Osborne, Scott C., and Robert L. Phillips. *Richard Harding Davis*, 97-98, 101-102.

EMMA F. DAWSON

"The Dramatic in My Destiny"
Chu, Limin. *The Image of China...*, 172-173.

DAZAI OSAMU

"Metamorphosis"
Wolfe, Alan. "The Failure of Allegory: A Reading of Dazai Osamu's 'Metamorphosis,'" *Selecta*, 2 (1981), 10-14.

WALTER DE LA MARE

"A. B. O."
Sullivan, Jack. *Elegant Nightmares*..., 92–94.

"Crewe"
Punter, David. *The Literature of Terror*..., 310–311.

"Mr. Kempe"
Punter, David. *The Literature of Terror*..., 307–309.

"Out of the Deep"
Punter, David. *The Literature of Terror*..., 301–303.

"A Recluse"
Briggs, Julia. *Night Visitors*..., 189–190.

"Seaton's Aunt"
Briggs, Julia. *Night Visitors*..., 191–193.
Punter, David. *The Literature of Terror*..., 309–310.

"Strangers and Pilgrims"
Briggs, Julia. *Night Visitors*..., 194–195.

"The Trumpet"
Allen, Walter. *The Short Story*..., 89–91.

LESTER DEL REY

"Instinct"
Warrick, Patricia S. *The Cybernetic Imagination*..., 114–115.

"Though Dreamers Die"
Warrick, Patricia S. *The Cybernetic Imagination*..., 107–108.

MAHASVETA DEVI

"Draupadi"
Spivak, Gayatri Chakravorty. "'Draupadi' by Mahasveta Devi," *Critical Inquiry*, 8 (1981), 381–392.

OLIVE DIBERT

"A Chinese Lily"
Chu, Limin. *The Image of China*..., 185.

PHILIP K. DICK

"Autofac"
Warrick, Patricia S. "The Labyrinthian Process of the Artificial: Dick's Androids and Mechanical Constructs," in Remington, Thomas J., Ed. *Selected Proceedings*..., 125.
_____. *The Cybernetic Imagination*..., 211–212.

"The Defenders"
Warrick, Patricia S. "The Labyrinthian Process...," 124–125.

"The Electric Ant"
Warrick, Patricia S. *The Cybernetic Imagination*..., 228–229.

"The Preserving Machine"
Warrick, Patricia S. "The Labyrinthian Process...," 123–124.

"Second Variety"
Warrick, Patricia S. "The Labyrinthian Process...," 124.
_____. *The Cybernetic Imagination*..., 211–212.

CHARLES DICKENS

"No. 1 Branch Line—The Signalman"
Seed, David. "Mystery in Everyday Things: Charles Dickens' 'Signalman,'" *Criticism*, 23 (1981), 42–57.

FRANCIS J. DICKIE

"The Creed of Ah Sin"
Chu, Limin. *The Image of China*..., 178.

JOAN DIDION

"When Did Music Come This Way? Children, Dear, Was It Yesterday?"
Brady, H. Jennifer. "Points West, Then and Now: The Fiction of Joan Didion," *Contemp Lit*, 20 (1979), 460–463.

ISAK DINESEN [BARONESS KAREN BLIXEN]

"The Blank Page"
Gubar, Susan. "'The Blank Page' and Issues of Female Creativity," *Critical Inquiry*, 8 (1981), 243–263.

"The Cardinal's Third Tale"
Burstein, Janet H. "Two Locked Caskets: Selfhood and 'Otherness' in the Works of Isak Dinesen," *Texas Stud Lit & Lang*, 20 (1978), 628–629.

"The Caryatids"
Lydenberg, Robin. "Against the Law of Gravity: Female Adolescence in Isak
    Dinesen's *Seven Gothic Tales*," *Mod Fiction Stud*, 24 (1979), 529-530.

"A Consolatory Tale"
Burstein, Janet H. "Two Locked Caskets...," 621-623.

"The Deluge at Norderney"
Brink, J. R. "Hamlet or Timon: Isak Dinesen's 'Deluge at Norderney,'" *Int'l Fiction
    R*, 5 (1978), 148-150.

"The Heroine"
Barker, Gerard A. *Instructor's Manual...*, 32-33.

"The Monkey"
Lydenberg, Robin. "Against the Law of Gravity...," 525-529.

"The Pearls"
Altenbernd, Lynn, and Leslie L. Lewis. *Instructor's Manual...*, 3rd ed., 19-20.

"Peter and Rose"
Burstein, Janet H. "Two Locked Caskets...," 625-626.

"The Ring"
Burstein, Janet H. "Two Locked Caskets...," 629-630.

"The Road Round Pisa"
Burstein, Janet H. "Two Locked Caskets...," 617-620.

"The Sailor-Boy's Tale"
Burstein, Janet H. "Two Locked Caskets...," 624-625.

"The Young Man with the Carnation"
Burstein, Janet H. "Two Locked Caskets...," 620-621.

DING LING

"A Certain Night"
Feng, Xiaxiong. "Ding Ling's Reappearance on the Literary Stage," *Chinese Lit*,
    [n.v.] , i (1980), 17-22.

"Du Wanxiang"
Feng, Xiaxiong. "Ding Ling's Reappearance...," 31-57.

"Night"
Feng, Xiaxiong. "Ding Ling's Reappearance...," 23-30.

HEIMITO VON DODERER

"Divertimento I"
Bachem, Michael. "Chaos, Order and Humanization in Doderer's Early Works,"
 Mod Lang Stud, 5, ii (1975), 70-73.

"Divertimento III"
Bachem, Michael. *Heimito von Doderer*, 44-45.

"Divertimento IV"
Bachem, Michael. *Heimito von Doderer*, 45-46.

"Divertimento V"
Bachem, Michael. *Heimito von Doderer*, 46-47.

"Divertimento VI"
Bachem, Michael. *Heimito von Doderer*, 47-48.

"Encounter at Dawn"
Bachem, Michael. *Heimito von Doderer*, 55-57.

"Jutta Bamberger"
Bachem, Michael. *Heimito von Doderer*, 35-41.

"A Person of Porcelain"
Bachem, Michael. *Heimito von Doderer*, 61.

"The Torment of the Leather Pouches"
Bachem, Michael. *Heimito von Doderer*, 59-60.

"Trethofen"
Bachem, Michael. *Heimito von Doderer*, 119-120.

"The Trumpets of Jericho"
Bachem, Michael. *Heimito von Doderer*, 111-116.

Politzer, Heinz. "Realismus und Realität in Heimito von Doderers 'Posaunen von
 Jericho,'" *Germ R*, 38 (January, 1963), 37-51.
Shaw, Michael. "Doderer's 'Posaunen von Jericho,'" *Symposium*, 21 (1967), 141-154.
Tschirky, René. ...*Doderers "Posaunen von Jericho"*..., 96-203.

"Two Lies, or Classical Tragedy in a Village"
Bachem, Michael. *Heimito von Doderer*, 57-59.

JAMES PATRICK DONLEAVY

"At Longitude and Latitude"
Heuermann, Hartmut. "Typisch amerikanisch? Zum literaturwissenschaftlichen
 Problem der Nationaltypik am Beispiel von James P. Donleavys 'At Longi-
 tude and Latitude,'" *Literature in Wissenschaft und Unterricht*, 14 (1981), 1-21.

"The Romantic Life of Alphonse A"
Norstedt, Johann A. "Irishmen and Irish-Americans in the Fiction of J. P. Donleavy," in Casey, Daniel J., and Robert E. Rhodes, Eds. *Irish-American Fiction...*, 122-123.

JOSÉ DONOSO

"Ana María"
McMurray, George R. *José Donoso*, 35-36.

"Celebration on a Grand Scale"
McMurray, George R. *José Donoso*, 45-46.

"Charleston"
McMurray, George R. *José Donoso*, 41-43, 49-50.

"China"
Castillo-Felíu, Guillermo I. "Aesthetic Impetus Versus Reality in Three Stories of José Donoso," *Stud Short Fiction*, 17 (1980), 134-135.
McMurray, George R. *José Donoso*, 34.

"The Closed Door"
Castillo-Felíu, Guillermo I. "Aesthetic Impetus...," 135-136.
McMurray, George R. *José Donoso*, 46-48, 50-51.

"The Güero"
McMurray, George R. *José Donoso*, 37-38.

"A Lady"
McMurray, George R. *José Donoso*, 46, 51.

"Namesakes"
McMurray, George R. *José Donoso*, 55.

"Paseo"
McMurray, George R. *José Donoso*, 38-41, 51-52.

"Santelices"
Castillo-Felíu, Guillermo I. "Aesthetic Impetus...," 136-138.
McMurray, George R. *José Donoso*, 43-45.

"Summertime"
McMurray, George R. *José Donoso*, 34-35.

"Two Letters"
McMurray, George R. *José Donoso*, 36.

FYODOR DOSTOEVSKY

"Bobok"
Jackson, Robert L. *The Art...*, 294-303.

"A Boy at Christ's Christmas Party"
Jackson, Robert L. *The Art*. . . , 260-271.
Naumann, Marina T. "Dostoevsky's 'The Boy at Christ's Christmas-Tree Party':
A Paraphrase of Andersen's 'The Little Match Girl,'"*Revue de Littérature
Comparée*, 219-220, iii-iv (1981), 317-330.

"A Christmas Party and a Wedding"
Jackson, Robert L. "The Garden of Eden in Dostoevsky's 'A Christmas Party
and a Wedding' and Chekhov's 'Because of Little Apples,'" *Revue de Littérature
Comparée*, 219-220, iii-iv (1981), 331-341.

"The Double"
Leatherbarrow, William J. *Fedor Dostoevsky*, 39-43.
MacAndrew, Elizabeth. *The Gothic Tradition*. . . , 212-213.
Neuhäuser, Rudolf. "Re-Reading *Poor Folk* and 'The Double,'" *Int'l Dostoevsky
Soc Bull*, 6 (1976), 29-32.

"The Dream of a Ridiculous Man"
Baker, Sheridan, and George Perkins. *Instructor's Manual*. . . , 36-37.
Lauth, Reinhard. "Der 'Traum eines lächerlichen Menschen' als Auseinder-
setzung mit Rousseau und Fichte," *Dostoevsky Stud*, 1 (1980), 89-101.
Leatherbarrow, William J. *Fedor Dostoevsky*, 136-137.
Rohrberger, Mary. *Instructor's Manual*. . . , 9-10.
Rosen, Nathan. "The Defective Memory of the Ridiculous Man," *Canadian-Am
Slavic Stud*, 12 (1978), 323-338.

"A Faint Heart"
Leatherbarrow, William J. *Fedor Dostoevsky*, 57-59.

"The Grand Inquisitor"
Grossvogel, David I. *Mystery*. . . , 71-73.
Jackson, Robert L. *The Art*. . . , 335-345.
Perring, Ronald E. "'The Grand Inquisitor,'" *Stud Hum*, 7, ii (1979), 52-57.

"The Landlady"
Leatherbarrow, William J. *Fedor Dostoevsky*, 45-48.

"The Little Hero"
Koehler, Ludmila. "'The Little Hero' of a Great Writer," *Int'l Dostoevsky Soc Bull*,
8 (1978), 22-30.

"A Meek One"
Basile, Bruno. "La finestra e l'icona: Patologia del monologo interiore ne 'La mite'
di F. M. Dostoevskij," in Raimondi, Ezio, and Bruno Basile, Eds. *Dal "Novellino"
a Moravia*. . . , 131-166.
Grossman, Leonid. "About 'The Meek One,'" *Soviet Lit*, 12 (1981), 57-59.

"Mr. Prokharchin"
Leatherbarrow, William J. *Fedor Dostoevsky*, 44-45.

"Notes from Underground"
Hall, J. R. "Abstraction in Dostoyevsky's 'Notes from Underground,'" *Mod Lang
R*, 76 (1981), 129-137.

Leatherbarrow, William J. *Fedor Dostoevsky*, 63–68.
Riggan, William. *Picaros, Madmen*..., 118–128.

"The Peasant Marey"
Jackson, Robert L. "The Triple Vision: Dostoevsky's 'The Peasant Marey,'" *Yale R*, 67 (1978), 225–235; rpt. in his *The Art*..., 20–32.

"White Nights"
Leatherbarrow, William J. *Fedor Dostoevsky*, 47–48.

ARTHUR CONAN DOYLE

"The Adventure of the Speckled Band"
Kennedy, X. J. *Instructor's Manual*..., 2nd ed., 34–35.

"The Case of Lady Sannox"
Punter, David. *The Literature of Terror*..., 318–319.

"The Five Orange Pips"
Christensen, Peter. "The Ineffectual Superman of 'The Five Orange Pips,'" *Baker Street J*, 27 (1977), 157–161.

"The Hound of the Baskervilles"
Christensen, Peter. "The Nature of Evil in 'The Hound of the Baskervilles,'" *Baker Street J*, 29 (1979), 209–211.

"The New Catacomb"
Punter, David. *The Literature of Terror*..., 317–318.

"Wisteria Lodge"
Clark, Edward F. "'Wisteria Lodge' Revisited: A Model Cop, a Model Laundry Item and a Not-So-Model Culinary Artist," *Baker Street J*, 31 (March, 1981), 24–31.

"The Yellow Face"
Drazen, Patrick E. "Next Stop, Norbury: Reflections on 'The Yellow Face,'" *Baker Street J*, 29 (1979), 16–20.

THEODORE DREISER

"Butcher Rogaum's Door"
Hakutani, Yoshinobu. "The Making of Dreiser's Early Short Stories: The Philosopher and the Artist," *Stud Am Fiction*, 6 (1978), 55–57; rpt. in his *Young Dreiser*..., 160–163.

"Chains"
Griffin, Joseph. "Dreiser's Short Stories and the Dream of Success," *Études Anglaises*, 31 (1978), 299–300.

"Fulfilment"
Griffin, Joseph. "Dreiser's Short Stories...," 300.

"Nigger Jeff"
Hakutani, Yoshinobu. "The Making...," 58-60; rpt. in his *Young Dreiser*...,
    163-165.

"The Shining Slave Makers"
Hakutani, Yoshinobu. "The Making...," 51-54; rpt. in his *Young Dreiser*...,
    154-160.

"When the Old Century Was New"
Griffin, Joseph P. "'When the Old Century Was New': An Early Dreiser Parody,"
    Stud Short Fiction, 17 (1980), 285-289.
Hakutani, Yoshinobu. "The Making...," 60-61; rpt. in his *Young Dreiser*...,
    165-167.

ANNETTE VON DROSTE-HÜLSHOFF

"Die Judenbuche"
Mellen, Philip A. "Ambiguity and Intent in 'Die Judenbuche,'" *Germ Notes*, 8
    (1977), 8-10.
Schneider, Ronald. "Moglichkeiten und Grenzen des Frürealismus im Bieder-
    meier: 'Die Judenbuch' der Annette von Droste-Hülshoff," *Der Deutschunterricht*,
    31, ii (1979), 85-94.

PAUL LAURENCE DUNBAR

"At Shaft 11"
Revell, Peter. *Paul Laurence Dunbar*, 116-117.

"The Boy and the Bayonet"
Revell, Peter. *Paul Laurence Dunbar*, 128-129.

"A Council of State"
Revell, Peter. *Paul Laurence Dunbar*, 117-120.

"The Finding of Zach"
Revell, Peter. *Paul Laurence Dunbar*, 130-131.

"The Last Fiddling of Mordaunt's Jim"
Revell, Peter. *Paul Laurence Dunbar*, 134-136.

"The Lynching of Jube Benson"
Revell, Peter. *Paul Laurence Dunbar*, 123-124.

"Mr. Cornelius Johnson, Office-Seeker"
Revell, Peter. *Paul Laurence Dunbar*, 117-118.

"One Man's Fortunes"
Revell, Peter. *Paul Laurence Dunbar*, 124-126.

"The Scapegoat"
Revell, Peter. *Paul Laurence Dunbar*, 121-122.

"The Strength of Gideon"
Revell, Peter. *Paul Laurence Dunbar*, 111-112.

"Viney's Free Papers"
Revell, Peter. *Paul Laurence Dunbar*, 111-112.

MARGUERITE DURAS

"Moderato cantabile"
Bassoff, Bruce. "Death and Desire in Marguerite Duras' 'Moderato cantabile,'"
Mod Lang Notes, 94 (1979), 720-730.

FRIEDRICH DÜRRENMATT

"Das Sterben der Pythia"
Spycher, Peter. "Friedrich Dürrenmatt's Story 'Das Sterben der Pythia': Farewell
to Theatre and a Return to Fiction and Essays?" *World Lit Today*, 55 (1981),
614-617.

MARIA EDGEWORTH

"Angelina; or, L'amie Inconnue"
Harden, O. Elizabeth M. *Maria Edgeworth's Art. . .*, 111-115.
Hawthorne, Mark D. *Doubt and Dogma. . .*, 36-37.

"The Bracelets"
Newcomer, James. *Maria Edgeworth*, 34-35.

"The Contrast"
Hawthorne, Mark D. *Doubt and Dogma. . .*, 53-54.

"False Key"
Harden, O. Elizabeth M. *Maria Edgeworth's Art. . .*, 21-23.

"Forester"
Harden, O. Elizabeth M. *Maria Edgeworth's Art. . .*, 108-111.
Hawthorne, Mark D. *Doubt and Dogma. . .*, 33-36.

"The Good Aunt"
Hawthorne, Mark D. *Doubt and Dogma. . .*, 32-33.

"The Good French Governess"
Hawthorne, Mark D. *Doubt and Dogma. . .*, 26-31.

"The Grateful Negro"
Hawthorne, Mark D. *Doubt and Dogma. . .*, 54-55.

"Lame Jervas"
Hawthorne, Mark D. *Doubt and Dogma. . .*, 52-53.

"Lazy Lawrence"
Harden, O. Elizabeth M. *Maria Edgeworth's Art*..., 23.

"The Lottery"
Hawthorne, Mark D. *Doubt and Dogma*..., 50-52.

"Madame de Fleury"
Hawthorne, Mark D. *Doubt and Dogma*..., 71-74.

"The Manufacturers"
Hawthorne, Mark D. *Doubt and Dogma*..., 55-57.

"The Modern Griselda"
Harden, O. Elizabeth M. *Maria Edgeworth's Art*..., 135-137.
Hawthorne, Mark D. *Doubt and Dogma*..., 60-62.

"Orlandino"
Harden, O. Elizabeth M. *Maria Edgeworth's Art*..., 225-226.

"Tomorrow"
Hawthorne, Mark D. *Doubt and Dogma*..., 57-58.

JOSEPH VON EICHENDORFF

"From the Life of a Good-for-Nothing"
Nygaard, Loisa. "Eichendorffs 'Aus dem Leben eines Taugenichts': 'Eine leise Persiflage' der Romantik," *Stud Romanticism*, 19 (1980), 193-216.

GEORGE ELIOT [MARY ANN EVANS]

"Janet's Repentance"
Carlisle, Janice. *The Sense of an Audience*, 19-22.
Carroll, David. "'Janet's Repentance' and the Myth of the Organic," *Nineteenth-Century Fiction*, 35 (1980), 331-348.
Stone, Donald D. *The Romantic Impulse*..., 204-205.

"The Lifted Veil"
Swann, Charles. "Déjà vu: Déjà lu: 'The Lifted Veil' as an Experiment in Art," *Lit & Hist*, 5 (1979), 40-57.
Wilt, Judith. *Ghosts of the Gothic*..., 183-187.

"The Sad Fortunes of the Rev. Amos Barton"
Carlisle, Janice. *The Sense of an Audience*, 172-176.

STANLEY ELKIN

"Fifty Dollars"
Bargen, Doris G. ...*Stanley Elkin*, 92-97.

"I Look Out for Ed Wolfe"
Bargen, Doris G. . . . *Stanley Elkin*, 83–91.

"In the Alley"
Bargen, Doris G. . . . *Stanley Elkin*, 50–52.

"The Party"
Bargen, Doris G. . . . *Stanley Elkin*, 67–70.

"A Poetics for Bullies"
Bargen, Doris G. . . . *Stanley Elkin*, 46–50.

"A Sound of Distant Thunder"
Bargen, Doris G. . . . *Stanley Elkin*, 59–63.

SARAH BARNWELL ELLIOTT

"As a Little Child"
Mackenzie, Clara C. *Sarah Barnwell Elliott*, 79–80.

"An Ex-Brigadier"
Mackenzie, Clara C. *Sarah Barnwell Elliott*, 110–111.

"Fortune's Vassals"
Mackenzie, Clara C. *Sarah Barnwell Elliott*, 141–142.

"Hands All Round"
Mackenzie, Clara C. *Sarah Barnwell Elliott*, 113–114.

"Hybrid Roses"
Mackenzie, Clara C. *Sarah Barnwell Elliott*, 81–82.

"An Idle Man"
Mackenzie, Clara C. *Sarah Barnwell Elliott*, 78–79.

"An Incident"
Mackenzie, Clara C. *Sarah Barnwell Elliott*, 93–95.

"Mrs. Gollyhaw's Candy-Stew"
Mackenzie, Clara C. *Sarah Barnwell Elliott*, 74–75.

"Readjustments"
Mackenzie, Clara C. *Sarah Barnwell Elliott*, 126–127.

"A Simple Heart"
Mackenzie, Clara C. *Sarah Barnwell Elliott*, 72–74.

"Some Data"
Mackenzie, Clara C. *Sarah Barnwell Elliott*, 88–90.

"Squire Kayley's Conclusions"
Mackenzie, Clara C. *Sarah Barnwell Elliott*, 95-96.

"Stephen's Margaret"
Mackenzie, Clara C. *Sarah Barnwell Elliott*, 80-81.

"*We* People"
Mackenzie, Clara C. *Sarah Barnwell Elliott*, 127-130.

"Without the Courts"
Mackenzie, Clara C. *Sarah Barnwell Elliott*, 96-97.

HARLAN ELLISON

"Adrift Just Off the Coast of Langerhans"
Rubens, Philip M. "Descents into Private Hells: Harlan Ellison's 'Psy-Fi,'"
Extrapolation, 20 (1979), 380-382.

"A Boy and His Dog"
Wendell, Carolyn. "The Alien Species: A Study of Women Characters in the
Nebula Award Winners, 1965-1973," *Extrapolation*, 20 (1979), 346.

"The Deathbird"
Rubens, Philip M. "Descents...," 383-384.

"Delusion for a Dragon Slayer"
Rubens, Philip M. "Descents...," 379-380.

"I Have No Mouth and I Must Scream"
Erlich, Richard D. "Trapped in the Bureaucratic Pinball Machine: A Vision of
Dystopia in the Twentieth Century," in Remington, Thomas J., Ed. *Selected
Proceedings...*, 33.

"The Place with No Name"
Rubens, Philip M. "Descents...," 382-383.

RALPH ELLISON

"Afternoon"
O'Meally, Robert G. *The Craft...*, 60-63.

"And Hickman Arrives"
O'Meally, Robert G. *The Craft...*, 121-126.

"Backwacking: A Plea to the Senator"
O'Meally, Robert G. *The Craft...*, 156-158.

"Battle Royal"
Howard, Daniel F., and William Plummer. *Instructor's Manual...*, 3rd ed., 61-62;
rpt. Howard, Daniel F., and John Ribar. *Instructor's Manual...*, 4th ed., 62.

*Mizener, Arthur. *A Handbook...*, 4th ed., 15–18.
Sadler, Lynn V. "Ralph Ellison and the Bird-Artist," *So Atlantic Bull*, 44, iv (1979), 21–22.

"The Birthmark"
O'Meally, Robert G. *The Craft...*, 59–60.

"Cadillac Flambé"
O'Meally, Robert G. *The Craft...*, 150–156.

"A Coupla Scalped Indians"
Blake, Susan L. "Ritual and Rationalization: Black Folklore in the Works of Ralph Ellison," *PMLA*, 94 (1979), 124.
O'Meally, Robert G. *The Craft...*, 113–118.

"Did You Ever Dream Lucky?"
O'Meally, Robert G. *The Craft...*, 109–113.

"Flying Home"
Blake, Susan L. "Ritual and Rationalization...," 124–126.
Okeke-Ezigbo, Emeka. "Buzzard/Eagle Symbolism in Ralph Ellison's 'Flying Home,'" *Notes Contemp Lit*, 9, v (1979), 2–3.
O'Meally, Robert G. *The Craft...*, 69–74.
Sadler, Lynn V. "...Bird-Artist," 23–25.
Smith, Elliott L., and Andrew W. Hart, Eds. *The Short Story...*, 115–117.

"Heine's Bull"
O'Meally, Robert G. *The Craft...*, 30–31.

"It Always Breaks Out"
O'Meally, Robert G. *The Craft...*, 130–133.

"Juneteenth"
O'Meally, Robert G. *The Craft...*, 133–138.

"King of the Bingo Game"
Madden, David. *Instructor's Manual...*, 5th ed., 89.
O'Meally, Robert G. *The Craft...*, 74–76.

"Mister Toussan"
Blake, Susan L. "Ritual and Rationalization...," 123–124.
O'Meally, Robert G. *The Craft...*, 63–66.

"Night-Talk"
O'Meally, Robert G. *The Craft...*, 138–144.

"Out of the Hospital and Under the Bar"
O'Meally, Robert G. *The Craft...*, 106–109.

"The Roof, the Steeple, and the People"
O'Meally, Robert G. *The Craft...*, 126–130.

"Slick Gonna Learn"
O'Meally, Robert G. *The Craft.* . ., 57–59.

"A Song of Innocence"
O'Meally, Robert G. *The Craft.* . ., 144–150.

"Sweet-the-Monkey"
O'Meally, Robert G. *The Craft.* . ., 34–35.

"That I Had the Wings"
O'Meally, Robert G. *The Craft.* . ., 66–68.

CONCHA ESPINA

"The Foundling"
Bretz, Mary L. *Concha Espina*, 62–64.

"The Girl Who Disappeared"
Bretz, Mary L. *Concha Espina*, 93–95.

"The Gray File"
Bretz, Mary L. *Concha Espina*, 113–114.

"Love's Cure"
Bretz, Mary L. *Concha Espina*, 93.

"The Man and the Mastiff"
Bretz, Mary L. *Concha Espina*, 112–113.

"Marilis"
Bretz, Mary L. *Concha Espina*, 124.

"The Prince of Song"
Bretz, Mary L. *Concha Espina*, 61.

"Rural Tragedy"
Bretz, Mary L. *Concha Espina*, 112.

"Talín"
Bretz, Mary L. *Concha Espina*, 60–61.

"Wax Flame"
Bretz, Mary L. *Concha Espina*, 92–93.

CARADOC EVANS

"Joseph's House"
Allen, Walter. *The Short Story* . . ., 220–222.

PAUL P. FARIS

"The Cup That Told"
Chu, Limin. *The Image of China*..., 194–195.

PHILIP JOSÉ FARMER

"After King Kong Fell"
Wymer, Thomas L. "Philip José Farmer: The Trickster as Artist," in Clareson,
Thomas D., Ed. *Voices for the Future*..., II, 39–41.

"The Captain's Daughter"
Wymer, Thomas L. "Philip José Farmer...," 42–43.

"My Sister's Brother"
Wymer, Thomas L. "Philip José Farmer...," 43–44.

JAMES T. FARRELL

"Jim O'Neill"
O'Connell, Barry. "The Lost World of James T. Farrell's Short Stories," in Casey,
Daniel J., and Robert E. Rhodes, Eds. *Irish-American Fiction*..., 60–61.

"Joe Eliot"
Higgs, Robert J. *Laurel & Thorn*..., 158–159.

WILLIAM FAULKNER

"Barn Burning"
Bradford, M. E. "Family and Community in Faulkner's 'Barn Burning,'" *Southern
R*, 17 (1981), 332–339.
Cox, James M. "On William Faulkner and 'Barn Burning,'" in Skaggs, Calvin,
Ed. *The American Short Story*, II, 403–406.
Fowler, Virginia C. "Faulkner's 'Barn Burning': Sarty's Conflict Reconsidered,"
Coll Lang Assoc J, 24 (1981), 513–522.
Hadley, Charles. "Seeing and Telling: Narrational Functions in the Short Story,"
in Petit, J[ean-] P[ierre], Ed. *Discourse and Style*, II, 63–68.
Kennedy, X. J. *Instructor's Manual*..., 2nd ed., 19–22.
Volpe, Edmond L. "'Barn Burning': A Definition of Evil," in Carey, Glenn O.,
Ed. *Faulkner: The Unspeakable Imagination*..., 75–82.

"The Bear"
Aiken, Charles S. "A Geographical Approach to William Faulkner's 'The Bear,'"
Geographical R, 71 (1981), 446–459.
Allen, Walter. *The Short Story*..., 181–183.
Church, Margaret. "Faulkner and Frazer: The Bear," *Int'l Fiction R*, 7 (1980), 126.
Ford, Daniel G. "'The Bear': Faulkner's Tale of Two Worlds," *Pubs Arkansas Philol
Assoc*, 7, i (1981), 18–22.
Kerr, Elizabeth. ...*Gothic Domain*, 145–147.

MacKethan, Lucinda H. *The Dream of Arcady*..., 170–179.
Scharr, John H. "Community or Contrast? William Faulkner and the Dual Legacy," in Diggins, John P., and Mark E. Kann, Eds. *The Problem*..., 93–111.
Stein, Paul S. "Ike McCaslin: Traumatized in a Hawthornian Wilderness," *Southern Lit J*, 12, ii (1980), 65–82.
Wittenberg, Judith B. *Faulkner*..., 197–201.

"Carcassonne"
Hamblin, Robert W. "'Carcassonne': Faulkner's Allegory of Art and the Artist," *Southern R*, 15 (1979), 355–365.

"A Courtship"
Bradford, M. E. "Faulkner's 'A Courtship': An Accommodation of Culture," *So Atlantic Q*, 80 (1981), 355–359.

"Delta Autumn"
Altenbernd, Lynn, and Leslie L. Lewis. *Instructor's Manual*..., 3rd ed., 20–22.
Jenkins, Lee. *Faulkner and Black-White Relations*..., 238–243.
Kerr, Elizabeth. ...*Gothic Domain*, 147–148.
*Mizener, Arthur, Ed. *Modern Short Stories*..., 4th ed., 678–680.

"Dry September"
Allen, Walter. *The Short Story*..., 184–186.
Barker, Gerard A. *Instructor's Manual*..., 59–60.
*Howard, Daniel F., and William Plummer. *Instructor's Manual*..., 3rd ed., 45; rpt. Howard, Daniel F., and John Ribar. *Instructor's Manual*..., 4th ed., 42.
Pryse, Marjorie. *The Mark*..., 119–120.
Stewart, Jack F. "The Infernal Climate of Faulkner's 'Dry September,'" *Research Stud*, 47 (1979), 238–243.

"An Error in Chemistry"
Klinkowitz, Jerome. *The Practice of Fiction*..., 64–66.

"The Fire and the Hearth"
Jenkins, Lee. *Faulkner and Black-White Relations*..., 252–260.
Kerr, Elizabeth M. ...*Gothic Domain*, 141–143.
*Mizener, Arthur. *A Handbook*..., 4th ed., 171–176.
Pilkington, John. *The Heart*..., 253–258.
Wittenberg, Judith B. *Faulkner*..., 201–202.

"Go Down, Moses"
Kerr, Elizabeth. ...*Gothic Domain*, 160–161.
Pilkington, John. *The Heart*..., 285–288.

"Golden Land"
Winchell, Mark R. "William Faulkner's 'Golden Land': Some Time in Hell," *Notes Mississippi Writers*, 14, i (1981), 12–17.

"Hand upon the Water"
Klinkowitz, Jerome. *The Practice of Fiction*..., 61–62.

"The Hill" [later expanded into "Nympholepsy"]
Watson, James G. "Faulkner's Short Stories and the Making of Yoknapatawpha County," in Fowler, Doreen, and Ann J. Abadie, Eds. *Fifty Years...*, 205-214.

"Knight's Gambit"
Klinkowitz, Jerome. *The Practice of Fiction...*, 66-69.
Skei, Hans H. "Faulkner's 'Knight's Gambit': Detection and Ingenuity," *Notes Mississippi Writers*, 13, ii (1981), 79-93.

"Mistral"
Paddock, Lisa. "'Trifles with a Tragic Profundity': The Importance of 'Mistral,'" *Mississippi Q*, 32 (1979), 413-422.

"Monk"
Klinkowitz, Jerome. *The Practice of Fiction...*, 58-61.
Volpe, Edmond L. "Faulkner's 'Monk': The Detective Story and the Mystery of the Human Heart," *Faulkner Stud*, 1 (1980), 86-90.

"An Odor of Verbena"
Pilkington, John. *The Heart...*, 211-215.
Wittenberg, Judith B. *Faulkner...*, 163-166.

"Old Man"
Douglas, Kenneth, and Sarah N. Lawall. "Masterpieces of the Modern World," in Mack, Maynard, *et al.*, Eds. *...World Masterpieces*, II, 4th ed., 1275-1276.
Wilcox, Earl J. "Christian Coloring in Faulkner's 'The Old Man,'" *Christianity & Lit*, 29, ii (1980), 63-74.

"The Old People"
Stewart, Jack F. "Structure, Language, and Vision in Faulkner's 'The Old People,'" *Ball State Univ Forum*, 22, iii (1981), 51-57.

"Pantaloon in Black"
Jenkins, Lee. *Faulkner and Black-White Relations...*, 243-252.
Kerr, Elizabeth. *...Gothic Domain*, 143-145.
Pilkington, John. *The Heart...*, 258-259.
Wittenberg, Judith B. *Faulkner...*, 202-203.

"Raid"
*Mizener, Arthur. *A Handbook...*, 4th ed., 179-185.

"Red Leaves"
Pryse, Marjorie. *The Mark...*, 121-122.

"The Rosary"
Folks, Jeffrey J. "William Faulkner's 'The Rosary' and Florence L. Barclay," *Stud Short Fiction*, 18 (1981), 445-447.

"A Rose for Emily"
Ahrends, Günter. *...Kurzgeschichte*, 164-166.
*Brooks, Cleanth, and Robert P. Warren. *Understanding Fiction*, 3rd ed., 227-231.

Fetterley, Judith. *The Resisting Reader...*, 34–45.

Garrison, Joseph M. "'Bought Flowers' in 'A Rose for Emily,'" *Stud Short Fiction*, 16 (1979), 341–344.

Hendricks, William O. "'A Rose for Emily': A Syntagmatic Analysis," *PTL: J Descriptive Poetics and Theory Lit*, 2 (1977), 257–295.

Hunter, William B. "A Chronology for Emily," *Notes Mod Am Lit*, 4 (1980), Item 18.

Lupack, Barbara T. "The Two Tableaux in Faulkner's 'A Rose for Emily,'" *Notes Contemp Lit*, 11, iii (1981), 6–7.

Rohrberger, Mary. *Instructor's Manual...*, 25.

Scherting, Jack. "Emily Grierson's Oedipus Complex: Motif, Motive, and Meaning in Faulkner's 'A Rose for Emily,'" *Stud Short Fiction*, 17 (1980), 397–405.

"Skirmish at Sartoris"

Pilkington, John. *The Heart...*, 206–209.

"Smoke"

Klinkowitz, Jerome. *The Practice of Fiction...*, 56–58.

"Spotted Horses"

McDermott, John V. "Mrs. Armstid: Faulkner's Moral 'Snag,'" *Stud Short Fiction*, 16 (1979), 179–182.

Male, Roy R. *...Cloistral Fiction*, 52–55.

Pilkington, John. *The Heart...*, 236–237.

"That Evening Sun"

Allen, Walter. *The Short Story...*, 186–188.

Barker, Gerard A. *Instructor's Manual...*, 37–39.

Hamblin, Robert W. "Before the Fall: The Theme of Innocence in 'That Evening Sun,'" *Notes Mississippi Writers*, 11 (1979), 86–94.

Pitcher, E. W. "Motive and Metaphor in Faulkner's 'That Evening Sun,'" *Stud Short Fiction*, 18 (1981), 131–135.

Scott, Virgil, and David Madden. *Instructor's Manual...*, 4th ed., 17–18; Madden, David. *Instructor's Manual...*, 5th ed., 38–41.

"Thrift"

Skei, Hans H. "A Forgotten Faulkner Story: 'Thrift,'" *Mississippi Q*, 32 (1979), 453–460.

"Tomorrow"

Klinkowitz, Jerome. *The Practice of Fiction...*, 62–64.

"Uncle Willy"

Polk, Noel. "Faulkner and Respectability," in Fowler, Doreen, and Ann J. Abadie, Eds. *Fifty Years...*, 114–119.

"Was"

Kerr, Elizabeth M. *...Gothic Domain*, 139–141.

Pilkington, John. *The Heart...*, 251–253.

"Wash"

Ahrends, Günter. *...Kurzgeschichte*, 166–168.

ARTHUR HUFF FAUSET

"Symphonesque"
Perry, Margaret. *Silence to the Drums* . . . , 124–128.

JESSIE REDMON FAUSET

"Double Trouble"
Sylvander, Carolyn W. *Jessie Redmon Fauset* . . . , 135–137.

"Emmy"
Sylvander, Carolyn W. *Jessie Redmon Fauset* . . . , 131–132.

"Mary Elizabeth"
Sylvander, Carolyn W. *Jessie Redmon Fauset* . . . , 136–137.

"The Sleeper Wakes"
Sylvander, Carolyn W. *Jessie Redmon Fauset* . . . , 133–135.

JACQUES FERRON

"Les Méchins"
Amprimoz, Alexandre L. "Sémiotique de l'organisation textuelle d'un conte: 'Les Méchins' de Jacques Ferron," *Présence Francophone*, 23 (1981), 131–141.

DOROTHY CANFIELD FISHER

"The Knot Hole"
Altenbernd, Lynn, and Leslie L. Lewis. *Instructor's Manual* . . . , 3rd ed., 22–23.

RUDOLPH FISHER

"The City of Refuge"
Deutsch, Leonard J. "'The Streets of Harlem': The Short Stories of Rudolph Fisher," *Phylon*, 40 (1979), 160–161.
McCluskey, John. "'Aim High and Go Straight': The Grandmother Figure in the Short Fiction of Rudolph Fisher," *Black Am Lit*, 15 (1981), 55–56.
Perry, Margaret. *Silence to the Drums* . . . , 112–114.

"Common Meter"
Deutsch, Leonard J. "'The Streets of Harlem' . . . ," 165.

"Dust"
Deutsch, Leonard J. "'The Streets of Harlem'. . . ," 165–166.

"Ezekiel"
Deutsch, Leonard J. "'The Streets of Harlem'. . . ," 166.

"Fire by Night"
Deutsch, Leonard J. "'The Streets of Harlem'...," 163–164.

"Guardian of the Law"
Deutsch, Leonard J. "'The Streets of Harlem'...," 166–167.
McCluskey, John. "'Aim High...,'" 58.

"High Yaller"
Deutsch, Leonard J. "'The Streets of Harlem'...," 162.

"Lindy Hop"
McCluskey, John. "'Aim High...,'" 57–58.

"Miss Cynthie"
Deutsch, Leonard J. "'The Streets of Harlem'...," 167–168.
McCluskey, John. "'Aim High...,'" 58–59.
Perry, Margaret. *Silence to the Drums*..., 115.

"The Promised Land"
Deutsch, Leonard J. "'The Streets of Harlem'...," 162–163.
McCluskey, John. "'Aim High...,'" 57.

"Ringtail"
McCluskey, John. "'Aim High...,'" 56.

"The South Lingers On"
Deutsch, Leonard J. "'The Streets of Harlem'...," 161.

F. SCOTT FITZGERALD

"Absolution"
Allen, Joan M. *Candles*..., 93–111.
Cushman, Keith. "Scott Fitzgerald's Scrupulous Meanness: 'Absolution' and 'The Sisters,'" *Fitzgerald/Hemingway Annual 1979*, [n.v.] (1980), 115–121.
Scott, Virgil, and David Madden. *Instructor's Manual*..., 4th ed., 21–23; Madden, David. *Instructor's Manual*..., 5th ed., 75–77.
Stavola, Thomas J. *Scott Fitzgerald*..., 126–130.

"The Baby Party"
Rohrberger, Mary. *Instructor's Manual*..., 24.

"Babylon Revisited"
Allen, Joan M. *Candles*..., 119–121.
Gervais, Ronald J. "The Snow of Twenty-Nine: 'Babylon Revisited' as *Ubi Sunt* Lament," *Coll Lit*, 7 (1980), 47–52.
Howard, Daniel F., and William Plummer. *Instructor's Manual*..., 3rd ed., 43; rpt. Howard, Daniel F., and John Ribar. *Instructor's Manual*..., 4th ed., 40.
*Mizener, Arthur. *A Handbook*..., 4th ed., 10–13.
Way, Brian. ...*Social Fiction*, 90–92.

"Basil and Cleopatra"
Messenger, Christian K. *Sport...*, 196-197.

"Benediction"
Allen, Joan M. *Candles...*, 43-45.

"Bernice Bobs Her Hair"
Way, Brian. *...Social Fiction*, 56-57.

"The Bowl"
Way, Brian. *...Social Fiction*, 74-75.

"Crazy Sunday"
Way, Brian. *...Social Fiction*, 93-95.

"The Curious Case of Benjamin Button"
Gery, John. "The Curious Grace of Benjamin Button," *Stud Short Fiction*, 17 (1980), 495-497.

"The Diamond as Big as the Ritz"
Allen, Joan M. *Candles...*, 85-88.
Way, Brian. *...Social Fiction*, 67-71.

"The Freshest Boy"
Allen, Joan M. *Candles...*, 29-30.

"Gods of Darkness"
Lewis, Janet. "Fitzgerald's 'Philippe, Count of Darkness,'" *Fitzgerald/Hemingway Annual 1975*, [n.v.] (1976), 15-16.

"The Ice Palace"
Gervais, Ronald J. "A Miracle of Rare Device: Fitzgerald's 'The Ice Palace,'" *Notes Mod Am Lit*, 5, iii (1981), Item 21.
Way, Brian. *...Social Fiction*, 55-56.

"In the Darkest Hour"
Lewis, Janet. "...'Philippe, Count of Darkness,'" 14-15.

"The Jelly-Bean"
Way, Brian. *...Social Fiction*, 60.

"The Last of the Belles"
Way, Brian. *...Social Fiction*, 82-84.

"Majesty"
Way, Brian. *...Social Fiction*, 45-46.

"May Day"
Ahrends, Günter. *...Kurzgeschichte*, 145-147.
Allen, Walter. *The Short Story...*, 142-146.
Perlis, Alan. "The Narrative Is All: A Study of F. Scott Fitzgerald's 'May Day,'" *Western Hum R*, 33 (1979), 65-72.
Way, Brian. *...Social Fiction*, 78-79.

"A Night at the Fair"
Allen, Joan M. *Candles...*, 23-25.

"One Trip Abroad"
Way, Brian. *...Social Fiction*, 89-90.

"The Ordeal"
Allen, Joan M. *Candles...*, 42-43.

"The Perfect Life"
Allen, Joan M. *Candles...*, 31-32.

"The Rich Boy"
Way, Brian. *...Social Fiction*, 84-87.

"The Rough Crossing"
Way, Brian. *...Social Fiction*, 88-89.

"The Sisters"
Cushman, Keith. "Scott Fitzgerald's Scrupulous Meanness...," 115-121.

"That Kind of Party"
Allen, Joan M. *Candles...*, 10-12.

"Winter Dreams"
Altenbernd, Lynn, and Leslie L. Lewis. *Instructor's Manual...*, 3rd ed., 24.

CHARLES MACOMB FLANDRAU

"Wanderlust"
Gunn, Drewey W. *American and British Writers...*, 51-52.

GUSTAVE FLAUBERT

"Bouvard and Pécuchet"
Cogny, Pierre. "La Parodie dans 'Bouvard et Pécuchet': Essai de lecture du chapitre 1," in Anon., Ed. *Flaubert et le comble de l'art...*, 39-47.
Crouzet, Michel. "Sur le grotesque triste dans 'Bouvard et Pécuchet,'" in Anon., Ed. *Flaubert et le comble de l'art...*, 49-74.
Donato, Eugenio. "The Museum's Furnace: Notes Toward a Contextual Reading of 'Bouvard and Pécuchet,'" in Harari, Josué V., Ed. *Textual Strategies...*, 213-238.
Gaillard, Françoise. "Une Inenarrable Histoire," in Anon., Ed. *Flaubert et le comble de l'art...*, 75-87.
Greene, John. "Structure et épistemologie dans 'Bouvard et Pécuchet,'" in Anon., Ed. *Flaubert et le comble de l'art...*, 111-128.
Herschberg-Pierrot, Anne. "Le Cliché dans 'Bouvard et Pécuchet,'" in Anon., Ed. *Flaubert et le comble de l'art...*, 31-37.
McKenna, Andrew J. "Writing in the Novel: Remarks on 'Bouvard et Pécuchet,'" *Lang & Style*, 14, ii (1981), 83-91.

Raitt, A. W. "L'Eternel Présent dans les romans de Flaubert," in Anon., Ed. *Flaubert et le comble de l'art...*, 139–147.

Seylaz, Jean-Luc. "Un Aspect de la narration flaubertienne: Quelques réflexions sur l'emploi du 'on' dans 'Bouvard et Pécuchet,'" in Anon., Ed. *Flaubert et le comble de l'art...*, 23–30.

Welsh, Alexander. *...Hero as Quixote*, 179–182.

"Hérodias"

O'Connor, John R. "Flaubert: *Trois Contes* and the Figure of the Double Cone," *PMLA*, 95 (1980), 822–824.

Zants, Emily. "*Trois contes*: A New Dimension in Flaubert," *Nottingham French Stud*, 18, i (1979), 37–44.

"St. Julien"

Biasi, Pierre-Marc de. "Un Conte à l'orientale: La Tentation de l'Orient dans 'La Légende de Saint Julien L'Hospitalier,'" *Romantisme*, 11 (1981), 47–66.

O'Connor, John R. "...Double Cone," 817–822.

Zants, Emily. "*Trois contes...*," 37–44.

"A Simple Heart"

Chambers, Ross. "Simplicité de coeur et duplicité textuelle: Étude d' 'Un Coeur simple,'" *Mod Lang Notes*, 96 (1981), 771–791.

O'Connor, John R. "...Double Cone," 813–817.

Zants, Emily. "*Trois contes...*," 37–44.

MARY HALLOCK FOOTE

"A Cloud on the Mountain"
Johnson, Lee A. *Mary Hallock Foote*, 62–63.

"The Cup of Trembling"
Johnson, Lee A. *Mary Hallock Foote*, 95–96.

"The Fate of a Voice"
Johnson, Lee A. *Mary Hallock Foote*, 64–68.

"Friend Barton's 'Concern'"
Johnson, Lee A. *Mary Hallock Foote*, 37–40.

"Gideon's Knock"
Johnson, Lee A. *Mary Hallock Foote*, 126–128.

"How the Pump Stopped at the Morning Watch"
Johnson, Lee A. *Mary Hallock Foote*, 105–107.

"In Exile"
Johnson, Lee A. *Mary Hallock Foote*, 33–36.

"The Maid's Progress"
Johnson, Lee A. *Mary Hallock Foote*, 108–109.

"The Picture in the Fire-Place Bedroom"
Johnson, Lee A. *Mary Hallock Foote*, 25.

"Pilgrims to Mecca"
Johnson, Lee A. *Mary Hallock Foote*, 109-111.

"The Story of Alcázar"
Johnson, Lee A. *Mary Hallock Foote*, 47-49.

"A Story of the Dry Season"
Johnson, Lee A. *Mary Hallock Foote*, 40-42.

"A Touch of Sun"
Johnson, Lee A. *Mary Hallock Foote*, 111-113.

"The Trumpeter"
Johnson, Lee A. *Mary Hallock Foote*, 94-95.

"The Watchman"
Johnson, Lee A. *Mary Hallock Foote*, 86-87.

SHELBY FOOTE

"Child by Fever"
Phillips, Robert L. "Shelby Foote's Bristol in 'Child by Fever,'" *Southern Q*, 19 (1980), 172-183.

E. M. FORSTER

"Albergo Empedocle"
Cavaliero, Glen. *A Reading*..., 43-44.
McDowell, Frederick P. W. "Forster's Posthumously Published Tales and Some Reflections on His Fiction," *Virginia Woolf Q*, 2 (1980), 272-273.

"Arthur Snatchfold"
Adams, Stephen. *The Homosexual as Hero*..., 121-122.
McDowell, Frederick P. W. "Forster's Posthumously Published Tales...," 275-276.
Malek, James S. "Forster's 'Arthur Snatchfold': Respectability vs. Apollo," *Notes Contemp Lit*, 10, iv (1980), 8-9.

"The Celestial Omnibus"
Cavaliero, Glen. *A Reading*..., 51-52.

"The Classical Annex"
McDowell, Frederick P. W. "Forster's Posthumously Published Tales...," 274-275.

"The Curate's Friend"
Cavaliero, Glen. *A Reading*..., 46-48.

"Dr. Woolacott"
McDowell, Frederick P. W. "Forster's Posthumously Published Tales...," 276-277.
Malek, James S. "Salvation in Forster's 'Dr. Woolacott,'" *Stud Short Fiction*, 18 (1981), 319-320.

"The Eternal Moment"
Allen, Walter. *The Short Story...*, 111-112.
Cavaliero, Glen. *A Reading...*, 55-56.

"The Life to Come"
Adams, Stephen. *The Homosexual as Hero...*, 119-120.
Herz, Judith S. "From Myth to Scripture: An Approach to Forster's Later Short Fiction," *Engl Lit Transition*, 24 (1981), 209-211.
McDowell, Frederick P. W. "Forster's Posthumously Published Tales...," 277-278.

"The Machine Stops"
Altenbernd, Lynn, and Leslie L. Lewis. *Instructor's Manual...*, 3rd ed., 25.
Cavaliero, Glen. *A Reading...*, 50-51.
Erlich, Richard D. "Trapped in the Bureaucratic Pinball Machine: A Vision of Dystopia in the Twentieth Century," in Remington, Thomas J., Ed. *Selected Proceedings...*, 35.
Warrick, Patricia S. *The Cybernetic Imagination...*, 44-46.

"The Obelisk"
McDowell, Frederick P. W. "Forster's Posthumously Published Tales...," 275.

"The Other Boat"
Adams, Stephen. *The Homosexual as Hero...*, 124-125.
Cavaliero, Glen. *A Reading...*, 144-145.
McDowell, Frederick P. W. "Forster's Posthumously Published Tales...," 278-279.

"Other Kingdom"
Cavaliero, Glen. *A Reading...*, 48-49.

"The Point of It"
Cavaliero, Glen. *A Reading...*, 53-54.

"The Purple Hat"
McDowell, Frederick P. W. "Forster's Posthumously Published Tales...," 271-272.

"The Road from Colonus"
Cavaliero, Glen. *A Reading...*, 54-55.

"The Rock"
Cavaliero, Glen. *A Reading...*, 172-173.
McDowell, Frederick P. W. "Forster's Posthumously Published Tales...," 273.

"The Story of a Panic"
Allen, Walter. *The Short Story...*, 110-111.
Cavaliero, Glen. *A Reading...*, 44-46.

"The Story of the Siren"
Cavaliero, Glen. *A Reading...*, 49–50.

"The Torque"
McDowell, Frederick P. W. "Forster's Posthumously Published Tales...," 275.

"What Does It Matter?"
Cavaliero, Glen. *A Reading...*, 141–142.

JOHN FOWLES

"The Cloud"
Huffaker, Robert. *John Fowles*, 128–130.
Olshen, Barry N. *John Fowles*, 103–106.

"The Ebony Tower"
Olshen, Barry N. *John Fowles*, 94–99.

"The Enigma"
Huffaker, Robert. *John Fowles*, 125–128.
Olshen, Barry N. *John Fowles*, 101–102.

"Poor Koko"
Bellamy, Michael O. "John Fowles's Version of Pastoral: Private Valleys and the
    Parity of Existence," *Critique*, 21, ii (1979), 78–79.
Huffaker, Robert. *John Fowles*, 123–125.
Olshen, Barry N. *John Fowles*, 99–100.

JANET FRAME

"Keel and Kool"
Evans, P. D. "'Farthest from the Heart': The Autobiographical Parables of Janet
    Frame," *Mod Fiction Stud*, 27 (1981), 37–38.

"The Lagoon"
Evans, P. D. "'Farthest from the Heart'...," 34–36.

LEONHARD FRANK

"Die Kriegswitwe"
Dietrick, Augustinus P. "Two Representative Expressionist Responses to the
    Challenge of the First World War: Carl Sternheim's *eigene Nuance* and Leonhard
    Frank's Utopia," in Genno, Charles N., and Heinz Wetzel, Eds. *The First World
    War...*, 28–29.

"Das Liebespaar"
Dietrick, Augustinus P. "Two Representative Expressionist Responses...," 29–30.

"Der Vater"
Dietrick, Augustinus P. "Two Representative Expressionist Responses...," 27-28.

MARY E. WILKINS FREEMAN

"Christmas Jenny"
Sherman, Sarah W. "The Great Goddess in New England: Mary Wilkins Freeman's 'Christmas Jenny,'" *Stud Short Fiction*, 17 (1980), 157-164.

"The Little Maid"
Williams, Blanche C. *Our Short Story Writers*, 175-176.

"A New England Nun"
Walker, Dorothea. "Freeman's Nun and Brown's Witch: A New Look at the New England Spinster," *Nassau R*, 3, i (1975), 2-4.

"The Revolt of Mother"
DeEulis, Marilyn D. "'Her Box of a House': Spatial Restriction as Psychic Signpost in Mary Wilkins Freeman's 'The Revolt of Mother,'" *Markham R* , 8 (1979), 51-52.
McElrath, Joseph R. "The Artistry of Mary E. Wilkins Freeman's 'The Revolt,'" *Stud Short Fiction*, 17 (1980), 255-261.
Williams, Blanche C. *Our Short Story Writers*, 169-171.

CELIA FREMLIN

"Don't Be Frightened"
Pearson, Carol, and Katherine Pope. *The Female Hero...*, 194-195.

BRIAN FRIEL

"Among the Ruïns"
Maxwell, D. E. S. *Brian Friel*, 35-36.

"The Diviner"
Maxwell, D. E. S. *Brian Friel*, 44.

"The Flower of Kiltymore"
Maxwell, D. E. S. *Brian Friel*, 33-34.

"Foundry House"
Maxwell, D. E. S. *Brian Friel*, 38-42.

"The Gold in the Sea"
Maxwell, D. E. S. *Brian Friel*, 42-44.

"The Highwayman and the Saint"
Maxwell, D. E. S. *Brian Friel*, 44-45.

"The Illusionists"
Maxwell, D. E. S. *Brian Friel*, 36-37.

"Johnny and Mick"
Maxwell, D. E. S. *Brian Friel*, 15-18.

"Mr. Sing My Heart's Delight"
Maxwell, D. E. S. *Brian Friel*, 34-35.

"My Father and the Sergeant"
Maxwell, D. E. S. *Brian Friel*, 37-38.

"The Potato Gatherers"
Maxwell, D. E. S. *Brian Friel*, 30-31.

"The Saucer of Larks"
Maxwell, D. E. S. *Brian Friel*, 31-32.

BARBARA FRISCHMUTH

"Baum des vergessenen Hundes"
Haberland, Paul M. "The Role of Art in the Writings of Barbara Frischmuth,"
   Mod Austrian Lit, 14, i-ii (1981), 92-93.

"Bleiben lassen"
Haberland, Paul M. "The Role of Art...," 91-92.

DANIEL FUCHS

"The Amazing Mystery of Storick, Dorschi, Pflaumer, Inc."
Miller, Gabriel. *Daniel Fuchs*, 151.

"The Apathetic Bookie Joint"
Miller, Gabriel. *Daniel Fuchs*, 145.

"A Clean Quiet House"
Miller, Gabriel. *Daniel Fuchs*, 146-147.

"Crap Game"
Miller, Gabriel. *Daniel Fuchs*, 144-145.

"Ecossaise, Berceuse, Polonaise"
Miller, Gabriel. *Daniel Fuchs*, 121-123.

"The First Smell of Spring, and Brooklyn"
Miller, Gabriel. *Daniel Fuchs*, 148-149.

"A Girl Like Cele"
Miller, Gabriel. *Daniel Fuchs*, 151-152.

"The Golden West"
Miller, Gabriel. *Daniel Fuchs*, 126–128.

"Love in Brooklyn"
Miller, Gabriel. *Daniel Fuchs*, 148–149.

"The Man from Mars"
Miller, Gabriel. *Daniel Fuchs*, 148.

"Man in the Middle of the Ocean"
Miller, Gabriel. *Daniel Fuchs*, 147–148.

"The Morose Policeman"
Miller, Gabriel. *Daniel Fuchs*, 145–146.

"Okay, Mr. Pappendas, Okay"
Miller, Gabriel. *Daniel Fuchs*, 152.

"People on a Planet"
Miller, Gabriel. *Daniel Fuchs*, 144.

"There's Always Honolulu"
Miller, Gabriel. *Daniel Fuchs*, 150.

"Twilight in Southern California"
Miller, Gabriel. *Daniel Fuchs*, 123–126.

CARLOS FUENTES

"All Cats Are Gray"
Gyurko, Lanin. "Fuentes and the Ancient Aztec Past: The Role of Moctezuma in 'Todos los gatos son pardos,'" in Lévy, Isaac J., and Juan Loveluck, Eds. *Simposi Carlos Fuentes...*, 193–213.

"Aura"
Titiev, Janice G. "Witchcraft in Carlos Fuentes' 'Aura,'" *Revista de Estudios Hispánicos*, 15 (1981), 396–405.

"The Cost of Life"
Blasi, Alberto. "'El costa de la vida': Una cápsula metafísica," in Lévy, Isaac J., and Juan Loveluck, Eds. *Simposi Carlos Fuentes...*, 65–73.

"The Doll Queen"
Durán, Gloria B. *The Archetypes of Carlos Fuentes...*, 198–199.

"Tlactocatzine, the One from the Flemish Garden"
Feijóo, Gladys. "Lo fantástico por el camino topológico en el cuento 'Tlactocatzine, del jardín en Flandes,'" in Lévy, Isaac J., and Juan Loveluck, Eds. *Simposi Carlos Fuentes...*, 75–85.

"What Fortune Brought"
Gyurko, Lanin. "Pop Art and Pop Life in Fuentes' 'Fortuna lo que ha querido,'"
    Horizontes, 45 (1979), 5-20.

ERNEST J. GAINES

"The Sky Is Gray"
*Mizener, Arthur. *A Handbook...*, 4th ed., 197-200.
Pecile, Jordon. "On Ernest J. Gaines and 'The Sky Is Gray,'" in Skaggs, Calvin,
    Ed. *The American Short Story*, II, 452-458.

JOHN GALSWORTHY

"The Japanese Quince"
Smith, Elliott L., and Andrew W. Hart, Eds. *The Short Story...*, 99-101.

GABRIEL GARCÍA MÁRQUEZ

"Baltazar's Wonderful Afternoon"
Foster, David W. "García Márquez and the *Escritura* of Complicity: 'La prodigiosa
    tarde de Baltazar,'" *Stud Short Fiction*, 16 (1979), 33-40.
————. ...*Spanish-American Short Story*, 39-50.

"Big Mama's Funeral"
Chase, Victoria F. "(De)mitificación en 'Los funerales de la Mamá Grande,'" *Texto
    Crítico*, 6, xvi-xvii (1980), 233-247.
Foster, David W. ...*Spanish-American Short Story*, 51-62.
González, Echevarría, Roberto. "'Big Mama's Wake,'" *Diacritics*, 4, ii (1974), 55-57.
Sims, Robert. "The Creation of Myth in Garcia Marquez's 'Los funerales de la
    Mamá Grande,'" *Hispania*, 61, i (1978), 14-23.

"Blacamán the Good, Vendor of Miracles"
Janes, Regina. *Gabriel García Márquez...*, 78-80.

"Death Constant Beyond Love"
Janes, Regina. *Gabriel García Márquez...*, 82-83.
Neghme Echeverría, Lidia. "La ironía trágica en un relato de García Márquez,"
    Eco, 27, vi (October, 1974), 627-646.

"The Handsomest Drowned Man in the World"
Davis, Mary E. "The Voyage Beyond the Map: 'El ahogado más hermoso del
    mundo,'" *Kentucky Romance Q*, 26 (1979), 25-33.
Janes, Regina. *Gabriel García Márquez...*, 76-78.
Seabra, Célia M. "A palavra como objeto de valor poético em García Márquez,"
    Revista Letras, 25 (January, 1976), 77-90.

"The Incredible and Sad Tale of Innocent Eréndira and Her Heartless
Grandmother"

Hancock, Joel. "Gabriel García Márquez's 'Eréndira' and the Brothers Grimm,"
Stud Twentieth Century Lit, 3 (1978), 43–52.
Janes, Regina. *Gabriel García Márquez* . . . , 85–87.
Rohrberger, Mary. *Instructor's Manual* . . . , 42.

"The Last Voyage of the Ghost Ship"
Janes, Regina. *Gabriel García Márquez* . . . , 80–82.

"Nabo"
Janes, Regina. *Gabriel García Márquez* . . . , 23–25.

"The Sea of Lost Time"
Vargas Llosa, Mario. "'El mar del tiempo perdido': un cuento de Gabriel García
Márquez," *Eco*, 22 (March/April, 1971), 481–504.

"The Third Resignation"
Zapata Olivella, Manuel. "Realidad y fabulación in García Márquez: Autocrítica
y reiteración como elementos estilísticos," *Revista Nacional de Cultura*, 30
(September–December, 1970), 21–27.

"A Very Old Man with Enormous Wings"
Borgeson, Paul W. "Los pobres ángeles de Gabriel García Márquez y Joaquín
Pasos," *Crítica Hispánica*, 3 (1981), 111–123.
Janes, Regina. *Gabriel García Márquez* . . . , 75–76.
Madden, David. *Instructor's Manual* . . . , 5th ed., 45–48.

HAMLIN GARLAND

"Among the Corn Rows"
Hiscoe, David W. "Feeding and Consuming in Garland's *Main-Travelled Roads*,"
Western Am Lit, 15 (1980), 11–13.

"A Branch Road"
Hiscoe, David W. "Feeding and Consuming . . . ," 6–9.

"Hippy the Dare-Devil" [originally titled "Story of Hippy"]
Underhill, Lonnie E., and Daniel F. Littlefield, Eds. *Hamlin Garland's
Observations* . . . , 34.

"The Iron Khiva"
Underhill, Lonnie E., and Daniel F. Littlefield, Eds. *Hamlin Garland's Observations* . . . , 16.

"Mrs. Ripley's Trip"
Hiscoe, David W. "Feeding and Consuming . . . ," 13–14.

"The Return of a Private"
Ahrends, Günter. . . . *Kurzgeschichte*, 113–115.
Hiscoe, David W. "Feeding and Consuming . . . ," 11.

"The Silence Eaters"
Underhill, Lonnie E., and Daniel F. Littlefield, Eds. *Hamlin Garland's Observations*..., 38–39.

"The Sitting Bull's Visit"
Underhill, Lonnie E., and Daniel F. Littlefield, Eds. *Hamlin Garland's Observations*..., 39–40.

"The Spartan Mother"
Underhill, Lonnie E., and Daniel F. Littlefield, Eds. *Hamlin Garland's Observations*..., 43–44.

"Under the Lion's Paw"
Hiscoe, David W. "Feeding and Consuming...," 14–15.

"Up the Coulé"
Hiscoe, David W. "Feeding and Consuming...," 4–6, 9–11.

VSEVOLOD GARSHIN

"The Action at Ayaslar"
Yarwood, Edmund. *Vsevolod Garshin*, 33–34.

"The Bears"
Yarwood, Edmund. *Vsevolod Garshin*, 80–81.

"The Coward"
Yarwood, Edmund. *Vsevolod Garshin*, 94–95.

"The Meeting"
Yarwood, Edmund. *Vsevolod Garshin*, 75–77.

"Night"
Yarwood, Edmund. *Vsevolod Garshin*, 67–68.

DANIEL GARZA

"Everybody Knows Tobie"
Robinson, Cecil. *Mexico*..., 316–318.

ELIZABETH GASKELL

"Christmas Storms and Sunshine"
Easson, Angus. *Elizabeth Gaskell*, 204.

"Cousin Phillis"
Easson, Angus. *Elizabeth Gaskell*, 221–226.
Stone, Donald D. *The Romantic Impulse*..., 166–167.

"The Crooked Branch" [originally titled "The Ghost in the Garden"]
Duthie, Enid L. *The Themes* . . . , 146–147.
Easson, Angus. *Elizabeth Gaskell*, 212–213.

"Curious If True"
Duthie, Enid L. *The Themes* . . . , 148–149.
Easson, Angus. *Elizabeth Gaskell*, 220–221.

"A Dark Night's Work"
Duthie, Enid L. *The Themes* . . . , 95–96.
Easson, Angus. *Elizabeth Gaskell*, 217–219.
Ganz, Margaret. *Elizabeth Gaskell* . . . , 203–206.

"The Doom of the Griffiths"
Duthie, Enid L. *The Themes* . . . , 147–148.
Ganz, Margaret. *Elizabeth Gaskell* . . . , 213–217.

"The Grey Woman"
Easson, Angus. *Elizabeth Gaskell*, 200–202, 216–217.
Ganz, Margaret. *Elizabeth Gaskell* . . . , 207–210.

"Half a Lifetime Ago"
Duthie, Enid L. *The Themes* . . . , 133–134.

"Libbie Marsh's Three Eras"
Duthie, Enid L. *The Themes* . . . , 123–124.

"Lois the Witch"
Duthie, Enid L. *The Themes* . . . , 142–145.
Easson, Angus. *Elizabeth Gaskell*, 215–216.
Ganz, Margaret. *Elizabeth Gaskell* . . . , 217–221.

"Mr. Harrison's Confession"
Easson, Angus. *Elizabeth Gaskell*, 207.

"The Moorland Cottage"
Duthie, Enid L. *The Themes* . . . , 47–48.
Easson, Angus. *Elizabeth Gaskell*, 206–207.
Ganz, Margaret. *Elizabeth Gaskell* . . . , 201–203.
Stone, Donald D. *The Romantic Impulse* . . . , 145–146.

"Morton Hall"
Easson, Angus. *Elizabeth Gaskell*, 210.
Ganz, Margaret. *Elizabeth Gaskell* . . . , 203–206.

"My French Master"
Easson, Angus. *Elizabeth Gaskell*, 210–211.

"My Lady Ludlow"
Easson, Angus. *Elizabeth Gaskell*, 214.
Ganz, Margaret. *Elizabeth Gaskell* . . . , 155–161.

"The Old Nurse's Story"
Duthie, Enid L. *The Themes*..., 140-141.
Ganz, Margaret. *Elizabeth Gaskell*..., 210-212.

"The Poor Clare"
Duthie, Enid L. *The Themes*..., 141-142.
Easson, Angus. *Elizabeth Gaskell*, 213-214.
Ganz, Margaret. *Elizabeth Gaskell*..., 213-215.

"Right at Last" [originally titled "The Sin of a Father"]
Easson, Angus. *Elizabeth Gaskell*, 214-215.

"The Sexton's Hero"
Easson, Angus. *Elizabeth Gaskell*, 203-204.

"The Squire's Story"
Duthie, Enid L. *The Themes*..., 145-146.
Ganz, Margaret. *Elizabeth Gaskell*..., 207-209.

WILLIAM GASS

"Order of Insects"
Rodrigues, Eusebio L. "A Nymph at Her Orisons: An Analysis of William Gass's 'Order of Insects,'" *Stud Short Fiction*, 17 (1980), 348-351.

WIRT GERRARE

"The Girl from Iloilo: A Picturesque Story of the Orient"
Chu, Limin. *The Image of China*..., 193-194.

ANDRÉ GIDE

"El Hadj"
Cryle, Peter. "Sur 'Le Renégat' et 'El Hadj, ou Le Traité du Faux Prophète' de André Gide," *Revue des Lettres Modernes*, Nos. 360-365 (1973), 113-118; rpt. Suther, Judith D., Ed. *Essays*..., 301-306.

"The Immoralist"
Kusch, Manfred. "The Gardens of 'L'Immoraliste,'" *French Forum*, 4 (1979), 206-218.
Levy, Zvi H. "'L'Immoraliste' et le mythe d'Oedipe," *Les Lettres Romanes*, 35, i-ii (1981), 3-34.
Mistacco, Vicki. "Reading 'The Immoralist': The Relevance of Narrative Roles," *Bucknell R*, 26 (1981), 64-74.
Pratt, Mary L. "Un mapa ideologico: Gide, Camus y Algeria," *Escritura*, 4, vii (1979), 77-92.

"The Pastoral Symphony"
Bognot, Lorène. "La Journée du 21 mai dans 'La Symphonie pastorale': Microcosme du roman," *Chimères*, [n.v.] (Fall, 1976-Spring, 1977), 16-19.

Cardinal, John P. "Musical Blindness: A Study of Gide's 'La Symphonie Pastorale,'" *Mod Langs*, 60, i (1979), 19-23.
Dutescu-Sturdza, Rodica. "Les Actes de langage en poétique: L'Argumentation hésitante chez A. Gide," *Revue Roumaine de Linguistique*, 26, i (1981), 69-74.
Festa McCormick, Diana. "La Nostalgie de la jeunesse dans la 'Symphonie' gidienne," *Rivista di Letterature*, 30 (1977), 145-154.

"Strait Is the Gate"
Levy, Lui. "Gide's 'Porte étroite,'" *Explicator*, 37, iv (1979), 22-24.

CHARLOTTE PERKINS GILMAN

"The Yellow Wall-Paper"
Altenbernd, Lynn, and Leslie L. Lewis. *Instructor's Manual...*, 3rd ed., 26-27.
Baker, Sheridan, and George Perkins. *Instructor's Manual...*, 10-11.

GEORGE GISSING

"Fleet-Footed Hester"
Tintner, Adeline R. "Gissing's 'Fleet-Footed Hester': The Atalanta of Hackney Downs," *Études anglaises*, 34 (1981), 443-447.

ELLEN GLASGOW

"The Artless Age"
Raper, Julius R. "Invisible Things: The Short Stories of Ellen Glasgow," *Southern Lit J*, 9 (Spring, 1977), 76; rpt. in his *From the Sunken Garden...*, 63-64.

"Dare's Gift"
Raper, Julius R. "Invisible Things...," 81-83; rpt. in his *From the Sunken Garden...*, 69-70.

"The Difference"
Raper, Julius R. "Invisible Things...," 74-76; rpt. in his *From the Sunken Garden...*, 61-63.

"Jordan's End"
Raper, Julius R. "Invisible Things...," 87-89; rpt. in his *From the Sunken Garden...*, 74-78.

"The Past"
Raper, Julius R. "Invisible Things...," 83-84; rpt. in his *From the Sunken Garden...*, 70-71.

"The Professional Instinct"
Raper, Julius R. "Invisible Things...," 67-70; rpt. in his *From the Sunken Garden...*, 54-60.

"Romance and Sally Byrd"
Raper, Julius R. "Invisible Things...," 76–79; rpt. in his *From the Sunken Garden*...,
65–66.

"The Shadowy Third"
Raper, Julius R. "Invisible Things...," 80–81; rpt. in his *From the Sunken Garden*...,
67–69.

"Thinking Makes It So"
Raper, Julius R. "Invisible Things...," 73–74; rpt. in his *From the Sunken Garden*...,
60–61.

"Whispering Leaves"
Raper, Julius R. "Invisible Things...," 84–87; rpt. in his *From the Sunken Garden*...,
71–75.

GAIL GODWIN

"Layover"
Mickelson, Anna Z. *Reaching Out*..., 81–82.

"Some Side Effects of Time Travel"
Mickelson, Anna Z. *Reaching Out*..., 72–73.

JOHANN WOLFGANG VON GOETHE

"Fairy Tale"
Bangerter, Lowell A. "The Serpent-Ring in Goethe's 'Das Märchen,'" *Germ Life & Letters*, 33 (1980), 111–115.

NIKOLAI GOGOL

"The Carriage"
Fanger, Donald. *The Creation*..., 122–124.

"Diary of a Madman"
Fanger, Donald. *The Creation*..., 115–118.
Peace, Richard. *The Enigma of Gogol*, 124–130.
Riggan, William. *Picaros, Madmen*..., 111–118.

"Ivan Fyodorovich Shponka and His Aunt"
Friedberg Seeley, Frank. "Notes on Gogol's Short Stories," *Annali: Sezione Slava* (Naples), 19 (1976), 12–15.
Gippius, V. V. *Gogol*, 69–70.

"Kolyaska"
Friedberg Seeley, Frank. "...Gogol's Short Stories," 15–17.

"The Nevsky Prospect"
Fanger, Donald. *The Creation*..., 111-113.
Friedberg Seeley, Frank. "...Gogol's Short Stories," 32-38.
Gippius, V. V. *Gogol*, 48-50.
Peace, Richard. *The Enigma of Gogol*, 95-112.

"The Nose"
Fanger, Donald. *The Creation*..., 118-122.
Friedberg Seeley, Frank. "...Gogol's Short Stories," 23-30.
Peace, Richard. *The Enigma of Gogol*..., 130-141.
Spycher, P. C. "N. V. Gogol's 'The Nose': A Satirical Comic Fantasy Born of an
    Impotence Complex," *Slavic & East European J*, 7 (1963), 361-374.

"Old-World Landowners"
Fanger, Donald. *The Creation*..., 96-97.
Friedberg Seeley, Frank. "...Gogol's Short Stories," 19-21.
Peace, Richard. *The Enigma of Gogol*, 31-47.

"The Overcoat"
Barksdale, E. C. *Daggers of the Mind*..., 94-95.
Chizhevsky, Dmitri. "On Gogol's 'The Overcoat,'" in Meyer, Priscilla, and Stephen
    Rudy, Eds. *Dostoevsky and Gogol*..., 137-160.
Fanger, Donald. *The Creation*..., 153-163.
Friedberg Seeley, Frank. "...Gogol's Short Stories," 39-44.
McFarlin, Harold A. "'The Overcoat' as a Civil Service Episode," *Canadian-Am
    Slavic Stud*, 13 (1979), 235-253.
Tejani, Bahadur. "The Origins of Modern Russian Literature: Critical Analysis
    of Gogol's 'Overcoat,'" *Lit Criterion*, 14, iv (1979), 65-69.

"The Portrait"
Barksdale, E. C. *Daggers of the Mind*..., 91-94.
Fanger, Donald. *The Creation*..., 113-115.
Friedberg Seeley, Frank. "...Gogol's Short Stories," 30-32.
Gippius, V. V. *Gogol*, 50-53.
Peace, Richard. *The Enigma of Gogol*, 112-124.
Ziolkowski, Theodore. *Disenchanted Images*..., 112-118.

"The Quarrel Between Ivan Ivanovich and Ivan Nikiforovich"
Alexander, Alex E. "The Two Ivans' Sexual Underpinnings," *Slavic & East European
    J*, 25, iii (1981), 24-37.
Fanger, Donald. *The Creation*..., 102-108.
Friedberg Seeley, Frank. "...Gogol's Short Stories," 17-19.
Gippius, V. V. *Gogol*, 70-71.
Peace, Richard. *The Enigma of Gogol*, 74-89.

"St. John's Eve"
Fanger, Donald. *The Creation*..., 86-87.

"The Sorochinsty Fair"
Fanger, Donald. *The Creation*..., 91-92.

"Taras Bulba"
Bahrij-Pikulyk, R. "Superheroes, Gentlemen or Pariahs? The Cossacks in Nikolai Gogol's 'Taras Bulba' and Panteleimon Kulish's *Black Council*," *J Ukrainian Stud*, 5, ii (1980), 30–47.
Gippius, V. V. *Gogol*, 111–112.
Peace, Richard. *The Enigma of Gogol*, 47–53.
Sirskyj, W. "Ideological Overtones in Gogol's 'Taras Bulba,'" *Ukrainian Q*, 35 (1979), 279–287.

"A Terrible Vengeance"
Fanger, Donald. *The Creation*..., 237–238.
Peace, Richard. *The Enigma of Gogol*, 16–24.

"Viy"
Fanger, Donald. *The Creation*..., 100–102.
Peace, Richard. *The Enigma of Gogol*, 53–73.

GERTRUDIS GÓMEZ DE AVELLANEDA

"The Baroness of Joux"
Harter, Hugh A. *Gertrudis Gómez de Avellaneda*, 161–162.

"The Beautiful Toda and the Twelve Wild Boars"
Harter, Hugh A. *Gertrudis Gómez de Avellaneda*, 163–164.

"The Cacique of Tumerqué"
Harter, Hugh A. *Gertrudis Gómez de Avellaneda*, 166–168.

"The Lady of Amboto"
Harter, Hugh A. *Gertrudis Gómez de Avellaneda*, 162–163.

"The Water Nymph of the Blue Lake"
Harter, Hugh A. *Gertrudis Gómez de Avellaneda*, 164–165.

"The White Vulture"
Harter, Hugh A. *Gertrudis Gómez de Avellaneda*, 165–166.

JOSÉ LUIS GONZÁLEZ

"La noche que volvimos a ser gentes"
Escalera Ortiz, Juan. "Estilo, técnica y temática en 'La noche que volvimos a ser gentes' de José Luis González," *Revista/Review Interamericana*, 10 (1980), 320–325.

NADINE GORDIMER

"Livingstone's Companions"
Allen, Walter. *The Short Story*..., 353–355.

"The Smell of Death and Flowers"
Allen, Walter. *The Short Story*..., 355–357.

CAROLINE GORDON

"The Last Day in the Field"
Scott, Virgil, and David Madden. *Instructor's Manual*..., 4th ed., 2–4; Madden, David. *Instructor's Manual*..., 5th ed., 3–4.

WILLIAM GOYEN

"The Armadillo Basket"
Phillips, Robert. *William Goyen*, 72–73.

"Bridge of Music, River of Sand"
Phillips, Robert. *William Goyen*, 108–109.

"Children of Old Somebody"
Phillips, Robert. *William Goyen*, 108–109.

"Ghost and Flesh, Water and Dirt"
Phillips, Robert. *William Goyen*, 51–52.

"The Letter in the Cedarchest"
Phillips, Robert. *William Goyen*, 49–50.

"Old Wildwood"
Phillips, Robert. *William Goyen*, 71–72.

"Pore Perrie"
Phillips, Robert. *William Goyen*, 50–51.

"A Shape of Light"
Phillips, Robert. *William Goyen*, 55–57.

"The Thief Coyote"
Phillips, Robert. *William Goyen*, 104–105.

"The White Rooster"
*Phillips, Robert. *William Goyen*, 47–49.

"Zamour" [originally titled "A Tale of Inheritance"]
Phillips, Robert. *William Goyen*, 74–76.

GORDON GRANT

"The Provocation of Ah Sing"
Chu, Limin. *The Image of China*..., 186–187.

SHIRLEY ANN GRAU

"The Beach Party"
Schlueter, Paul. *Shirley Ann Grau*, 124–125.

"The Bright Day"
Schlueter, Paul. *Shirley Ann Grau*, 114–115.

"Eight O'Clock One Morning"
Schlueter, Paul. *Shirley Ann Grau*, 135–136.

"Fever Flower"
Schlueter, Paul. *Shirley Ann Grau*, 115–117.

"The Girl with the Flaxen Hair"
Schlueter, Paul. *Shirley Ann Grau*, 113–114.

"The Homecoming"
Schlueter, Paul. *Shirley Ann Grau*, 123–124.

"Joshua"
Schlueter, Paul. *Shirley Ann Grau*, 121–122.

"The Land and the Water"
Schlueter, Paul. *Shirley Ann Grau*, 127–128.

"The Last Gas Station"
Schlueter, Paul. *Shirley Ann Grau*, 128–130.

"The Lonely April"
Schlueter, Paul. *Shirley Ann Grau*, 136–137.

"The Man Outside"
Schlueter, Paul. *Shirley Ann Grau*, 132–133.

"Miss Yellow Eyes"
Schlueter, Paul. *Shirley Ann Grau*, 111–112.

"One Summer"
Schlueter, Paul. *Shirley Ann Grau*, 119–121.

"The Other Way"
Schlueter, Paul. *Shirley Ann Grau*, 131–132.

"The Patriarch"
Schlueter, Paul. *Shirley Ann Grau*, 103–104.

"Sea Change"
Schlueter, Paul. *Shirley Ann Grau*, 133–134.

"The Thieves" [originally titled "The Man Below"]
Schlueter, Paul. *Shirley Ann Grau*, 130–131.

"Three"
Schlueter, Paul. *Shirley Ann Grau*, 125–126.

"The Way Back"
Schlueter, Paul. *Shirley Ann Grau*, 137–138.

"The Way of a Man"
Schlueter, Paul. *Shirley Ann Grau*, 117–119.

"White Girl, Fine Girl"
Schlueter, Paul. *Shirley Ann Grau*, 107–109.

"The Wind Shifting West"
Schlueter, Paul. *Shirley Ann Grau*, 122–123.

GRAHAM GREENE

"The Basement Room"
Barker, Gerard A. *Instructor's Manual* . . ., 64–65.

"Brother"
Scott, Virgil, and David Madden. *Instructor's Manual* . . ., 4th ed., 51–53; Madden,
David. *Instructor's Manual* . . ., 5th ed., 10–11.

"The Innocent"
Mizener, Arthur. *A Handbook* . . ., 4th ed., 47–48.

I. GREKOVA

"Beyond the Entryway"
Brown, Deming. . . .*Literature Since Stalin*, 164–165.

"Ladies' Hairdresser"
Brown, Deming. . . .*Literature Since Stalin*, 165–167.

FRANZ GRILLPARZER

"The Poor Player" [same as "The Poor Fiddler"]
Mahlendorf, Ursula. "Franz Grillparzer's 'The Poor Fiddler': The Terror of
Rejection," *Am Imago*, 36 (1979), 118–146.
Porter, James. "Reading Representation in Franz Grillparzer's 'Der arme
Spielmann,'" *Deutsche Vierteljahrsschrift*, 55 (1981), 293–322.
Reinhardt, George W. "Jacob's Self-Delusion in Grillparzer's 'Der arme Spiel-
mann,'" *Univ Dayton R*, 15, i (1981), 27–32.
Roe, Ian F. "'Der arme Spielmann' and the Role of Compromise in Grillparzer's
Work," *Germ R*, 56 (1981), 134–139.
Thompson, Bruce. *Franz Grillparzer*, 121–130.
Turner, D. "Some Observations on the Theme of the Bachelor in the German
Novelle from Grillparzer to Storm," in Thunecke, Jörg, Ed. *Formen Realistischer
Erzählkunst* . . ., 55.

Waldeck, Peter B. *The Split Self...*, 103–111.

ALEXANDER GRIN [ALEXANDER STEPANOVICH GRINEVSKY]

"The Lanfier Colony"
Luker, Nicholas J. L. "Alexander Grin: A Survey," *Russian Lit Tri-Q*, 8 (Winter, 1974), 349–350.

"Oranges"
Luker, Nicholas J. L. "Alexander Grin...," 347.

"Reno Island"
Luker, Nicholas J. L. "Alexander Grin...," 348–349.

RALPH GUSTAFSON

"The Human Fly"
Keitner, Wendy. *Ralph Gustafson*, 76–77.

"The Paper-Spike"
Keitner, Wendy. *Ralph Gustafson*, 74–75.

"The Pigeon"
Keitner, Wendy. *Ralph Gustafson*, 67–68.

"Shower of Gold"
Keitner, Wendy. *Ralph Gustafson*, 73–74.

"Snow"
Keitner, Wendy. *Ralph Gustafson*, 66–67.

"Summer Storm"
Keitner, Wendy. *Ralph Gustafson*, 65–66.

"Surrey Harvest"
Keitner, Wendy. *Ralph Gustafson*, 61–62.

"The Tangles of Neaera's Hair"
Keitner, Wendy. *Ralph Gustafson*, 77–79.

"The Vivid Air"
Keitner, Wendy. *Ralph Gustafson*, 70–71.

J. B. HALDANE

"The Last Judgment"
Parrinder, Patrick. "Science Fiction as Truncated Epic," in Slusser, George E., George R. Guffey, and Mark Rose, Eds. *Bridges...*, 100–101.

ALBERT HALPER

"A Farewell to the Rising Sun"
Hart, John E. *Albert Halper*, 38–40.

"On the Shore"
Hart, John E. *Albert Halper*, 33–34.

"Prelude"
Hart, John E. *Albert Halper*, 110–111.

LESLIE HALVARD

"Arch Anderson"
Allen, Walter. *The Short Story*..., 276–279.

"Belcher's Hod"
Allen, Walter. *The Short Story*..., 275–276.

"No Use Blaming Him"
Allen, Walter. *The Short Story*..., 279–280.

MARION E. HAMILTON

"Wong"
Chu, Limin. *The Image of China*..., 213–214.

PETER HANDKE

"Kindergeschichte"
Oelkers, Jürgen. "Müssen uns Dichter sagen was 'Erziehung ist?' Pädagogische
Anmerkungen zu Peter Handkes 'Kindergeschichte,'" *Neue Sammlung*,
21 (1981), 273–280.

"Die linkshändige Frau"
Klein, Michael. "Peter Handke: 'Die linkshändige Frau': Fiktion eines Märchens,"
in Holzner, Johann, Michael Klein, and Wolfgang Wiesmüller, Eds. *Studien
zur Literatur*..., 235–252.

"Wunschloses Unglück"
Love, Ursula. "'Als sei ich...ihr GESCHUNDENES HERZ': Identifizierung
und negative Kreativität in Peter Handkes Erzählung 'Wunschloses Unglück,'"
Seminar, 17 (1981), 130–146.

JAMES HANSON

"Behind the Devil Screen"
Chu, Limin. *The Image of China*..., 199–200.

"The Divorce of Ah Lum"
Chu, Limin. *The Image of China...*, 217-218.

"The Princess and the Pauper"
Chu, Limin. *The Image of China...*, 196-197.

"The Winning of Josephine Chang"
Chu, Limin. *The Image of China...*, 199-200.

WILL N. HARBEN [WILLIAM NATHANIEL HARBEN]

"Abrum, Ca'line and Asphalt" [originally titled "The Matrimonial Troubles of Abraham and Caroline"]
Murphy, James K. *Will N. Harben*, 61.

"The Heresy of Abner Calihan"
Murphy, James K. *Will N. Harben*, 75-76.

"A Humble Abolitionist"
Murphy, James K. *Will N. Harben*, 69-70.

"Jim Trundle's Crisis"
Murphy, James K. *Will N. Harben*, 74.

"A Prophet Without Honor"
Murphy, James K. *Will N. Harben*, 62-63.

"A Rural Visitor"
Murphy, James K. *Will N. Harben*, 73.

"The Sale of Uncle Rastus"
Murphy, James K. *Will N. Harben*, 72.

"The Tender Link"
Murphy, James K. *Will N. Harben*, 76.

"The Tragic Story of Sunset Rock, Tennessee"
Murphy, James K. *Will N. Harben*, 53-54.

"The Whipping of Uncle Henry"
Murphy, James K. *Will N. Harben*, 70-71.

THOMAS HARDY

"Barbara of the House of Grebe"
Scott, James F. "Thomas Hardy's Use of the Gothic: An Examination of Five Representative Works," *Nineteenth-Century Fiction*, 17 (1963), 375-376.
Sumner, Rosemary. "Hardy Ahead of His Time: 'Barbara of the House of Grebe,'" *Notes & Queries*, 225 (1980), 230-231.
_____. *Thomas Hardy...*, 22-29.

"The Committeeman of 'The Terror'"
Scott, James F. "Thomas Hardy's Use...," 372-373.

"The Doctor's Legend"
Scott, James F. "Thomas Hardy's Use...," 376-377.

"The Duchess of Hamptonshire"
Reilly, J. J. "Short Stories of Thomas Hardy," *Catholic World*, 128 (1929), 410-411.

"The Fiddler of the Reels"
Giordano, Frank R. "Characterization and Conflict in Hardy's 'The Fiddler of
   the Reels,'" *Texas Stud Lit & Lang*, 17 (1975), 617-633.
Sumner, Rosemary. *Thomas Hardy...*, 21-22.

"The Grave by the Handpost"
Haarder, Andreas. "Fatalism and Symbolism in Hardy: An Analysis of 'The Grave
   by the Handpost,'" *Orbis Litterarum*, 34 (1979), 227-237.

"A Mere Interlude"
Quinn, Maire A. "Thomas Hardy and the Short Story," in Pinion, F. B., Ed.
   Budmouth Essays..., 84-85.

"The Romantic Adventures of a Milkmaid"
Benazon, Michael. "'The Romantic Adventures of a Milkmaid': Hardy's Modern
   Romance," *Engl Stud Canada*, 5 (1979), 56-65.
Wing, George. "Tess and the Romantic Milkmaid," *R Engl Lit*, 3 (1962), 22-30.

"The Three Strangers"
Roberts, James L. "Legend and Symbol in Hardy's 'The Three Strangers,'"
   Nineteenth-Century Fiction, 17 (1962), 191-194.

"Tony Kytes, The Arch-Deceiver"
Quinn, Maire A. "Thomas Hardy...," 76-77.

"A Tragedy of Two Ambitions"
Reilly, J. J. "Short Stories...," 411-412.

"What the Shepherd Saw"
Quinn, Maire A. "Thomas Hardy...," 81-82.

"The Withered Arm"
Scott, James F. "Thomas Hardy's Use...," 371-372.

CHARLES R. HARKER

"The Revenge of a Heathen"
Chu, Limin. *The Image of China...*, 181-182.

BRET HARTE

"The Ancestors of Peter Atherly"
Scheick, William J. *The Half-Breed*..., 78.

"Convert of the Mission"
Robinson, Cecil. *Mexico*..., 305-306.

"The Devotion of Enríquez"
Robinson, Cecil. *Mexico*..., 143-144.

"The Legend of Monte del Diablo"
Robinson, Cecil. *Mexico*..., 285-286.

"The Passing of Enríquez"
*Robinson, Cecil. *Mexico*..., 157-158.

"A Pupil of Chestnut Ridge"
Robinson, Cecil. *Mexico*..., 171-172, 253-254.

"Tennessee's Partner"
*Brooks, Cleanth, and Robert P. Warren. *Understanding Fiction*, 3rd ed., 118-121.
Burton, Linda. "For Better or Worse—Tennessee and His Partner: A New Approach to Bret Harte," *Arizona Q*, 36 (1980), 211-216.
Conner, William F. "The Euchring of Tennessee: A Reëxamination of Bret Harte's 'Tennessee's Partner,'" *Stud Short Fiction*, 17 (1980), 113-120.

GERHART HAUPTMANN

"Carnival"
Washington, Ida H. "The Symbolism of Contrast in Gerhart Hauptmann's 'Fasching,'" *Germ Q*, 52 (1979), 248-251.

"Signalman Thiel"
Atkinson, Ross. "Patterns of Restraint in Hauptmann's 'Bahnwärter Thiel,'" *Proceedings Pacific Northwest Conference Foreign Langs*, 29, i (1978), 57-61.
Clouser, Robin A. "The Spiritual Malaise of a Modern Hercules, Hauptmann's 'Bahnwärter Thiel,'" *Germ R*, 55 (1980), 98-106.

HAZEL H. HAVERMALE

"The Canton Shawl"
Chu, Limin. *The Image of China*..., 204.

JOHN HAWKES

"Charivari"
Scholes, Robert. *Fabulation and Metafiction*, 174-177.

"The Owl"
Laing, Jeffrey. "The Doctored Voice: Sexual Imagery and Medical Jargon in John
   Hawkes's 'The Owl,'" *Notes Contemp Lit*, 10, v (1980), 6-7.
Scholes, Robert. "John Hawkes as Novelist: The Example of the Owl," *Hollins
   Critic*, 14 (June, 1977), 1-10.

NATHANIEL HAWTHORNE

"Alice Doane's Appeal"
Downing, David. "Beyond Convention: The Dynamics of Imagery and Response
   in Hawthorne's Early Sense of Evil," *Am Lit*, 51 (1980), 468-476.
Gollin, Rita K. . . . *Truth of Dreams*, 105-108.
Swann, Charles. "'Alice Doane's Appeal': Or, How to Tell a Story," *Lit & Hist*,
   5 (1977), 4-25.
Williamson, James L. "Vision and Revision in 'Alice Doane's Appeal,'" *Am
   Transcendental Q*, 40 (1978), 348-353.

"The Ambitious Guest"
Plambeck, Vernon L. "Hearth Imagery and the Element of Home in Hawthorne's
   'The Ambitious Guest,'" *Platte Valley R*, 9, i (1981), 68-71.

"The Ancestral Footsteps"
Gollin, Rita K. . . . *Truth of Dreams*, 208-209.

"The Birthmark"
Ahrends, Günter. . . . *Kurzgeschichte*, 75-78.
Burns, Shannon. "Alchemy and 'The Birth-Mark,'" *Am Transcendental Q*, No. 42
   (Spring, 1979), 147-158.
Fetterley, Judith. *The Resisting Reader* . . . , 22-33.
Gatta, John. "Aylmer's Alchemy in 'The Birthmark,'" *Philol Q*, 57 (1978), 399-413.
Gollin, Rita K. . . . *Truth of Dreams*, 112-114.
MacAndrew, Elizabeth. *The Gothic Tradition* . . . , 175-176.
Micklus, Robert. "Hawthorne's Jekyll and Hyde: The Aminadab in Aylmer," *Lit
   & Psych*, 29 (1979), 148-159.
Proudfit, Charles L. "Eroticization of Intellectual Functions as an Oedipal
   Defense: A Psychoanalytic View of Nathaniel Hawthorne's 'The Birthmark,'"
   Int'l R Psycho-Analysis, 7 (1980), 375-383.
Quinn, James, and Ross Baldessarini. "'The Birth-Mark': A Deathmark," *Hartford
   Stud Lit*, 13 (1981), 91-98.
Rees, John O. "Aminadab in 'The Birth-Mark': The Name Again," *Names*,
   28 (1981), 171-182.

"The Canterbury Pilgrims"
Gollin, Rita K. . . . *Truth of Dreams*, 81-82.

"The Devil in Manuscript"
Gollin, Rita K. . . . *Truth of Dreams*, 83-84.

"Earth's Holocaust"
Mellow, James R. *Nathaniel Hawthorne* . . . , 235-236.

"Ethan Brand"
Brown, Christopher. "'Ethan Brand': A Portrait of the Artist," *Stud Short Fiction*, 17 (1980), 171-174.
Mellow, James R. *Nathaniel Hawthorne...*, 283-285.
Pandeya, Prabhat K. "Hawthorne's 'Ethan Brand': Discovering the Unpardonable Sin," *J Engl*, 7 (1980), 134-143.

"Feathertop"
Attebery, Brian. *The Fantasy Tradition...*, 44-47.

"The Gray Champion"
Male, Roy R. *...Cloistral Fiction*, 47-49.
Pike, Burton. *The Image of the City...*, 23-25.

"The Hall of Fantasy"
Gollin, Rita K. *...Truth of Dreams*, 41-42.

"The Haunted Mind"
Gollin, Rita K. *...Truth of Dreams*, 98-101.
Hostetler, Norman. "Imagination and Point of View in 'The Haunted Mind,'" *Am Transcendental Q*, 39 (1978), 263-267.
Johnson, Claudia D. *The Productive Tension...*, 25-27.

"The Hollow of the Three Hills"
Downing, David. "Beyond Convention...," 463-468.
Gollin, Rita K. *...Truth of Dreams*, 103-105.
Rohrberger, Mary. *Instructor's Manual...*, 4.

"The Maypole of Merry Mount"
Altenbernd, Lynn, and Leslie L. Lewis. *Instructor's Manual...*, 3rd ed., 28-29.
Messenger, Christian K. *Sport...*, 20-21.

"The Minister's Black Veil"
Ahrends, Günter. *...Kurzgeschichte*, 73-75.
Barry, Elaine. "Beyond the Veil: A Reading of Hawthorne's 'The Minister's Black Veil,'" *Stud Short Fiction*, 17 (1980), 15-20.
Colacurcio, Michael J. "Parson Hooper's Power of Blackness: Sin and Self in 'The Minister's Black Veil,'" *Prospects*, 5 (1980), 331-411.
Smith, Elliott L. and Wanda V. *Instructor's Manual...*, 11-12.

"Monsieur du Miroir"
Irwin, John T. *American Hieroglyphics...*, 258-265.
Mellow, James R. *Nathaniel Hawthorne...*, 95-97.

"My Kinsman, Major Molineux"
Abrams, Robert E. "The Psychology of Cognition in 'My Kinsman, Major Molineux,'" *Philol Q*, 58 (1979), 336-347.
Allen, Walter. *The Short Story...*, 30-33.
Bier, Jesse. "Hawthorne's 'My Kinsman, Major Molineux,'" *Explicator*, 38, iv (1980), 40-41.
Gollin, Rita K. *...Truth of Dreams*, 115-123.
Johnson, Claudia D. *The Productive Tension...*, 27-30.

Lease, Benjamin. *Anglo-American Encounters...*, 74–75.
Mellow, James R. *Nathaniel Hawthorne...*, 61–63.
Scott, Virgil, and David Madden. *Instructor's Manual...*, 4th ed., 72–74.

"The New Adam and Eve"
Mellow, James R. *Nathaniel Hawthorne...*, 236–238.
Shurr, William H. "Eve's Bower: Hawthorne's Transition from Public Doctrines to Private Truths," in Thompson, G. R., and Virgil L. Lokke, Eds. *Ruined Eden...*, 156–160.

"An Old Woman's Tale"
Gollin, Rita K. *...Truth of Dreams*, 102–103.

"Peter Goldthwaite's Treasure"
Gollin, Rita K. *...Truth of Dreams*, 92–93.

"The Prophetic Pictures"
Ziolkowski, Theodore. *Disenchanted Images...*, 118–122.

"Rappaccini's Daughter"
Gollin, Rita K. *...Truth of Dreams*, 110–112.
Karlow, Martin. "'Rappaccini's Daughter' and the Art of Dreaming," *Univ Hartford Stud Lit*, 13 (1981), 122–138.
MacAndrew, Elizabeth. *The Gothic Tradition...*, 171–172.
Shurr, William H. "Eve's Bower...," 149–156.

"Roger Malvin's Burial"
Robinson, E. Arthur. "'Roger Malvin's Burial': Hawthorne and the American Environment," *Nathaniel Hawthorne J*, [n.v.] (1977), 147–166.
Rohrberger, Mary. *Instructor's Manual...*, 5.
Samson, John. "Hawthorne's Oak Tree," *Am Lit*, 52 (1980), 457–461.

"Sylph Etherege"
Gollin, Rita K. *...Truth of Dreams*, 110–112.

"The Village Uncle"
Gollin, Rita K. *... Truth of Dreams*, 85–86.

"Wakefield"
Madden, David. *Instructor's Manual...*, 5th ed., 67–69.

"The Wives of the Dead"
Selzer, John L. "Psychological Romance in Hawthorne's 'The Wives of the Dead,'" *Stud Short Fiction*, 16 (1979), 311–315.

"Young Goodman Brown"
Ahrends, Günter. *...Kurzgeschichte*, 69–72.
Allen, Walter. *The Short Story...*, 33–38.
Bell, Michael D. *...The Sacrifice of Relation*, 134–136.
*Brooks, Cleanth, and Robert P. Warren. *Understanding Fiction*, 3rd ed., 29–32.
Cifelli, Edward. "Typology: A New Ambiguity in 'Young Goodman Brown,'" *Coll Engl Assoc Critic*, 41, iii (1979), 16–17.

Gollin, Rita K. ... *Truth of Dreams*, 123–128.
Jayne, Edward. "Pray Tarry with Me, Young Goodman Brown," *Lit & Psych*, 29 (1979), 100–113.
Johnson, Claudia D. *The Productive Tension*..., 30–35.
Mellow, James R. *Nathaniel Hawthorne*..., 59–60.
Mosher, Harold F. "The Source of Ambiguity in Hawthorne's 'Young Goodman Brown': A Structuralist Approach," *ESQ: J Am Renaissance*, 26, i (1980), 16–25.
Williamson, James L. "'Young Goodman Brown': Hawthorne's 'Devil in Manuscript,'" *Stud Short Fiction*, 18 (1981), 155–162.
Winslow, Joan D. "The Stranger Within: Two Stories by Oates and Hawthorne," *Stud Short Fiction*, 17 (1980), 263–268.

MUHAMMAD HUSAYN HAYKAL

"The Atonement for the Sin of True Love"
Smith, Charles D. "Love, Passion and Class in the Fiction of Muhammad Husayn Haykal," *J Am Oriental Soc*, 99 (1979), 254–256.

"Love Is Blind"
Smith, Charles D. "Love, Passion and Class...," 256–257.

"The Power of Passionate Love"
Smith, Charles D. "Love, Passion and Class...," 254.

HAIM [HAYIM] HAZAR

"The Sermon"
Alexander, Edward. *The Resonance of Dust*..., 74–77.

ANNE HÉBERT

"The Death of Stella"
Amprimoz, Alexandre L. "Semiotique de la segmentation d'un texte narratif: 'La Mort de Stella' d'Anne Hébert," *Présence Francophone*, 19 (1979), 97–105.

"The Torrent"
Roy-Hewitson, Lucille. "Anne Hébert: 'Le Torrent' ou l'integration au cosmos," *French R*, 53 (1980), 826–833.
Rubinger, Catherine. "Actualité de deux contes-témoins: 'Le Torrent' d'Anne Hébert et 'Un Jardin au bout du monde' de Gabrielle Roy," *Présence Francophone*, 20 (1980), 121–126.

EDITH HECHT

"His First Client"
Chu, Limin. *The Image of China*..., 214.

SADEQ HEDAYAT

"Buried Alive"
Mostaghel, Deborah M. "'No Common Point'? A Reading of Two Works by Sadeq Hedayat," *Lit East & West*, 21 (1977), 295-296.

"The Man Who Killed His Passions"
Mostaghel, Deborah M. "'No Common Point'?...," 294-295.

"Three Drops of Blood"
Mostaghel, Deborah M. "'No Common Point'?...," 296-300.

HEINRICH HEINE

"Florentine Night"
Grözinger, Elvira. "Die 'doppelte Buchhaltung': Eine Bemerkung zu Heines 'Florentinischen Nächten,'" *Heine J*, 18 (1979), 65-83.

ROBERT A. HEINLEIN

"All Your Zombies—"
Franklin, H. Bruce. *Robert A. Heinlein...*, 120-124.

"Blowups Happen"
Franklin, H. Bruce. *Robert A. Heinlein...*, 36-37.

"By His Bootstraps"
Franklin, H. Bruce. *Robert A. Heinlein...*, 55-57.

"Coventry"
Franklin, H. Bruce. *Robert A. Heinlein...*, 34-36.

"The Devil Makes the Law"
Franklin, H. Bruce. *Robert A. Heinlein...*, 23-24.

"The Elephant Circuit"
Franklin, H. Bruce. *Robert A. Heinlein...*, 109-110.

"Gulf"
Franklin, H. Bruce. *Robert A. Heinlein...*, 94-96.

"Jerry Is a Man"
Franklin, H. Bruce. *Robert A. Heinlein...*, 93-94.

"Let There Be Light"
Franklin, H. Bruce. *Robert A. Heinlein...*, 22-23.

"Life-Line"
Franklin, H. Bruce. *Robert A. Heinlein...*, 18-19.

"Logic of Empire"
Franklin, H. Bruce. *Robert A. Heinlein...*, 24-27.

"Lost Legion"
Franklin, H. Bruce. *Robert A. Heinlein...*, 47-49.

"The Man Who Sold the Moon"
Franklin, H. Bruce. *Robert A. Heinlein...*, 72-73.

"The Menace from Earth"
Franklin, H. Bruce. *Robert A. Heinlein...*, 70-71.

"Misfit"
Franklin, H. Bruce. *Robert A. Heinlein...*, 19-20.

"Project Nightmare"
Franklin, H. Bruce. *Robert A. Heinlein...*, 102-103.

"Requiem"
Franklin, H. Bruce. *Robert A. Heinlein...*, 20-21.

"Sky Lift"
Franklin, H. Bruce. *Robert A. Heinlein...*, 69-70.

"Solution Unsatisfactory"
Franklin, H. Bruce. *Robert A. Heinlein...*, 60-62.

"They"
Franklin, H. Bruce. *Robert A. Heinlein...*, 45-46.

"Universe"
Franklin, H. Bruce. *Robert A. Heinlein...*, 43-44.
Rose, Mark. *Alien Encounter...*, 42-43.

"The Unpleasant Profession of Jonathan Hoag"
Franklin, H. Bruce. *Robert A. Heinlein...*, 46-47.

"Waldo"
Franklin, H. Bruce. *Robert A. Heinlein...*, 52-55.

"The Year of the Jackpot"
Franklin, H. Bruce. *Robert A. Heinlein...*, 101-102.

LILLIAN HELLMAN

"Julia"
Bernikow, Louise. *Among Women*, 147-149.

ERNEST HEMINGWAY

"After the Storm"
Williams, Wirt. *The Tragic Art...*, 97–98.

"An Alpine Idyll"
Williams, Wirt. *The Tragic Art...*, 95–96.

"Banal Story"
Kvam, Wayne. "Hemingway's 'Banal Story,'" *Fitzgerald/Hemingway Annual 1974*, [n.v.] (1975), 181–191.
Williams, Wirt. *The Tragic Art...*, 93–94.

"The Battler"
Breidlid, Anders. "Courage and Self-Affirmation in Ernest Hemingway's 'Lost Generation' Fiction," *Edda*, [n.v.] (1979), 283.
Dahiya, Bhim S. *The Hero in Hemingway...*, 41–43.
Kyle, Frank B. "Parallel and Complementary Themes in Hemingway's Big Two-Hearted River Stories and 'The Battler,'" *Stud Short Fiction*, 16 (1979), 296–298.

"Big Two-Hearted River"
Adair, William. "Landscapes of the Mind: 'Big Two-Hearted River,'" *Coll Lit*, 4 (1977), 144–151.
Ahrends, Günter. *...Kurzgeschichte*, 149–151.
Breidlid, Anders. "Courage and Self-Affirmation...," 284–285.
Cooley, John R. "Nick Adams and 'The Good Old Place,'" *Southern Hum R*, 14 (1980), 63–66.
Gibb, Robert. "He Made Him Up: 'Big Two-Hearted River' as Doppelgänger," *Hemingway Notes*, 5, i (1979), 20–24.
Hoffman, Steven K. "*Nada* and the Clean, Well-Lighted Place: The Unity of Hemingway's Short Fiction," *Essays Lit*, 6 (1979), 101–102.
*Howard, Daniel F., and William Plummer. *Instructor's Manual...*, 3rd ed., 49–50; rpt. Howard, Daniel F., and John Ribar. *Instructor's Manual...*, 4th ed., 45–46.
Kyle, Frank B. "Parallel and Complementary Themes...," 298–300.
Muller, Gilbert H. "*In Our Time*: Hemingway and the Discontent of Civilization," *Renascence*, 29 (1977), 190–191.
Williams, Wirt. *The Tragic Art...*, 37–38.

"A Canary for One"
Williams, Wirt. *The Tragic Art...*, 92–93.

"The Capital of the World"
Williams, Wirt. *The Tragic Art...*, 11–12.

"Cat in the Rain"
Wagner, Linda W. "'Proud and Friendly and Gently': Women in Hemingway's Early Fiction," *Coll Lit*, 7 (1980), 241.

"A Clean, Well-Lighted Place"
Allen, Walter. *The Short Story...*, 147–148.
Hoffman, Steven K. "*Nada* and the Clean...," 94–96, 97–98.
Kennedy, X. J. *Instructor's Manual...*, 2nd ed., 18–19.

Kobler, J. F. "Hemingway's Four Dramatic Short Stories," *Fitzgerald/Hemingway Annual 1975*, [n.v.] (1976), 252–257.

"Cross-Country Snow"
Breidlid, Anders. "Courage and Self-Affirmation...," 283–284.

"Crossing the Mississippi"
Dahiya, Bhim S. *The Hero in Hemingway...*, 46.

"A Day's Wait"
Hays, Peter L. "Self-Reflexive Laughter in 'A Day's Wait,'" *Hemingway Notes*, 6, i (1980), 25.

"The Denunciation"
Gertzman, Jay A. "Hemingway's Writer-Narrator in 'The Denunciation,'" *Research Stud*, 47 (1979), 244–252.
Johnstone, Kenneth G. "Hemingway's 'The Denunciation': The Aloof American," *Fitzgerald/Hemingway Annual 1979*, [n.v.] (1980), 371–382.

"The Doctor and the Doctor's Wife"
Breidlid, Anders. "Courage and Self-Affirmation...," 281–282.
Dahiya, Bhim S. *The Hero in Hemingway...*, 28–30.

"The End of Something"
Dahiya, Bhim S. *The Hero in Hemingway...*, 37–41.
Vaidyanathan, T. G. "The Nick Adams Stories and the Myth of Initiation," in Naik, M. K., *et al.*, Eds. *Indian Studies...*, 207–208.
Wagner, Linda W. "'Proud and Friendly and Gently'...," 239–240.

"The Faithful Bull"
Widmayer, Jayne A. "Hemingway's Hemingway Parodied: The Hypocritical Griffon and the Dumb Ox," *Stud Short Fiction*, 18 (1981), 433–438.

"Fathers and Sons"
Boutelle, Ann E. "Hemingway and 'Papa': Killing of the Father in the Nick Adams Fiction," *J Mod Lit*, 9 (1981), 141–146.
Williams, Wirt. *The Tragic Art...*, 104–105.

"Fifty Grand"
Allen, Walter. *The Short Story...*, 155–157.
Messenger, Christian K. *Sport...*, 256.
Williams, Wirt. *The Tragic Art...*, 96–97.

"The Gambler, the Nun, and the Radio"
Hoffman, Steven K. "*Nada* and the Clean...," 99–100, 105.
*Mizener, Arthur. *A Handbook...*, 4th ed., 78–82.
Williams, Wirt. *The Tragic Art...*, 100–101.

"The Good Lion"
Widmayer, Jayne A. "Hemingway's Hemingway Parodied...," 433–438.

"Hills Like White Elephants"
Fletcher, Mary D. "Hemingway's 'Hills Like White Elephants,'" *Explicator*, 38, iv (1980), 16–18.
Kobler, J. F. "Hemingway's 'Hills Like White Elephants,'" *Explicator*, 38, iv (1980), 6–7.
Organ, Dennis. "Hemingway's 'Hills Like White Elephants,'" *Explicator*, 37 (1979), 11.
Wagner, Linda W. "'Proud and Friendly and Gently'. . .," 241.
Weeks, Lewis E. "Hemingway's Hills: Symbolism in 'Hills Like White Elephants,'" *Stud Short Fiction*, ·17 (1980), 75–77.

"Homage to Switzerland"
Williams, Wirt. *The Tragic Art. . .*, 99–100.

"In Another Country"
Cass, Colin S. "The Look of Hemingway's 'In Another Country,'" *Stud Short Fiction*, 18 (1981), 309–313.
Jakobs, Rudolf. "Ein Interpretationsversuch von Hemingways Kurzgeschichte 'In Another Country' als Beitrag zur Diskussion affektiver Lernziele in Fremdsprachenunterricht," *Neusprachliche Mitteilungen*, 34 (1981), 223–229.
Rohrberger, Mary. *Instructor's Manual. . .*, 25–26.
Scott, Virgil, and David Madden. *Instructor's Manual. . .*, 4th ed., 19–21; Madden, David. *Instructor's Manual*, 5th ed., 23–25.

"Indian Camp"
Breidlid, Anders. "Courage and Self-Affirmation. . .," 281.
Dahiya, Bhim S. *The Hero in Hemingway. . .*, 25–28.
Vaidyanathan, T. G. "The Nick Adams Stories. . .," 208–210.

The Indians Move Away"
Dahiya, Bhim S. *The Hero in Hemingway. . .*, 34–35.

"The Killers"
Ahrends, Günter. . . .*Kurzgeschichte*, 151–152.
Barker, Gerard A. *Instructor's Manual. . .*, 40–41.
*Brooks, Cleanth, and Robert P. Warren. *Understanding Fiction*, 3rd ed., 194–202.
Dahiya, Bhim S. *The Hero in Hemingway. . .*, 35–37.
Hoffman, Steven K. "*Nada* and the Clean. . .," 96–97.
Kobler, J. F. ". . .Dramatic Short Stories," 250–252.
Marx, Paul. "Hemingway and the Ethnics," in Filler, Louis, Ed. *Seasoned Authors. . .*, 47–50.
Williams, Wirt. *The Tragic Art. . .*, 94–95.

"The Last Good Country"
Cooley, John R. "Nick Adams. . .," 57.
Dahiya, Bhim S. *The Hero in Hemingway. . .*, 45–46.
Johnson, David R. "'The Last Good Country': Again the End of Something," *Fitzgerald/Hemingway Annual 1979*, [n.v.] (1980), 363–370.
Wagner, Linda W. "'Proud and Friendly and Gently'. . .," 244–245.

"The Light of the World"
Elliott, Gary D. "Hemingway's 'The Light of the World,'" *Explicator*, 40, i (1981), 48–50.

"A Man of the World"
Williams, Wirt. *The Tragic Art*..., 195-197.

"My Old Man"
Baker, Sheridan, and George Perkins. *Instructor's Manual*..., 14-15.
Nakajima, Kenji. *"Lacrimae Rerum* in 'My Old Man,'" *Kyushu Am Lit*, 22 (May, 1981), 18-23.
Williams, Wirt. *The Tragic Art*..., 38-39.

"A Natural History of the Dead"
Williams, Wirt. *The Tragic Art*..., 102-103.

"Night Before Landing"
Dahiya, Bhim S. *The Hero in Hemingway*..., 47-48.

"Now I Lay Me"
Boutelle, Ann E. "Hemingway and 'Papa'...," 139-140.
Cooley, John R. "Nick Adams...," 61-62.
Hoffman, Steven K. *"Nada* and the Clean...," 98.

"The Old Man and the Sea"
Barbour, James, and Robert Sattelmeyer. "Baseball and Baseball Talk in 'The Old Man and the Sea,'" *Fitzgerald/Hemingway Annual 1975*, [n.v.] (1976), 281-287.
Bennett, Fordyce R. "Manolin's Father," *Fitzgerald/Hemingway Annual 1979*, [n.v.] (1980), 417-418.
Green, Gregory. "The Old Superman and the Sea: Nietzsche, the Lions, and the 'Will to Power,'" *Hemingway Notes*, 5, i (1979), 14-19.
Messenger, Christian K. *Sport*..., 293-296.
Price, S. Devlin. "Hemingway's 'The Old Man and the Sea,'" *Explicator*, 38, iii (1980), 5.
Radeljković, Zvonimir. "A Long Journey to Hope: Hemingway's 'The Old Man and the Sea,'" in Thorson, James L., Ed. *Yugoslav Perspectives*..., 103-106.
Strauch, Edward H. "'The Old Man and the Sea': A Numerological View," *Aligah J Engl Stud*, 6 (1981), 89-100.
Williams, Wirt. *The Tragic Art*..., 175-182.

"On the Quai at Smyrna"
Benson, Jackson R. "Patterns of Connection and Their Development in Hemingway's *In Our Time*," *Rendezvous*, 5, ii (1970), 45-46.
Williams, Wirt. *The Tragic Art*..., 35-36.

"The Sea Change"
Hough, Julie. "Hemingway's 'The Sea Change': An Embracing of Reality," *Odyssey*, 2, ii (1978), 16-18.

"The Short Happy Life of Francis Macomber"
Bender, Bert. "Margot Macomber's Gimlet," *Coll Lit*, 8, i (1981), 12-20.
Cahalan, James M. "Hemingway's Last Word about the Ending of 'Macomber,'" *Hemingway Notes*, 5, i (1980), 33-34.
Fleming, Robert E. "When Hemingway Nodded: A Note on Firearms in 'The Short Happy Life of Francis Macomber,'" *Notes Mod Am Lit*, 5, iii (1981), Item 17.

Harkey, Joseph H. "The Africans and Francis Macomber," *Stud Short Fiction*, 17 (1980), 345–348.

Hellenga, Robert R. "Macomber *Redivivus*," *Notes Mod Am Lit*, 3, ii (1979), Item 10.

Herndon, Jerry A. "'Macomber' and the 'Fifth Dimension,'" *Notes Mod Am Lit*, 5, iv (1981), Item 24.

Hoffman, Steven K. "*Nada* and the Clean...," 102–103.

Hurley, C. Harold. "Hemingway's 'The Short Happy Life of Francis Macomber,'" *Explicator*, 38, iii (1980), 9.

McKenna, John J. "Macomber: The 'Nice Jerk,'" *Am Notes & Queries*, 17 (1979), 73–74.

Seydow, John J. "Francis Macomber's Spurious Masculinity," *Hemingway R*, 1, i (1981), 33–41.

Williams, Wirt. *The Tragic Art...*, 126–129.

"The Snows of Kilimanjaro"
Hoffman, Steven K. "*Nada* and the Clean...," 103–104.
Williams, Wirt. *The Tragic Art...*, 134–135.

"Soldier's Home"
Boyd, John D. "Hemingway's 'Soldier's Home,'" *Explicator*, 40, i (1981), 51–53.
Broer, Lawrence. "'Soldier's Home,'" *Lost Generation J*, 3, ii (1975), 31–32.
Jones, Horace P. "Hemingway's 'Soldier's Home,'" *Explicator*, 37 (1979), 17.
Monteiro, George. "Hemingway's 'Soldier's Home,'" *Explicator*, 40, i (1981), 50–51.
Nakajima, Kenji. "Hemingway's View of Alienation in 'Soldier's Home,'" *Kyushu Am Lit*, 20 (1979), 21–28.
Rovit, Earl. "On Ernest Hemingway and 'Soldier's Home,'" in Skaggs, Calvin, Ed. *The American Short Story*, I, 252–255.

"Ten Indians"
Boutelle, Ann E. "Hemingway and 'Papa'...," 135–136.
Dahiya, Bhim S. *The Hero in Hemingway...*, 32–33.

"Three Shots"
Dahiya, Bhim S. *The Hero in Hemingway...*, 23–25.

"The Three-Day Blow"
Breidlid, Anders. "Courage and Self-Affirmation...," 282–283.

"The Undefeated"
Williams, Wirt. *The Tragic Art...*, 90–92.

"A Way You'll Never Be"
Altenbernd, Lynn, and Leslie L. Lewis. *Instructor's Manual...*, 3rd ed., 30–31.
Cooley, John R. "Nick Adams...," 62.
Hagemann, E. R. "The Feather Dancer in 'A Way You'll Never Be,'" *Hemingway R*, 6, ii (1981), 25–27.
Hoffman, Steven K. "*Nada* and the Clean...," 98–99.
Williams, Wirt. *The Tragic Art...*, 98–99.

"Wine of Wyoming"
Williams, Wirt. *The Tragic Art...*, 101–102.

HERMANN HESSE

"Journey to the East"
Mileck, Joseph. *Hermann Hesse...*, 217-229.

"Klingsor's Last Summer"
Mileck, Joseph. *Hermann Hesse...*, 153-157.

"Siddhartha"
Chander, Harish. "Hermann Hesse's 'Siddhartha' and the Doctrine of Anatman," *So Asian R*, 3 (1979), 60-66.
Fickert, Kurt J. *Hermann Hesse's Quest...*, 84-86.
García Barros, Renato. "'Siddhartha': El largo y difícil camino hacia sí mismo," *Nueva Revista del Pacifico*, 6 (1977), 44-57.
Mileck, Joseph. *Hermann Hesse...*, 165-168.
Narasimhaiah, Sanjay. "Hermann Hesse's Siddhartha: Between the Rebellion and the Regeneration," *Lit Criterion*, 16 (1981), 50-60.

Du BOSE HEYWARD

"The Half Pint Flask"
Slavick, William H. *DuBose Heyward*, 92-96.

HIGUCHI ICHIYŌ

"Child's Play"
Danly, Robert L. *In the Shade...*, 135-140.

"Clouds in Springtime"
Danly, Robert L. *In the Shade...*, 82-83.

"Encounters on a Dark Night"
Danly, Robert L. *In the Shade...*, 81-82.

"In Obscurity"
Danly, Robert L. *In the Shade...*, 75-78.

"Old-Fashioned Credit Accounts, Modern Cash on the Line"
Danly, Robert L. *In the Shade...*, 116-118.

"On the Last Day of the Year"
Danly, Robert L. *In the Shade...*, 111-112.

"Separate Ways"
Danly, Robert L. *In the Shade...*, 145-146.

"The Sound of the Koto"
Danly, Robert L. *In the Shade...*, 79-81.

"The Thirteenth Night"
Danly, Robert L. *In the Shade...*, 143–145.

"Troubled Waters"
Danly, Robert L. *In the Shade...*, 140–143.

E[RNST] T[HEODOR] A[MADEUS] HOFFMANN

"The Adventure of New Year's Night"
Schneider, Peter. "Das Funktionieren von Literatur: Eine Skizze zu zwei
Erzählungen E. T. A. Hoffmanns," *Mitteilungen der E. T. A. Hoffmann-
Gesellschaft-Bamberg*, 27 (1981), 22–28.

"Counselor Krespel"
Ziolkowski, Theodore. *Disenchanted Images...*, 110–112.

"Don Juan"
Swales, Martin. "Narrative Sleight-of-Hand: Some Notes on Two German
Romantic Tales," *New Germ Stud*, 6 (1978), 4–13.
Wellbery, David E. "E. T. A. Hoffmann and Romantic Hermeneutics: An
Interpretation of Hoffmann's 'Don Juan,'" *Stud Romanticism*, 19 (1980),
455–473.

"The Doubles"
MacAndrew, Elizabeth. *The Gothic Tradition...*, 210–211.

"Knight Gluck"
Elardo, Ronald J. "The Maw as Infernal Medium in 'Ritter Gluck' and *Die
Bergwerke zu Falun*," *New Germ Stud*, 9, i (1981), 29–49.
Karoli, Christa. "'Ritter Gluck': Hoffmanns erstes Fantasiestück," in Prang,
Helmut, Ed. *E. T. A. Hoffmann*, 335–358.

"Little Zaches Called Cinnabar"
Walter, Jürgen. "E. T. A. Hoffmanns Märchen 'Klein Zaches Genannt Zinnober':
Versuch einer sozialgeschichtlichen Interpretation," in Prang, Helmut, Ed.
E. T. A. Hoffmann, 398–423.

"The Lost Reflection"
Ziolkowski, Theodore. *Disenchanted Images...*, 168–172.

"Mademoiselle de Scudery"
Gorski, Gisela. "Das 'Fräulein von Scuderi' als Detectivgeschichte," *Mitteilungen
der E. T. A. Hoffmann-Gesellschaft-Bamberg*, 27 (1981), 1–5.
Himmel, Hellmuth. "Schuld und Sühne der Scuderi: Zu Hoffmanns Novelle,"
in Prang, Helmut, Ed. *E. T. A. Hoffmann*, 215–236.
Holbeche, Yvonne. "The Relationship of the Artist to Power: E. T. A. Hoffmann's
'Das Fräulein von Scuderi,'" *Seminar*, 16 (1980), 1–11.
Kanzog, Klaus. "E. T. A. Hoffmanns Erzählung 'Das Fräulein von Scudery' als
Kriminalgeschichte," in Prang, Helmut, Ed. *E. T. A. Hoffmann*, 307–321.

Schneider, Peter. "Verbrechen, Künstlertum und Wahnsinn: Untersuchungen zur Figur des Cardillac in E. T. A. Hoffmanns 'Das Fräulein von Scuderi,'" *Mitteilungen der E. T. A. Hoffmann-Gesellschaft-Bamberg*, 26 (1980), 34–50.

"The Magnetizer"
Tatar, Maria M. *Spellbound...*, 130–135.

"Master Floh"
Pavlyshyn, Marko. "Interpretations of Word as Act: The Debate on E. T. A. Hoffmann's 'Meister Floh,'" *Seminar*, 17 (1981), 196–204.

"The Mines of Falun"
Elardo, Ronald J. "The Maw...," 29–49.
Tatar, Maria M. *Spellbound...*, 142–143.

"Nutcracker and Mouse King"
Elardo, Ronald J. "E. T. A. Hoffmann's 'Nussknacker und Mausekönig': The Mouse-Queen in the Tragedy of the Hero," *Germ R*, 55 (1980), 3–8.

"Princess Brambilla"
Mühlher, Robert. "'Princess Brambilla': Ein Beitrag zum Verständnis der Dichtung," in Prang, Helmut, Ed. *E. T. A. Hoffmann*, 185–214.

"The Sandman"
Grossvogel, David I. *Mystery...*, 18–19.
Tatar, Maria. "E. T. A. Hoffmann's 'Der Sandmann': Reflections and Romantic Irony," *Mod Lang Notes*, 95 (1980), 585–608.

"The Uncanny Guest"
Tatar, Maria M. *Spellbound...*, 133–135.

HUGO VON HOFMANNSTHAL

"Reitergeschichte"
Hansen, Carl V. "The Death of First Sergeant Anton Lerch in Hofmannsthal's 'Reitergeschichte': A Military Analysis," *Mod Austrian Lit*, 13, ii (1980), 17–26.

"Summer Time"
Wellbery, David E. "Narrative Theory and Textual Interpretation: Hofmannsthal's 'Sommerreise' As Test," *Deutsche Vierteljahrsschrift*, 54 (1980), 306–333.

"The Tale of the 672nd Night"
Barker, Andrew W. "The Triumph of Life in Hofmannsthal's 'Das Märchen der 672. Nacht,'" *Mod Lang R*, 74 (1979), 341–348.
Cohn, Dorrit. "'Als Traum Erzählt': The Case for a Freudian Reading of Hofmannsthal's 'Märchen der 672. Nacht,'" *Deutsche Vierteljahrsschrift*, 54 (1980), 284–305.
Ferrucci, Carlo. "La sublimazione mortale," *Nuova Corrente*, 81 (1980), 69–90; 82–83 (1980), 23–54.
Rieckmann, Jens. "Von der menschlichen Unzulänglichkeit: Zu Hofmannsthals 'Das Märchen der 672. Nacht,'" *Germ Q*, 54 (1981), 298–310.

EDUARDO LADISLAO HOMBERG

"El ruiseñor y el artista"
Cortés, Darío A. "'El ruiseñor y el artista': Un cuento fantástico de Eduardo L. Homberg," in Gordon, Alan M., and Evelyn Rugg, Eds. *Actas del Sexto Congreso Internacional*..., 188–191.

SIDNEY HOWARD

"The God They Left Behind Them"
White, Sidney H. *Sidney Howard*, 45–46.

"The Homesick Lady"
White, Sidney H. *Sidney Howard*, 47–48.

"A Likeness of Elizabeth"
White, Sidney H. *Sidney Howard*, 41–42.

"Mrs. Vietch: A Segment of Biography"
White, Sidney H. *Sidney Howard*, 43–44.

"The Stars in Their Courses"
White, Sidney H. *Sidney Howard*, 40.

"Such Women as Ellen Steele"
White, Sidney H. *Sidney Howard*, 46–47.

"Transatlantic"
White, Sidney H. *Sidney Howard*, 42–43.

WILLIAM DEAN HOWELLS

"Editha"
Bellamy, Michael O. "Eros and Thanatos in William Dean Howells's 'Editha,'" *Am Lit Realism*, 12 (1979), 283–287.
Furia, Philip. "'Editha': The Feminine View," *Am Lit Realism*, 12 (1979), 278–282.
Humma, John. "Howells's 'Editha': An American Allegory," *Markham R*, 8 (1979), 77–80.

"His Apparition"
Feigenoff, Charles. "'His Apparition': The Howells No One Believes In," *Am Lit Realism*, 13 (1980), 85–89.

BOHUMIL HRABAL

"Palaverers"
Heim, Michael. "Hrabal's Aesthetic of the Powerful Experience," in Birnbaum, Henrik, and Thomas Eekman, Eds. *Fiction and Drama*..., 201–206.

JESSLYN H. HULL

"A Yellow Angel"
Chu, Limin. *The Image of China*. . ., 218.

ZORA NEALE HURSTON

"Drenched in Light"
Howard, Lillie P. *Zora Neale Hurston*, 59-62.
Perry, Margaret. *Silence to the Drums*. . ., 121-122.

"The Gilded Six-Bits"
Howard, Lillie P. *Zora Neale Hurston*, 69-72.

"John Redding Goes to Sea"
Howard, Lillie P. *Zora Neale Hurston*, 58-59.
Perry, Margaret. *Silence to the Drums*. . ., 123-124.

"Muttsy"
Howard, Lillie P. *Zora Neale Hurston*, 65-66.

"Spunk"
Howard, Lillie P. *Zora Neale Hurston*, 62-64.

INTIZĀR HUSAIN

"The Dolorous City"
Memon, Muhammad U. "Reclamation of Memory, Fall, and the Death of the
    Creative Self: Three Moments in the Fiction of Intizār Husain," *Int'l J Middle
    East Stud*, 13 (1981), 85-87.

"The Lost Ones"
Memon, Muhammad U. "'The Lost Ones': A Requiem for the Self," *Edebiyat:
    J Middle Eastern Lit*, 3 (1978), 141-143; rpt. *Int'l J Middle East Stud*, 13 (1981),
    81-84.

"The Stairway"
Memon, Muhammad U. "Reclamation of Memory. . .," 75-81.

"The Yellow Cur"
Memon, Muhammad U. "Reclamation of Memory. . .," 84-85.

HWANG CHUN-MING

"Days of Looking at the Sea"
Goldblatt, Howard. "The Rural Stories of Hwang Chun-ming," in Faurot,
    Jeannette L., Ed. *Chinese Fiction from Taiwan*. . ., 119-121.

"The Drowning of an Old Cat"
Goldblatt, Howard. "The Rural Stories...," 116–119.

"The Fish"
Goldblatt, Howard. "The Rural Stories...," 113–115.

"The Gong"
Goldblatt, Howard. "The Rural Stories...," 125–128.

"His Son's Big Doll"
Birch, Cyril. "Images of Suffering in Taiwan Fiction," in Faurot, Jeannette L.,
   Ed. *Chinese Fiction from Taiwan*..., 74–75.
Goldblatt, Howard. "The Rural Stories...," 123–125.

"Ringworms"
Goldblatt, Howard. "The Rural Stories...," 121–123.

"The Story of Ch'ing-fan Kung"
Goldblatt, Howard. "The Rural Stories...," 115–116.

YOUSSEF IDRIS

"The Bottom of the City"
El-Gabalawy, Saad. "The Human Bond: Notes on Youssef Idris's Short Stories,"
   Int'l Fiction R, 6, ii (1979), 141–142.

"Farahat's Republic"
El-Gabalawy, Saad. "The Human Bond...," 140–141.

"The Fourth Case"
El-Gabalawy, Saad. "The Human Bond...," 138–139.

"Sayyed's Father"
El-Gabalawy, Saad. "The Human Bond...," 139–140.

EUGÈNE IONESCO

"Rhinoceros"
Danner, G. Richard. "Bérenger's Dubious Defense of Humanity in 'Rhinocéros,'"
   French R, 53 (1979) 207–214.

WASHINGTON IRVING

"The Adalantado of the Seven Cities"
Bowden, Mary W. *Washington Irving*, 178–179.

"The Adventure of My Aunt"
Doubleday, Neal F. *Variety of Attempt*..., 42–43.

"The Adventure of My Uncle"
Bowden, Mary W. *Washington Irving*, 97-98.
Doubleday, Neal F. *Variety of Attempt.* . ., 41-42.

"The Adventure of the German Student"
Bowden, Mary W. *Washington Irving*, 98-99.
Devlin, James E. "Irving's 'Adventure of the German Student,'" *Stud Am Fiction*,
    7 (1979), 92-95; rpt. *Lit & Psych*, 29 (1979), 120-122.

"The Adventure of the Mason"
Bowden, Mary W. *Washington Irving*, 135-136.

"The Adventure of the Mysterious Picture"
Doubleday, Neal F. *Variety of Attempt.* . ., 43-44.

"The Devil and Tom Walker"
Bowden, Mary W. *Washington Irving*, 106-107.

"Dolph Heyliger"
Bowden, Mary W. *Washington Irving*, 90-95.
Getz, John R. "Irving's 'Dolph Heyliger': Ghost Story or Tall Talk?" *Stud Short
    Fiction*, 16 (1979), 67-68.

"The Legend of Prince Ahmed Al Kemel"
Bowden, Mary W. *Washington Irving*, 139-140.

"The Legend of Sleepy Hollow"
Ahrends, Günter. . . . *Kurzgeschichte*, 59-63.
Bowden, Mary W. *Washington Irving*, 72-74.
Gross, Barry. "Washington Irving: The Territory Behind," *Markham R*, 10 (Fall-
    Winter, 1980-1981), 7-9.
Pajak, Edward F. "Washington Irving's Ichabod Crane: American Narcissism,"
    Am Imago, 38 (1981), 127-135.

"The Legend of the Three Beautiful Princesses"
Bowden, Mary W. *Washington Irving*, 137-138.

"The Legend of the Two Discreet Statues"
Bowden, Mary W. *Washington Irving*, 142-143.

"Rip Van Winkle"
Ahrends, Günter. . . . *Kurzgeschichte*, 63-66.
Dawson, William P. "'Rip Van Winkle' as Bawdy Satire: The Rascal and the
    Revolution," *ESQ: J Am Renaissance*, 27 (1981), 198-206.
Fetterley, Judith. *The Resisting Reader.* . ., 1-11.
Gross, Barry. "Washington Irving. . .," 5-7.
Kann, David J. "'Rip Van Winkle': Wheels Within Wheels," *Am Imago*, 36 (1979),
    178-196.
Mengeling, Marvin E. "Irving's Knickerbocker 'Folktales,'" *Am Transcendental Q*,
    40 (1978), 357-362.

"The Spectre Bridegroom"
Bowden, Mary W. *Washington Irving*, 72-73.

"The Storm Ship"
Doubleday, Neal F. *Variety of Attempt*..., 114–117.

"The Story of the Young Italian"
Bell, Michael D. ... *The Sacrifice of Relation*, 69–71.
Bowden, Mary W. *Washington Irving*, 100–102.

"The Stout Gentleman"
Male, Roy R. ... *Cloistral Fiction*, 33–34.

"The Student of Salamanca"
Bell, Michael D. ... *The Sacrifice of Relation*, 67–69.
Bowden, Mary W. *Washington Irving*, 83–86.

"Wolfert Webber"
Bowden, Mary W. *Washington Irving*, 107–110.

FAZIL ISKANDER

"On a Summer Day"
Brown, Deming. ... *Literature Since Stalin*, 207–208.

SHIRLEY JACKSON

"The Daemon Lover"
Barker, Gerard A. *Instructor's Manual*..., 56–58.

"The Flower Garden"
Mizener, Arthur. *A Handbook*..., 4th ed., 93–95.

"The Lottery"
Allen, Barbara. "A Folkloristic Look at Shirley Jackson's 'The Lottery,'" *Tennessee Folklore Soc Bull*, 46 (1980), 119–124.
Altenbernd, Lynn, and Leslie L. Lewis. *Instructor's Manual*..., 3rd ed., 31–32.
Bagchee, Shyamal. "Design of Darkness in Shirley Jackson's 'The Lottery,'" *Notes Contemp Lit*, 9, iv (1979), 8–9.
Smith, Elliott L. and Wanda V. *Instructor's Manual*..., 18–19.
Williams, Richard H. "A Critique of the Sampling Plan Used in Shirley Jackson's 'The Lottery,'" *J Mod Lit*, 7 (1979), 543–544.

"Seven Types of Ambiguity"
Welch, Dennis M. "Manipulation in Shirley Jackson's 'Seven Types of Ambiguity,'" *Stud Short Fiction*, 18 (1981), 27–31.

W. W. JACOBS

"The Monkey's Paw"
Baker, Sheridan, and George Perkins. *Instructor's Manual*..., 6.
Smith, Elliott L., and Andrew W. Hart, Eds. *The Short Story*..., 78–80.

JENS PETER JACOBSEN

"Doctor Faust"
Jensen, Niels L. *Jens Peter Jacobsen*, 125–126.

"Mrs. Fönss"
Jensen, Niels L. *Jens Peter Jacobsen*, 126–129.

"Mogens"
Jensen, Niels L. *Jens Peter Jacobsen*, 108–113.

"The Plague in Bergamo"
Jensen, Niels L. *Jens Peter Jacobsen*, 117–122.

"A Shot in the Fog"
Jensen, Niels L. *Jens Peter Jacobsen*, 113–115.

"Strangers"
Jensen, Niels L. *Jens Peter Jacobsen*, 107–108.

"There Should Have Been Roses" [same as "From the Sketchbook"]
Jensen, Niels L. *Jens Peter Jacobsen*, 122–126.

"Two Worlds"
Jensen, Niels L. *Jens Peter Jacobsen*, 115–117.

DAN JACOBSON

"Beggar My Neighbour"
*Mizener, Arthur. *A Handbook*..., 4th ed., 101–104.

"The Zulu and the Zeide"
Allen, Walter. *The Short Story*..., 360–361.

HENRY JAMES

"The Aspern Papers"
Bell, Barbara C. "Beyond Irony in Henry James: 'The Aspern Papers,'" *Stud Novel*, 13 (1981), 282–293.
Jensen-Osinski, Barbara. "The Key to the Palpable Past: A Study of Miss Tina in 'The Aspern Papers,'" *Henry James R*, 3, i (1981), 4–10.
Kappeler, Suzanne. *Writing and Reading*..., 14–43.

"The Beast in the Jungle"
Betsky-Zweig, S. "From Pleached Garden to Jungle and Waste Land: Henry James's Beast," in Bakker, J., and D. R. M. Wilkinson, Eds. *From Cooper to Philip Roth*..., 45–55.
Dupettay, Annick. "La Bête et le dandy ou la rencontre au coin plaisant," *Confluents*, 6, ii (1980), 105–122.

Gargano, James W. "The 'Look' as a Major Event in James's Short Fiction," *Arizona Q,* 35 (1979), 318–320.

Harris, Janice H. "Bushes, Bears, and 'The Beast in the Jungle,'" *Stud Short Fiction,* 18 (1981), 147–154.

Salmon, Rachel. "Naming and Knowing in Henry James's 'The Beast in the Jungle': The Hermeneutics of a Sacred Text,"*Orbis Litterarum,* 36 (1981), 302–322.

Shapland, Elizabeth. "Duration and Frequency: Prominent Aspects of Time in Henry James' 'The Beast in the Jungle,'" *Papers Lang & Lit,* 17 (1981), 33–47.

Sicker, Philip. *Love and the Quest...,* 119–120.

"The Beldonald Holbein"
Kappeler, Suzanne. *Writing and Reading...,* 99–101.

"The Bench of Desolation"
Sicker, Philip. *Love and the Quest...,* 169–170.

Zablotny, Elaine. "Henry James and the Demonic Vampire and Madonna," *Psychocultural R,* 3 (1979), 222–224.

"Benvolio"
Fogel, Daniel M. *Henry James...,* 162–163.

"Daisy Miller"
Barnett, Louise K. "Jamesian Feminism: Women in 'Daisy Miller,'" *Stud Short Fiction,* 16 (1979), 281–287.

Kirk, Carey H. "'Daisy Miller': The Reader's Choice," *Stud Short Fiction,* 17 (1980), 275–283.

Meyers, Jeffrey. "Velázquez and 'Daisy Miller,'" *Stud Short Fiction,* 16 (1979), 171–178.

Pearson, Carol, and Katherine Pope. *The Female Hero...,* 109–110.

Tassel, Janet Q. "The Sick and the Well: Playing at Life in 'Daisy Miller,'" *Stud Hum,* 8, ii (1981), 18–20.

Wilson, Frankie, and Max Westbrook. "Daisy Miller and the Metaphysician," *Am Lit Realism,* 13 (1980), 270–279.

"A Day of Days"
Fogel, Daniel M. *Henry James...,* 143.

"De Grey"
Zablotny, Elaine. "Henry James and the Demonic...," 207–210.

"The Death of the Lion"
Kappeler, Suzanne. *Writing and Reading...,* 83–86.

"The Diary of a Man of Fifty"
Zablotny, Elaine. "Henry James and the Demonic...," 216–221.

"Eugene Pickering"
Fogel, Daniel M. *Henry James...,* 155–157.

Marks, Patricia. "Culture and Rhetoric in Henry James's 'Poor Richard' and 'Eugene Pickering,'" *So Atlantic Bull,* 44, i (1979), 64–71.

"The Figure in the Carpet"
Kappeler, Suzanne. *Writing and Reading...*, 75–79.
Lock, Peter W. "'The Figure in the Carpet': The Text as Riddle and Force,"
Nineteenth-Century Fiction, 36 (1981), 157–175.
Miller, J. Hillis. "'The Figure in the Carpet,'" *Poetics Today*, 1, iii (1980), 107–118.
Salmon, Rachel. "A Marriage of Opposites: Henry James's 'The Figure in the
Carpet' and the Problem of Ambiguity," *Engl Lit Hist*, 47 (1980), 788–803.
White, Allon. *The Uses of Obscurity...*, 51–52.

"Flickerbridge"
Kappeler, Suzanne. *Writing and Reading...*, 105–110.

"Fordham Castle"
Dyson, J. Peter. "Death and Separation in 'Fordham Castle,'" *Stud Short Fiction*,
16 (1979), 41–47.
Sicker, Philip. *Love and the Quest...*, 170–171.
Vanderbilt, Kermit. "'Complicated Music at Short Order' in 'Fordham Castle,'"
Henry James R, 2 (1980), 61–66.

"Four Meetings"
Gargano, James W. "The 'Look'...," 310–313.
Martin, W. R. "The Narrator's 'Retreat' in James's 'Four Meetings,'" *Stud Short
Fiction*, 17 (1980), 497–499.

"The Great Good Place"
Whelan, Robert E. "God, Henry James, and 'The Great Good Place,'" *Research
Stud*, 47 (1979), 212–220.

"In the Cage"
Salzberg, Joel. "Mr. Mudge as Redemptive Fate: Juxtaposition in James's 'In the
Cage,'" *Stud Novel*, 11 (1979), 63–76.
Schor, Naomi. "Fiction as Interpretation/Interpretation as Fiction," in Suleiman,
Susan R., and Inge Crossman, Eds. *The Reader in the Text...*, 170–173.

"John Delavoy"
Kappeler, Suzanne. *Writing and Reading...*, 160–161.
White, Allon. *The Uses of Obscurity...*, 50–51.

"The Jolly Corner"
Ahrends, Günter. *...Kurzgeschichte*, 122–125.
Bereyziat, Jean. "Ironie, indices et dérobade: 'The Jolly Corner' et la question
du sens," *Confluents*, 6, ii (1980), 7–56.
Bier, Jesse. "Henry James's 'The Jolly Corner': The Writer's Fable and the Deeper
Matter," *Arizona Q*, 35 (1979), 321–334.
Boisson, Claude, Philippe Thoiron, and Paul Veyriras. "Du son au sens dans 'The
Jolly Corner' de Henry James: Analyse d'un texte et esquisse d'une methode,"
Confluents, 6, ii (1980), 57–104.
Delfattore, Joan. "The 'Other' Spencer Brydon," *Arizona Q*, 35 (1979), 335–341.
Fogel, Daniel M. *Henry James...*, 151–152.
*Mizener, Arthur. *A Handbook...*, 4th ed., 61–65.

"A Landscape Painter"
Fogel, Daniel M. *Henry James*. . . , 142–143.
Levy, Leo B. "Consciousness in Three Early Tales of Henry James," *Stud Short Fiction*, 18 (1981), 407–409.
Zablotny, Elaine. "Henry James and the Demonic. . . ," 203–207.

"The Last of the Valerii"
Altenbernd, Lynn, and Leslie L. Lewis. *Instructor's Manual*. . . , 3rd ed., 32–33.
Berkson, Dorothy. "Tender-Minded Idealism and Erotic Repression in James's 'Madame de Mauves' and 'The Last of the Valerii'," *Henry James R*, 2, ii (1981), 78–86.
Fogel, Daniel M. *Henry James*. . . , 148–149.
Sicker, Philip. *Love and the Quest*. . . , 38–40.
Ziolkowski, Theodore. *Disenchanted Images*. . . , 61–65.

"The Lesson of the Master"
Kappeler, Suzanne. *Writing and Reading*. . . , 78–81.
Miller, Vivienne. "Henry James and the Alienation of the Artist: 'The Lesson of the Master'," *Engl Stud Africa*, 23 (1980), 9–20.
*Mizener, Arthur. *A Handbook*. . . , 4th ed., 67–69.
Seed, David. "James's 'The Lesson of the Master'," *Explicator*, 39, i (1980), 9–10.

"The Liar"
Berland, Alwyn. *Culture and Conduct*. . . , 41–43.
Gargano, James W. "The 'Look'. . . ," 313–315.

"A Light Man"
Fogel, Daniel M. *Henry James*. . . , 149–151.
Sweeney, Gerald M. "Henry James and the 'New England Conscience'—Once Again," *New England Q*, 54 (1981), 255–258.

"Longstaff's Marriage"
Sicker, Philip. *Love and the Quest*. . . , 41–42.

"Madame de Mauves"
Allen, Walter. *The Short Story*. . . , 44–47.
Berkson, Dorothy. "Tender-Minded Idealism. . . ," 78–86.
Fogel, Daniel M. *Henry James*. . . , 152–154.
Gargano, James W. "The 'Look'. . . ," 306–310.
Safranek, William P. "Longmore in 'Madame de Mauves': The Making of a Pragmatist," *Arizona Q*, 35 (1979), 293–302.

"The Madonna of the Future"
Sicker, Philip. *Love and the Quest*. . . , 30–32.

"Maud-Evelyn"
Sicker, Philip. *Love and the Quest*. . . , 100–101.

"Miss Gunton of Poughkeepsie"
Allen, Walter. *The Short Story*. . . , 43–44.

"A Most Extraordinary Case"
Sicker, Philip. *Love and the Quest*. . . , 36–37.

"My Friend Bingham"
Fogel, Daniel M. *Henry James*. . . , 144–146.
Levy, Leo B. "Consciousness. . .," 409–410.

"The Next Time"
Kappeler, Suzanne. *Writing and Reading*. . . , 86–89.

"Nona Vincent"
Kappeler, Suzanne. *Writing and Reading*. . . , 98–99.

"Osborne's Revenge"
Levy, Leo B. "Consciousness. . .," 410–412.

"The Papers"
Tintner, Adeline R. "'The Papers': Henry James Rewrites *As You Like It*," *Stud Short Fiction*, 17 (1980), 165–170.

"A Passionate Pilgrim"
Fogel, Daniel M. *Henry James*. . . , 151–152.

"Paste"
Barker, Gerard A. *Instructor's Manual*. . . , 28–30.
Scott, Virgil, and David Madden. *Instructor's Manual*. . . , 4th ed., 58–60; Madden, David. *Instructor's Manual*. . . , 5th ed., 15–17.

"Poor Richard"
Fogel, Daniel M. *Henry James*. . . , 146–148.
Marks, Patricia. "Culture and Rhetoric. . .," 61–64.
Zablotny, Elaine. "Henry James and the Demonic. . .," 211–216.

"Professor Fargo"
Tatar, Maria M. *Spellbound*. . . , 232–235.

"The Pupil"
Lay, Mary M. "The Real Beast: Surrogate Brothers in James's 'The Pupil' and *The Princess Casamassima*," *Am Lit Realism*, 13 (1980), 73–84.

"The Real Right Thing"
Kappeler, Suzanne. *Writing and Reading*. . . , 76–81.

"The Real Thing"
Ahrends, Günter. . . . *Kurzgeschichte*, 126–129.
Gargano, James W. "The 'Look'. . .," 315–318.
Ron, Moshe. "A Reading of 'The Real Thing,'" *Yale French Stud*, 58 (1979), 190–212.

"A Round of Visits"
Bradbury, Nicola. *Henry James*. . . , 212–216.
Sicker, Philip. *Love and the Quest*. . . , 172–174.

"The Story in It"
Kappeler, Suzanne. *Writing and Reading*. . . , 101–105.
Tremper, Ellen. "Henry James's 'The Story in It': A Successful Aesthetic Adventure," *Henry James R*, 3, i (1981), 11–16.

"The Story of a Masterpiece"
Sicker, Philip. *Love and the Quest*. . . , 27–30.
Zablotny, Elaine. "Henry James and the Demonic. . .," 221.

"The Story of a Year"
Fogel, Daniel M. *Henry James*. . . , 140–142.

"The Sweetheart of M. Briseux"
Tintner, Adeline. "Henry James's Mona Lisa," *Essays Lit*, 8, i (1981), 105–108.

"The Tone of Time"
*Mizener, Arthur. *A Handbook*. . . , 4th ed., 57–60.

"A Tragedy of Error"
Savarese, John E. "Henry James's First Story: A Study of Error," *Stud Short Fiction*,
    17 (1980), 431–435.

"The Tree of Knowledge"
White, Allon. *The Uses of Obscurity*. . . , 156–157.

"The Turn of the Screw"
Allen, John J. "The Governess and the Ghost in 'The Turn of the Screw,'" *Henry
    James R*, 1 (1979), 73–80.
Braches, Ernst. "De diepe gronden van 'The Turn of the Screw,'" *Revisor*, 8,
    v (1981), 26–39.
Brooke-Rose, Christina. "The Squirm of the True: A Structural Analysis of Henry
    James's 'The Turn of the Screw,'" *PTL: J Descriptive Poetics and Theory Lit*, 1
    (1976), 513–546.
Cook, David A., and Timothy J. Corrigan. "Narrative Structure in 'The Turn
    of the Screw': A New Approach to Meaning," *Stud Short Fiction*, 17 (1980),
    55–65.
Curtsinger, E. C. "'The Turn of the Screw' As Writer's Parable," *Stud Novel*,
    17 (1980), 344–358.
Goetz, William R. "The Frame of 'The Turn of the Screw': Framing the Reader
    In," *Stud Short Fiction*, 18 (1981), 71–74.
Gruner, Dennis. "The Demon Child in 'The Turn of the Screw,'" *Psychocultural
    R*, 2 (1978), 221–239.
Hill, Robert W. "A Counterclockwise Turn in James's 'The Turn of the Screw,'"
    Twentieth Century Lit, 27 (1981), 53–71.
Holloway, Marcella M. "Another Turn of James' 'The Turn of the Screw,'" *Coll
    Engl Assoc Critic*, 16, 2 (1979), 9–17.
Kauffman, Linda. "The Author of Our Woe: Virtue Recorded in 'The Turn of
    the Screw,'" *Nineteenth-Century Fiction*, 36 (1981), 176–192.
MacAndrew, Elizabeth. *The Gothic Tradition*. . . , 230–233.
Mazella, Anthony J. "An Answer to the Mystery of 'The Turn of the Screw,'" *Stud
    Short Fiction*, 17 (1980), 327–333.
Milne, Fred L. "Atmosphere as Triggering Device in 'The Turn of the Screw,'"
    Stud Short Fiction, 18 (1981), 293–299.
Punter, David. *The Literature of Terror*. . . , 292–300.
Schleifer, Ronald. "The Trap of the Imagination: The Gothic Tradition, Fiction,
    and 'The Turn of the Screw,'" *Criticism*, 22 (1980), 297–319.
Schrero, Elliot M. "Exposure in 'The Turn of the Screw,'" *Mod Philol*, 78 (1981),
    261–274.

Stone, Albert E. "Henry James and Childhood: 'The Turn of the Screw,'" in Hague, John A., Ed. *American Character*..., 279-292.
Taylor, Anne R. *Male Novelists*..., 168-176.
Wirth-Nesher, Hans. "The Strange Case of 'The Turn of the Screw' and 'Heart of Darkness,'" *Stud Short Fiction*, 16 (1979), 323-324.

"The Velvet Glove"
Curtsinger, E. C. "Henry James's Farewell in 'The Velvet Glove,'" *Stud Short Fiction*, 18 (1981), 163-169.

"Washington Square"
Dean, Martha B. "Washington Square: Not So Simple As It Seems," *West Virginia Univ Philol Papers*, 26 (August, 1980), 105-112.
Maini, Darshan S. "'Washington Square': A Centennial Essay," *Henry James R*, 1 (1979), 89-101.

M[ONTAGUE] R[HODES] JAMES

"The Ash-Tree"
Briggs, Julia. *Night Visitors*..., 130-132.

"Count Magnus"
Sullivan, Jack. *Elegant Nightmares*..., 69-70.

"The Mezzotint"
Sullivan, Jack. *Elegant Nightmares*..., 82-85.

SARAH ORNE JEWETT

"Andrew's Fortune"
Donovan, Josephine. *Sarah Orne Jewett*, 58-59.

"An Autumn Holiday"
Donovan, Josephine. *Sarah Orne Jewett*, 51-52.

"The Best China Saucer"
Donovan, Josephine. *Sarah Orne Jewett*, 23-24.

"Beyond the Toll-Gate"
Donovan, Josephine. *Sarah Orne Jewett*, 24-25.

"A Bit of Shore Life"
Donovan, Josephine. *Sarah Orne Jewett*, 26-28.

"The Captains"
Donovan, Josephine. *Sarah Orne Jewett*, 36-37.

"The Circus at Denby"
Donovan, Josephine. *Sarah Orne Jewett*, 37-38.

"The Courting of Sister Wisby"
Donovan, Josephine. "A Woman's Vision of Transcendence: A New Interpretation
  of the Works of Sarah Orne Jewett," *Massachusetts R*, 21 (1980), 377-378.
_____. *Sarah Orne Jewett*, 79-80.

"Cunner-Fishing"
Donovan, Josephine. *Sarah Orne Jewett*, 38-39.

"The Dulham Ladies"
Donovan, Josephine. *Sarah Orne Jewett*, 56-58.

"A Dunnet Shepherdess"
Donovan, Josephine. *Sarah Orne Jewett*, 112-113.

"The Failure of David Berry"
Donovan, Josephine. *Sarah Orne Jewett*, 90-91.

"The Flight of Betsey Lane"
Donovan, Josephine. *Sarah Orne Jewett*, 93-94.

"The Foreigner"
Donovan, Josephine. *Sarah Orne Jewett*, 114-116.
Kraus, Mary C. "Sarah Orne Jewett and Temporal Continuity," *Colby Lib Q*, 15
  (1979), 161-163.

"The Girl with the Cannon Dresses"
Donovan, Josephine. *Sarah Orne Jewett*, 21-22.

"A Guest at Home"
Donovan, Josephine. *Sarah Orne Jewett*, 25-26.

"The Guests of Mrs. Timms"
Donovan, Josephine. *Sarah Orne Jewett*, 84-85.

"In Dark New England Days"
Donovan, Josephine. *Sarah Orne Jewett*, 85-86.

"In Shadow"
Donovan, Josephine. *Sarah Orne Jewett*, 39-40.

"Jenny Garrow's Lovers"
Donovan, Josephine. *Sarah Orne Jewett*, 19-20.

"The King of Folly Island"
Donovan, Josephine. *Sarah Orne Jewett*, 76-77.

"The Landscape Chamber"
Donovan, Josephine. *Sarah Orne Jewett*, 77-78.

"A Late Supper"
Donovan, Josephine. *Sarah Orne Jewett*, 44-45.

"Law Lane"
Donovan, Josephine. *Sarah Orne Jewett*, 80-81.

"A Lost Lover"
Donovan, Josephine. *Sarah Orne Jewett*, 42-44.

"Martha's Lady"
Donovan, Josephine. *Sarah Orne Jewett*, 118-119.
Hobbs, Glenda. "Pure and Passionate: Female Friendship in Sarah Orne Jewett's 'Martha's Lady,'" *Stud Short Fiction*, 17 (1980), 21-29.

"Miss Chauncey"
Donovan, Josephine. *Sarah Orne Jewett*, 40.

"Miss Peck's Promotion"
Donovan, Josephine. *Sarah Orne Jewett*, 87-88.

"Miss Sydney's Flowers"
Donovan, Josephine. *Sarah Orne Jewett*, 41-42.

"Miss Tempy's Watchers"
Donovan, Josephine. *Sarah Orne Jewett*, 82-84.

"Mr. Bruce"
Donovan, Josephine. *Sarah Orne Jewett*, 20-21.

"The Mistress of Sydenham Plantation"
Donovan, Josephine. *Sarah Orne Jewett*, 94-95.

"My Lady Brandon and the Widow Jim"
Donovan, Josephine. *Sarah Orne Jewett*, 35-36.

"Nancy's Doll"
Donovan, Josephine. *Sarah Orne Jewett*, 29-30.

"The Only Rose"
Donovan, Josephine. *Sarah Orne Jewett*, 92-93.
Mayer, Charles W. "'The Only Rose': A Central Jewett Story," *Colby Lib Q*, 17 (1981), 26-33.

"The Shipwrecked Buttons"
Donovan, Josephine. *Sarah Orne Jewett*, 22-23.

"The Shore House"
Donovan, Josephine. *Sarah Orne Jewett*, 34-35.

"Tom's Husband"
Donovan, Josephine. *Sarah Orne Jewett*, 52-53.

"A Village Shop"
Donovan, Josephine. *Sarah Orne Jewett*, 88-89.

"The Waiting Place"
Donovan, Josephine. *Sarah Orne Jewett*, 104–105.

"A White Heron"
Donovan, Josephine. "A Woman's Vision...," 375–376.
⸻. *Sarah Orne Jewett*, 69–72.

RICHARD MALCOLM JOHNSTON

"An Adventure of Mr. Joel Boozle"
Hitchcock, Bert. *Richard Malcolm Johnston*, 77.

"The Combustion of Jim Rakestraw"
Hitchcock, Bert. *Richard Malcolm Johnston*, 74–75.

"The Early Majority of Mr. Thomas Watts"
Hitchcock, Bert. *Richard Malcolm Johnston*, 60–61.

"The Expensive Treat of Colonel Moses Grice"
Hitchcock, Bert. *Richard Malcolm Johnston*, 57–59.

"The Goosepond School"
Hitchcock, Bert. *Richard Malcolm Johnston*, 50–53.

"How Mr. Bill Williams Took the Responsibility"
Hitchcock, Bert. *Richard Malcolm Johnston*, 53–55.

"Investigations Concerning Mr. Jonas Lively"
Hitchcock, Bert. *Richard Malcolm Johnston*, 55–57.

"Mr. Fortner's Marital Claim"
Hitchcock, Bert. *Richard Malcolm Johnston*, 77–78.

"Mr. Neelus Peeler's Condition"
Hitchcock, Bert. *Richard Malcolm Johnston*, 63–64.

"Old Friends and New Friends"
Hitchcock, Bert. *Richard Malcolm Johnston*, 65–66.

"The Pursuit of Mr. Adiel Slack"
Hitchcock, Bert. *Richard Malcolm Johnston*, 62–63.

"The Various Languages of Billy Moon"
Hitchcock, Bert. *Richard Malcolm Johnston*, 59–60.

JAMES JONES

"A Bottle of Cream"
Giles, James R. *James Jones*, 110–112.

"Greater Love"
Giles, James R. *James Jones*, 115-117.

"The Ice-Cream Headache"
Giles, James R. *James Jones*, 101-105.

"Just Like the Girl"
Giles, James R. *James Jones*, 105-108.

"The Pistol"
Giles, James R. *James Jones*, 91-100.
Shepherd, Allen. "'A Deliberately Symbolic Little Novella': James Jones's 'The Pistol,'" *So Dakota R*, 10 (1972), 111-129.

"The Temper of Steel"
Giles, James R. *James Jones*, 119-121.

"The Tennis Game"
Giles, James R. *James Jones*, 108-110.

"Two Legs for the Two of Us"
Giles, James R. *James Jones*, 117-119.

"The Valentine"
Giles, James R. *James Jones*, 112-113.

"The Way It Is"
Giles, James R. *James Jones*, 113-115.

RAYMOND F. JONES

"Noise Level"
Shippey, T. A. "The Cold War in Science Fiction, 1940-1969," in Parrinder, Patrick, Ed. *Science Fiction...*, 99-101.

NEIL JORDAN

"A Love"
Norris, David. "Imaginative Response versus Authority Structures: A Theme of the Anglo-Irish Short Story," in Rafroidi, Patrick, and Terence Brown, Eds. *The Irish Short Story*, 74-76.

JAMES JOYCE

"After the Race"
Blayac, Alain. "'After the Race' ou les avatars d'un texte polysemique," *Cahiers Victoriens et Edouardiens*, 14 (October, 1981), 39-46.
Gordon, John. *...Metamorphoses*, 18-19.

"Araby"
Altenbernd, Lynn, and Leslie L. Lewis. *Instructor's Manual*..., 3rd ed., 34–35.
*Brooks, Cleanth, and Robert P. Warren. *Understanding Fiction*, 3rd ed., 125–128.
Chatman, Seymour. "Analgorithm," *James Joyce Q*, 18 (1981), 292–299.
Egan, Joseph J. "Romantic Ireland, Dead and Gone: Joyce's 'Araby' as National Myth," *Colby Lib Q*, 15 (1979), 188–193.
Gordon, John. . . .*Metamorphoses*, 16–18.
*Mizener, Arthur. *A Handbook*..., 4th ed., 146–147.
Sosnoski, James J. "On the Anvil of Theoretical Debate: *Story and Discourse* as Literary Theory," *James Joyce Q*, 18 (1981), 267–276.
———. "*Story and Discourse* and the Practice of Literary Criticism: 'Araby,' a Test Case," *James Joyce Q*, 18 (1981), 255–265.

"The Boarding House"
Gordon, John. . . .*Metamorphoses*, 20.
Smith, Elliott L. and Wanda V. *Instructor's Manual*..., 18.

"Clay"
Gordon, John. . . .*Metamorphoses*, 21–22.
Laroque, François. "Hallowe'en Customs in 'Clay': A Study of James Joyce's Use of Folklore in *Dubliners*," *Cahiers Victoriens et Edouardiens*, 14 (October, 1981), 47–56.
Rohrberger, Mary. *Instructor's Manual*..., 19–20.
*Scholes, Robert. *Elements of Fiction*, 68–73; 2nd ed., 66–77.
Solomon, Albert J. "The Mysteries of the Hymeneal Future: Tradition and Games in 'Clay,'" *James Joyce Q*, 17 (1980), 303–306.

"Counterparts"
Gordon, John. . . .*Metamorphoses*, 21.

"The Dead"
Allen, Walter. *The Short Story*..., 117–120.
Boyd, John D. "Gabriel Conroy's Secret Sharer," *Stud Short Fiction*, 17 (1980), 499–501.
Eggers, Tilly. "What Is a Woman...a Symbol Of?" *James Joyce Q*, 18 (1981), 379–385.
Gordon, John. . . .*Metamorphoses*, 25–27.
Higgins, Joanna. "A Reading of the Last Sentence of 'The Dead,'" *Engl Lang Notes*, 17 (1980), 203–207.
*Howard, Daniel F., and William Plummer. *Instructor's Manual*..., 3rd ed., 25–26; rpt. Howard, Daniel F., and John Ribar. *Instructor's Manual*..., 4th ed., 25.
Kiely, Robert. *Beyond Egotism*..., 87–91.
McDermott, Hubert. "Conroy and Coffin in Joyce's 'The Dead,'" *Notes & Queries*, 27 (1980), 533.
Torchiana, Donald T. "James Joyce's Method in *Dubliners*," in Rafroidi, Patrick, and Terence Brown, Eds. *The Irish Short Story*, 137–140.
———. "The Ending of 'The Dead': I Follow Saint Patrick," *James Joyce Q*, 18 (1981), 123–132.

"An Encounter"
Gordon, John. . . .*Metamorphoses*, 17.

"Eveline"
Gordon, John. . . . *Metamorphoses*, 18.
Skerl, Jennie. "A New Look at Vladimir Propp's Narrative Grammar: The Example of Joyce's 'Eveline,'" *Essays Lit*, 8 (1981), 151–171.

"Grace"
Allen, Walter. *The Short Story*. . . , 115–116.
Gordon, John. . . . *Metamorphoses*, 24–25.

"Ivy Day in the Committee Room"
Gordon, John. . . . *Metamorphoses*, 23.
Maguin, J. M. "Le Fonctionnement symbolique de 'Ivy Day in the Committee Room,'" *Cahiers Victoriens et Edouardiens*, 14 (October, 1981), 57–69.

"A Little Cloud"
Cope, Jackson I. *Joyce's Cities*. . . , 17–20.
Gordon, John. . . . *Metamorphoses*, 20.
Kiely, Robert. *Beyond Egotism*. . . , 134–136.
Scott, Virgil, and David Madden. *Instructor's Manual*. . . , 4th ed., 9–11; Madden, David. *Instructor's Manual*. . . , 5th ed., 21–23.

"A Mother"
Gordon, John. . . . *Metamorphoses*, 23–24.

"A Painful Case"
Bershtel, Sara. "A Note on the Forgotten Apple in James Joyce's 'A Painful Case,'" *Stud Short Fiction*, 16 (1979), 237–240.
Gordon, John. . . . *Metamorphoses*, 22–23.

"The Sisters"
Gordon, John. . . . *Metamorphoses*, 13–17.
Newell, Kenneth B. "The Sin of Knowledge in Joyce's 'The Sisters,'" *Ball State Univ Forum*, 20, iii (1979), 44–53.

"Two Gallants"
Gordon, John. . . . *Metamorphoses*, 19–20.
O'Toole, L. M. "Narrative Structure and Living Texture: Joyce's 'Two Gallants,'" *PTL: J Descriptive Poetics and Theory Lit*, 1 (1976), 441–458.

FRANZ KAFKA

"Before the Law"
Detsch, Richard. "Delusion in Kafka's Parables 'Vor dem Gesetz,' 'Das Schweigen der Sirenen'; and 'Von den Gleichnissen': A Hermeneutic Approach," *Mod Austrian Lit*, 14, i–ii (1981), 15–16.
Steinberg, Erwin R. "Kafka's 'Before the Law': A Religious Archetype with Multiple Referents," *Cithara*, 18, i (1978), 27–45.
Thiher, Allen. "Kafka's Legacy," *Mod Fiction Stud*, 26 (1981), 559–560.

"The Burrow"
Bänziger, Hans. "Das nameslose Tier und sein Territorium: Zu Kafkas Dichtung 'Der Bau,'" *Deutsche Vierteljahrsschrift*, 53 (1979), 300-325.
Coetzee, J. M. "Time, Tension and Aspect in Kafka's 'The Burrow,'" *Mod Lang Notes*, 96 (1981), 556-579.
Snyder, Verne P. "Kafka's 'Burrow': A Speculative Analysis," *Twentieth Century Lit*, 27 (1981), 113-126.
Stine, Peter. "Franz Kafka and the Animals," *Contemp Lit*, 22 (1981), 75-76.
Sussman, Henry. "The All-Embracing Metaphor: Reflections on Kafka's 'The Burrow,'" *Glyph*, 1 (1977), 100-131.

* "The Cares of a Family Man"
Stine, Peter. ". . . Animals," 68-70.

"Children on a Country Road"
Thieberger, Richard. "Noch einmal: 'Kinder auf der Landstrasse': Zur Thema: Ist Kafka Realist?" *Jahrbuch für Internationale Germanistik*, 11, ii (1979), 53-57.

"A Country Doctor"
Harroff, Stephen. "The Structure of 'Ein Landarzt': Rethinking Mythopoesis in Kafka," *Symposium*, 34 (1980), 42-55.
Kurz, Paul K. *On Modern German Literature*, 149-172.
Rohrberger, Mary. *Instructor's Manual. . .*, 35.
Stockholder, Katherine. "'A Country Doctor': The Narrator as Dreamer," *Am Imago*, 35 (1978), 331-346.
Waldeck, Peter B. *The Split Self. . .*, 151-152.

"The Description of a Struggle"
Waldeck, Peter B. *The Split Self. . .*, 143-145.

"Eleven Sons"
Böschenstein, Bernhard. "'Elf Söhne,'" in David, Claude, Ed. *Franz Kafka. . .*, 136-151.
Lewis, Hanna B. "Kafka's 'Elf Söhne': A Further Discussion," *Orbis Litterarum*, 35 (1980), 274-278.
Mitchell, Breon. "Franz Kafka's 'Elf Söhne': A New Look at the Puzzle," *Germ Q*, 47 (1974), 191-203.

"A Fratricide"
Mitchell, Breon. "Ghosts from the Dungeons of the World Within: Franz Kafka's 'Ein Brudermord,'" *Monatshefte*, 73 (1981), 51-61.

"The Giant Mole" [same as "The Village Schoolteacher"]
Stine, Peter. ". . . Animals," 65-66.

"The Great Wall of China"
Alexander, Edward. *The Resonance of Dust. . .*, 6-7.

"A Hunger Artist"
Garrison, Joseph M. "Getting into the Cage: A Note on Kafka's 'A Hunger Artist,'" *Int'l Fiction R*, 8, i (1981), 61-63.

Howard, Daniel F., and William Plummer. *Instructor's Manual...*, 3rd ed., 30;
rpt. Howard, Daniel F., and John Ribar. *Instructor's Manual*, 4th ed., 30.
Madden, David. *Instructor's Manual...*, 5th ed., 74-75.
Mahony, Patrick. "A Hunger Artist': Content and Form," *Am Imago*, 35 (1978),
357-374.
Pott, Hans-George. "Allegorie und Sprachverlust: Zu Kafkas 'Hungerkünstler'
Zyklus und der Idee einer Kleinen Literatur," *Euphorion*, 73 (1979), 435-450.

"The Hunter Gracchus"
Raboin, Claudine. "Die Gestalten an der Grenze: Zu den Erzählungen und
Fragmenten 1916-1918," in David, Claude, Ed. *Franz Kafka...*, 126-130.
Rohrberger, Mary. *Instructor's Manual...*, 34.

"In the Gallery"
Fickert, Kurt J. "The Function of the Subjective in Kafka's 'Auf der Galerie,'"
Germ Notes, 10 (1979), 33-36.
Ritter, Naomi. "Up in the Gallery: Kafka and Prévert," *Mod Lang Notes*, 96 (1981),
632-637.

"In the Penal Colony"
Fowler, Doreen F. "'In the Penal Colony': Kafka's Unorthodox Theology," *Coll
Lit*, 6 (1979), 113-120.
Hadomi, Leah. "The Utopian Dimension of Kafka's 'In the Penal Colony,'" *Orbis
Litterarum*, 35 (1980), 235-249.
Pascal, Roy. "Kafka's 'In der Strafkolonie': Narrative Structure and Interpretation,"
Oxford Germ Stud, 11 (1980), 123-145.
Steinberg, Erwin R. "Die zwei Kommandanten in Kafkas 'In der Strafkolonie,'"
in Caputo-Mayr, Maria L., Ed. *Franz Kafka...*, 144-153.
Thiher, Allen. "Kafka's Legacy," 558-559.

"Investigations of a Dog"
Stine, Peter. "...Animals," 72-75.

"Jackals and Arabs"
Stine, Peter. "...Animals," 70-71.

"Josephine the Singer"
Sattler, Emil E. "Erzählperspektive in Kafkas 'Josephine,'" in Caputo-Mayr, Maria
L., Ed. *Franz Kafka...*, 235-242.
Stine, Peter. "...Animals," 77-79.
Wiley, Marion E. "Kafka's Piping Mice as Spokesmen for Communication," *Mod
Fiction Stud*, 25 (1979), 253-258.

"The Judgment"
Brun, Jacques. "La Figure du père dans deux nouvelles de Kafka: 'Le Verdict'
et 'La Metamorphose,'" *Les Langues Modernes*, 75 (1981), 415-429.
Fickert, Kurt. "A Fairy-Tale Motif in Kafka's 'The Judgment,'" *Int'l Fiction R*, 6
(1979), 118-120.
Swales, Martin. "Why Read Kafka?" *Mod Lang R*, 76 (1981), 357-366.
Thiher, Allen. "Kafka's Legacy," 548-551.
Waldeck, Peter B. *The Split Self...*, 145-149.

"A Knock on the Manor Gate"
Galle, Roland. "Angstbildung im historischen Wandel von literarischer Erfahrung,"
    Neohelicon, 8 (1981), 43–61.

"Metamorphosis"
Brun, Jacques. "La Figure du père...," 415–429.
Jackson, Rosemary. *Fantasy*..., 160–161.
Jofen, Jean. "'Metamorphosis,'" *Am Imago*, 35 (1978), 347–356.
Nehamas, Alexander. "The Postulated Author: Critical Monism as a Regulative
    Ideal," *Critical Inquiry*, 8 (1981), 133–149.
Schepers, Gerhard. "Images of *Amae* in Kafka: With Special Reference to
    'Metamorphosis,'" *Humanities*, 15 (July, 1980), 66–83.
Skulsky, Harold. *Metamorphosis*..., 171–194.
Sokel, Walter H. "Von Marx zum Mythos: Das Problem der Selbstentfremdung
    in Kafkas 'Verwandlung,'" *Monatshefte*, 73 (1981), 6–22.
Stine, Peter. "...Animals," 63–65.
Thiher, Allen. 'Kafka's Legacy," 551–557.
Waldeck, Peter B. *The Split Self*..., 110–111.

"An Old Manuscript"
Alexander, Edward. *The Resonance of Dust*..., 5–6.

"A Report to an Academy"
Frye, Lawrence O. "Word Play: Irony's Way to Freedom in Kafka's 'Ein Bericht
    für eine Akademie,'" *Deutsche Vierteljahrsschrift*, 55 (1981), 457–475.
Stine, Peter. "...Animals," 71–72.

"The Silence of the Sirens"
Detsch, Richard. "Delusion in Kafka's Parables...," 16–17.
Moses, Stéphane. "Franz Kafka: 'Le Silence des Sirènes,'" *Hebrew Univ Stud Lit*,
    4 (1976), 48–70.

KAJII MOTOJIRO

"The Ascension of K"
Lippit, Noriko M. *Reality and Fiction*..., 115.

"The Lemon"
Lippit, Noriko M. *Reality and Fiction*..., 113–114.

"The Scroll of Darkness"
Lippit, Noriko M. *Reality and Fiction*..., 115.

"Under the Cherry Tree"
Lippit, Noriko M. *Reality and Fiction*..., 116.

PATRICK KAVANAGH

"The Lay of the Crooked Knight"
Nemo, John. *Patrick Kavanagh*, 83–84.

KAWABATA YASUNARI

"The Moon in the Water"
Petersen, Gwenn B. *The Moon...*, 129-136.

"Of Birds and Beasts"
Petersen, Gwenn B. *The Moon...*, 157-159.

"One Arm"
Petersen, Gwenn B. *The Moon...*, 178-180.

"Reencounter"
Petersen, Gwenn B. *The Moon...*, 180-181.

YURI KAZAKOV

"Adam and Eve"
Brown, Deming. *...Literature Since Stalin*, 160-161.

GOTTFRIED KELLER

"Der Landvogt von Greifensee"
Turner, D. "Some Observations on the Theme of the Bachelor in the German Novelle from Grillparzer to Storm," in Thunecke, Jörg, Ed. *Formen Realistischer Erzählkunst...*, 56-57.

"Das Verloren Lachen"
Paul, Jean-Marie. "'Das Verloren Lachen' de G. Keller," *Études Germaniques*, 36 (1981), 43-55.

"A Village Romeo and Juliet"
Swales, M[artin]. "Keller's Realism: Some Observations on 'Romeo und Julia auf dem Dorfe,'" in Thunecke, Jörg, Ed. *Formen Realistischer Erzählkunst...*, 159-167.

E. LINCOLN KELLOGG

"A Partly Celestial Tale"
Chu, Limin. *The Image of China...*, 198.

MAEVE KELLY

"The Last Campaign"
Harmon, Maurice. "First Impressions: 1968-1978," in Rafroidi, Patrick, and Terence Brown, Eds. *The Irish Short Story*, 67-68.

DANIEL KEYES

"Flowers for Algernon"
Smith, Elliott L., and Andrew W. Hart, Eds. *The Short Story*..., 218–221.

BENEDICT KIELY

"Blackbird in a Bramble Bough"
Casey, Daniel J. *Benedict Kiely*, 32–33.

"Down Then by Derry"
Casey, Daniel J. *Benedict Kiely*, 36–38.

"A Room in Linden"
Casey, Daniel J. *Benedict Kiely*, 39–40.

"The White Wild Bronco"
Casey, Daniel J. *Benedict Kiely*, 34–36.

GRACE KING

"The Balcony"
Kirby, David. *Grace King*, 40–41.

"Bonne Maman"
Jones, Anne G. *Tomorrow Is Another Day*..., 117–121.

"A Crippled Hope"
Kirby, David. *Grace King*, 43–44.

"Destiny"
Kirby, David. *Grace King*, 49–50.

"La Grande Demoiselle"
Kirby, David. *Grace King*, 41–42.

"The Little Convent Girl"
Jones, Anne G. *Tomorrow Is Another Day*..., 121–126.

"Making Progress"
Kirby, David. *Grace King*, 50–51.

"A Quarrel with God"
Kirby, David. *Grace King*, 47–49.

"The Story of a Day"
Kirby, David. *Grace King*, 42–43.

RUDYARD KIPLING

"At the End of the Passage"
McClure, John A. *Kipling and Conrad*..., 35-36.

"Baa, Baa, Black Sheep"
McClure, John A. *Kipling and Conrad*..., 12-14.

"Beyond the Pale"
McClure, John A. *Kipling and Conrad*..., 45-48.

"The Dream of Duncan Parrenness"
Briggs, Julia. *Night Visitors*..., 108-109.

"The Edge of the Evening"
Houlton, E. N. "'The Edge of the Evening,'" *Kipling J*, 46 (December, 1979), 5-10.

"Friendly Brook"
Allen, Walter. *The Short Story*..., 70-71.

"The Galley-Slave"
McClure, John A. *Kipling and Conrad*..., 26-28.

"The Gardener"
Madden, David. *Instructor's Manual*..., 5th ed., 78-81.
Smith, Elliott L., and Andrew W. Hart, Eds. *The Short Story*..., 88-91.

"The Head of the District"
Green, Martin. "Literary Boston: The Change of Taste at the End of the Century," in Nagel, James, and Richard Astro, Eds. *American Literature*..., 120-121.
McClure, John A. *Kipling and Conrad*..., 24-26.

"His Chance in Life"
McClure, John A. *Kipling and Conrad*..., 51-54.

"The Judgment of Dungara"
McClure, John A. *Kipling and Conrad*..., 25-26.

"Lispeth"
McClure, John A. *Kipling and Conrad*..., 75-76.

"The Madness of Private Ortheris"
McClure, John A. *Kipling and Conrad*..., 42-45.

"The Man Who Would Be King"
Baker, Sheridan, and George Perkins. *Instructor's Manual*..., 7-8.
*Brooks, Cleanth, and Robert P. Warren. *Understanding Fiction*, 3rd ed., 104-106.
Pollak, Oliver B. "'The Man Who Would Be King,'" *Kipling J*, 46 (September, 1979), 10-13.

"Mrs. Bathurst"
Williams, T. L. "The Tramps in 'Mrs. Bathurst,'" *Kipling J*, 46 (December, 1979),
13-14.

"On Greenhow Hill"
McClure, John A. *Kipling and Conrad*. . . , 19-20.

"The Phantom Rickshaw"
McClure, John A. *Kipling and Conrad*. . . , 36-37.

"The Prophet and the Country"
Lewis, Lisa A. F. "'The Prophet and the Country'–The Nastiest Story," *Kipling
J*, 47 (1980), 31-38.

"The Return of Imray"
McClure, John A. *Kipling and Conrad*. . . , 37-42.

"The Son of His Father"
McClure, John A. *Kipling and Conrad*. . . , 64-68.

"The Strange Ride of Morrowbie Jukes"
McClure, John A. *Kipling and Conrad*. . . , 33-34.

"Swept and Garnished"
Briggs, Julia. *Night Visitors*. . . , 168-169.

"To Be Filed for Reference"
McClure, John A. *Kipling and Conrad*. . . , 48-50.

"Wireless"
Allen, Walter. *The Short Story*. . . , 68-70.

"The Wish-House"
Allen, Walter. *The Short Story*. . . , 71-72.

HEINRICH VON KLEIST

"The Duel"
Belhalfaousi, Barbara. "'Der Zweikampf' von Heinrich von Kleist: oder die Dialek-
tik von Absolutheit und ihrer Trübung," *Études Germaniques*, 36 (1981), 22-42.
McGlathery, James M. "Kleist's 'Der Zweikampf' as Comedy," in Ugrinsky, Alexej,
Frederick J. Churchill, Frank S. Lambasa, and Robert F. von Berg, Eds.
Heinrich von Kleist Studies, 87-92.

"The Earthquake in Chile"
Corkhill, Alan. "Kleists 'Das Erdbeben in Chili' und Brechts 'Der Augsburger
Kreidekreis': Ein Vergleich der Motivik und des Erzähstils," *Wirkendes Wort*,
31 (1981), 152-157.

"The Foundling"
Hassoun, Jacques. "L'Enfant trouvé, ou 'Je vais vous dire toute la vérité,'" *Littérature*,
43 (1981), 17-23.

Linn, Rolf N. "Kleist's 'Der Findling': The Pitfalls of Terseness," in Ugrinsky, Alexej, Frederick J. Churchill, Frank S. Lambasa, and Robert F. von Berg, Eds. *Heinrich von Kleist Studies*, 93–100.

"Michael Kohlhaas"
Morse, David. *Perspectives on Romanticism...*, 230–232.

"St. Cecilia or the Power of Music"
Heine, Thomas. "Kleist's 'St. Cecilia' and the Power of Politics," *Seminar*, 16 (1980), 71–82.

VIKTOR KONETSKY

"A Tale About Radio Operator Kamushkin"
Brown, Deming. ...*Literature Since Stalin*, 210–211.

ANATOLII KRITONOSOV

"Burn, Burn Brightly"
Shneidman, N. N. *Soviet Literature...*, 29–30.

JAMES F. KRONENBERG

"The Avenging Joss"
Chu, Limin. *The Image of China...*, 179–181.

HENRY KUTTNER and C[ATHERINE] L. MOORE

"Vintage Season"
Rose, Mark. *Alien Encounter...*, 107–108.

CARMEN LAFORET

"The Cat's Secret"
Johnson, Roberta. *Carmen Laforet*, 117–118.

"The Christmas Gift"
Johnson, Roberta. *Carmen Laforet*, 109–110.

"The Condemned"
Johnson, Roberta. *Carmen Laforet*, 126–128.

"The Dead Woman"
Johnson, Roberta. *Carmen Laforet*, 107–109.

"An Engagement"
Johnson, Roberta. *Carmen Laforet*, 132–136.

"The Inferno"
Johnson, Roberta. *Carmen Laforet*, 112–113.

"The Last Night"
Johnson, Roberta. *Carmen Laforet*, 100–101.

"The Last Summer"
Johnson, Roberta. *Carmen Laforet*, 121–123.

"The Little Girl"
Johnson, Roberta. *Carmen Laforet*, 130–132.

"The Newlyweds"
Johnson, Roberta. *Carmen Laforet*, 113–115.

"Off to School"
Johnson, Roberta. *Carmen Laforet*, 106–107.

"The Photograph"
Johnson, Roberta. *Carmen Laforet*, 105–106.

"The Piano"
Illanes Adaro, Graciela. *La Novelística de Carmen Laforet*, 102–105.
Johnson, Roberta. *Carmen Laforet*, 128–130.

"The Pleasure Trip"
Johnson, Roberta. *Carmen Laforet*, 123–126.

"The Return"
Johnson, Roberta. *Carmen Laforet*, 103–104.

"Rosamunda"
Johnson, Roberta. *Carmen Laforet*, 101–102.

"The Unburdening"
Johnson, Roberta. *Carmen Laforet*, 115–117.

ALEX LA GUMA

"Blankets"
Green, Robert. "Chopin in the Ghetto: The Short Stories of Alex La Guma,"
World Lit Written Engl, 20 (1981), 11–12.

"The Gladiators"
Green, Robert. "Chopin in the Ghetto. . .," 9–10.

"The Lemon Orchard"
Green, Robert. "Chopin in the Ghetto. . .," 10–11.

"A Matter of Taste"
Green, Robert. "Chopin in the Ghetto. . .," 10.

"Nocturne"
Green, Robert. "Chopin in the Ghetto. . .," 5-7.

"Out of Darkness"
Green, Robert. "Chopin in the Ghetto. . .," 7-8.

"Slipper Satin"
Green, Robert. "Chopin in the Ghetto. . .," 9.

"A Walk in the Night"
Green, Robert. "Chopin in the Ghetto. . .," 12-16.

TOMMASO LANDOLFI

"Gogol's Wife"
Madden, David. *Instructor's Manual*. . ., 5th ed., 103-107.

"Hands"
Rohrberger, Mary. *Instructor's Manual*. . ., 38-39.

VALERY LARBAUD

"Amants, heureux amants. . ."
Brown, John L. *Valery Larbaud*, 107-111.

"Beauté, mon beau souci"
Brown, John L. *Valery Larbaud*, 103-107.

"Devoirs de vacances"
Brown, John L. *Valery Larbaud*, 90-91.

"Mon plus secret conseil"
Brown, John L. *Valery Larbaud*, 111-114.

"La Paix et le salut"
Brown, John L. *Valery Larbaud*, 93.

RING LARDNER

"Anniversary"
Evans, Elizabeth. *Ring Lardner*, 67-68.

"Champion"
Evans, Elizabeth. *Ring Lardner*, 63-64.
Higgs, Robert J. *Laurel & Thorn*. . ., 112-113.
Messenger, Christian K. *Sport*. . ., 120-121.

"Contract"
Evans, Elizabeth. "Ring Lardner's Bridge-Playing Spoil Sports," *Notes Contemp Lit*, 11, i (1981), 5.

"A Day with Conrad Green"
Evans, Elizabeth. *Ring Lardner*, 69-70.

"The Golden Honeymoon"
Goldberg, Gerald J. "On Ring Lardner and 'The Golden Honeymoon,'" in Skaggs, Calvin, Ed. *The American Short Story*, II, 222-226.

"Gullible's Travels"
Evans, Elizabeth. *Ring Lardner*, 64-65.

"Haircut"
*Brooks, Cleanth, and Robert P. Warren. *Understanding Fiction*, 3rd ed., 171-173.
Evans, Elizabeth. *Ring Lardner*, 61-63.
Smith, Elliott L., and Andrew W. Hart, Eds. *The Short Story*..., 193-197.

"Liberty Hall"
Evans, Elizabeth. *Ring Lardner*, 55-56.

"The Love Nest"
Evans, Elizabeth. *Ring Lardner*, 66-67.

"Mr. and Mrs. Fix-It"
Evans, Elizabeth. *Ring Lardner*, 53-55.

"My Roomy"
Evans, Elizabeth. *Ring Lardner*, 79-80.

"Old Folks' Christmas"
Evans, Elizabeth. *Ring Lardner*, 70-71.

"Poodle"
Evans, Elizabeth. *Ring Lardner*, 99-101.

"Reunion"
Evans, Elizabeth. *Ring Lardner*, 82-83.

"Rhythm"
Evans, Elizabeth. *Ring Lardner*, 111-118.

"Some Like Them Cold"
Allen, Walter. *The Short Story*..., 132-134.

"Three Without Doubled"
Evans, Elizabeth. *Ring Lardner*, 84-85; rpt., with changes, in her "Ring Lardner's Bridge-Playing Spoil Sports," *Notes Contemp Lit*, 11, i (1981), 5-6.

"Who Dealt?"
Evans, Elizabeth. *Ring Lardner*, 86-87; rpt., with changes, in her "...Spoil Sports," 6.

"Zone of Quiet"
Evans, Elizabeth. *Ring Lardner*, 56-57.

MARGARET LAURENCE

"The Drummer of All the World"
Morley, Patricia. *Margaret Laurence*, 68.
*Thomas, Clara. *The Manawaka World...*, 36–39.

"Godman's Master"
Callaghan, Barry. "The Writings of Margaret Laurence," in New, William, Ed. *Margaret Laurence*, 127–128.
Kreisel, Henry. "The African Stories of Margaret Laurence," in New, William, Ed. *Margaret Laurence*, 105–107.
Morley, Patricia. *Margaret Laurence*, 69–70.
Woodcock, George. "The Human Elements: Margaret Laurence's Fiction," in Helwig, David, Ed. *The Human Elements...*, 147.

"A Gourdful of Glory"
Osachoff, Margaret. "Colonialism in the Fiction of Margaret Laurence," *Southern R*, 13 (1980), 228.

"The Half-Husky"
Morley, Patricia. *Margaret Laurence*, 119.

"The Loons"
Morley, Patricia. *Margaret Laurence*, 117–119.

"The Merchant of Heaven"
Morley, Patricia. *Margaret Laurence*, 70.

"The Perfume Sea"
Morley, Patricia. *Margaret Laurence*, 70–71.
*Thomas, Clara. *The Manawaka World...*, 45–46.

"The Rain Child"
Morley, Patricia. *Margaret Laurence*, 68–69.

"The Sound of Singing"
Morley, Patricia. *Margaret Laurence*, 111–114.
Thomas, Clara. *The Manawaka World...*, 100–101.

"To Set Our House in Order"
Morley, Patricia. *Margaret Laurence*, 114–117.

"The Tomorrow-Tamer"
Callaghan, Barry. "The Writings...," 128.
Read, S. E. "The Maze of Life: The Work of Margaret Laurence," in New, William, Ed. *Margaret Laurence*, 48.
*Thomas, Clara. *The Manawaka World...*, 39.

"The Voice of Adamo"
*Thomas, Clara. *The Manawaka World...*, 41–42.
Woodcock, George. "The Human Elements...," 147.

MARY LAVIN

"A Likely Story"
Kelly, A. A. *Mary Lavin*..., 126-127.

"Lilacs"
Kelly, A. A. *Mary Lavin*..., 29-30.

"Limbo"
Kelly, A. A. *Mary Lavin*..., 86-87.

"The Little Prince"
Kelly, A. A. *Mary Lavin*..., 54-56.

"The Long Ago"
Kelly, A. A. *Mary Lavin*..., 50-51.

"The Long Holidays"
Kelly, A. A. *Mary Lavin*..., 142-143.

"The Lost Child"
Kelly, A. A. *Mary Lavin*..., 106-108.

"Love Is for Lovers"
Kelly, A. A. *Mary Lavin*..., 72-73.

"Loving Memory"
Kelly, A. A. *Mary Lavin*..., 56-58.

"A Memory"
Kelly, A. A. *Mary Lavin*..., 79-82.

"Miss Holland"
Kelly, A. A. *Mary Lavin*..., 24-26.

"My Molly"
Kelly, A. A. *Mary Lavin*..., 124-126.

"The Nun's Mother"
Kelly, A. A. *Mary Lavin*..., 92-95.

"One Evening"
Kelly, A. A. *Mary Lavin*..., 135-136.

"The Pastor of Six Mile Bush"
Kelly, A. A. *Mary Lavin*..., 99-101.

"Posy"
Kelly, A. A. *Mary Lavin*..., 38-39.

"A Pure Accident"
Kelly, A. A. *Mary Lavin*..., 101-103.

"Sarah"
Kelly, A. A. *Mary Lavin*..., 143-144.

"Say Could That Lady Be I?"
Kelly, A. A. *Mary Lavin* . . . , 151–153.

"The Shrine"
Kelly, A. A. *Mary Lavin* . . . , 103–105.

"A Single Lady"
Kelly, A. A. *Mary Lavin* . . . , 28–29.

"The Small Bequest"
Kelly, A. A. *Mary Lavin* . . . , 36–37.

"A Story with a Pattern"
Kelly, A. A. *Mary Lavin* . . . , 115–117.

"Sunday Brings Sunday"
Kelly, A. A. *Mary Lavin* . . . , 48–49.

"The Widow's Son"
Kelly, A. A. *Mary Lavin* . . . , 118–119.

"The Will"
Allen, Walter. *The Short Story* . . . , 307–309.
Kelly, A. A. *Mary Lavin* . . . , 30–31.

"A Woman Friend"
Kelly, A. A. *Mary Lavin* . . . , 77–79.

"The Young Girls"
Kelly, A. A. *Mary Lavin* . . . , 49–50.

WARNER LAW

"The Harry Hastings Method"
Scott, Virgil, and David Madden. *Instructor's Manual* . . . , 4th ed., 49–51; Madden,
David. *Instructor's Manual* . . . , 5th ed., 8–10.

D. H. LAWRENCE

"Adolf"
Hobsbaum, Philip. *A Reader's Guide* . . . , 39–40.

"The Blind Man"
Scott, Virgil, and David Madden. *Instructor's Manual* . . . , 4th ed., 6–9; Madden,
David. *Instructor's Manual* . . . , 5th ed., 17–19.

"The Border Line"
Becker, George J. *D. H. Lawrence*, 119–120.

"The Christening"
Hobsbaum, Philip. *A Reader's Guide* . . . , 30–31.

"Daughters of the Vicar"
Allen, Walter. *The Short Story*..., 104–105.
Becker, George J. *D. H. Lawrence*, 115–116.
Kiely, Robert. *Beyond Egotism*..., 65–66.

"England, My England"
Hobsbaum, Philip. *A Reader's Guide*..., 33–34.

"Fanny and Annie"
Cushman, Keith. "The Achievement of *England, My England and Other Stories*,"
    in Partlow, Robert B., and Harry T. Moore, Eds. ...*The Man Who Lived*,
    31–32.
Hobsbaum, Philip. *A Reader's Guide*..., 38–39.
Niven, Alistair. *D. H. Lawrence*..., 84–85.

"The Fox"
Allen, Walter. *The Short Story*..., 108–109.
Brown, Christopher. "The Eyes Have It: Vision in 'The Fox,'" *Wascana R*, 15,
    ii (1980), 61–68.
Jones, Lawrence. "Physiognomy and the Sensual Will in 'The Ladybird' and 'The
    Fox,'" *D. H. Lawrence R*, 13 (1980), 11–24.
Ruderman, Judith G. "Lawrence's 'The Fox' and Verga's 'The She-Wolf': Variations
    on the Theme of the 'Devouring Mother,'" *Mod Lang Notes*, 94 (1979), 153–165.

"Jimmy and the Desperate Woman"
Allen, Walter. *The Short Story*..., 106–108.
Hobsbaum, Philip. *A Reader's Guide*..., 122–123.

"The Ladybird"
Hobsbaum, Philip. *A Reader's Guide*..., 104–106.
Jones, Lawrence. "Physiognomy...," 7–11.

"The Man Who Died"
Lucente, Gregory L. *The Narrative of Realism*..., 118–123.

"The Man Who Loved Islands"
Clark, L. D. *The Minoan Distance*..., 356–359.

"The Man Who Was Through with the World"
Hobsbaum, Philip. *A Reader's Guide*..., 125–126.

"The Miner at Home"
Hobsbaum, Philip. *A Reader's Guide*..., 28.

"None of That"
Gunn, Drewey W. *American and British Writers*..., 143–144.

"Odour of Chrysanthemums"
Allen, Walter. *The Short Story*..., 102–104.
Becker, George J. *D. H. Lawrence*, 114–115.
Hobsbaum, Philip. *A Reader's Guide*..., 26–28.
Howard, Daniel F., and William Plummer. *Instructor's Manual*..., 3rd ed., 36;
    rpt. Howard, Daniel F., and John Ribar. *Instructor's Manual*..., 4th ed., 35.

*Mizener, Arthur. *A Handbook...*, 4th ed., 121–122.
Piccolo, Anthony. "Ritual Strategy: Concealed Form in the Short Stories of D. H. Lawrence," *Mid-Hudson Lang Stud*, 2 (1979), 89–92.

"The Princess"
Clark, L. D. *The Minoan Distance...*, 317–320.
MacDonald, Robert H. "Images of Negative Union: The Symbolic World of D. H. Lawrence's 'The Princess,'" *Stud Short Fiction*, 16 (1979), 289–293.

"The Prussian Officer",
Allen, Walter. *The Short Story...*, 99–100.
*Howard, Daniel F., and John Ribar. *Instructor's Manual...*, 4th ed., 34.
Rohrberger, Mary. *Instructor's Manual...*, 20–21.
Wilt, Judith. *Ghosts of the Gothic...*, 281–282.

"St. Mawr"
Becker, George J. *D. H. Lawrence*, 128–131.
Clark, L. D. "D. H. Lawrence as a Southwestern Author," *Phoenix* (Korea), 23 (1981), 17–24.
Dix, Carol. *D. H. Lawrence and Women*, 110–111.
Hobsbaum, Philip. *A Reader's Guide...*, 110–114.
Michaels, Jennifer E. "The Horse as a Life-Symbol in the Prose Works of D. H. Lawrence," *Int'l Fiction R*, 5 (1978), 120–121.
Scheff, Doris. "Interpreting 'Eyes' in D. H. Lawrence's 'St. Mawr,'" *Am Notes & Queries*, 19 (1980), 48–51.

"The Shades of Spring"
Altenbernd, Lynn, and Leslie L. Lewis. *Instructor's Manual...*, 3rd ed., 36.
Smith, Elliott L. and Wanda V. *Instructor's Manual...*, 13.

"The Shadow in the Rose Garden"
Kiely, Robert. *Beyond Egotism...*, 89–90.
*Mizener, Arthur. *A Handbook...*, 4th ed., 124–127.
Smith, Elliott L., and Andrew W. Hart, Eds. *The Short Story...*, 259–262.

"A Sick Collier"
Hobsbaum, Philip. *A Reader's Guide...*, 28–29.

"Strike Pay"
Hobsbaum, Philip. *A Reader's Guide...*, 29–30.

"Sun"
Clark, L. D. *The Minoan Distance...*, 347–348.
Hobsbaum, Philip. *A Reader's Guide...*, 126–128.
Piccolo, Anthony. "Sun and Sex in the Last Stories of D. H. Lawrence," in Grenander, M. E., Ed. *Helios...*, 170–173.

"Things"
Hobsbaum, Philip. *A Reader's Guide...*, 123–124.

"Tickets, Please"
*Brooks, Cleanth, and Robert P. Warren. *Understanding Fiction*, 3rd ed., 161–163.

Cushman, Keith. "The Achievement...," 30–31.
Hobsbaum, Philip. *A Reader's Guide*..., 36.
Ryan, Kiernan. "The Revenge of the Women: Lawrence's 'Tickets, Please,'" *Lit & Hist*, 7 (1981), 210–222.

"The Virgin and the Gipsy"
Gutierrez, Donald. *Lapsing Out*..., 55–66.
Guttenberg, Barnett. "Realism and Romance in Lawrence's 'The Virgin and the Gipsy,'" *Stud Short Fiction*, 17 (1980), 99–103.
Hobsbaum, Philip. *A Reader's Guide*..., 115–118.

"The White Stocking"
Hobsbaum, Philip. *A Reader's Guide*..., 24–25.
*Mizener, Arthur. *A Handbook*..., 4th ed., 128–133.

"Wintry Peacock"
Cushman, Keith. "The Achievement...," 37.

"The Woman Who Rode Away"
Allen, Walter. *The Short Story*..., 100–101.
Clark, L. D. *The Minoan Distance*..., 309–311.
————. "...Southwestern Authors," 17–24.
Gunn, Drewey W. *American and British Writers*..., 137–138.
Macniven, Ian S. "D. H. Lawrence's Indian Summer," in Partlow, Robert B., and Harry T. Moore, Eds. *...The Man Who Lived*, 44–45.
Piccolo, Anthony. "Sun and Sex...," 169–170.

"You Touched Me"
Hobsbaum, Philip. *A Reader's Guide*..., 36–37.
Piccolo, Anthony. "Ritual Strategy...," 94–97.

HENRY LAWSON

"A Child in the Dark"
Allen, Walter. *The Short Story*..., 94–96.

"The Drover's Wife"
Mitchell, Adrian. "Fiction," in Kramer, Leonie, Ed. *The Oxford History*..., 70–71.

"Going Blind"
Kiernan, Brian. "Ways of Seeing: Henry Lawson's 'Going Blind,'" *Australian Lit Stud*, 9 (1980), 298–308.

"The Union Buries Its Dead"
Allen, Walter. *The Short Story*..., 92–94.
Mitchell, Adrian. "Fiction," 71–72.

JEAN-MARIE GUSTAVE LE CLÉZIO

"The Day Beaumont Became Acquainted with His Pain"
Waelti-Walters, Jennifer R. *J. M. G. Le Clézio*, 34–36.

"A Day of Old Age"
Waelti-Walters, Jennifer R. *J. M. G. Le Clézio*, 39-40.

"Fever"
Waelti-Walters, Jennifer R. *"Narrative Movement in J. M. G. Le Clézio's 'Fever,'"* Stud
Short Fiction, 14 (1977), 247-249; rpt., with changes, in her *J. M. G. Le Clézio*,
32-34.

"Martin"
Waelti-Walters, Jennifer R. "Narrative Movement...," 249-250; rpt., with changes,
in her *J. M. G. Le Clézio*, 37-38.

ALWYN LEE

"Something for Bradshaw's Tombstone"
Robinson, Cecil. *Mexico...*, 178-179.

VERNON LEE

"Amour Dure"
Briggs, Julia. *Night Visitors...*, 119-122.

"Oke of Okehurst"
Briggs, Julia. *Night Visitors...*, 121-122.

J. SHERIDAN LE FANU

"An Authentic Narrative of the Ghost of a Hand"
McCormack, W. J. *Sheridan Le Fanu...*, 142-143.

"Carmilla"
MacAndrew, Elizabeth. *The Gothic Tradition...*, 166-167.
McCormack, W. J. *Sheridan Le Fanu...*, 190-191.
Veeder, William. "'Carmilla': The Arts of Repression," *Texas Stud Lit & Lang*, 22
(1980), 197-223.

"The Fortune of Sir Robert Ardagh"
McCormack, W. J. *Sheridan Le Fanu...*, 73-74.

"Green Tea"
Sullivan, Jack. *Elegant Nightmares...*, 12-31.

"The Haunted Baronet"
McCormack, W. J. *Sheridan Le Fanu...*, 148-150.

"The Last Heir of Castle Connor"
McCormack, W. J. *Sheridan Le Fanu...*, 74-75.
Sullivan, Jack. *Elegant Nightmares...*, 38-39.

"Mr. Justice Harbottle"
Sullivan, Jack. *Elegant Nightmares*. . ., 44–55.

"The Mysterious Lodger"
McCormack, W. J. *Sheridan Le Fanu*. . ., 117–120.
Sullivan, Jack. *Elegant Nightmares*. . ., 40–41.

URSULA K. LE GUIN

"The Day Before the Revolution"
Arbur, Rosemarie. "Beyond Feminism, the Self Intact: Woman's Place in the Work
of Ursula K. Le Guin," in Remington, Thomas J., Ed. *Selected Proceedings*. . .,
159–161.

"The Masters"
Koper, Peter T. "Science and Rhetoric in the Fiction of Ursula K. Le Guin," in
De Bolt, Joe, Ed. *Ursula K. Le Guin*. . ., 66–69.

"Mazes"
Bucknall, Barbara J. *Ursula K. Le Guin*, 129–130.

"The New Atlantis"
Bucknall, Barbara J. *Ursula K. Le Guin*, 124–126.

"The Ones Who Walk Away from Omelas"
Kennedy, X. J. *Instructor's Manual*. . ., 2nd ed., 33–34.

"Vaster Than Empires and More Slow"
Bucknall, Barbara J. *Ursula K. Le Guin*, 137–138.

STANISLAW LEM

"The Computer That Fought a Dragon"
Warrick, Patricia S. *The Cybernetic Imagination*. . ., 194–195.

"The Hunt"
Warrick, Patricia S. *The Cybernetic Imagination*. . ., 196–197.

"The Mask"
Rose, Mark. *Alien Encounter*. . ., 157–165.

"The Sanatorium of Dr. Vliperdius"
Warrick, Patricia S. *The Cybernetic Imagination*. . ., 193–194.

"The Sixth Sally"
Warrick, Patricia S. *The Cybernetic Imagination*. . ., 195–196.

SIEGFRIED LENZ

"The Amusement Doctor"
Murdoch, Brian. "Ironic Reversal in the Short Stories of Siegfried Lenz,"
Neophilologus, 58 (1974), 408-409.

"Favorite Food for Hyenas"
Schwenckendiek, B. "Fünf moderne Satiren im Deutschunterricht," *Der Deutschunterricht*, 18, iii (1966), 45-47.

"The Lightship"
Murdoch, Brian, and Malcolm Read. *Siegfried Lenz*, 50-54.

"Mein verdrossenes Gesicht"
Murdoch, Brian. "Ironic Reversal...," 407-408.

"Opportunity for Renunciation"
Murdoch, Brian, and Malcolm Read. *Siegfried Lenz*, 115-117.

NIKOLAI LESKOV

"Administrative Grace"
Lantz, K. A. *Nikolay Leskov*, 139-140.

"The Amazon"
Lantz, K. A. *Nikolay Leskov*, 47-50.

"The Apparition in the Engineers' Castle"
Lantz, K. A. *Nikolay Leskov*, 122-123.

"At the Edge of the World"
Lantz, K. A. *Nikolay Leskov*, 87-90.
_____. "Leskov's 'At the Edge of the World': The Search for an Image of Christ,"
    Slavic & East European J, 25, i (1981), 34-43.
Muckle, James Y. *Nikolai Leskov...*, 114-116.

"The Beast"
Lantz, K. A. *Nikolay Leskov*, 123-124.
Muckle, James Y. *Nikolai Leskov...*, 117.

"The Beast Pen"
Lantz, K. A. *Nikolay Leskov*, 144-145.

"The Best Implorer of God"
Lantz, K. A. *Nikolay Leskov*, 110-111.

"The Bishop's Judgement"
Muckle, James Y. *Nikolai Leskov...*, 116.

"The Brigand of Askalon"
Lantz, K. A. *Nikolay Leskov*, 113-114.

"A Cancelled Affair"
Lantz, K. A. *Nikolay Leskov*, 39–40.

"Cheramour"
Lantz, K. A. *Nikolay Leskov*, 106–107.

"Christ Visits a Peasant"
Muckle, James Y. *Nikolai Leskov . . .*, 121–123.

"Conscience-Stricken Danila"
Lantz, K. A. *Nikolay Leskov*, 112–113.

"Deathless Golovan"
Lantz, K. A. *Nikolay Leskov*, 104–105.

"Deception"
Lantz, K. A. *Nikolay Leskov*, 124–125.

"The Devil Chase"
Muckle, James Y. *Nikolai Leskov . . .*, 123–124.

"The Enchanted Pilgrim"
Lantz, K. A. *Nikolay Leskov*, 84–87.
Muckle, James Y. *Nikolai Leskov . . .*, 33–35.

"Episcopal Justice"
Lantz, K. A. *Nikolay Leskov*, 90–92.

"Exorcising the Devil"
Lantz, K. A. *Nikolay Leskov*, 96–97.

"Fish Soup Without Fish"
Lantz, K. A. *Nikolay Leskov*, 136–137.

"The Hour of God's Will"
Lantz, K. A. *Nikolay Leskov*, 117–118.

"Innocent Prudentsy"
Lantz, K. A. *Nikolay Leskov*, 115–116.
Muckle, James Y. *Nikolai Leskov . . .*, 135.

"A Kolyvan Husband"
Lantz, K. A. *Nikolay Leskov*, 99–100.

"Kotin the Provider and Platonida"
Lantz, K. A. *Nikolay Leskov*, 50–52.

"The Kreutzer Sonata"
Lantz, K. A. *Nikolay Leskov*, 127–128.

"Lady Macbeth of Mtsensk"
Lantz, K. A. *Nikolay Leskov*, 45–47.

"The Left-Handed Craftsman" [same as "The Lefthander" or "Lefty"]
Keenan, William. "Leskov's 'Left-Handed Craftsman' and Zamyatin's *Flea*: Irony into Allegory," *Forum Mod Lang Stud*, 16 (1980), 66–78.
Lantz, K. A. *Nikolay Leskov*, 97–99.

"The Life of a Peasant Woman"
Lantz, K. A. *Nikolay Leskov*, 42–43.

"A Man Without Shame"
Lantz, K. A. *Nikolay Leskov*, 95–96.

"The March Hare"
Lantz, K. A. *Nikolay Leskov*, 145–146.

"The Mountain"
Lantz, K. A. *Nikolay Leskov*, 114–115.

"The Musk-Ox"
Lantz, K. A. *Nikolay Leskov*, 41–42.

"Nightowl"
Lantz, K. A. *Nikolay Leskov*, 140–142.

"The Prince's Slanders"
Muckle, James Y. *Nikolai Leskov...*, 106–107.

"A Product of Nature"
Lantz, K. A. *Nikolay Leskov*, 131–132.

"The Sealed Angel"
Lantz, K. A. *Nikolay Leskov*, 81–84.

"The Sentry"
Lantz, K. A. *Nikolay Leskov*, 108–109.

"Spiritual Torment"
Muckle, James Y. *Nikolai Leskov...*, 134.

"The Toupee Artist"
Lantz, K. A. *Nikolay Leskov*, 129–130.

"Unmercenary Engineers"
Lantz, K. A. *Nikolay Leskov*, 105–106.

"The White Eagle"
Lantz, K. A. *Nikolay Leskov*, 121–122.
O'Connor, Katherine T. "The Specter of Political Corruption: Leskov's 'White Eagle,'" *Russian Lit Tri-Q*, 8 (Winter, 1974), 393–406.

"A Will of Iron"
Lantz, K. A. *Nikolay Leskov*, 94–95.

A Winter's Day"
Lan†z, K. A. *Nikolay Leskov*, 142-143.

DORIS LESSING

"Between Men"
Millar, Helen J. "Doris Lessing's Short Stories: A Woman's Right to Choose?"
Lit North Queensland, 6 (1978), 32-33.

"The Day Stalin Died"
Allen, Walter. *The Short Story . . .*, 352-353.

"The De Wets Come to Kloof Grange"
Millar, Helen J. "Doris Lessing's Short Stories: The Male's Point of View," *Lit
North Queensland*, 6 (1978), 48-49.

"Dialogue"
Allen, Orphia J. "Structure and Motif in Doris Lessing's *A Man and Two Women*,"
Mod Fiction Stud, 26 (1980), 71-72.

"England versus England"
Allen, Orphia J. "Structure and Motif. . .," 66-67.

"Flight"
Millar, Helen J. ". . .The Male's Point of View," 47.

"The Habit of Loving"
Millar, Helen J. ". . .The Male's Point of View," 45-46.

"He"
Millar, Helen J. ". . .Right to Choose?" 28-29.

"Homage to Isaac Babel"
Allen, Orphia J. "Structure and Motif. . .," 67-68.
Altenbernd, Lynn, and Leslie L. Lewis. *Instructor's Manual . . .*, 3rd ed., 39.

"Lucy Grange"
Millar, Helen J. ". . .Right to Choose?" 29-30.

"Not a Very Nice Story"
Millar, Helen J. ". . .Right to Choose?" 26.

"Notes for a Case History"
Millar, Helen J. ". . .Right to Choose?" 33-35.

"The Nuisance"
Smith, Elliott L., and Andrew W. Hart, Eds. *The Short Story . . .*, 184-185.

"Old Chief Mshlanga"
Allen, Walter. *The Short Story . . .*, 348-349.

"One Off the Short List"
Clements, Frances M. "Lessing's 'One Off the Short List' and the Definition of
    Self," *Frontiers*, 1 (Fall, 1975), 106–109.
Millar, Helen J. ". . .Right to Choose?" 30–32.

"Our Friend Judith"
Altenbernd, Lynn, and Leslie L. Lewis. *Instructor's Manual*. . ., 3rd ed., 37–38.
Millar, Helen J. ". . .Right to Choose?" 35–36.

"Out of the Fountain"
Auderlen, Eckhard. "Verbindlichkeit und Relativität der Werte in Doris Lessings
    'Out of the Fountain,'" *Anglistik & Englischunterricht*, 9 (December, 1979), 61–84.

"The Pig"
Butcher, Margaret K. "'Two Forks of a Road': Divergence and Convergence in
    the Short Stories of Doris Lessing," *Mod Fiction Stud*, 26 (1980), 55–61.

"The Second Hut"
Allen, Walter. *The Short Story*. . ., 350–351.

"The Story of Non-Marrying Man"
Millar, Helen J. ". . .The Male's Point of View," 49–51.

"The Sun Between Their Feet"
Allen, Orphia J. "Interpreting 'The Sun Between Their Feet,'" *Doris Lessing
    Newsletter*, 5, ii (1981), 1–2.

"To Room Nineteen"
Allen, Orphia J. "Structure and Motif. . .," 65–66.
Dean, Sharon. "Marriage, Motherhood, and Lessing's 'To Room Nineteen,'" *Doris
    Lessing Newsletter*, 5, i (1981), 14.
Howard, Daniel F., and William Plummer. *Instructor's Manual*. . ., 3rd ed., 67–68;
    rpt. Howard, Daniel F., and John Ribar. *Instructor's Manual*. . ., 4th ed., 68–69.
Millar, Helen J. ". . .Right to Choose?" 26–28.
Pearson, Carol, and Katherine Pope. *The Female Hero*. . ., 47–48.

"The Trinket Box"
Butcher, Margaret K. "'Two Forks of a Road'. . .," 55–61.

"An Unposted Love Letter"
Madden, David. *Instructor's Manual*. . ., 5th ed., 109–112.

"The Witness"
Millar, Helen J. ". . .The Male's Point of View," 44–45.

"The Woman"
Millar, Helen J. ". . .The Male's Point of View," 43–44.

"A Woman on a Roof"
Millar, Helen J. ". . .The Male's Point of View," 42–43.

ALUN LEWIS

"Almost a Gentleman"
Devine, Kathleen. "Alun Lewis's 'Almost a Gentleman,'" *Anglo-Welsh R*, 67
(1980), 79–84.

"Cold Spell"
Allen, Walter. *The Short Story...*, 303–304.

"The Wanderers"
Allen, Walter. *The Short Story...*, 301–303.

WYNDHAM LEWIS

"Cantleman's Spring Mate"
*Jameson, Frederic. *Fables of Aggression...*, 26–29.
Lafourcade, Bernard. "The Taming of the Wild Body," in Meyers, Jeffrey, Ed.
Wyndham Lewis..., 157–158.

LUCY F. LINDSAY

"Sang"
Chu, Limin. *The Image of China...*, 212.

CLARICE LISPECTOR

"Daydream of a Drunken Housewife"
Lindstrom, Naomi. "A Feminist Discourse Analysis of Clarice Lispector's 'Daydream of a Drunken Housewife,'" *Latin Am Lit*, 9 (1981), 7–16.

JACK LONDON

"The Bones of Kahelili"
*McClintock, James I. "Jack London's Use of Carl Jung's *Psychology of the
Unconscious,*" in Ownbey, Ray W., Ed. *Jack London...*, 51–52.

"The Call of the Wild"
Frey, Charles. "Contradiction in 'The Call of the Wild,'" *Jack London Newsletter*,
12 (1979), 35–37.

"The Chinago"
*Hendricks, King. "Jack London: Master Craftsman of the Short Story," in
Ownbey, Ray W., Ed. *Jack London...*, 27–30.

"The Great Interrogation"
*Wilcox, Earl. "The Kipling of the Klondike: Naturalism in London's Early
Fiction," in Ownbey, Ray W., Ed. *Jack London...*, 84–86.

"The Law of Life"
*Hendricks, King. "Jack London...," 25-27.
Maffi, Mario. "'The Law of Life': Jack London and the Dialect of Nature," *Jack London Newsletter*, 12 (1979), 42-45.

"Law-Giving"
Gunn, Drewey W. *American and British Writers...*, 68-69.

"Love of Life"
*Hendricks, King. "Jack London...," 22-25.

"The Men of Forty-Mile"
*Wilcox, Earl. "The Kipling of the Klondike...," 87-88.

"The Mexican"
Gunn, Drewey W. *American and British Writers...*, 56-57.
Pettit, Arthur G. *Images of the Mexican American...*, 185-186.
Robinson, Cecil. *Mexico...*, 182-183.

"The Priestly Prerogative"
*Wilcox, Earl. "The Kipling of the Klondike...," 90-91.

"The Red One"
Brown, Ellen. "A Perfect Sphere: Jack London's 'The Red One,'" *Jack London Newsletter*, 11 (1978), 81-85.
Campbell, Jeanne. "Falling Stars: Myth in 'The Red One,'" *Jack London Newsletter*, 11 (1978), 86-96.

"Shin Bones"
*McClintock, James I. "Jack London's Use...," 49-51.

"The Son of the Wolf"
*Wilcox, Earl. "The Kipling of the Klondike...," 82-83.

"The Tears of Ah Kim"
*McClintock, James I. "Jack London's Use...," 46-48.

"To Build a Fire"
Baker, Sheridan, and George Perkins. *Instructor's Manual...*, 36.
Barker, Gerard A. *Instructor's Manual...*, 3-5.
*Hendricks, King. "Jack London...," 19-22.

"The Water Babies"
*McClintock, James I. "Jack London's Use...," 48-49.

"When Alice Told Her Soul"
*McClintock, James I. "Jack London's Use...," 46.

"Which Make Men Remember"
*Wilcox, Earl. "The Kipling of the Klondike...," 88-89.

"The White Silence"
*Wilcox, Earl. "The Kipling of the Klondike...," 80-82.

JOSÉ LÓPEZ RUBIO

"Aunt Germana"
Holt, Marion P. *José López Rubio*, 34-35.

LORELLE [unidentified]

"The Battle of the Wabash"
Chu, Limin. *The Image of China...*, 165-167.

H. P. LOVECRAFT

"The Call of Cthulhu"
Aquino, Michael A. "Lovecraftian Ritual—Ceremony of the Nine Angels: 'The Call of Cthulhu,'" *Nyctalops*, No. 13 (May, 1977), 13-15.
Bertin, Eddy C. "The Cthulhu Mythos," *Nyctalops*, 1, iv (June, 1971), 3-6, 43; rpt. *Drab*, 4, iii (October, 1978), 18-20, 22-24.
Carter, Lin. "The Cthulhu Mythos," in Carter, Lin, Ed. *The Spawn...*, 1-4; rpt. *Nueva Dimensión*, No. 79 (July, 1976), 30-31.

"The Outsider"
Mosig, Dirk W. "The Four Faces of 'The Outsider,'" *Nyctalops*, 2, ii (July, 1974), 3-10; rpt. *Il Re in Giallo*, 1, ii (1976), 29-47.
_____. "An Analytic Interpretation: 'The Outsider,' Allegory of the Psyche," *Quarber Merkur*, 15, i (March, 1977), 50-55.

"The Whisperer in Darkness"
Leiber, Fritz. "'The Whisperer' Re-Examined," *Haunted*, 2, ii (December, 1964), 22-25; rpt. in his *The Book of Fritz Leiber*, 143-147.
Wheelock, Alan S. "Dark Mountain: H. P. Lovecraft and the 'Vermont Horror,'" *Vermont History*, 155 (1977), 221-228.

"The White Ship"
Mosig, Dirk W. "'The White Ship': A Psychic Odyssey," *Whisper*, 2, i (November, 1974), 35-37, 39-40; rpt. Joshi, S. T., Ed. *...Four Decades of Criticism*, 186-190.

MALCOLM LOWRY

"The Bravest Boat"
Cross, Richard K. *Malcolm Lowry...*, 88-90.

"Elephant and Colosseum"
Bareham, T. E. "Strange Poems of God's Mercy: The Lowry Short Stories," in Smith, Anne, Ed. *The Art...*, 164-165.
Cross, Richard K. *Malcolm Lowry...*, 95-97.

"The Forest Path to the Spring"
Bareham, T. E. "Strange Poems...," 166–168.
Cross, Richard K. *Malcolm Lowry*..., 99–106.
Epstein, Perle. "'The Forest Path to the Spring': An Exercise in Contemplation,"
   in Smith, Anne, Ed. *The Art*..., 130–143.
MacDonald, R. D. "Canada in Lowry's Fiction," *Mosaic*, 14, ii (1981), 40–46.

"Ghostkeeper"
Cross, Richard K. *Malcolm Lowry*..., 86–88.

"Gin and Goldenrod"
Bareham, T. E. "Strange Poems...," 165–166.
Cross, Richard K. *Malcolm Lowry*..., 98–99.

"Hotel Room in Chartres"
Cross, Richard K. *Malcolm Lowry*..., 13–15.

"In Le Havre"
Cross, Richard K. *Malcolm Lowry*..., 16–17.

"In the Black Hills"
Cross, Richard K. *Malcolm Lowry*..., 85–86.

"Present Estate of Pompeii"
Cross, Richard K. *Malcolm Lowry*..., 97–99.

"Strange Comfort Afforded by the Profession"
Cross, Richard K. *Malcolm Lowry*..., 93–95.

"Through the Panama"
Bareham, T. E. "Strange Poems...," 158–159.
Cross, Richard K. *Malcolm Lowry*..., 90–93.

LU HSÜN [LU XÜN or CHOU SHU-JEN]

"A Madman's Diary"
Shu, James C. T. "Iconoclasm in Wang Wen-hsing's *Chia-pien*, in Faurot, Jeannette
   L., Ed. *Chinese Fiction from Taiwan*..., 185–187.

"The True Story of Ah Q"
Ge, Baoquan. "On the World Significance of 'The True Story of Ah Q,'" *Chinese
   Lit*, 7 (1981), 110–123.

MARTA LYNCH

"Entierro de carnaval"
Lindstrom, Naomi. "Woman's Voice in the Short Stories of Marta Lynch," in Minc,
   Rose S., Ed. ...*Latin American Short Story*, 149.

"Historía con gato"
Lindstrom, Naomi. "Woman's Voice...," 149–150.

"Triptico"
Lindstrom, Naomi. "Woman's Voice...," 150–151.

ANDREW LYTLE

"Mister McGregor"
*Mizener, Arthur. *A Handbook*..., 4th ed., 202–206.

CHARLES W. McCABLE

"Only a Squaw Man—Kind Feelings Lodge in Many Unlikely Places"
Chu, Limin. *The Image of China*..., 219–220.

MARY McCARTHY

"Artists in Uniform"
Hardy, Willene S. *Mary McCarthy*, 30–31.
*Mizener, Arthur. *A Handbook*..., 4th ed., 19–26.

"Cruel and Barbarous Treatment"
Hardy, Willene S. *Mary McCarthy*, 32–34.
Stock, Irvin. *Fiction as Wisdom*..., 163–164.

"The Genial Host"
Hardy, Willene S. *Mary McCarthy*, 43–47.

"Ghostly Father, I Confess"
Hardy, Willene S. *Mary McCarthy*, 47–50.
Stock, Irvin. *Fiction as Wisdom*..., 165–166.

"The Man in the Brooks Brothers Suit"
Hardy, Willene S. *Mary McCarthy*, 37–42.

"Portrait of the Intellectual as a Yale Man"
Stock, Irvin. *Fiction as Wisdom*..., 164–165.

"Rogue's Gallery"
Hardy, Willene S. *Mary McCarthy*, 34–36.

JOHN LUDLUM McCONNEL

"The Ranger's Chase"
Hallway, John E. "Early Illinois Author John L. McConnel and 'The Ranger's Chase,'" *J Illinois State Hist Soc*, 73 (1980), 177–188.

CARSON McCULLERS

"Art and Mr. Mahoney"
McDowell, Margaret B. *Carson McCullers*, 128–129.
Philips, Robert. "Freaking Out: The Short Stories of Carson McCullers," *Southern R*, 63 (Winter, 1978), 71.

"The Ballad of the Sad Café"
Allen, Walter. *The Short Story...*, 313–318.
Autunes, Futin B. "'The Ballad of the Sad Café' and 'The Sojourner': Common Themes and Images," *Estudos Anglo-Americanos*, 3–4 (1979–1980), 191–199.
Clark, Charlene K. "Male-Female Pairs in Carson McCullers' 'The Ballad of the Sad Café' and *The Member of the Wedding*," *Notes Contemp Lit*, 9, i (1979), 11–12.
Kahane, Claire. "Gothic Mirrors and Feminine Identity," *Centennial R*, 24 (1980), 60–61.
MacAndrew, Elizabeth. *The Gothic Tradition...*, 245–246.
McDowell, Margaret B. *Carson McCullers*, 65–80.

"Breath from the Sky"
McDowell, Margaret B. *Carson McCullers*, 117–119.

"Correspondence"
McDowell, Margaret B. *Carson McCullers*, 123–124.

"A Domestic Dilemma"
McDowell, Margaret B. *Carson McCullers*, 132–134.

"The Haunted Boy"
McDowell, Margaret B. *Carson McCullers*, 119.

"The Instant of the Hour After"
McDowell, Margaret B. *Carson McCullers*, 132–133.

"The Jockey"
McDowell, Margaret B. *Carson McCullers*, 125–126.

"Like That"
McDowell, Margaret B. *Carson McCullers*, 119–121.

"Madame Zilensky and the King of Finland"
McDowell, Margaret B. *Carson McCullers*, 126–128.

"The Sojourner"
Autunes, Futin B. "...Common Themes and Images," 191–199.
Brooks, Cleanth, and Robert P. Warren. *Instructor's Manual...*, 3rd ed., 28–29.
McDowell, Margaret B. *Carson McCullers*, 134–135.
Philips, Robert. "Freaking Out...," 70.
Smith, Elliott L. and Wanda V. *Instructor's Manual...*, 17.

"Sucker"
McDowell, Margaret B. *Carson McCullers*, 119–121.
Philips, Robert. "Freaking Out...," 66–67.

*"A Tree, A Rock, A Cloud"
McDowell, Margaret B. *Carson McCullers*, 129–131.
Philips, Robert. "Freaking Out...," 70–71.
Rohrberger, Mary. *Instructor's Manual...*, 30–31.
Scott, Virgil, and David Madden. *Instructor's Manual...*, 4th ed., 4–6; Madden, David. *Instructor's Manual...*, 5th ed., 4–5.
Smith, Elliott L., and Andrew W. Hart, Eds. *The Short Story...*, 136–138.

"Who Has Seen the Wind?"
McDowell, Margaret B. *Carson McCullers*, 132.

"Wunderkind"
McDowell, Margaret B. *Carson McCullers*, 121–123.

JOHN McGAHERN

"Peaches"
Brown, Terence. "John McGahern's *Nightlines*: Tone, Technique, and Symbolism," in Rafroidi, Patrick, and Terence Brown, Eds. *The Irish Short Story*, 298–299.

ARTHUR MACHEN

"The Novel of the Black Seal"
Briggs, Julia. *Night Visitors...*, 72–73.

"The Novel of the White Powder"
Briggs, Julia. *Night Visitors...*, 70–73.

BERNARD MacLAVERTY

"St. Paul Could Hit the Nail on the Head"
Kelly, Thomas. "*Secrets and Other Stories* by Bernard MacLaverty," *Éire*, 16, i (1981), 156–157.

"Secrets"
Kelly, Thomas. "*Secrets and Other Stories...*," 157–158.

NORMAN MACLEAN

"A River Runs Through It"
Hesford, Walter. "Fishing for the Words of Life: Norman Maclean's 'A River Runs Through It,'" *Rocky Mt R*, 34 (1980), 33–45.

SEAN MacMATHUNA

"A Straight Run down to Kilcash"
Norris, David. "Imaginative Response versus Authority Structures: A Theme of
    the Anglo-Irish Short Story," in Rafroidi, Patrick, and Terence Brown, Eds.
    The Irish Short Story, 70–71.

JAMES ALAN McPHERSON

"Gold Coast"
*Mizener, Arthur. *A Handbook...*, 4th ed., 89–92.
Scott, Virgil, and David Madden. *Instructor's Manual...*, 4th ed., 104–106.

NORMAN MAILER

"A Calculus at Heaven"
Bailey, Jennifer. *Norman Mailer...*, 7–9.

"The Man Who Studied Yoga"
Bailey, Jennifer. *Norman Mailer...*, 21–23.
Gordon, Andrew. *An American Dreamer...*, 87–94.
Michaels, I. Lloyd. "Shaggy Dog Storytelling in Mailer's 'The Man Who Studied
    Yoga,'" *Stud Hum*, 8, ii (1981), 34–39.

"Maybe Next Year"
Gordon, Andrew. *An American Dreamer...*, 55–57.

"The Time of Her Time"
Bailey, Jennifer. *Norman Mailer...*, 32–35.
Gordon, Andrew. *An American Dreamer...*, 113–128.

CLARENCE MAJOR

"Art"
Bolling, Doug. "A Reading of Clarence Major's Short Fiction," *Black Am Lit Forum*,
    13 (1979), 52–53.

"Dear Freud"
Bolling, Doug. "...Major's Short Fiction," 52.

"Escape the Close Circle"
Bolling, Doug. "...Major's Short Fiction," 54.

"Fish, Tomatoes, Mama & Book"
Bolling, Doug. "...Major's Short Fiction," 55.

"Newhouse"
Bolling, Doug. "...Major's Short Fiction," 53.

"Number Four"
Bolling, Doug. "...Major's Short Fiction," 53.

"The Pecan Pie"
Bolling, Doug. "...Major's Short Fiction," 55-56.

"The Vase and the Rose"
Bolling, Doug. "...Major's Short Fiction," 53-54.

BERNARD MALAMUD

"Angel Levine"
Avery, Evelyn G. *Rebels and Victims...*, 99-101.
Canham, Laurel. "Matrix and Allegory in Selected Malamud Short Stories,"
    Linguistics in Lit, 2, iii (1977), 81-86.
Hershinow, Sheldon. *Bernard Malamud*, 122-124.

"Black Is My Favorite Color"
Avery, Evelyn G. *Rebels and Victims...*, 101-103.
Howard, Daniel F., and William Plummer. *Instructor's Manual...*, 3rd ed., 59;
    rpt. Howard, Daniel F., and John Ribar. *Instructor's Manual...*, 4th ed., 65.

"The Cost of Living"
Allen, Walter. *The Short Story...*, 343-344.

"The German Refugee"
Allen, Walter. *The Short Story...*, 346-347.

"Glass Blower of Venice"
Ducharme, Robert. *Art and Idea...*, 139-140.
Hershinow, Sheldon. *Bernard Malamud*, 85.

"Idiots First"
Hershinow, Sheldon. *Bernard Malamud*, 126-127.
Kliemann, Kristin. "A Perspective on Bernard Malamud's 'Idiots First,'" *Linguistics
    in Lit*, 2, iii (1977), 27-40.
Madden, David. *Instructor's Manual...*, 5th ed., 51-54.
Rohrberger, Mary. *Instructor's Manual...*, 39.

"The Jewbird"
Allen, Walter. *The Short Story...*, 344-346.
Hershinow, Sheldon. *Bernard Malamud*, 124-126.
Kennedy, J. Gerald. "Parody as Exorcism: 'The Raven' and 'The Jewbird,'" *Genre*,
    13 (1980), 161-169.

"The Lady of the Lake"
Alexander, Edward. *The Resonance of Dust...*, 125-126.
Schmidt-von Bardeleben, Renate. "Bernard Malamuds 'The Lady of the Lake':
    Judischamerikanische Selbstdarstellung und britisch-englische Literatur-
    tradition," in Erlebach, Peter, Wolfgang G. Müller, and Klaus Reuter, Eds.
    Geschichtlichkeit..., 257-271.

"The Last Mohican"
Ducharme, Robert. *Art and Idea*..., 133–135.
Hershinow, Sheldon. *Bernard Malamud*, 76–79.
Yokota, Kazunori. "On B. Malamud's 'The Last Mohican,'" *Chu-Shikoku Stud Am Lit*, 12 (1976), 32–37.

"The Loan"
Canham, Laurel. "Matrix and Allegory...," 63–65.

"The Magic Barrel"
Ahrends, Günter. ...*Kurzgeschichte*, 196–200.
Hershinow, Sheldon. *Bernard Malamud*, 128–131.
Howard, Daniel F., and John Ribar. *Instructor's Manual*..., 4th ed., 66.
Scott, Virgil, and David Madden. *Instructor's Manual*..., 4th ed., 91–93.
Storey, Michael L. "Pinye Salzman, Pan and 'The Magic Barrel,'" *Stud Short Fiction*, 18 (1981), 180–183.

"The Mourners"
Canham, Laurel. "Matrix and Allegory...," 76–81.
Hershinow, Sheldon. *Bernard Malamud*, 120–122.

"Naked Nude"
Ducharme, Robert. *Art and Idea*..., 136–137.
Hershinow, Sheldon. *Bernard Malamud*, 80–81.

"Pictures of the Artist"
Ducharme, Robert. *Art and Idea*..., 138–139.
Hershinow, Sheldon. *Bernard Malamud*, 83–85.

"A Pimp's Revenge"
Ducharme, Robert. *Art and Idea*..., 137–138.

"The Silver Crown"
Avery, Evelyn G. *Rebels and Victims*..., 45–46.
Canham, Laurel. "Matrix and Allegory...," 72–76.
Hershinow, Sheldon. *Bernard Malamud*, 131–133.

"Still Life"
Ducharme, Robert. *Art and Idea*..., 135–136.
Hershinow, Sheldon. *Bernard Malamud*, 79–80.

"Take Pity"
Canham, Laurel. "Matrix and Allegory...," 70–72.
*Mizener, Arthur. *A Handbook*..., 4th ed., 156–159.

"The Talking Horse"
Burch, Beth and Paul W. "Myth on Myth: Bernard Malamud's 'The Talking Horse,'" *Stud Short Fiction*, 16 (1979), 350–353.

EDUARDO MALLEA

"Human Reason"
Lichtblau, Myron I. "Narrative Voice in Eduardo Mallea's 'La razon humana,'" in Minc, Rose S., Ed. ...*Latin American Short Story*, 120–125.

ANDRÉ PIEYRE DE MANDIARGUES

"Le Diamant"
Campanani, Susan. "Alchemy in Pieyre de Mandiargues' 'Le Diamant,'" *French R*, 50 (1977), 602–609.

"La Spirale"
Saad, Gabriel. "L'Espagne mythique d'André Pieyre de Mandiargues," *Recherches et Études*, 1 (1979), 61–70.

FREDERICK MANFRED

"Arrow of Love"
Wright, Robert C. *Frederick Manfred*, 127–129.

"Country Love"
Wright, Robert C. *Frederick Manfred*, 131.

"Footsteps in the Alfalfa"
Wright, Robert C. *Frederick Manfred*, 135–136.

"Lew and Luanne"
Wright, Robert C. *Frederick Manfred*, 129–131.

"The Mink Coat"
Wright, Robert C. *Frederick Manfred*, 132–136.

HEINRICH MANN

"The Marvelous"
Gross, David. *The Writer and Society...*, 43–45.

"Pippo Spano"
Gross, David. *The Writer and Society...*, 84–85.

"Resignation"
Gross, David. *The Writer and Society...*, 131.

"Das Wunderbare"
Gross, David. *The Writer and Society...*, 43–45.

THOMAS MANN

"The Bajazzo"
Lindsay, J. M. "Thomas Mann's First Stories: Some New Directions in German
Realism," in Thunecke, Jörg, Ed. *Formen Realistischer Erzählkunst...*, 268-269.

"The Blood of the Walsungs"
Apter, T. E. *Thomas Mann...*, 47-50.
Erlich, Gloria C. "Race and Incest in Mann's 'Blood of the Walsungs,'" *Stud
Twentieth Century Lit*, 2 (1978), 113-126.
Sjobren, Christine. "Wendelin and the Theme of Transformation in Thomas
Mann's *Wälsungenblut*," *Comp Lit Stud*, 14 (1977), 346-359.

"Death in Venice"
Apter, T. E. *Thomas Mann...*, 50-57.
Cadieux, André. "The Jungle of Dionysus: The Self in Mann and Nietzsche,"
Psych & Lit, 3 (1979), 53-63.
Heller, Peter. "Der 'Tod in Venedig' und Thomas Manns 'Grund-Motiv,'" in
Schultze, Hans H., and Gerald Chapple, Eds. *Thomas Mann...*, 35-83.
Parkes, Ford B. "The Image of the Tiger in Thomas Mann's 'Tod in Venedig,'"
Stud Twentieth Century Lit, 3 (1978), 73-83.
Rockwood, Heidi M. "Mann's 'Death in Venice,'" *Explicator*, 39, iv (1981), 34.
Swales, Martin. *Thomas Mann...*, 37-45.

"Disillusionment"
Lindsay, J. M. "Thomas Mann's First Stories...," 267.

"Disorder and Early Sorrow"
Bolkoski, Sidney. "Thomas Mann's 'Disorder and Early Sorrow': The Writer as
Social Critic," *Contemp Lit*, 22 (1981), 218-233.

"Fallen"
Lindsay, J. M. "Thomas Mann's First Stories...," 265-266.
Winston, Richard. *Thomas Mann...*, 56-57.

"Gerächt"
Lindsay, J. M. "Thomas Mann's First Stories...," 270.

"The Hungry"
Winston, Richard. *Thomas Mann...*, 168-170.

"The Infant Prodigy"
Rohrberger, Mary. *Instructor's Manual...*, 17.
Smith, Elliott L., and Andrew W. Hart, Eds. *The Short Story...*, 268-269.

"Little Herr Friedemann"
Lindsay, J. M. "Thomas Mann's First Stories...," 267-268.

"Luischen"
Lindsay, J. M. "Thomas Mann's First Stories...," 270-271.

"Mario and the Magician"
Apter, T. E. *Thomas Mann*..., 136–139.
Mandel, Siegfried. "Mann's 'Mario and the Magician,' or Who Is Silvestra?" *Mod Fiction Stud*, 25 (1980), 593–611.
Speirs, R. C. "Some Psychological Observations on Domination, Acquiescence and Revolt in Thomas Mann's 'Mario und der Zauberer,'" *Forum Mod Lang Stud*, 16 (1980), 319–330.
Swales, Martin. *Thomas Mann*..., 77–80.
Tatar, Maria M. *Spellbound*..., 257–264.
Wehner, James V. "The Nature of Evil in Melville's 'Billy Budd' and Mann's 'Mario und der Zauberer,'" *Comparatist*, 4 (1980), 31–46.

"Railway Accident"
Winston, Richard. *Thomas Mann*..., 264–265.

"Royal Highness"
Swales, Martin. *Thomas Mann*..., 36–37.

"Tobias Mindernickel"
Lindsay, J. M. "Thomas Mann's First Stories...," 269.

"Tonio Kröger"
Apter, T. E. *Thomas Mann*..., 31–34.
Douglas, Kenneth, and Sarah N. Lawall. "Masterpieces of the Modern World," in Mack, Maynard, *et al.*, Eds. ... *World Masterpieces*, II, 4th ed., 1252–1253.
Swales, Martin. *Thomas Mann*..., 29–34.

"The Transposed Heads"
Ganeshan, V. "'The Transformed Heads' by Thomas Mann: An Indian Legend or a Metaphysical Jest?" *J School Lang*, 5, i–ii (1977–1978), 1–13.

"Tristan"
Swales, Martin. *Thomas Mann*..., 34–36.

"The Wardrobe"
Lindsay, J. M. "Thomas Mann's First Stories...," 269–270.
Winston, Richard. *Thomas Mann*..., 115–116.

"The Will to Happiness"
Lindsay, J. M. "Thomas Mann's First Stories...," 266–267.

BALRAJ MANRA

"The Box of Matches"
Adkins, Joan F. "An Analysis of Three Short Stories," *Indian Lit*, 21, i (1978), 60–62.

CAPTAIN MANSFIELD [given name unknown]

"A Deal in Dope"
Chu, Limin. *The Image of China*..., 190–191.

KATHERINE MANSFIELD [KATHERINE BEAUCHAMP]

"At the Bay"
Allen, Walter. *The Short Story*..., 174-175.
Hanson, Clare, and Andrew Gurr. *Katherine Mansfield*, 99-106.

"Bliss"
Allen, Walter. *The Short Story*..., 168-170.
Hanson, Clare, and Andrew Gurr. *Katherine Mansfield*, 58-65.
Zorn, Marilyn. "Visionary Flowers: Another Study of Katherine Mansfield's 'Bliss,'" *Stud Short Fiction*, 17 (1980), 141-147.

"The Daughters of the Late Colonel"
Bernikow, Louise. *Among Women*, 88-89.
Rohrberger, Mary. *Instructor's Manual*..., 21-22.

"Her First Ball"
*Mizener, Arthur. *A Handbook*..., 4th ed., 153-155.

"Je ne parle pas français"
Hanson, Clare, and Andrew Gurr. *Katherine Mansfield*, 64-70.

"The Lady's Maid"
Smith, Elliott L.,. and Andrew W. Hart, Eds. *The Short Story*..., 169-171.

"The Life of Ma Parker"
Allen, Walter. *The Short Story*..., 166-167.

"The Man Without a Temperament"
Rohrberger, Mary. *Instructor's Manual*..., 22-23.
Ross, Gordon N. "Klaymongso in Mansfield's 'The Man Without a Temperament,'" *Stud Short Fiction*, 18 (1981), 179-180.

"A Married Man's Story"
Hanson, Clare, and Andrew Gurr. *Katherine Mansfield*, 106-113.

"Miss Brill"
Hanson, Clare, and Andrew Gurr. *Katherine Mansfield*, 75-82.

"Prelude"
Allen, Walter. *The Short Story*..., 171-173.
Hanson, Clare. "Katherine Mansfield and Symbolism: The 'Artist's Method' in 'Prelude,'" *J Commonwealth Lit*, 16, i (1981), 25-39.

"Something Childish but Very Natural"
Dowling, David. "Mansfield's 'Something Childish but Very Natural,'" *Explicator*, 38, iii (1980), 44-46.

"The Tiredness of Rosabel"
Allen, Walter. *The Short Story*..., 165-166.
Hanson, Clare, and Andrew Gurr. *Katherine Mansfield*, 29-30.

"The Voyage"
Hanson, Clare, and Andrew Gurr. *Katherine Mansfield*, 95–99.

"The Wind Blows"
Hanson, Clare, and Andrew Gurr. *Katherine Mansfield*, 45–49.

"The Woman at the Store"
Hanson, Clare, and Andrew Gurr. *Katherine Mansfield*, 37–40.

"The Young Girl"
Kobler, J. F. "The Sexless Narrator of Mansfield's 'The Young Girl,'" *Stud Short Fiction*, 17 (1980), 269–274.

WALLACE MARKFIELD

"The Country of the Crazy Horse"
Friedman, Melvin J. "The Enigma of Unpopularity and Critical Neglect: The Case of Wallace Markfield," in Filler, Louis, Ed. *Seasoned Authors...*, 35.

RENÉ MARQUÉS

"The Blue Kite"
Martin, Eleanor J. *René Marqués*, 66–67.

"The Child in the Tree"
Martin, Eleanor J. *René Marqués*, 64.

"The Crucifixion of Miss Bunning"
Martin, Eleanor J. *René Marqués*, 65–66.

"Death"
Martin, Eleanor J. *René Marqués*, 57.

"The Dragon's Hour"
Martin, Eleanor J. *René Marqués*, 61–63.

"Fear"
Martin, Eleanor J. *René Marqués*, 56–57.

"In a City Called San Juan"
Martin, Eleanor J. *René Marqués*, 67–68.

"In the Stern, There Lies a Body"
Martin, Eleanor J. *René Marqués*, 63–64.

"The Informer"
Martin, Eleanor J. *René Marqués*, 65.

"Island in Manhattan"
Martin, Eleanor J. *René Marqués*, 51–52.

"The Knife and the Stone"
Martin, Eleanor J. *René Marqués*, 66.

"The Little Miracle of Saint Anthony"
Martin, Eleanor J. *René Marqués*, 54–55.

"The Oath"
Martin, Eleanor J. *René Marqués*, 55–56.

"Purification on Christ Street"
Martin, Eleanor J. *René Marqués*, 59–60.

"Three Men Near the River"
Martin, Eleanor J. *René Marqués*, 58–59.

"Two Turns of the Key and a Guardian Angel"
Martin, Eleanor J. *René Marqués*, 60–61.

DON MARQUIS

"The Ancient Mariner"
Lee, Lynn. *Don Marquis*, 97–99.

"The Glass Eater's Story"
Lee, Lynn. *Don Marquis*, 100–101.

"The Magic Melody"
Lee, Lynn. *Don Marquis*, 102–103.

"Miss Higginbotham Declines"
Lee, Lynn. *Don Marquis*, 130–131.

"The Report of a Trial Which Was Not Printed"
Lee, Lynn. *Don Marquis*, 135–138.

"The Saddest Man"
Lee, Lynn. *Don Marquis*, 95–97.

"Satan Goes to Church"
Lee, Lynn. *Don Marquis*, 134–135.

"Twiller Van Durden's Miracle"
Lee, Lynn. *Don Marquis*, 132–134.

PAULE MARSHALL

"Reena"
Hull, Gloria T. "'To Be a Black Woman in America': A Reading of Paule Marshall's
'Reena,'" *Obsidian*, 4, iii (1978), 5–15.

EZEQUIEL MARTINEZ ESTRADA

"Examen sin conciencia"
Escudero Valentin, Rogelio. "Enfoque sociohistórico de 'Examen sin conciencia,' cuento de Ezequiel Martinez Estrada," *Revista de Estudios Hispánicos* (Puerto Rico), 7 (1980), 59–74.

MASAMUNE HAKUCHŌ

"Autumn of This Year"
Rolf, Robert. *Masamune Hakuchō*, 150–153.

"By the Inlet"
Rolf, Robert. *Masamune Hakuchō*, 83–85.

"Clay Doll"
Rolf, Robert. *Masamune Hakuchō*, 75–78.

"The Dead and the Living"
Rolf, Robert. *Masamune Hakuchō*, 86–88.

"Discord and Harmony"
Rolf, Robert. *Masamune Hakuchō*, 42–43.

"Dust"
Rolf, Robert. *Masamune Hakuchō*, 50–52.

"Early Summer This Year"
Rolf, Robert. *Masamune Hakuchō*, 149–150.

"Elder Brother Rii"
Rolf, Robert. *Masamune Hakuchō*, 153–154.

"Ghost Picture"
Rolf, Robert. *Masamune Hakuchō*, 52–56.

"Hell"
Rolf, Robert. *Masamune Hakuchō*, 67–69.

"I Killed a Man, and Yet"
Rolf, Robert. *Masamune Hakuchō*, 109–110.

"Illusion"
Rolf, Robert. *Masamune Hakuchō*, 96–103.

"Nightmare"
Rolf, Robert. *Masamune Hakuchō*, 91–95.

"Old Friend"
Rolf, Robert. *Masamune Hakuchō*, 45–50.

"Peace of Mind"
Rolf, Robert. *Masamune Hakuchō*, 56–58.

"The Smell of the Cowshed"
Rolf, Robert. *Masamune Hakuchō*, 88–91.

"Solitude"
Rolf, Robert. *Masamune Hakuchō*, 39–42.

"Spring This Year"
Rolf, Robert. *Masamune Hakuchō*, 148–149.

"Suffocation"
Rolf, Robert. *Masamune Hakuchō*, 78–82.

"Various People"
Rolf, Robert. *Masamune Hakuchō*, 95–96.

"Wasted Effort"
Rolf, Robert. *Masamune Hakuchō*, 69–72.

"Whither?"
Rolf, Robert. *Masamune Hakuchō*, 63–67.

JOHN MATHEUS

"Anthropoi"
Perry, Margaret. *Silence to the Drums* . . ., 116–117.

"Fog"
Perry, Margaret. *Silence to the Drums* . . ., 117–118.

ANTUN GUSTAV MATOŠ

"The Balcony"
Pantzer, Eugene E. *Antun Gustav Matoš*, 35–37.

W. SOMERSET MAUGHAM

"The Colonel's Lady"
Pearson, Carol, and Katherine Pope. *The Female Hero* . . ., 242–243.

"The Letter"
Fink, Guido. "'Smiling Unconcern': Tre racconti di W. S. Maugham," in Lombardo, Agostino, Ed. *Studi inglesi* . . ., 261–280.

"Mackintosh"
Allen, Walter. *The Short Story* . . ., 159–160.

"The Outstation"
Fink, Guido. "'Smiling Unconcern'...," 261-280.

"P & O"
Fink, Guido. "'Smiling Unconcern'...," 261-280.

"Rain" [same as "Sadie Thompson"]
Allen, Walter. *The Short Story...*, 158-159.
Scott, Virgil, and David Madden. *Instructor's Manual...*, 4th ed., 14-16.

"Sanatorium"
Costa, Richard H. "Maugham's 'Partial Self': The 'Unexpected View' on the Way to 'The Death of Ivan Ilych,'" *Coll Engl Assoc Critic*, 43, iv (1981), 3-7.

"The Yellow Streak"
Morgan, Ted. *Maugham*, 295-296.

GUY DE MAUPASSANT

"Christmas Night"
Donaldson-Evans, Mary. "'Nuit de Noël' and 'Conte de Noël': Ironic Diptych in Maupassant's Work," *French R*, 54 (1980), 66-77.

"Darkness"
Morris, D. Hampton. "Variations on a Theme: Five Tales of Horror by Maupassant," *Stud Short Fiction*, 17 (1980), 475-481.

"Don Juan"
Tanabe, Hideki. "Zwei literarische Konfrontationen mit dem 'Don Juan'— Erlebnis: E. T. A. Hoffmanns 'Don Juan' und E. Mörikes Mozart-novelle," *Hitotsubashi*, 22, i (1981), 31-41.

"He"
Morris, D. Hampton. "Variations on a Theme...," 475-481.

"The Horla"
Delabroy, Jean. "Corps inconnaissable," in Gohin, Yves, and Robert Ricatte, Eds. *Recherches en sciences des textes*, 125-134.
Morris, D. Hampton. "Variations on a Theme...," 475-481.
Neefs, Jacques. "La Representation fantastique dans 'Le Horla' de Maupassant," *Cahiers de l'Association Internationale*, 32 (1980), 231-245.
Ziolkowski, Theodore. *Disenchanted Images...*, 190-192.

"The Jewels"
Barker, Gerard A. *Instructor's Manual...*, 28-30.
Maugham, W. Somerset. "The Short Story," in March, Edward, Ed. *Essays by Diverse Hands...*, 124-125.
Reid, Wallis, and Bonny Gildin. "Semantic Analysis Without the Sentence," in Clyne, Paul, William F. Hanks, and Carol L. Hofbauer, Eds. *The Elements...*, 163-174.

"The Lock of Hair"
Morris, D. Hampton. "Variations on a Theme...," 475-481.

"La Mère Sauvage"
Rohrberger, Mary. *Instructor's Manual...*, 11-12.

"The Necklace"
Brooks, Cleanth, and Robert P. Warren. *Instructor's Manual...*, 3rd ed., 16-17.
*_____. *Understanding Fiction*, 3rd ed., 72-74.
Scott, Virgil, and David Madden. *Instructor's Manual...*, 4th ed., 55-57; Madden,
    David. *Instructor's Manual...*, 5th ed., 13-15.
Smith, Elliott L. and Wanda V. *Instructor's Manual...*, 9-10.

"Une Partie de campagne"
Scott, C. "Divergent Paths of Pastoralism: Parallels and Contrasts in Maupassant's
    'Une Partie de compagne' and 'La Femme de Paul,'" *Forum Mod Lang Stud*,
    16 (1980), 270-280.

"Paul's Woman"
Scott, C. "Divergent Paths...," 270-280.

"Story of Christmas"
Donaldson-Evans, Mary. "...Ironic Diptych in Maupassant's Work," 66-77.

"Tallow Ball"
Donaldson-Evans, Mary. "The Decline and Fall of Elisabeth Rousset: Text and
    Context in Maupassant's 'Boule de suif,'" *Australian J French Stud*, 18, i (1981),
    16-34.

FRANÇOIS MAURIAC

"Thérèse Desqueyroux"
Fischler, Alexander. "Thematic Keys in François Mauriac's 'Thérèse Desqueyroux'
    and *Le Noeud de Viperes*," *Mod Lang Q*, 40 (1979), 378-383.

WILLIAM STARBUCK MAYO

"The Astonishing Adventure of James Botello"
Van Dusen, Gerald C. *William Starbuck Mayo*, 86-87.

"The Captain's Story"
Van Dusen, Gerald C. *William Starbuck Mayo*, 74-77.

"Don Sebastian: A Tale from the Chronicles of Portugal"
Van Dusen, Gerald C. *William Starbuck Mayo*, 73-74.

"A Legend of the Cape de Verdes"
Van Dusen, Gerald C. *William Starbuck Mayo*, 81-82.

"The Pious Constancy of Inez de Mencia Mont-Roy"
Van Dusen, Gerald C. *William Starbuck Mayo*, 88–90.

"A Real Pirate"
Van Dusen, Gerald C. *William Starbuck Mayo*, 82–86.

HERMAN MELVILLE

"The Apple-Tree Table"
Breinig, Helmbrecht. "Symbol, Satire, and the Will to Communicate in Melville's 'The Apple-Tree Table,'" *Am Stud*, 22, ii (1977), 269–285.

"Bartleby the Scrivener"
Ahrends, Günter. . . .*Kurzgeschichte*, 92–99.
Allen, Walter. *The Short Story*. . ., 38–39.
Anderson, Walter E. "Form and Meaning in 'Bartleby the Scrivener,'" *Stud Short Fiction*, 18 (1981), 383–399.
Brodwin, Stanley. "To the Frontiers of Eternity: Melville's Crossing in 'Bartleby the Scrivener,'" in Inge, M. Thomas, Ed. *Bartleby the Inscrutable*. . ., 174–196.
*Chase, Richard. "A Parable of the Artist," in Inge, M. Thomas, Ed. *Bartleby the Inscrutable*. . ., 78–83.
Coss, David L. "The Reader in 'Bartleby the Scrivener,'" *Pubs Missouri Philol Assoc*, 5 (1980), 39–43.
*Felheim, Marvin. "Meaning and Structure in 'Bartleby,'" in Inge, M. Thomas, Ed. *Bartleby the Inscrutable*. . ., 114–120.
Hardwick, Elizabeth. "Bartleby and Manhattan," *New York R Books*, 28 (July 16, 1981), 27–31.
*Marcus, Mordecai. "Melville's Bartleby as a Psychological Double," in Inge, M. Thomas, Ed. *Bartleby the Inscrutable*. . ., 107–113.
*Marx, Leo. "Melville's Parable of the Walls," in Inge, M. Thomas, Ed. *Bartleby the Inscrutable*. . ., 84–106.
Miller, Lewis H. "'Bartleby' and the Dead Letter," *Stud Am Fiction*, 8 (1980), 1–12.
Mollinger, Robert N. *Psychoanalysis and Literature*. . ., 85–96.
*Murray, Henry A. "Bartleby and I," in Inge, M. Thomas, Ed. *Bartleby the Inscrutable*. . ., 121–142.
Mushabac, Jane. *Melville's Humor*. . ., 110–120.
Oakland, John. "Romanticism in Melville's 'Bartleby' and *Pierre*," *Moderna Sprak*, 70 (1976), 209–219.
*Oliver, Egbert S. "A Second Look at 'Bartleby,'" in Inge, M. Thomas, Ed. *Bartleby the Inscrutable*. . ., 61–74.
Parker, Hershel. "The 'Sequel' in 'Bartleby,'" in Inge, M. Thomas, Ed. *Bartleby the Inscrutable*. . ., 159–165.
*Patrick, Walton R. "Melville's 'Bartleby' and the Doctrine of Necessity," in Inge, M. Thomas, Ed. *Bartleby the Inscrutable*. . ., 143–158.
Rosenberry, Edward H. *Melville*, 118–120.
Sliver, Alan. "The Lawyer and the Scrivener," *Partisan R*, 48 (1981), 409–424.
Stern, Milton R. "Towards 'Bartleby the Scrivener,'" in MacMillan, Duane J., Ed. *The Stoic Strain*. . ., 19–41.
Wadlington, Warwick. *The Confidence Game*. . ., 113–123.
Wilson, James C. "'Bartleby': The Walls of Wall Street," *Arizona Q*, 37 (1981), 335–346.

"The Bell Tower"
Karcher, Carolyn L. "Melville's 'The Bell-Tower' and 'Benito Cereno': Companion-Pieces on Slavery," *Essays Lit*, 6 (1979), 57-69.
_____. *Shadow over the Promised Land...*, 143-159.

"Benito Cereno"
Allen, Walter. *The Short Story...*, 39-42.
Avasthi, Adiya P. "Point of View in Herman Melville: An Analysis of 'Benito Cereno,'" *J Engl*, 8 (1980), 55-74.
Bakker, J. "Beyond Slavery," *Dutch Q R*, 7 (1977), 128-139.
Bell, Michael D. *...The Sacrifice of Relation*, 214-215.
D'Avanzo, Mario L. "Melville's 'San Dominick' and Ezekiel's Dry Bones," *Coll Lit*, 8 (1981), 186-188.
Dryden, Edgar A. *Melville's Thematics of Form...*, 199-209.
Grenander, M. E. "Melville's 'Benito Cereno,'" *Explicator*, 39, i (1980), 33-34.
Hallab, Mary Y. "Victims of 'Malign Machinations': Irving's *Christopher Columbus* and Melville's 'Benito Cereno,'" *J Narrative Technique*, 9 (1979), 200-202.
Karcher, Carolyn L. "...Companion-Pieces on Slavery," 57-69.
_____. *Shadow over the Promised Land...*, 127-143.
Mushabac, Jane. *Melville's Humor...*, 142-148.
Rosenberry, Edward H. *Melville*, 126-129.
Sundquist, Eric J. "Suspense and Tautology in 'Benito Cereno,'" *Glyph*, 8 (1981), 103-126.
Wadlington, Warwick. *The Confidence Game...*, 125-135.

"Billy Budd"
Aspiz, Harold. "The 'Lurch of the Torpedo-Fish': Electrical Concepts in 'Billy Budd,'" *ESQ: J Am Renaissance*, 26 (1980), 127-136.
Babin, James L. "Melville's 'Billy Budd,'" *Explicator*, 40, i (1981), 30-31.
Berga i Bague, Miquel. "Narrative Point of View in Melville's 'Billy Budd,'" *Anuario del Departamento de Inglés*, [n.v.] (1978), 39-42.
Canaday, Nicholas. "Distortion by History and Legend: The Pessimistic Ending of 'Billy Budd,'" *So Carolina R*, 13, ii (1981), 98-103.
Constantinescu, Ligia. "'Billy Budd': Irony as Double Allegiance," *Anales Ştiinţifice ale Universităţii Iaşi*, 25 (1979), 77-83.
Dryden, Edgar A. *Melville's Thematics of Form...*, 209-216.
Farnham, James F. "Captain Vere's Existential Failure," *Arizona Q*, 37 (1981), 362-370.
Hays, Peter L., and Richard D. Rust. "'Something Healing': Fathers and Sons in 'Billy Budd,'" *Nineteenth-Century Fiction*, 34 (1979), 326-336.
Holstein, Jay A. "The 'Inside' Role of Biblical Allusion in Melville's 'Billy Budd' (an Inside Narrative)," *Rendezvous*, 15, ii (1980), 35-46.
Hutchinson, George B. "The Conflict of Patriarchy and Balanced Sexual Principles in 'Billy Budd,'" *Stud Novel*, 13 (1981), 388-398.
Johnson, Barbara. "Melville's Fist: The Execution of 'Billy Budd,'" *Stud Romanticism*, 18 (1979), 567-599; rpt. in her *The Critical Difference...*, 79-109.
Matheson, Terence J. "A New Look at Melville's Claggart," *Stud Short Fiction*, 17 (1980), 445-453.
Mushabac, Jane. *Melville's Humor...*, 153-158.
Noriguchi, Shinichiro. "The Death of the Three Main Characters in 'Billy Budd,'" *Kyushu Am Lit*, 21 (1980), 8-12.
Rosenberry, Edward H. *Melville*, 101-113.

Rubin, Larry. "'Billy Budd': What Goes on Behind the Closed Door," *Am Imago*, 37 (1980), 65–67.
Scorza, Thomas J. *In the Time Before Steamboats*..., 69–195.
Sheldon, Leslie E. "Melville's 'Billy Budd,'" *Explicator*, 38, ii (1980), 44–46.
Sherrill, Rowland A. *The Prophetic Melville*..., 200–221.
Wadlington, Warwick. *The Confidence Game*..., 170–178.
Wehner, James V. "The Nature of Evil in Melville's 'Billy Budd' and Mann's 'Mario und der Zauberer,'" *Comparatist*, 4 (1980), 31–46.

"Cock-a-Doodle-Doo!"
Recken, Stephen. "Stokering in Tartarus: Melville's 'Cock-a-Doodle-Doo!'" *Stud Am Fiction*, 7, i (1979), 99–107.
Rowland, Beryl. "Melville and the Cock That Crew," *Am Lit*, 52 (1981), 593–606.

"The Encantadas"
Karcher, Carolyn L. *Shadow over the Promised Land*..., 109–120.
Moses, Carole. "Melville's Dark God: Christian Echoes in 'Sketch Nine' of 'The Encantadas,'" *Stud Short Fiction*, 16 (1979), 68–70.
Rosenberry, Edward H. *Melville*, 124–126.
Scheick, William J. *The Half-Breed*..., 59–60.

"The Fiddler"
Rosenberry, Edward H. *Melville*, 116–117.

"I and My Chimney"
Breinig, Helmbracht. "The Symbol of Complexity: 'I and My Chimney' and Its Significance in the Context of Melville's Later Writings," *Anglia*, 98 (1980), 51–67.
Irwin, John T. *American Hieroglyphics*..., 295–297.

"The Lightning-Rod Man"
Attebery, Brian. *The Fantasy Tradition*..., 55–56.
Verbier, Douglas L. "Who Is the Lightning-Rod Man?" *Stud Short Fiction*, 18 (1981), 273–277.

"The Paradise of Bachelors and the Tartarus of Maids"
Karcher, Carolyn L. *Shadow over the Promised Land*..., 120–127.
Mushabac, Jane. *Melville's Humor*..., 120–122.

"The Piazza"
Rosenberry, Edward H. *Melville*, 114–115.

CONRAD FERDINAND MEYER

"The Monk's Wedding"
Matthias, K. "Zwischen Gebundeheit und Freiheit: Die Tragik des Individuums in einer Übergangsepoche — Zur Interpretation von C. F. Meyers 'Die Hochzeit des Mönchs,'" in Thunecke, Jörg, Ed. *Formen Realistischer Erzähl-kunst*..., 179–208.

"Die Richterin"
Plater, Edward M. V. "Alcuin's 'harmlose Fabel' in C. F. Meyer's 'Die Richterin,'"
  Germ Life & Letters, 32 (1979), 318–326.

"The Suffering of a Boy"
Jacobson, Manfred R. "The King and the Court: A Reading of C. F. Meyer's
  'Das Leiden eines Knaben,'" *Seminar*, 15 (1979), 27–38.

PIERRE MILLE

"Barnavaux, général"
Hargreaves, Alec G. *The Colonial Experience. . .*, 140–141.

"Barnavaux, homme d'état"
Hargreaves, Alec G. *The Colonial Experience . . .*, 143–149.

"Les Chinois"
Hargreaves, Alec G. *The Colonial Experience. . .*, 126–129.

"Le Dieu"
Hargreaves, Alec G. *The Colonial Experience. . .*, 130–131.

"L'Evadé"
Hargreaves, Alec G. *The Colonial Experience. . .*, 155–156.

"La Précaution inutile"
Hargreaves, Alec G. *The Colonial Experience. . .*, 141–143.

"Un Prêtre qui pécha"
Hargreaves, Alec G. *The Colonial Experience. . .*, 119–120.

"Le Romancero"
Hargreaves, Alec G. *The Colonial Experience. . .*, 136–139.

HENRY MILLER

"Circe"
Shifreen, Lawrence. "Henry Miller's *Mezzotints*: The Undiscovered Roots of *Tropic
  of Cancer*," *Stud Short Fiction*, 16 (1979), 14–15.

"Dawn Travellers"
Shifreen, Lawrence. "Henry Miller's *Mezzotints. . .*," 12–13.

WALTER M. MILLER

"The Big Hunger"
Samuelson, David M. "The Lost Canticles of Walter M. Miller, Jr.," *Sci Fiction
  Stud*, 3 (1976), 8–9; rpt. Clareson, Thomas D., Ed. *Voices for the Future. . .*,
  II, 63.

"Blood Bank"
Samuelson, David M. "The Lost Canticles...," 13–14; rpt. Clareson, Thomas
D., Ed. *Voices for the Future...*, II, 69–70.

"Check and Checkmate"
Samuelson, David M. "The Lost Canticles...," 6; rpt. Clareson, Thomas D., Ed.
Voices for the Future..., II, 60–61.

"Cold Awakening"
Samuelson, David M. "The Lost Canticles...," 8; rpt. Clareson, Thomas D., Ed.
Voices for the Future..., II, 63.

"Command Performance"
Samuelson, David M. "The Lost Canticles...," 17; rpt. Clareson, Thomas D.,
Ed. *Voices for the Future...*, II, 74.

"Conditionally Human"
Samuelson, David M. "The Lost Canticles...," 17–18; rpt. Clareson, Thomas
D., Ed. *Voices for the Future...*, II, 17–18.

"Crucifixus Etiam"
Samuelson, David M. "The Lost Canticles...," 19–21; rpt. Clareson, Thomas
D., Ed. *Voices for the Future...*, II, 77–79.

"The Darfsteller"
Samuelson, David M. "The Lost Canticles...," in Clareson, David M., Ed. *Voices
for the Future...*, II, 79–81.

"Dark Benediction"
Samuelson, David M. "The Lost Canticles...," 18–19; rpt. Clareson, Thomas
D., Ed. *Voices for the Future...*, II, 76–77.

"Death of a Spaceman" [same as "Memento Homo"]
Samuelson, David M. "The Lost Canticles...," 9; rpt. Clareson, Thomas D., Ed.
Voices for the Future..., II, 63–64.

"Dumb Waiter"
Samuelson, David M. "The Lost Canticles...," in Clareson, Thomas D., Ed. *Voices
for the Future...*, II, 64–65.

"The Hoofer"
Samuelson, David M. "The Lost Canticles...," 9; rpt. Clareson, Thomas D., Ed.
Voices for the Future..., II, 64.

"I Made You"
Samuelson, David M. "The Lost Canticles...," 9–10; rpt. Clareson, Thomas D.,
Ed. *Voices for the Future...*, II, 64.

"It Takes a Thief" [same as "Big Joe and the Nth Generation"]
Samuelson, David M. "The Lost Canticles...," in Clareson, Thomas D., Ed. *Voices
for the Future...*, II, 61.

"No Moon for Me"
Samuelson, David M. "The Lost Canticles...," 8; rpt. Clareson, Thomas D., Ed.
  Voices for the Future..., II, 62–63.

"Please Me Plus Three"
Samuelson, David M. "The Lost Canticles...," 7; rpt. Clareson, Thomas D., Ed.
  Voices for the Future..., II, 61–62.

"Secret of the Death Dome"
Samuelson, David M. "The Lost Canticles...," in Clareson, David M., Ed. *Voices
  for the Future...*, II, 67–68.

"Six and Ten Are Johnny"
Samuelson, David M. "The Lost Canticles...," 11; rpt. Clareson, Thomas D.,
  Ed. *Voices for the Future...*, II, 67.

"The Soul-Empty Ones"
Samuelson, David M. "The Lost Canticles...," 6–7; rpt. Clareson, Thomas D.,
  Ed. *Voices for the Future...*, II, 61.

"The Ties That Bind"
Samuelson, David M. "The Lost Canticles...," 13; rpt. Clareson, Thomas D.,
  Ed. *Voices for the Future...*, II, 68–69.

"The Yokel"
Samuelson, David M. "The Lost Canticles...," 7–8; rpt. Clareson, Thomas D.,
  Ed. *Voices for the Future...*, II, 62.

MISHIMA YUKIO

"Love in the Morning"
Petersen, Gwenn B. *The Moon...*, 236–237.

"Patriotism"
Petersen, Gwenn B. *The Moon...*, 241–245.

"The Priest and His Love"
Petersen, Gwenn B. *The Moon...*, 256–257.

"The Sea and the Sunset"
Petersen, Gwenn B. *The Moon...*, 273–274.

"Seven Bridges"
Petersen, Gwenn B. *The Moon...*, 267–268.

FERENC MOLNÁR

"The Coal Pilferers"
Györgyey, Clara. *Ferenc Molnár*, 55–56.

"The Gnome and the Princess"
Györgyey, Clara. *Ferenc Molnár*, 57-58.

"Music"
Györgyey, Clara. *Ferenc Molnár*, 56-57.

"Princess Olga at the Funeral"
Györgyey, Clara. *Ferenc Molnár*, 60-61.

"The Secret of the Aruwima Forest"
Györgyey, Clara. *Ferenc Molnár*, 50.

JOHN MONTAGUE

"A Change of Management"
Allen, Walter. *The Short Story...*, 391-392.

EUGENE MONTALE

"Butterfly of Dinard"
West, Rebecca J. *Eugene Montale...*, 144-146.

"English Gentleman"
West, Rebecca J. *Eugene Montale...*, 152-153.

BRIAN MOORE

"Grieve for the Dear Departed"
Dahlie, Hallvard. *Brian Moore*, 25-26.

"Lion of the Afternoon"
Dahlie, Hallvard. *Brian Moore*, 27-28.

"Next Thing Was Kansas"
Dahlie, Hallvard. *Brian Moore*, 28-29.

"Off the Track"
Dahlie, Hallvard. *Brian Moore*, 29-30.

"Sassenach"
Dahlie, Hallvard. *Brian Moore*, 24-25.

"The Sight"
Dahlie, Hallvard. *Brian Moore*, 32.

"Uncle T"
Dahlie, Hallvard. *Brian Moore*, 30-31.

C[ATHERINE] L. MOORE

"Shambleau"
Rosinsky, Natalie M. "C. L. Moore's 'Shambleau': Woman as Alien or Alienated Woman?" in Remington, Thomas J., Ed. *Selected Proceedings*..., 68–74.

FRANK MOORHOUSE

"Dell Goes into Politics"
Kiernan, Brian. "Frank Moorhouse: A Retrospective," *Mod Fiction Stud*, 27 (1981), 82–83.

"The Dutch Letter"
Kiernan, Brian. "Frank Moorhouse...," 78.

"The Everlasting Secret Family"
Kiernan, Brian. "Frank Moorhouse...," 80–81.

"Imogene Continued"
Kiernan, Brian. "Frank Moorhouse...," 78–80.

"The Town Philosophers' Banquet"
Kiernan, Brian. "Frank Moorhouse...," 76–77.

MORI ŌGAI

"The Abe Family"
Bowring, Richard J. *Mori Ōgai*..., 202–204.

"Fumizukai"
Bowring, Richard J. *Mori Ōgai*..., 96–97.

"The Last Testament of Okitsu Yagoemon"
Bowring, Richard J. *Mori Ōgai*..., 197–201.

"Ōshio Heihachirō"
Bowring, Richard J. *Mori Ōgai*..., 210–214.

"The Revenge of Gojiingahara"
Bowring, Richard J. *Mori Ōgai*..., 208–210.

"Sahashi Jingorō"
Bowring, Richard J. *Mori Ōgai*..., 205–207.

"Sakai jiken"
Bowring, Richard J. *Mori Ōgai*..., 214–216.

"Tsuge Shirōzaemon"
Bowring, Richard J. *Mori Ōgai*..., 231–232.

EDUARD MÖRIKE

"Mozart on the Way to Prague"
Tanabe, Hideki. "Zwei literarische Konfrontationen mit dem 'Don Juan'– Erlebnis:
   E. T. A. Hoffmanns 'Don Juan' und E. Mörikes Mozart-novelle," *Hitotsubashi*,
   22, i (1981), 31-41.

WILLIAM MORRIS

"Frank's Sealed Letter"
Kirchhoff, Frederick. *William Morris*, 39-40.

"The Ring Given to Venus"
Ziolkowski, Theodore. *Disenchanted Images...*, 57-58.

"The Story of the Glittering Plain"
Kirchhoff, Frederick. *William Morris*, 137-141.

"The Story of the Unknown Church"
Kirchhoff, Frederick. *William Morris*, 34-36.

"The Water of the Wondrous Isles"
Kirchhoff, Frederick. *William Morris*, 155-161.

"The Well at the World's End"
Kirchhoff, Frederick. *William Morris*, 146-155.

"The Wood Beyond the World"
Kirchhoff, Frederick. *William Morris*, 141-145.

WRIGHT MORRIS

"The Ram in the Thicket"
Scott, Virgil, and David Madden. *Instructor's Manual...*, 4th ed., 24-27; Madden,
   David. *Instructor's Manual...*, 5th ed., 28-31.

TONI MORRISON

"1919"
Howard, Daniel F., and John Ribar. *Instructor's Manual...*, 4th ed., 79.

"SEEMOTHERMOTHERISVERYNICE"
Rosinsky, Natalie M. "Mothers and Daughters: Another Minority Group," in
   Davidson, Cathy N., and E. M. Broner, Eds. *The Lost Tradition...*, 281-283.

MOTI NANDY

"Coming to the Town"
Chakravarty, D. K. "Bengali Short Story Today," *Indian Lit*, 21, i (1978), 77.

"The United Front"
Chakravarty, D. K. "Bengali Short Story Today," 77–78.

MARY T. MOTT

"Poor Ah Toy"
Chu, Limin. *The Image of China*..., 207–209.

EZEKIEL MPHAHLELE

"Grieg on a Stolen Piano"
Moore, Gerald. *Twelve African Writers*, 57–58.

"He and the Cat"
Moore, Gerald. *Twelve African Writers*, 53–54.

"The Living and Dead"
Moore, Gerald. *Twelve African Writers*, 55–57.

"Man Must Live"
Moore, Gerald. *Twelve African Writers*, 53.

ALICE MUNRO

"Boys and Girls"
Wallace, Bronwen. "Women's Lives: Alice Munro," in Helwig, David, Ed. *The Human Elements*..., 58–59.

"Material"
Wallace, Bronwen. "Women's Lives...," 59–61.

"The Ottawa Valley"
Wallace, Bronwen. "Women's Lives...," 64–66.

"Tell Me Yes or No"
Wallace, Bronwen. "Women's Lives...," 62–63.

ROBERT MUSIL

"The Blackbird"
Luft, David. *Robert Musil*..., 183–184.
Mauser, Wolfgang. "'Es hat sich eben alles so ereignet': Zu Musils 'Die Amsel,'" in Goeppert, Sebastian, Ed. *Perspektiven*..., 101–123.

"The Enchanted House"
Luft, David. *Robert Musil*..., 91–92.

"Das Fliegenpapier"
Röttger, Brigitte. "Robert Musils 'Das Fliegenpapier': Eine strukturale Analyse anhand der Kategorien Ju. M. Lotmans," in Dietrich, Peter, Ed. *Sub Tua Platano*..., 509–512.

"The Perfection of Love"
Henninger, Peter. "On Literature and Condensation: Robert Musil's Early Nouvelles," *Glyph*, 5 (1979), 116–119.
Luft, David. *Robert Musil*..., 93–95.

"The Portuguese Lady"
Paulson, Ronald M. "A Re-examination and Re-interpretation of Some of the Symbols in Robert Musil's 'Die Portugiesin,'" *Mod Austrian Lit*, 13, ii (1980), 111–120.

"The Temptation of Silent Veronica"
Luft, David. *Robert Musil*..., 91–92.

"Tonka"
Luft, David. *Robert Musil*..., 48–49.
Wucherpfennig, Wolf. "'Tonka' oder die Angst vor Erkenntnis," in Goeppert, Sebastian, Ed. *Perspektiven*..., 233–259.

ALFRED MUSSET

"Les Deux Maîtresses"
Lehtonen, Maija. "'Les Deux Maîtresses' d'Alfred Musset," *Neuphilologische Mitteilungen*, 80 (1979), 209–221.

FRANZ NABL

"The Find"
Holzner, Johann. "Anerkennung und Kritik bürgerlicher Legensformen in Franz Nabls Erzählung 'Der Fund,'" in Bartsch, Kurt, Gerhard Melzer, and Johann Strutz, Eds. *Über Franz Nabl*..., 83–98.

VLADIMIR NABOKOV

"A Guide to Berlin"
Johnson, D. Barton. "A Guide to Nabokov's 'A Guide to Berlin,'" *Slavic & East European J*, 23 (1979), 353–361.

"The Leonardo"
Rohrberger, Mary. *Instructor's Manual*..., 36–37.

"Pnin"
Mizener, Arthur. *A Handbook*..., 4th ed., 135–140.

"Scenes from the Life of a Double Monster"
Pifer, Ellen. "Locating the Monster in Nabokov's 'Scenes from the Life of a Double
Monster," *Stud Am Fiction*, 9 (1981), 97–101.

"Signs and Symbols"
Hagopian, John V. "Decoding Nabokov's 'Signs and Symbols,'" *Stud Short Fiction*,
18 (1981), 115–119.
Rosenzweig, Paul J. "The Importance of Reader Response in Nabokov's 'Signs
and Symbols,'" *Essays Lit*, 7 (1980), 255–260.

"That in Aleppo Once"
Howard, Daniel F., and John Ribar. *Instructor's Manual...*, 4th ed., 51–52.

"Tyrants Destroyed"
Burns, Dan E. "*Bend Sinister* and 'Tyrants Destroyed': Short Story into Novel,"
Mod Fiction Stud, 25 (1979), 510–512.

"The Vane Sisters"
Eggenschwiler, David. "Nabokov's 'The Vane Sisters': Exuberant Pedantry and
a Biter Bit," *Stud Short Fiction*, 18 (1981), 33–39.

YURI NAGIBIN

"The Chase"
Brown, Deming. ...*Literature Since Stalin*, 155–156.

"Chetunov, Son of Chetunov"
Brown, Deming. ...*Literature Since Stalin*, 156–157.

"A Man and a Road"
Brown, Deming. ...*Literature Since Stalin*, 154–155.

R. K. NARAYAN

"A Horse and Two Goats"
Rao, V. Panduranga. "The Craftsmanship of R. K. Narayan," in Mohan, Ramesh,
Ed. *Indian Writing...*, 58–64.

GÉRARD DE NERVAL [GÉRARD LABRUNIE]

"The Golden Ass"
Knapp, Bettina L. *Gérard de Nerval...*, 93–94.

"L'Histoire de la Reine du Matin et de Soliman, des Génies"
Gilbert, Claire. *Nerval's Double...*, 89–99.

"L'Histoire du Calife Hakem"
Gilbert, Claire. *Nerval's Double...*, 46–58.

"The Illuminists"
Knapp, Bettina L. *Gérard de Nerval*..., 185-186.

"The Marquis de Fayolle"
Knapp, Bettina L. *Gérard de Nerval*..., 161-162.

"Le Roi de Bicêtre"
Gilbert, Claire. *Nerval's Double*..., 59-69.

"The Singular Biography of Raoul Spifame"
Knapp, Bettina L. *Gérard de Nerval*..., 69-71.

"Sylvie"
Gasché, Rudolphe. "The Mixture of Genres, the Mixture of Styles, and Figural Interpretation: 'Sylvie' by Gérard de Nerval," *Glyph*, 7 (1980), 102-130.
Gilbert, Claire. *Nerval's Double*..., 100-110.
Padgett, Jacqueline O. "Spirits and Their Bodies: Images of Woman in Nerval's 'Sylvie,'" *Kentucky Romance Q*, 27 (1980), 327-333.

FRANCES NEWMAN

"Rachel and Her Children"
Jones, Anne G. *Tomorrow Is Another Day*..., 280-283.

NGUGI WA THIONG'O

"And the Rain Came Down"
Little, Kenneth. ...*Urban Women's Image*..., 70-71.

"Minutes of Glory"
Little, Kenneth. ...*Urban Women's Image*..., 89-90.

"The Mubenzi Tribesman"
Little, Kenneth. ...*Urban Women's Image*..., 38-39.

ANAÏS NIN

"The All-Seeing"
Balakian, Anna. "The Poetic Reality of Anaïs Nin," in Zaller, Robert, Ed. *A Casebook*..., 120-121.
Franklin, Benjamin, and Duane Schneider. *Anaïs Nin*..., 56-57.

"Birth"
Franklin, Benjamin, and Duane Schneider. *Anaïs Nin*..., 59-60.

"Bread and Wafer"
Franklin, Benjamin, and Duane Schneider. *Anaïs Nin*..., 74-82.
Knapp, Bettina L. *Anaïs Nin*, 107-111.

"Winter of Artifice" [originally titled "Lilith"]
Franklin, Benjamin, and Duane Schneider. *Anaïs Nin...*, 27–33.
Jason, Philip K. "Doubles/Don Juans...," 83–85.
Knapp, Bettina L. *Anaïs Nin*, 77–86.
Kuntz, Paul G. "Art as Public Dream: The Practice and Theory of Anaïs Nin,"
    in Zaller, Robert, Ed. *A Casebook...*, 81–86.

LARRY NIVEN

"Neutron Star"
Nedelkovich, Alexander. "The Stellar Parallels: Robert Silverberg, Larry Niven,
    and Arthur C. Clarke," *Extrapolation*, 21 (1980), 348–360.

FRANK NORRIS

"After Strange Gods"
Chu, Limin. *The Image of China...*, 201–203.

"This Animal of Buldy Jones"
Messenger, Christian. "Frank Norris and the College Sportsman," *Am Lit Realism*,
    12 (1979), 291–292.

"Thoroughbred"
Chu, Limin. *The Image of China...*, 182–184.

"Travis Hallett's Halfback"
Messenger, Christian. "...College Sportsman," 288–291.

LINO NOVÁS CALVO

"'Allies' and 'Germans'"
Souza, Raymond D. *Lino Novás Calvo*, 60–64.

"Angusola and the Knives"
Souza, Raymond D. *Lino Novás Calvo*, 103–104.

"A Bad Man"
Souza, Raymond D. *Lino Novás Calvo*, 72–74.

"Between Neighbors"
Souza, Raymond D. *Lino Novás Calvo*, 81–82.

"A 'Bum'"
Souza, Raymond D. *Lino Novás Calvo*, 102–103.

"The Cow on the Rooftop"
Souza, Raymond D. *Lino Novás Calvo*, 112–116.

"The Dark Night of Ramón Yendía"
Souza, Raymond D. *Lino Novás Calvo*, 64–67.

"Don't Lay a Finger on Him"
Clinton, Stephen. "The Scapegoat Archetype as a Principle of Composition in
    Novás Calvo's 'Un dedo encima,'" *Hispania*, 62, i (1979), 56-61.
Souza, Raymond D. *Lino Novás Calvo*, 67-72.

"Down in Copey"
Souza, Raymond D. *Lino Novás Calvo*, 117-118.

"The Execution of Fernández"
Souza, Raymond D. *Lino Novás Calvo*, 97-98.

"The First Lesson"
Souza, Raymond D. *Lino Novás Calvo*, 75-78.

"The Grandmother Queen and Her Nephew Delfín"
Souza, Raymond D. *Lino Novás Calvo*, 98-99.

"In the Key"
Souza, Raymond D. *Lino Novás Calvo*, 35-39.

"The Invisible Husband"
Souza, Raymond D. *Lino Novás Calvo*, 105-108.

"Long Island"
Souza, Raymond D. *Lino Novás Calvo*, 74-75.

"My Uncle Antón Luna"
Souza, Raymond D. *Lino Novás Calvo*, 110-112.

"The Night the Dead Came out to Haunt Us"
Souza, Raymond D. *Lino Novás Calvo*, 39-44.

"The Ninth Moon"
Souza, Raymond D. *Lino Novás Calvo*, 79-80.

"No One to Kill"
Souza, Raymond D. *Lino Novás Calvo*, 108-109.

"The Oquendo Family"
Souza, Raymond D. *Lino Novás Calvo*, 91-92.

"The Other Key"
Fernandez, Sergio. "Lino Novás Calvo, hechizador de negros," *Universidad*, Nos.
    14-15 (April, 1957), 47-55.

"Palm Key"
Souza, Raymond D. *Lino Novás Calvo*, 87-89.

"The Place That's Calling Me"
Souza, Raymond D. *Lino Novás Calvo*, 93-94.

"The Room for Dying"
Souza, Raymond D. *Lino Novás Calvo*, 92-93.

"A Ruined Man"
Souza, Raymond D. *Lino Novás Calvo*, 18-20.

"The Secret of Narciso Campana"
Souza, Raymond D. *Lino Novás Calvo*, 109-110.

"A Singular Encounter"
Souza, Raymond D. *Lino Novás Calvo*, 21-22.

"The Spiderman"
Souza, Raymond D. *Lino Novás Calvo*, 99-101.

"A Thinking Man"
Souza, Raymond D. *Lino Novás Calvo*, 20-21.

"Tie That Man Down!"
Souza, Raymond D. *Lino Novás Calvo*, 90-91.

"The Vine"
Souza, Raymond D. *Lino Novás Calvo*, 22-27.

"The Vision of Tamaría"
Souza, Raymond D. *Lino Novás Calvo*, 84-87.

"Worse Than a Hell"
Souza, Raymond D. *Lino Novás Calvo*, 103-105.

FLORA NWAPA

"The Child Thief"
Brown, Lloyd W. *Women Writers in Black Africa*, 130-132.

"The Delinquent Adult"
Brown, Lloyd W. *Women Writers in Black Africa*, 132-134.

"Jide's Story"
Brown, Lloyd W. *Women Writers in Black Africa*, 129-130.

"The Loss of Eze"
Brown, Lloyd W. *Women Writers in Black Africa*, 129.

"My Soldier Brother"
Brown, Lloyd W. *Women Writers in Black Africa*, 123-124.

"The Road to Benin"
Brown, Lloyd W. *Women Writers in Black Africa*, 125-126.

"This Is Lagos"
Brown, Lloyd W. *Women Writers in Black Africa*, 124-125.

"The Traveller"
Brown, Lloyd W. *Women Writers in Black Africa*, 126-128.

JOYCE CAROL OATES

"Accomplished Desires"
Altenbernd, Lynn, and Leslie L. Lewis. *Instructor's Manual*. . ., 3rd ed., 44–45.

"& Answers"
Creighton, Joanne V. "Unliberated Women in Joyce Carol Oates's Fiction," *World Lit Written Engl*, 17 (1978), 170–171; rpt. in her *Joyce Carol Oates*, 123–124; Wagner, Linda W., Ed. *Critical Essays on Joyce Carol Oates*, 152–153.

"Angst"
Bender, Eileen T. "Between the Categories: Recent Short Fiction by Joyce Carol Oates," *Stud Short Fiction*, 17 (1980), 416–417.

"Archway"
Creighton, Joanne V. *Joyce Carol Oates*, 35–36.

"Assault"
Bender, Eileen T. "Between the Categories. . .," 421–423.
Mickelson, Anna Z. *Reaching Out*. . ., 18–20.

"Blindfold"
Creighton, Joanne V. *Joyce Carol Oates*, 121–122.

"Bodies"
*Sullivan, Walter. "The Artificial Demon: Joyce Carol Oates and the Dimensions of the Real," in Wagner, Linda W., Ed. *Critical Essays on Joyce Carol Oates*, 79.

"By the North Gate"
Creighton, Joanne V. *Joyce Carol Oates*, 27–29.

"The Census Taker"
Creighton, Joanne V. *Joyce Carol Oates*, 30.
Friedman, Ellen. *Joyce Carol Oates*, 17–20.

"A Descriptive Catalogue"
Creighton, Joanne V. *Joyce Carol Oates*, 130–131.

"Did You Ever Slip on Red Blood?"
*Grant, Mary K. "The Language of Tragedy and Violence," in Wagner, Linda W., Ed. *Critical Essays on Joyce Carol Oates*, 69–70.

"First Views of the Enemy"
Creighton, Joanne V. *Joyce Carol Oates*, 39–40.

"Four Summers"
Cushman, Keith. "A Reading of Joyce Carol Oates's 'Four Summers,'" *Stud Short Fiction*, 18 (1981), 137–146.

"Free"
Grant, Mary K. "The Language of Tragedy. . .," 64–65.

"How I Contemplated the World from the Detroit House of Correction and Began My Life Over Again"
Madden, David. *Instructor's Manual...*, 5th ed., 54–57.
Rohrberger, Mary. *Instructor's Manual...*, 46–47.

"In the Old World"
Creighton, Joanne V. *Joyce Carol Oates*, 29.

"In the Region of Ice"
Creighton, Joanne V. "Joyce Carol Oates's Craftsmanship in *The Wheel of Love*," *Stud Short Fiction*, 15 (1978), 381–383; rpt., with changes, in her *Joyce Carol Oates*, 118–120.
Friedman, Ellen. *Joyce Carol Oates*, 16–17.
Howard, Daniel F., and John Ribar. *Instructor's Manual...*, 4th ed., 88.
Liston, William T. "Her Brother's Keeper," *Southern Hum R*, 11 (1977), 195–203.

"In the Warehouse"
Creighton, Joanne V. *Joyce Carol Oates*, 122–123.

"The Lady with the Pet Dog"
Creighton, Joanne V. *Joyce Carol Oates*, 131–132.

"Loving/Losing/Loving a Man"
Mickelson, Anna Z. *Reaching Out...*, 29–30.

"Magna Mater"
Creighton, Joanne V. *Joyce Carol Oates*, 125–127.

"The Maniac"
Bender, Eileen T. "Between the Categories...," 420–421.

"The Metamorphosis" [originally titled "Others' Dreams"]
Creighton, Joanne V. *Joyce Carol Oates*, 132–133.

"Normal Love"
Allen, Walter. *The Short Story...*, 383–384.

"Norman and the Killer"
Creighton, Joanne V. *Joyce Carol Oates*, 32–34.

"Out of Place"
Mizener, Arthur. *A Handbook...*, 4th ed., 149–152.

"Pastoral Blood"
Creighton, Joanne V. *Joyce Carol Oates*, 31–32.

"Plagiarized Material"
Bender, Eileen T. "Between the Categories...," 417–419.
Creighton, Joanne V. *Joyce Carol Oates*, 139–140.

"Rewards of Fame"
Avant, John A. "*The Hungry Ghosts*," *New Republic*, 171 (August 31, 1974), 30–31; rpt. Wagner, Linda W., Ed. *Critical Essays on Joyce Carol Oates*, 36–37.

"Small Avalanche"
Creighton, Joanne V. *Joyce Carol Oates*, 121-122.

"The Son of God and His Sorrow"
Creighton, Joanne V. *Joyce Carol Oates*, 140-141.

"Stigmata"
Creighton, Joanne V. *Joyce Carol Oates*, 36-37.

"The Survival of Childhood"
Creighton, Joanne V. *Joyce Carol Oates*, 34-35.

"Swamps"
Creighton, Joanne V. *Joyce Carol Oates*, 27-29.

"Sweet Love Remembered"
Creighton, Joanne V. *Joyce Carol Oates*, 29-30.

"Unmailed, Unwritten Letters"
Creighton, Joanne V. "Joyce Carol Oates's Craftsmanship...," 378-379; rpt., with changes, in her *Joyce Carol Oates*, 115-116.

"Upon the Sweeping Flood"
Ahrends, Günter. ...*Kurzgeschichte*, 181-183.
Creighton, Joanne V. *Joyce Carol Oates*, 37-38.

"Waiting"
Allen, Walter. *The Short Story*..., 385-387.
Creighton, Joanne V. *Joyce Carol Oates*, 124-125.

"What Is the Connection Between Men and Women?"
Creighton, Joanne V. "Joyce Carol Oates's Craftsmanship...," 379-380; rpt. in her *Joyce Carol Oates*, 116-117.

"Where Are You Going, Where Have You Been?"
Creighton, Joanne V. "Joyce Carol Oates's Craftsmanship...," 380-381, 383; rpt., with changes, in her *Joyce Carol Oates*, 117-118.
Friedman, Ellen. *Joyce Carol Oates*, 10-13.
Gillis, Christina M. "'Where Are You Going, Where Have You Been?': Seduction, Space, and a Fictional Mode," *Stud Short Fiction*, 18 (1981), 65-70.
Harty, Kevin J. "Archetype and Popular Lyric in Joyce Carol Oates' 'Where Are You Going, Where Have You Been?'" *Pennsylvania Engl* , 8, i (1980-81), 26-28.
Male, Roy R. ...*Cloistral Fiction*, 71-72.
*Sullivan, Walter. "The Artificial Demon...," 77-78.
Wegs, Joyce M. "'Don't You Know Who I Am?': The Grotesque in Oates's 'Where Are You Going, Where Have You Been?'" *J Narrative Technique*, 5 (1975), 66-72; rpt. Wagner, Linda W., Ed. *Critical Essays on Joyce Carol Oates*, 87-92.
Winslow, Joan D. "The Stranger Within: Two Stories by Oates and Hawthorne," *Stud Short Fiction*, 17 (1980), 263-268.

"Where I Live and What I Live For"
Creighton, Joanne V. *Joyce Carol Oates*, 133-134.

"Wild Saturday"
*Sullivan, Walter. "The Artificial Demon...," 78–79.

"You"
*Sullivan, Walter. "The Artificial Demon...," 80–81.

PADRAIC O'CONAIRE

"Paidin Mhaire"
Murphy, Maureen. "The Short Story in Irish," *Mosaic*, 12, iii (1979), 84.

"The Woman on Whom God Put His Hand"
Murphy, Maureen. "The Short Story in Irish," 85.

"The Woman Who Was Made to Suffer"
Murphy, Maureen. "The Short Story in Irish," 84–85.

FLANNERY O'CONNOR

"The Artificial Nigger"
Kahane, Claire. "The Artificial Nigger," *Massachusetts R*, 19 (1978), 183–186.
*Mizener, Arthur. *A Handbook...*, 4th ed., 40–42.
Nisly, Paul W. "The Prison of the Self: Isolation in Flannery O'Connor's Fiction,"
     Stud Short Fiction, 17 (1980), 51–54.
Shloss, Carol. ...*Limits of Inference*, 118–123.

"A Circle in the Fire"
Shloss, Carol. ...*Limits of Inference*, 49–54.
Tedford, Barbara W. "Flannery O'Connor and the Social Classes," *Southern Lit
     J*, 13, ii (1981), 37–39.
Young, Thomas D. *The Past in the Present...*, 133–135.

"The Displaced Person"
Coles, Robert. *Flannery O'Connor's South*, 14–32.
Cox, James M. "On Flannery O'Connor and 'The Displaced Person,'" in Skaggs,
     Calvin, Ed. *The American Short Story*, I, 338–344.
Kahane, Claire. "The Artificial Nigger," 187–192.
Male, Roy R. ...*Cloistral Fiction*, 101–112.
Shloss, Carol. ...*Limits of Inference*, 74–79.
Tedford, Barbara W. "Flannery O'Connor...," 36–37.

"The Enduring Chill"
Kahane, Claire. "The Artificial Nigger," 186–187.
Tedford, Barbara W. "Flannery O'Connor...," 33.

"Everything That Rises Must Converge"
Altenbernd, Lynn, and Leslie L. Lewis. *Instructor's Manual...*, 3rd ed., 46–47.
Coles, Robert. *Flannery O'Connor's South*, 32–43.
Kahane, Claire. "The Artificial Nigger," 192–193.
Rohrberger, Mary. *Instructor's Manual...*, 31.

"The Geranium"
Kahane, Claire. "The Artificial Nigger," 193-196.

"Good Country People"
Allen, Walter. *The Short Story*..., 324-325.
Chew, Martha. "Flannery O'Connor's Double-Edged Satire: The Idiot Daughter
   versus the Lady Ph.D.," *Southern Q*, 19, ii (1981), 17-25.
Howard, Daniel F., and William Plummer. *Instructor's Manual*..., 3rd ed., 72;
   rpt. Howard, Daniel F., and John Ribar. *Instructor's Manual*..., 4th ed., 74.
Male, Roy R. ...*Cloistral Fiction*, 70-71.
Nisly, Paul W. "Wart Hogs from Hell: The Demonic and the Holy in Flannery
   O'Connor's Fiction," *Ball State Univ Forum*, 22, iii (1981), 45-50.
Orevicz, Cheryl Z. "Seduced by Language: The Case of Joy-Hulga Hopewell,"
   Stud Am Fiction, 7 (1979), 221-228.
Scott, Virgil, and David Madden. *Instructor's Manual*..., 4th ed., 29-31; Madden,
   David. *Instructor's Manual*..., 5th ed., 31-33.
Shloss, Carol. ...*Limits of Inference*, 42-48.
Young, Thomas D. *The Past in the Present*..., 123-125.

"A Good Man Is Hard to Find"
Ahrends, Günter. ...*Kurzgeschichte*, 176-179.
Allen, Walter. *The Short Story*..., 326-328.
Brooks, Cleanth, and Robert P. Warren. *Instructor's Manual*..., 3rd ed., 42-45.
Bryant, Hallman B. "Reading the Map in 'A Good Man Is Hard to Find,'" *Stud
   Short Fiction*, 18 (1981), 301-307.
Cobb, Joann P. "Pascal's Wager and Two Modern Losers," *Philosophy & Lit*, 3
   (1979), 192-195.
Coles, Robert. *Flannery O'Connor's South*, 119-122.
Kaplan, Carola. "Graham Greene's Pinkie Brown and Flannery O'Connor's Misfit:
   The Psychopathic Killer and the Mystery of God's Grace," *Renascence*, 32
   (1980), 116-128.
Montgomery, Marion. *Why Flannery O'Connor Stayed Home*, 129-130.

"Greenleaf"
Koon, William. "'Hep Me Not to Be So Mean': Flannery O'Connor's Subjectivity,"
   Southern R, 15 (1979), 324-325.
Rout, Kathleen. "Dream a Little Dream of Me: Mrs. May and the Bull in
   Flannery O'Connor's 'Greenleaf,'" *Stud Short Fiction*, 16 (1979), 233-235.
Ryan, Steven T. "The Three Realms of O'Connor's 'Greenleaf,'" *Christianity &
   Lit*, 29, i (1979), 39-51.
Shields, John C. "Flannery O'Connor's 'Greenleaf' and the Myth of Europa and
   the Bull," *Stud Short Fiction*, 18 (1981), 421-431.
Shloss, Carol. ...*Limits of Inference*, 65-73.

"Judgement Day"
Nisly, Paul W. "Wart Hogs...," 45-50.
Tolomeo, Diane. "Home to Her True Country: The Final Trilogy of Flannery
   O'Connor," *Stud Short Fiction*, 17 (1980), 339-340.

"The Life You Save May Be Your Own"
Chew, Martha. "Flannery O'Connor's Double-Edged Satire...," 17-25.
Koon, William. "'Hep Me Not to Be So Mean'...," 325.

"Parker's Back"
Coles, Robert. *Flannery O'Connor's South*, 88–93.
Napier, James J. "In 'Parker's Back': A Technical Slip by Flannery O'Connor," *Notes Contemp Lit*, 11, iv (1981), 5–6.
Shloss, Carol. . . . *Limits of Inference*, 113–118.
Slattery, Dennis P. "Faith in Search of an Image: The Iconic Dimension of Flannery O'Connor's 'Parker's Back,'" *So Central Bull*, 41 (1981), 120–123.
Tolomeo, Diane. "Home to Her True Country. . .," 337–338.

"Revelation"
Kennedy, X. J. *Instructor's Manual*. . ., 2nd ed., 22–23.
Napier, James J. "The Cave-Waiting Room in O'Connor's 'Revelation,'" *Notes Mod Am Lit*, 5, iv (1981), Item 23.
Nisly, Paul W. "Wart Hogs. . .," 45–50.
Shloss, Carol. . . . *Limits of Inference*, 109–113.
Tedford, Barbara W. "Flannery O'Connor. . .," 31–32.
Tolomeo, Diane. "Home to Her True Country. . .," 336–337.

"The River"
Browning, Preston M. "Flannery O'Connor's Devil Revisited," *Southern Hum R*, 10 (1976), 325–326.
Magliola, Robert. "Grounds and Common(s), and a Heideggerian Recension," *Papers Lang & Lit*, 17 (1981), 80–87.
Young, Thomas D. *The Past in the Present*. . ., 129–131.

"A Stroke of Good Fortune"
McDermott, John V. "O'Connor's 'A Stroke of Good Fortune,'" *Explicator*, 38, iv (1980), 13–14.
Mayer, Charles W. "The Comic Spirit in 'A Stroke of Good Fortune,'" *Stud Short Fiction*, 16 (1979), 70–74.

"A Temple of the Holy Ghost"
Allen, Suzanne. "Memoirs of a Southern Catholic Girlhood: Flannery O'Connor's 'A Temple of the Holy Ghost,'" *Renascence*, 31 (1979), 83–92.
Kahane, Claire. "Gothic Mirrors and Feminine Identity," *Centennial R*, 24 (1980), 61–63.
Young, Thomas D. *The Past in the Present*. . ., 126–129.

"A View of the Woods"
Riso, Don. "Blood and Land in 'A View of the Woods,'" *New Orleans R*, 1 (1979), 255–257.

FRANK O'CONNOR [MICHAEL FRANCIS O'DONOVAN]

"The Bridal Night"
Sherry, Ruth. "Frank O'Connor and Gaelic Ireland," in Drudy, P. J., Ed. *Irish Studies*, I, 44–46.

"The Drunkard"
*Brooks, Cleanth, and Robert P. Warren. *Understanding Fiction*, 3rd ed., 150–152.
Tomory, William M. *Frank O'Connor*, 126–127.

"First Confession"
Scott, Virgil, and David Madden. *Instructor's Manual*..., 4th ed., 36-38; Madden,
    David. *Instructor's Manual*..., 5th ed., 41-42.
Smith, Elliott L., and Andrew W. Hart, Eds. *The Short Story*..., 177-179.

"The Holy Door"
Allen, Walter. *The Short Story*..., 217-218.
Tomory, William M. *Frank O'Connor*, 105-106.

"In the Train"
Sherry, Ruth. "Frank O'Connor...," 43-44.

"Judas"
Rohrberger, Mary. *Instructor's Manual*..., 26-27.
Tomory, William M. *Frank O'Connor*, 124-126.

"The Long Road to Ummera"
Tomory, William M. *Frank O'Connor*, 97-98.

"The Mad Lomasneys"
Tomory, William M. *Frank O'Connor*, 102-104.

"The Majesty of the Law"
Sherry, Ruth. "Frank O'Connor...," 42-43.
Tomory, William M. *Frank O'Connor*, 91.

"Michael's Wife"
Tomory, William M. *Frank O'Connor*, 90-91.

"The Miser"
Tomory, William M. *Frank O'Connor*, 98-99.

"A Mother's Warning"
Tomory, William M. *Frank O'Connor*, 119-120.

"My Oedipus Complex"
Altenbernd, Lynn, and Leslie L. Lewis. *Instructor's Manual*..., 3rd ed., 48.
*Mizener, Arthur. *A Handbook*..., 4th ed., 32-34.
Tomory, William M. *Frank O'Connor*, 130-131.

"The New Teacher"
Tomory, William M. *Frank O'Connor*, 96-97.

"News for the Church"
Tomory, William M. *Frank O'Connor*, 116.

"The Patriarch"
Sherry, Ruth. "Frank O'Connor...," 38-39.

"Peasants"
Sherry, Ruth. "Frank O'Connor...," 39-41.

"A Romantic" [in *Bones of Contention*]
Tomory, William M. *Frank O'Connor*, 92-94.

"A Romantic" [in *More Stories*]
Tomory, William M. *Frank O'Connor*, 108-109.

"September Dawn"
Tomory, William M. *Frank O'Connor*, 32.

"The Star That Bids the Shepherd Fold"
Tomory, William M. *Frank O'Connor*, 115-117.

"The Teacher's Mass"
Tomory, William M. *Frank O'Connor*, 120-121.

"Uprooted"
Sherry, Ruth. "Frank O'Connor...," 46-48.
Tomory, William M. *Frank O'Connor*, 99-100.

SEAN O'FAOLAIN

"The Kitchen"
Bonaccorso, Richard. "Sean O'Faolain's *Foreign Affair*," *Éire*, 16, ii (1981), 143-144.

"Lovers at the Lake"
Allen, Walter. *The Short Story*..., 215-216.

"The Man Who Invented Sin"
Allen, Walter. *The Short Story*..., 214-215.

"Murder at Cobbler's Hulk"
Bonaccorso, Richard. "...*Foreign Affair*," 141.

"Up the Bare Stairs"
Bonaccorso, Richard. "...*Foreign Affair*," 142-143.

LIAM O'FLAHERTY

"Going into Exile"
Allen, Walter. *The Short Story*..., 211-213.

GRACE OGOT

"Elizabeth"
Conde, Maryse. "Three Female Writers in Modern Africa: Flora Nwapa, Ama Ata Aidoo, and Grace Ogot," *Présence Africaine*, No. 82 (1972), 142.
Little, Kenneth. ...*Urban Women's Image*..., 115-116.

"The Honourable Minister"
Little, Kenneth. . . . *Urban Women's Image*. . . , 25–27.

"The Old White Witch"
Brown, Lloyd W. *Women Writers in Black Africa*, 28–29.
Conde, Maryse. "Three Female Writers. . . ," 140–141.

"The Other Woman"
Little, Kenneth. . . . *Urban Women's Image*. . . , 42–44.

"The White Veil"
Brown, Lloyd W. *Women Writers in Black Africa*, 30.
Conde, Maryse. "Three Female Writers. . . ," 141–142.
Little, Kenneth. . . . *Urban Women's Image*. . . , 24–25.

JOHN O'HARA

"Andreas"
Walker, Nancy. "'All that you need to know': John O'Hara's Achievement in the
Novella," *John O'Hara J*, 4, i (1981), 73–74.

"A Case History"
Walker, Nancy. ". . . Achievement in the Novella," 68–69.

"The Doctor's Son"
Allen, Walter. *The Short Story*. . . , 245–246.

"The Engineer"
Walker, Nancy. ". . . Achievement in the Novella," 64.

"A Few Trips and Some Poetry"
Walker, Nancy. ". . . Achievement in the Novella," 76–78.

"The Girl on the Baggage Truck"
Walker, Nancy. ". . . Achievement in the Novella," 66.

"Imagine Kissing Pete"
Walker, Nancy. ". . . Achievement in the Novella," 66–67.

"James Francis and the Star"
Walker, Nancy. ". . . Achievement in the Novella," 74–76.

"Nineteen Minutes Away"
Walker, Nancy. ". . . Achievement in the Novella," 63–64.

"Pat Collins"
Allen, Walter. *The Short Story*. . . , 247–248.
Walker, Nancy. ". . . Achievement in the Novella," 69–71.

"The Skeleton"
Walker, Nancy. ". . . Achievement in the Novella," 71–72.

"We're Friends Again"
Walker, Nancy. ". . .Achievement in the Novella," 67.

O. HENRY [WILLIAM SYDNEY PORTER]

"The Furnished Room"
*Brooks, Cleanth, and Robert P. Warren. *Understanding Fiction*, 3rd ed., 43–46.

"The Shamrock and the Palm"
McCreery, David J. "Imitating Life: O. Henry's 'The Shamrock and the Palm,'"
  Mississippi Q, 34 (1981), 113–121.

"While the Auto Waits"
Allen, Walter. *The Short Story. . .*, 59–60.

SEAMUS O'KELLY

"The Weaver's Grave"
Clune, Anne. "Seamus O'Kelly," in Rafroidi, Patrick, and Terence Brown, Eds.
  The Irish Short Story, 151–154.
Norris, David. "Imaginative Response versus Authority Structures: A Theme of
  the Anglo-Irish Short Story," in Rafroidi, Patrick, and Terence Brown, Eds.
  The Irish Short Story, 52–54.

DIANE OLIVER

"Neighbors"
*Mizener, Arthur. *A Handbook. . .*, 4th ed., 28–30.

TILLIE OLSEN

"I Stand Here Ironing"
Frye, Joanna S. "'I Stand Here Ironing': Motherhood as Experience and Meta-
  phor," *Stud Short Fiction*, 18 (1981), 287–292.
Howard, Daniel F., and John Ribar. *Instructor's Manual. . .*, 4th ed., 60.

"O Yes"
Bernikow, Louise. *Among Women*, 264–265.

"Tell Me a Riddle"
Howard, Daniel F., and John Ribar. *Instructor's Manual. . .*, 4th ed., 59.
Pearson, Carol, and Katherine Pope. *The Female Hero. . .*, 44–45.

JUAN CARLOS ONETTI

"Avenida de Mayo"
Diez, Luis A. "'Avenida de Mayo' y 'El posible Baldi': Dos varaciones onettianas
sobre el tema 'The Man of the Crowd' de Edgar Allan Poe," in Minc, Rose
S., Ed. *Latin American Fiction Today*, 93-96.

"Jacob y el otro"
Guyman, Matthew. "Tangled Trails: In the Footsteps of Juan Carlos Onetti:
Meditations on His Short Story 'Jacob y el otro,'" *Papers in Romance*, 3, i
(1981), 35-45.

"El posible Baldi"
Diez, Luis A. "'Avenida de Mayo' y 'El posible Baldi': Dos varaciones. . . ," 96-98.

OLIVER ONIONS

"The Beckoning Fair One"
Briggs, Julia. *Night Visitors. . .*, 161.
Sullivan, Jack. *Elegant Nightmares. . .*, 133-134.

AMOS OZ

"Lands of the Jackal"
Yudkin, Leon I. "The Jackal and the Other Place: The Stories of Amos Oz,"
J Semitic Stud, 23 (1978), 331-332.

"Late Love"
Yudkin, Leon I. "The Jackal. . . ," 335.

"My Michael"
Yudkin, Leon I. "The Jackal. . . ," 333.

"The Nomad and the Viper"
Yudkin, Leon I. "The Jackal. . . ," 332-333.

"Repair of the World"
Yudkin, Leon I. "The Jackal. . . ," 334-335.

CYNTHIA OZICK

"The Suitcase"
Bernikow, Louise. *Among Women*, 265-267.

JOSÉ EMILIO PACHECO

"El castillo en la aguja"
Prada Oropeza, Renato, *et al.* [9]. "Análisis semiótico de 'El castillo en la aguja'
de José Emilio Pacheco," *Semiosis*, 1 (July-December, 1978), 5-20.

THOMAS NELSON PAGE

"Marse Chan"
Ridgely, J. V. *Nineteenth-Century Southern Literature*, 96–98.

PAI HSIEN-YUNG

"Lament for Bygone Days"
Ou-yang Tzu. "The Fictional World of Pai Hsien-yung," in Faurot, Jeannette L.,
Ed. *Chinese Fiction from Taiwan...*, 173–174.

GRACE PALEY

"A Conversation with My Father"
DeKouven, Marianne. "Mrs. Hegel-Shtein's Tears," *Partisan R*, 48 (1981), 217–220.
Howard, Daniel F., and John Ribar. *Instructor's Manual...*, 4th ed., 71.

"Distance"
Mickelson, Anna Z. *Reaching Out...*, 226–227.

"Enormous Changes at the Last Minute"
Howard, Daniel F., and John Ribar. *Instructor's Manual...*, 4th ed., 72.

"Faith in the Afternoon"
DeKouven, Marianne. "Mrs. Hegel-Shtein's Tears," 220–222.

"The Immigrant Story"
Mickelson, Anna Z. *Reaching Out...*, 223–224.

"A Long Distance Runner"
Crawford, John W. "Archetypal Patterns in Grace Paley's 'Runner,'" *Notes Contemp Lit*, 11, iv (1981), 10–12.

"The Loudest Voice"
Smith, Elliott L. and Wanda V. *Instructor's Manual...*, 5.

"Wants"
Mickelson, Anna Z. *Reaching Out...*, 231–232.

EMILIA PARDO BAZÁN

"La dama joven"
Charnon-Deutsch, Lou. "Naturalism in the Short Fiction of Emilia Pardo Bazán," *Hispanic J*, 3, i (1981), 80–82.

"Náufragas"
Charnon-Deutsch, Lou. "Naturalism...," 77–78.

"La niña martir"
Charnon-Deutsch, Lou. "Naturalism...," 76–77.

DOROTHY PARKER

"But the One on the Right"
Smith, Elliott L., and Andrew W. Hart, Eds. *The Short Story*..., 164–166.

JOAQUÍN PASOS

"The Poor Angel"
Borgeson, Paul W. "Los pobres ángeles de Gabriel García Márquez y Joaquín
Pasos," *Critica Hispánica*, 3 (1981), 111–123.

R. J. PEARSALL

"The Revelation"
Chu, Limin. *The Image of China*..., 168–169.

Y. L. PERETZ [ITZHAK L. PERETZ]

"The Apron"
Adler, Ruth. *Women of the Shtetl*..., 108.

"The Defense of the Accused"
Adler, Ruth. *Women of the Shtetl*..., 66–67.

"An Informer"
Adler, Ruth. *Women of the Shtetl*..., 54.

"The Love Affair"
Adler, Ruth. *Women of the Shtetl*..., 74–75.

"The Mental Ward"
Adler, Ruth. *Women of the Shtetl*..., 45–46.

"The Messenger"
Adler, Ruth. *Women of the Shtetl*..., 44–45.

"The Mute"
Adler, Ruth. *Women of the Shtetl*..., 85–86.

"A Night of Terror"
Adler, Ruth. *Women of the Shtetl*..., 75–76.

"No Luck"
Adler, Ruth. *Women of the Shtetl*..., 101.

"A Question"
Adler, Ruth. *Women of the Shtetl*..., 62–63.

"The Reader"
Adler, Ruth. *Women of the Shtetl*..., 109–110.

"The Shtaymil"
Adler, Ruth. *Women of the Shtetl...*, 50–51.

"The Sick Boy"
Adler, Ruth. *Women of the Shtetl...*, 92–93.

"A Strange Being"
Adler, Ruth. *Women of the Shtetl...*, 86–87.

"The Trust" [same as "Seven Years of Plenty"]
Adler, Ruth. *Women of the Shtetl...*, 63–64.

"The Woman Mrs. Hannah"
Adler, Ruth. *Women of the Shtetl...*, 35–36.

"A Woman's Wrath"
Adler, Ruth. *Women of the Shtetl...*, 38–39.

HARRY MARK PETRAKIS

"The Wooing of Ariadne"
Smith, Elliott L. and Wanda V. *Instructor's Manual...*, 15.

ANN PETRY

"The Witness"
Madden, David. "Ann Petry: 'The Witness,'" *Stud Black Lit*, 6, iii (1975), 24–26;
  rpt. Scott, Virgil, and David Madden. *Instructor's Manual...*, 4th ed., 121–124;
  Madden, David. *Instructor's Manual...*, 5th ed., 107–109.

ELIZABETH STUART PHELPS

"An Angel over the Right Shoulder"
Pearson, Carol, and Katherine Pope. *The Female Hero...*, 42–43.

PI-I-HUNG

"Children after Divorce"
Link, E. Perry. *Mandarin Ducks...*, 224–225.

ALBERT PIKE

"A Mexican Tale"
Robinson, Cecil. *Mexico...*, 128–129.

BORIS PIL'NYAK

"Krasnoye derevo"
Falchikov, Michael. "Rerouting the Train of Time — Boris Pil'nyak's 'Karasnoye derevo,'" *Mod Lang R*, 75 (1980), 138-147.

LUIGI PIRANDELLO

"The Doctor's Duty"
Licastro, Emanuele. "The Theme of Escape in Luigi Pirandello's Short Stories," *Paideia*, 6 (1979), 51.

"The Epistle Singer"
Licastro, Emanuele. "The Theme of Escape...," 46.

"Horse in the Moon"
Rohrberger, Mary. *Instructor's Manual...*, 16-17.

"I Have So Much to Tell You"
Licastro, Emanuele. "The Theme of Escape...," 44.

"If. . ."
Licastro, Emanuele. "The Theme of Escape...," 45.

"The Journey" [same as "The Trip"]
Licastro, Emanuele. "The Theme of Escape...," 50.

"Let's Burn the Hay"
Licastro, Emanuele. "The Theme of Escape...," 47.

"Let's Not Think About It Any More"
Licastro, Emanuele. "The Theme of Escape...," 44-45.

"The Light of the Other House"
Licastro, Emanuele. "The Theme of Escape...," 53.

"Near Death"
Licastro, Emanuele. "The Theme of Escape...," 50-51.

"The Readied Room"
Licastro, Emanuele. "The Theme of Escape...," 49.

"The Stuffed Bird" [same as "The Straw Bird"]
Licastro, Emanuele. "The Theme of Escape...," 51-52.

"The Train Has Whistled"
Licastro, Emanuele. "The Theme of Escape...," 48.

"The Truth"
Licastro, Emanuele. "The Theme of Escape...," 52-53.

"War"
*Brooks, Cleanth, and Robert P. Warren. *Understanding Fiction*, 3rd ed., 77-80.

"The Wheelbarrow"
Licastro, Emanuele. "The Theme of Escape...," 48-49.

WILLIAM PLOMER

"Ula Masonda"
Allen, Walter. *The Short Story*..., 233-235.

"When the Sardines Came"
Allen, Walter. *The Short Story*..., 231-233.

EDGAR ALLAN POE

"The Assignation"
Bell, Michael D. ... *The Sacrifice of Relation*, 122-123.
Bickman, Martin. *The Unsounded Centre*..., 63-67.
Pitcher, Edward W. "Poe's 'The Assignation': A Reconsideration," *Poe Stud*, 13,
    i (1980), 1-4.

"Berenice"
Blythe, Hal, and Charlie Sweet. "Poe's Satiric Use of Vampirism in 'Berenice,'"
    Poe Stud, 14 (1981), 21-22.
Phillips, Elizabeth. *Edgar Allan Poe*..., 116-120.

"The Black Cat"
Brooke-Rose, Christine. "The Readerhood of Man," in Suleiman, Susan, and Inge
    Crossman, Eds. *The Reader in the Text*..., 135-141.
_____. *A Rhetoric*..., 117-122.
McElroy, John H. "The Kindred Artist; or, The Case of the Black Cat," *Stud
    Am Humor*, 3, ii (1976), 103-117.
Madden, David. *Instructor's Manual*..., 5th ed., 49-50.
Phillips, Elizabeth. *Edgar Allan Poe*..., 131-136.

"The Cask of Amontillado"
Jacoby, Jay. "Fortunato's Premature Demise in 'The Cask of Amontillado,'" *Poe
    Stud*, 12 (1979), 30-31.
Kozikowski, Stanley J. "A Reconsideration of Poe's 'The Cask of Amontillado,'"
    Am Transcendental Q, 39 (1978), 269-280.
Spisak, James W. "Narration as Seduction, Seduction as Narration," *Coll Engl Assoc
    Critic*, 16, ii (1979), 26-29.

"A Descent into the Maelström"
Engel, Leonard W. "Edgar Allan Poe's Use of the Enclosure Device in 'A Descent
    into the Maelström,'" *Essays Arts & Sciences*, 8 (1979), 21-26.
Irwin, John T. *American Hieroglyphics*..., 66-69.

"The Domain of Arnheim"
Horn, Andrew. "'A Refined Thebiad': Wealth and Social Disengagement in Poe's
'The Domain of Arnheim,'" *ESQ: J Am Renaissance*, 27, iv (1981), 191–197.

"The Fall of the House of Usher"
Ahrends, Günter. *. . . Kurzgeschichte*, 84–89.
Allen, Walter. *The Short Story. . .*, 25–29.
Attebery, Brian. *The Fantasy Tradition. . .*, 38–41.
Bell, Michael D. *. . . The Sacrifice of Relation*, 108–112.
Fisher, Benjamin F. "Playful 'Germanism' in 'The Fall of the House of Usher':
    The Storyteller's Art," in Thompson, G. R., and Virgil L. Lokke, Eds. *Ruined
    Eden. . .*, 355–374.
Frank, Frederick S. "Poe's House of the Seven Gothics: The Fall of the Narrator
    in 'The Fall of the House of Usher,'" *Orbis Litterarum*, 34 (1979), 331–351.
Hermann, Claudine, and Nicholas Kostis. "'The Fall of the House of Usher' or
    the Art of Duplication," *Sub-Stance*, No. 26 (1980), 36–42.
Matheson, Terence J. "Fatalism in 'The Fall of the House of Usher,'" *Engl Stud
    Canada*, 6 (1980), 421–429.
Mollinger, Robert N. *Psychoanalysis and Literature. . .*, 73–84.
Phillips, Elizabeth. *Edgar Allan Poe. . .*, 120–126.
Quinn, Patrick F. "A Misreading of Poe's 'The Fall of the House of Usher,'" in
    Thompson, G. R., and Virgil L. Lokke, Eds. *Ruined Eden. . .*, 303–312.
––––––. "'Usher' Again: Trust the Teller!" in Thompson, G. R., and Virgil L.
    Lokke, Eds. *Ruined Eden. . .*, 341–353.
Ricardou, Jean. "The Story Within the Story," trans. Joseph Kestner, *James Joyce
    Q*, 18 (1981), 324–327.
Saliba, David R. "Usher's Narrator Veiled," *Poe Stud*, 14, ii (1981), 31.
Sharp, Roberta. "Usher and Rosicrucianism: Speculation," *Poe Stud*, 12 (1979),
    34–35.
Simpson, Lewis P. *The Brazen Face. . .*, 99–102.
Stoehr, Taylor. "'Unspeakable Horror' in Poe," *So Atlantic Q*, 78 (1979), 324–328.
Thompson, G. R. "Poe and the Paradox of Terror: Structures of Heightened
    Consciousness in 'The Fall of the House of Usher,'" in Thompson, G. R.,
    and Virgil L. Lokke, Eds. *Ruined Eden. . .*, 313–340.

"The Gold Bug"
Hennelly, Mark M. "Le Grand Captain Kidder and His Bogus Bug," *Stud Short
    Fiction*, 17 (1980), 77–79.
Irwin, John T. *American Hieroglyphics. . .*, 56–57.
Krumme, Peter. *Augenblicke. . .*, 38–41.

"Hop-Frog"
MacAndrew, Elizabeth. *The Gothic Tradition. . .*, 169–170.

"The Imp of the Perverse"
Spanier, Sandra W. "'Nests of Boxes': Form, Sense, and Style in Poe's 'The Imp
    of the Perverse,'" *Stud Short Fiction*, 17 (1980), 307–316.

"Ligeia"
Bennett, Maurice J. "'The Madness of Art': Poe's 'Ligeia' as Metafiction," *Poe
    Stud*, 14, i (1981), 1–6.
Bickman, Martin. *The Unsounded Centre. . .*, 74–79.

Byers, John R. "The Opium Chronology of Poe's 'Ligeia,'" *So Atlantic Bull*, 45, i (1980), 40–46.

Heller, Terry. "Poe's 'Ligeia' and the Pleasures of Terror," *Gothic*, 2, ii (1980), 39–49.

Lewis, Paul. "The Intellectual Function of Gothic Fiction: Poe's 'Ligeia' and Tieck's 'Wake Not the Dead,'" *Comp Lit Stud*, 16 (1979), 211–214.

Richard, Claude. "'L' ou l'indicibilité de Dieux: Une Lecture de 'Ligeia,'" *Delta*, 12 (April, 1981), 11–34.

Saliba, David R. "The Nightmare in Miniature: 'Ligeia,'" *Am Transcendental Q*, 40 (1978), 357–362.

Stahlberg, Lawrence. "'And the Will Therein Lieth, Which Dieth Not': A Reconsideration of Ligeia's 'Gigantic Volition,'" *Am Transcendental Q*, 43 (Summer, 1979), 199–209.

Stoehr, Taylor. "'Unspeakable Horror'. . .," 319–322.

"Loss of Breath"
Kiell, Norman. *Varieties of Sexual Experience*. . ., 688–691.

"The Man of the Crowd"
Mazurek, Ray. "Art, Ambiguity, and the Artist in Poe's 'The Man of the Crowd,'" *Poe Stud*, 12 (1979), 25–28.

Phillips, Elizabeth. *Edgar Allan Poe*. . ., 127–128.

"The Man That Was Used Up"
Alekna, Richard A. "'The Man That Was Used Up': Further Notes on Poe's Satirical Targets," *Poe Stud*, 12 (1979), 36.

Scott, Virgil, and David Madden. *Instructor's Manual*. . ., 4th ed., 68–71.

"The Masque of the Red Death"
Ahrends, Günter. . . .*Kurzgeschichte*, 81–84.

Busson, Robert. "From the Eastern to the Western or Black Chamber: La Face cachée du 'Masque de la Mort Rouge,'" *Confluents*, 6, ii (1980), 123–131.

"Morella"
Bell, Michael D. . . . *The Sacrifice of Relation*, 115–116.

Bickman, Martin. *The Unsounded Centre*. . ., 67–73.

"The Murders in the Rue Morgue"
Knight, Stephen. *Form and Ideology*. . ., 39–52.

Porter, Dennis. *The Pursuit of Crime*. . ., 22–25.

"The Mystery of Marie Roget"
Knight, Stephen. *Form and Ideology*. . ., 52–58.

"The Narrative of Arthur Gordon Pym"
Aldiss, Brian W. *Billion Year Spree*. . ., 50–52.

Frank, Frederick S. "The Gothic at Absolute Zero: Poe's 'Narrative of Arthur Gordon Pym,'" *Extrapolation*, 21 (1980), 21–30.

Fukuchi, Curtis. "Poe's Providential 'Narrative of Arthur Gordon Pym,'" *ESQ: J Am Renaissance*, 27 (1981), 147–156.

Irwin, John T. *American Hieroglyphics*. . ., 188–205.

Krumme, Peter. *Augenblicke*. . ., 97–128.

Rosenzweig, Paul. "The Search for Identity: The Enclosure Motif in 'The Narrative of Arthur Gordon Pym,'" *ESQ: J Am Renaissance*, 26 (1980), 111-126.
Scheick, William J. *The Half-Breed...*, 20-21.

"The Oval Portrait"
MacAndrew, Elizabeth. *The Gothic Tradition...*, 217-218.
Mollinger, Robert N. "Edgar Allan Poe's 'The Oval Portrait': Fusion of Multiple Identities," *Am Imago*, 36 (1979), 147-153.
Ziolkowski, Theodore. *Disenchanted Images...*, 122-123.

"The Pit and the Pendulum"
Lease, Benjamin. *Anglo-American Encounters...*, 71-73.
Phillips, Elizabeth. *Edgar Allan Poe...*, 136-137.

"A Predicament"
Winder, Barbara D. "Two Poe Stories: The Presentation of Taboo Themes Through Humorous Reversals," *Thalia*, 1, ii (1978), 29-33.

"The Purloined Letter"
Altenbernd, Lynn, and Leslie L. Lewis. *Instructor's Manual...*, 3rd ed., 48-49.
Grossvogel, David I. *Mystery...*, 93-107.
Holland, Norman N. "Re-Covering 'The Purloined Letter': Reading as a Personal Transaction," in Suleiman, Susan R., and Inge Crossman, Eds. *The Reader in the Text...*, 350-370.
Knight, Stephen. *Form and Ideology...*, 58-65.
Krumme, Peter. *Augenblicke...*, 70-96.

"The Sphinx"
Krumme, Peter. *Augenblicke...*, 31-38.
Male, Roy R. *...Cloistral Fiction*, 33-34.

"The System of Dr. Tarr and Professor Fether"
Winder, Barbara D. "Two Poe Stories...," 29-33.

"A Tale of the Ragged Mountains"
Tatar, Maria M. *Spellbound...*, 199-200.

"The Tell-Tale Heart"
Baker, Sheridan, and George Perkins. *Instructor's Manual...*, 9-10.
Frank, F. S. "Neighborhood Gothic: Poe's 'Tell-Tale Heart,'" *Sphinx*, 3, iv (1981), 53-60.
Phillips, Elizabeth. *Edgar Allan Poe...*, 128-131.
Pitcher, Edward W. "The Physiognomical Meaning of Poe's 'The Tell-Tale Heart,'" *Stud Short Fiction*, 16 (1979), 231-233.
Tucker, B. D. "'The Tell-Tale Heart' and the 'Evil Eye,'" *Southern Lit J*, 13, ii (1981), 92-98.

"The Unparalleled Adventures of One Hans Pfaall"
Hillegas, Mark R. "The Literary Background to Science Fiction," in Parrinder, Patrick, Ed. *Science Fiction...*, 14-16.

"William Wilson"
Barker, Gerard A. *Instructor's Manual...*, 69-71.

MacAndrew, Elizabeth. *The Gothic Tradition*..., 220-221.
Orr, Leonard. "The 'Other' and 'Bad Faith': The Proto-Existentialism of Poe's 'William Wilson,'" *Stud Hum*, 9, i (1981), 33-38.
West, William. "Staying Alive: Poe's 'William Wilson,'" *enclitic*, 2, ii (1978), 34-49.
Ziolkowski, Theodore. *Disenchanted Images*..., 180-182.

FREDERIK POHL

"Day Million"
Samuelson, David N. "Critical Mass: The Science Fiction of Frederik Pohl," *Sci-Fiction Stud*, 7 (1980), 87-88.

"In the Problem Pit"
Samuelson, David N. "Critical Mass...," 89.

"The Merchant of Venus"
Samuelson, David N. "Critical Mass...," 89.

"The Tunnel Under the World"
Samuelson, David N. "Critical Mass...," 83-84.

"We Purchased People"
Samuelson, David N. "Critical Mass...," 90.

JOHN POLIDORI

"The Vampyre"
Punter, David. *The Literature of Terror*..., 118-119.
Twitchell, James B. *The Living Dead*..., 108-113.

HENRIK PONTOPPIDAN

"Charity"
Mitchell, P. M. *Henrik Pontoppidan*, 41-42.

"A Deathblow"
Mitchell, P. M. *Henrik Pontoppidan*, 43-44.

"The End of a Life"
Mitchell, P. M. *Henrik Pontoppidan*, 25-28.

"The Votive Ship" [same as "The Ship Model"]
Mitchell, P. M. *Henrik Pontoppidan*, 28-29.

KATHERINE ANNE PORTER

"The Circus"
Fetterley, Judith. "The Struggle for Authenticity: Growing Up Female in *The Old Order*," *Kate Chopin Newsletter*, 2, ii (1976), 13-15.

"The Cracked Looking-Glass"
*Warren, Robert P. "Irony with a Center," in Warren, Robert P., Ed. *Katherine Anne Porter . . .*, 102.

"A Day's Work"
Allen, Walter. *The Short Story . . .*, 193–194.

"The Fig Tree"
Fetterley, Judith. "The Struggle. . .," 16–17.
Rohrberger, Mary. *Instructor's Manual . . .*, 23–24.

"Flowering Judas"
Altenbernd, Lynn, and Leslie L. Lewis. *Instructor's Manual . . .*, 3rd ed., 50–51.
Gunn, Drewey W. *American and British Writers . . .*, 111–113.
Scott, Virgil, and David Madden. *Instructor's Manual . . .*, 4th ed., 32–34; Madden, David. *Instructor's Manual . . .*, 5th ed., 82–83.
*Warren, Robert P. "Irony with a Center," 96–98.

"The Grave"
*Brooks, Cleanth. "On 'Old Mortality,'" in Warren, Robert P., Ed. *Katherine Anne Porter . . .*, 112–116.
Fetterley, Judith. "The Struggle. . .," 17–18.
Howard, Daniel F., and William Plummer. *Instructor's Manual . . .*, 3rd ed., 40; rpt. Howard, Daniel F., and John Ribar. *Instructor's Manual . . .*, 4th ed., 38.
*Mizener, Arthur. *A Handbook . . .*, 4th ed., 36–38.

"Holiday"
*Core, George. "'Holiday': A Version of Pastoral," in Warren, Robert P., Ed. *Katherine Anne Porter . . .*, 117–125.

"The Jilting of Granny Weatherall"
Cobb, Joann P. "Pascal's Wager and Two Modern Losers," *Philosophy & Lit*, 3 (1979), 189–192.
Heilbrun, Carolyn G. "On Katherine Anne Porter and 'The Jilting of Granny Weatherall,'" in Skaggs, Calvin, Ed. *The American Short Story*, II, 296–299.
Howard, Daniel F., and William Plummer. *Instructor's Manual . . .*, 3rd ed., 39.
Mayer, David R. "Porter's 'The Jilting of Granny Weatherall,'" *Explicator*, 38, iv (1980), 33–34.

"The Last Leaf"
Fetterley, Judith. "The Struggle. . .," 15–16.

"The Leaning Tower"
Allen, Walter. *The Short Story . . .*, 194–196.

"María Concepción"
Gunn, Drewey W. *American and British Writers . . .*, 106–108.
Robinson, Cecil. *Mexico . . .*, 218–220.

"Noon Wine"
Male, Roy R. . . .*Cloistral Fiction*, 99–101.

Smith, Elliott L. and Wanda V. *Instructor's Manual...*, 21–23.
*Warren, Robert P. "Irony with a Center," 98–102.

"Old Mortality"
Allen, Walter. *The Short Story...*, 189–191.
Walsh, Thomas F. "Miranda's Ghost in 'Old Mortality,'" *Coll Lit*, 6 (1979), 57–63.
*Warren, Robert P. "Irony with a Center," 102–107.

"The Old Order"
Allen, Walter. *The Short Story...*, 191–192.
Fetterley, Judith. "The Struggle...," 11–12.

"Pale Horse, Pale Rider"
Allen, Walter. *The Short Story...*, 192–193.
Douglas, Kenneth, and Sarah N. Lawall. "Masterpieces of the Modern World,"
    in Mack, Maynard, *et al.*, Eds. *...World Masterpieces*, II, 4th ed., 1272–1273.
Gernes, Sonia. "Life after Life: Katherine Anne Porter's Version," *J Pop Culture*,
    14 (1981), 669–675.
Walsh, Thomas F. "The Dream Self in 'Pale Horse, Pale Rider,'" *Wascana R*, 14,
    ii (1979), 61–69.

"The Source"
Fetterley, Judith. "The Struggle...," 11.

"That Tree"
Gunn, Drewey W. *American and British Writers...*, 113–114.

"The Witness"
Fetterley, Judith. "The Struggle...," 13.

J. F. POWERS

"The Forks"
Scott, Virgil, and David Madden. *Instructor's Manual...*, 4th ed., 38–40.

"A Losing Game"
*Mizener, Arthur. *A Handbook...*, 4th ed., 97–100.

MUNSHI PREM CHAND [DHANPAT RAI SHRIVASTAV]

"The Bad Omen"
Orr, Inge C. "Premchand's Use of Folklore in His Short Stories," *Asian Folklore
    Stud*, 36, i (1977), 37–38.

"The Co-Wives"
Orr, Inge C. "Premchand's Use of Folklore...," 40–43.

"Despair"
Orr, Inge C. "Premchand's Use of Folklore...," 38–39.

J. B. PRIESTLEY

"The Pavilion of Masks"
DeVitis, A. A., and Albert E. Kalson. *J. B. Priestley*, 114–115.

V. S. PRITCHETT

"The Camberwell Beauty"
Allen, Walter. *The Short Story...*, 273–274.

"It May Never Happen"
Allen, Walter. *The Short Story...*, 270–273.

"The Saint"
Allen, Walter. *The Short Story...*, 268–270.

AGNES L. PROVOST

"Heathen"
Chu, Limin. *The Image of China...*, 209–211.

JAMES PURDY

"Don't Call Me by My Right Name"
Ahrends, Günter. *...Kurzgeschichte*, 203–205.

ALEXANDER PUSHKIN

"The Captain's Daughter"
Debreczeny, Paul. "The Execution of Captain Mironov: A Crossing of the Tragic
   and Comic," in Kodjak, Andrej, Krystyna Pomorska, and Kiril Taranovsky,
   Eds. *Alexander Puškin...*, 67–78.
Kodjak, Andrej. "Puškin's Utopian Myth," in Kodjak, Andrej, Krystyna Pomorska,
   and Kiril Taranovsky, Eds. *Alexander Puškin...*, 121–123.

"The Coffinmaker" [same as "The Undertaker"]
Bethea, David M., and Sergei Davydov. "Pushkin's Saturnine Cupid: The Poetics
   of Parody in *The Tales of Belkin*," *PMLA*, 96 (1981), 16–18.

"The Golden Cockerel"
Kodjak, Andrej. "Puškin's Utopian Myth," 123–124.

"The Lady Peasant"
Bethea, David M., and Sergei Davydov. "Pushkin's Saturnine Cupid...," 13.

"Mistress into Maid"
Kodjak, Andrej. "Puškin's Utopian Myth," 120–121.

"The Queen of Spades"
Barksdale, E. C. *Daggers of the Mind*..., 76–83.

"The Shot"
Bethea, David M., and Sergei Davydov. "Pushkin's Saturnine Cupid...," 10–11.

"The Stationmaster"
Bethea, David M., and Sergei Davydov. "Pushkin's Saturnine Cupid...," 12–13.

"The Tale of Tsar Saltan"
Kodjak, Andrej. "Puškin's Utopian Myth," 119–120.

THOMAS PYNCHON

"Entropy"
Ahrends, Günter. ...*Kurzgeschichte*, 213–217.
Jackson, Rosemary. *Fantasy*..., 166–167.
Mackey, Douglas A. *The Rainbow Quest*..., 8–10.
*Mizener, Arthur. *A Handbook*..., 4th ed., 106–113.
Plater, William M. *The Grim Phoenix*..., 50–56.
Schaub, Thomas H. *Pynchon*..., 22–24.
Seed, David. "Order in Thomas Pynchon's 'Entropy,'" *J Narrative Technique*, 11 (1981), 135–153.
Stark, John O. *Pynchon's Fiction*..., 19–20.

"Low-lands"
Mackey, Douglas A. *The Rainbow Quest*..., 7–8.
Stark, John O. *Pynchon's Fiction*..., 161–165.

"Mortality and Mercy in Vienna"
Mackey, Douglas A. *The Rainbow Quest*..., 6–7.
White, Allon. "Ironic Equivalence: A Reading of Thomas Pynchon's 'Mortality and Mercy in Vienna,'" *Critical Q*, 23, iii (1981), 55–62.

"The Secret Integration"
Mackey, Douglas A. *The Rainbow Quest*..., 10–12.

WILHELM RAABE

"Else von der Tanne"
Daemmrich, Horst S. *Wilhelm Raabe*, 51–52.

"Die Gänse von Bützow"
Daemmrich, Horst S. *Wilhelm Raabe*, 59–61.

"Gedelöcke"
Daemmrich, Horst S. *Wilhelm Raabe*, 50–51.

"Die Hämelschen Kinder"
Daemmrich, Horst S. *Wilhelm Raabe*, 51.

"Holunderblüte"
Daemmrich, Horst S. *Wilhelm Raabe*, 50-51.

"Höxter und Corvey"
Daemmrich, Horst S. *Wilhelm Raabe*, 63-64.

"Der Marsch nach Hause"
Daemmrich, Horst S. *Wilhelm Raabe*, 61-63.

"Die schwartze Galeere"
Daemmrich, Horst S. *Wilhelm Raabe*, 45-46.

"Der Student von Wittenberg"
Daemmrich, Horst S. *Wilhelm Raabe*, 43-45.

"Zum wilden Mann"
Daemmrich, Horst S. *Wilhelm Raabe*, 97-100.

MOHAN RAKESH

"Another Life"
Weir, Ann L. "Behind the Facade: Communication Between Characters in the
Stories of Mohan Rakesh," *J So Asian Lit*, 13, i-vi (1977-1978), 56-57.

"Ek Aur Zindagi"
Sinha, Raghuvir. "Mohan Rakesh—A Visionary Short Story Writer," *Indian Lit*,
21, i (1978), 95-100.

"Miss Pall"
Weir, Ann L. "Behind the Facade...," 56.

"The Strangers"
Weir, Ann L. "Behind the Facade...," 59-61.

"Suhagine"
Sinha, Raghuvir. "Mohan Rakesh...," 106-114.

"The Wound"
Weir, Ann L. "Behind the Facade...," 54-55.

FLORENCE ENGLE RANDALL

"The Watchers"
Smith, Elliott L., and Andrew W. Hart, Eds. *The Short Story...*, 153-154.

RAJA RAO

"The Cow of the Barricades"
*Naik, M. K. "Narrative Strategy in Raja Rao's *The Cow of the Barricades and Other Stories*," in Mohan, Ramesh, Ed. *Indian Writing*..., 51-52.

"Narsiga"
*Naik, M. K. "Narrative Strategy...," 52-54.

VALENTIN GRIGOREVICH RASPUTIN

"The Final Term"
Shneidman, N. N. *Soviet Literature*..., 77-79.

"Live and Remember"
Shneidman, N. N. *Soviet Literature*..., 79-80.

"Money for Maria"
Brown, Deming. ...*Literature Since Stalin*, 250-251.
Shneidman, N. N. *Soviet Literature*..., 76-77.

"Parting with Matera"
Pankin, Boris. "Matera—Farewells and Encounters," *Soviet Stud Lit*, 18, iii (1981), 46-75.
Shneidman, N. N. *Soviet Literature*..., 81-83.

JOHN REED

"Endymion"
Gunn, Drewey W. *American and British Writers*..., 61-62.

ALFONSO REYES

"La cena"
Robb, James W. "'La cena' de Alfonso Reyes, cuento oniico: Surrealismo o realismo mágico," *Thesaurus*, [n.v.] (1981), 36.

MACK REYNOLDS

"Pacifist"
Warrick, Patricia. "Mack Reynolds: The Future as Socio-Economic Possibility," in Clareson, Thomas D., Ed. *Voices for the Future*..., II, 151.

"Revolution"
Warrick, Patricia. "...Socio-Economic Possibility," 151-152.

JEAN RHYS

"From a French Prison"
Staley, Thomas F. *Jean Rhys* . . ., 27.

"Goodbye Marcus, Goodbye Rose"
Staley, Thomas F. *Jean Rhys* . . ., 128–129.

"La Gross Fifi"
Staley, Thomas F. *Jean Rhys* . . ., 30–31.

"Hunger"
Staley, Thomas F. *Jean Rhys* . . ., 28–29.

"I Spy a Stranger"
Wolfe, Peter. *Jean Rhys*, 54–57.

"Illusion"
Wolfe, Peter. *Jean Rhys*, 36–37.

"In a Café"
Wolfe, Peter. *Jean Rhys*, 37–38.

"Mannequin"
Wolfe, Peter. *Jean Rhys*, 39–40.

"Rapunzel, Rapunzel"
Staley, Thomas F. *Jean Rhys* . . ., 130.

"Sleep It Off, Lady"
Wolfe, Peter. *Jean Rhys*, 58–60.

"Tigers Are Better-Looking"
Wolfe, Peter. *Jean Rhys*, 47–49.

"Till September Petronella"
Staley, Thomas F. *Jean Rhys* . . ., 122–125.

"Vienne"
Staley, Thomas F. *Jean Rhys* . . ., 31–34.

JULIO RAMÓN RIBEYRO

"Los gallinazos sin plumas"
Gerdes, Dick C. "Julio Ramón Ribeyro: Un analisis de sus cuentos," *Kentucky Romance Q,* 26 (1979), 51–53.

"Interior L"
Gerdes, Dick C. "Julio Ramón Ribeyro. . .," 53–54.

"Silvio en el rosedal"
Luchting, Wolfgang A. "'Mundo en el parque': *La palabra del mudo 111* –'Silvio en el rosedal' de Julio Ramón Ribeyro," *Explicación de Textos Literarios*, 10, i (1981), 35-47.

MARY ROBERTS RINEHART

"The Better Man"
Cohn, Jan. *Improbable Fiction...*, 210-211.

"His Father's Son"
Cohn, Jan. *Improbable Fiction...*, 34-35.

"Lightning Never Strikes Twice"
Cohn, Jan. *Improbable Fiction...*, 211-212.

"The Second Marriage"
Cohn, Jan. *Improbable Fiction...*, 212-213.

"Seven Days"
Cohn, Jan. *Improbable Fiction...*, 48-49.

"The Tall Tree"
Cohn, Jan. *Improbable Fiction...*, 192-193.

"The Temporary Death of Mrs. Ayres"
Cohn, Jan. *Improbable Fiction...*, 229-230.

"Three Pirates of Penzance"
Cohn, Jan. *Improbable Fiction...*, 51-52.

AUGUSTO ROA BASTOS

"El pájaro mosca"
Saad, Gabriel. "'El pájaro mosca': Palabra de la madre, escritura del padre," *Cuadernos Hispanoamericanos*, 375 (1981), 490-503.

ALAIN ROBBE-GRILLET

"The Secret Room"
Brooks, Cleanth, and Robert P. Warren. *Understanding Fiction*, 3rd ed., 257-258.
Madden, David. *Instructor's Manual...*, 5th ed., 59-62.

LUIS ROMERO

"At the Edge of Time"
González-del-Valle, Luis, and Bradley A. Shaw. *Luis Romero*, 80-81.

"The Beach"
González-del-Valle, Luis, and Bradley A. Shaw. *Luis Romero*, 93-94.

"The Boat"
González-del-Valle, Luis, and Bradley A. Shaw. *Luis Romero*, 91-92.

"Elena's Birthday"
González-del-Valle, Luis, and Bradley A. Shaw. *Luis Romero*, 92-93.

"Foot Soldier's Soliloquy"
González-del-Valle, Luis, and Bradley A. Shaw. *Luis Romero*, 83-85.

"Mister Plural Anyone"
González-del-Valle, Luis, and Bradley A. Shaw. *Luis Romero*, 74-77.

"Repatriates' Soliloquy"
González-del-Valle, Luis, and Bradley A. Shaw. *Luis Romero*, 86.

"Sentinel's Soliloquy"
González-del-Valle, Luis, and Bradley A. Shaw. *Luis Romero*, 85.

"A Shadow Passed By"
González-del-Valle, Luis, and Bradley A. Shaw. *Luis Romero*, 79-80.

"They Call This Judgment..."
González-del-Valle, Luis, and Bradley A. Shaw. *Luis Romero*, 77-79.

FRANK ROONEY

"Cyclists' Raid"
Male, Roy R. . . . *Cloistral Fiction*, 66-68.

MIKHAIL MIKHAĬLOVICH ROSHCHIN

"Vospominanie"
Pankin, Boris. "The Past That Is Always with You," *Soviet Stud Lit*, 18, i (1981–1982), 30-50.

SINCLAIR ROSS

"Circus in Town"
McMullen, Lorraine. *Sinclair Ross*, 35-36.

"Cornet at Night"
McMullen, Lorraine. *Sinclair Ross*, 36-40.

"A Day with Pegasus"
McMullen, Lorraine. *Sinclair Ross*, 34-35.

"The Lamp at Noon"
McMullen, Lorraine. *Sinclair Ross*, 31–33.

"No Other Way"
McMullen, Lorraine. *Sinclair Ross*, 24–27.

"One's a Heifer"
McMullen, Lorraine. *Sinclair Ross*, 45–48.

"The Outlaw"
McMullen, Lorraine. *Sinclair Ross*, 41–44.

"The Painted Door"
McMullen, Lorraine. *Sinclair Ross*, 27–31.

DANTE GABRIEL ROSSETTI

"Saint Agnes of Intercession"
Ziolkowski, Theodore. *Disenchanted Images...*, 106–108.

JOSEPH ROTH

"Die Legende vom heiligen Trinker"
Browning, Barton W. "Joseph Roth's 'Legende vom heiligen Trinker': Essence
    and Elixir," in Strelka, Joseph P., Robert F. Bell, and Eugene Dobson, Eds.
    Protest..., 81–95.
Mornin, Edward. "Drinking in Joseph Roth's Novels and Tales," *Int'l Fiction R*,
    6, i (1979), 83–84.

PHILIP ROTH

"The Conversion of the Jews"
Guttmann, Allen. *The Jewish Writer...*, 65–66.
Jones, Judith P., and Guinevera A. Nance. *Philip Roth*, 28–31.
Landis, Joseph C. "The Sadness of Philip Roth: An Interim Report," in Pinsker,
    Sanford, Ed. *Critical Essays...*, 166–168.
Madden, David. *Instructor's Manual...*, 5th ed., 101–102.
Pinsker, Sanford. "Joseph in Chederland: A Note on 'The Conversion of the Jews,'"
    Stud Am Jewish Lit, 1, ii (1979), 36–37.
Roth, David S. "'The Conversion of the Jews': What Hath Mother Wrought?"
    Bull West Virginia Assoc Coll Engl Teachers, 3, ii (1976), 39–42.

"Courting Disaster"
Jones, Judith P., and Guinevera A. Nance. *Philip Roth*, 103–105.

"Defender of the Faith"
DaCrema, Joseph J. "Roth's 'Defender of the Faith,'" *Explicator*, 39, i (1980), 19–20.
Guttmann, Allen. *The Jewish Writer...*, 66–67.
Isaac, Dan. "In Defense of Philip Roth," *Chicago R*, 17, ii–iii (1964), 91–92.
*Mizener, Arthur. *A Handbook...*, 4th ed., 84–88.

"Eli the Fanatic"
Guttmann, Allen. *The Jewish Writer...*, 70–71.
Isaac, Dan. "In Defense...," 92–94.
Jones, Judith P., and Guinevera A. Nance. *Philip Roth*, 31–36.
Knopp, Josephine Z. *The Trial of Judaism...*, 104–109.
Landis, Joseph C. "The Sadness...," 168–169.
Rockland, Michael A. "The Jewish Side of Philip Roth," *Stud Am Jewish Lit*, 1,
    ii (1979), 33–34.

"Epstein"
Isaac, Dan. "In Defense...," 95.
Jones, Judith P., and Guinevera A. Nance. *Philip Roth*, 24–27.

"Ferdinand"
Morse, J. Mitchell. "Brand Names and Others," *Hudson R*, 22 (1969), 319.

"Goodbye, Columbus"
Cohen, Sarah B. "Philip Roth's Would-Be Patriarchs and Their *Shikses* and Shrews,"
    in Pinsker, Sanford, Ed. *Critical Essays...*, 210–212.
Guttmann, Allen. *The Jewish Writer...*, 67–70.
Isaac, Dan. "In Defense...," 87–90.
Landis, Joseph C. "The Sadness...," 168.
Rockland, Michael A. "The Jewish Side...," 32–33.

"It Was"
Morse, J. Mitchell. "Brand Names...," 319–320.

"My True Story"
Jones, Judith P., and Guinevera A. Nance. *Philip Roth*, 106–111.

"On the Air"
Jones, Judith P., and Guinevera A. Nance. *Philip Roth*, 152–157.

"Salad Days"
Jones, Judith P., and Guinevera A. Nance. *Philip Roth*, 101–102.

"You Can't Tell a Man by the Song He Sings"
Jones, Judith P., and Guinevera A. Nance. *Philip Roth*, 132–133.

FREDERICK ROTHERMEL

"Foo Soon, the Heathen"
Chu, Limin. *The Image of China...*, 188–189.

CONSTANCE ROURKE

"The Porch"
Bellman, Samuel I. *Constance Rourke*, 35–37.

"Portrait of a Young Woman"
Bellman, Samuel I. *Constance Rourke*, 37-39.

GABRIELLE ROY

"A Garden at the End of the World"
Rubinger, Catherine. "Actualité de deux contes-témoins: 'Le Torrent' d'Anne Hébert et 'Un Jardin au bout du monde' de Gabrielle Roy," *Présence Francophone*, 20 (1980), 121-126.

JUAN RULFO

"Anacleto Morones"
Molloy, Sylvia. "Desentendimiento y socarronetía en 'Anacleto Morones' de Juan Rulfo," *Escritura*, 6, xi (1981), 163-171.

"Es que somos muy pobres"
Arango, Manuel A. "Aspectos sociales en tres cuentos de *El llano en llanas* de Juan Rulfo: 'Macario,' 'Nos han dado la tierra' y 'Es que somos muy pobres,'" *Cuadernos Hispanoamericanos*, 375 (1981), 627-634.

"El llano en llanas"
Mocega-Gonzalez, Esther P. "La revolución y el hombre en el cuento 'El llano en llanas,'" *Cuadernos Americanos*, 225 (1979), 214-229.

"Luvina"
Echavarren, Roberto. "Contexto y puesta en escena en 'Luvina' de Juan Rulfo," *Dispositio*, 5-6, xv-xvi (1980-1981), 155-177.
Foster, David W. ...*Spanish-American Short Story*, 31-38.

"Macario"
Arango, Manuel A. "Aspectos sociales...," 627-634.

"Nos han dado la tierra"
Arango, Manuel A. "Aspectos sociales...," 627-634.

DAMON RUNYON

"Baseball Hattie"
Higgs, Robert J. *Laurel & Thorn*..., 113-114.

"Bred for Battle"
Higgs, Robert J. *Laurel & Thorn*..., 97-99.

JOANNA RUSS

"Daddy's Girl"
Pearson, Carol, and Katherine Pope. *The Female Hero*..., 182-183.

FERDINAND VON SAAR

"Schloss Kostenitz"
Spielmann, Hans R. "Geschichtsdarstellung in der franzikojosephinischen Epik
(Ferdinand von Saar): 'Schloss Kostenitz'—Alfred Kubin: *Die andere Seite*—
Joseph Roth: *Radetzkymarsch*," *Österreich in Geschichte und Literatur,* 24 (1980),
238–256.

SAKI [HECTOR HUGH MUNRO]

"Filboid Studge"
Langguth, A. J. *Saki...*, 177–178.

"Gabriel-Ernest"
Langguth, A. J. *Saki...*, 158–162.

"The Interlopers"
Hartwell, Ronald. "Fallen Timbers—a Death Trap: A Comparison of Bierce and
Munro," *Research Stud,* 49 (1981), 61–66.

"The Mappined Life"
Stahl, John D. "Saki's *Enfant Terrible* in 'The Open Window,'" *Lang Q,* 15,
iii–iv (1977), 8.

"Mrs. Packletide's Tiger"
Langguth, A. J. *Saki...*, 174–176.

"The Open Window"
Langguth, A. J. *Saki...*, 214–216.
Smith, Elliott L., and Andrew W. Hart, Eds. *The Short Story...*, 37–38.
Stahl, John D. "Saki's *Enfant Terrible...*," 5–6, 8.

"Sredni Vashtar"
Allen, Walter. *The Short Story...*, 86–87.
Stahl, John D. "Saki's *Enfant Terrible...*," 7.

"Tobermory"
Allen, Walter. *The Short Story...*, 87–88.

J. D. SALINGER

"De Daumier-Smith's Blue Period"
*Galloway, David. *The Absurd Hero...*, 2nd rev. ed., 209–211.
Lundquist, James. *J. D. Salinger*, 102–106.

"Down at the Dinghy"
Bryan, James. "The Admiral and Her Sailor in Salinger's 'Down at the Dinghy,'"
Stud Short Fiction, 17 (1980), 174–178.
*Galloway, David. *The Absurd Hero...*, 2nd rev. ed., 215–216.
Lundquist, James. *J. D. Salinger*, 97–98.

"The Fire Sermon"
Lundquist, James. *J. D. Salinger*, 84-86.

"For Esmé—with Love and Squalor"
*Galloway, David. *The Absurd Hero*..., 2nd rev. ed., 214-215.
Lundquist, James. *J. D. Salinger*, 98-101.
Wenke, John. "Sergeant X, Esmé, and the Meaning of Words," *Stud Short Fiction*,
    18 (1981), 251-259.

"Franny"
*Galloway, David. *The Absurd Hero*..., 2nd rev. ed., 217-219.
Lundquist, James. *J. D. Salinger*, 120-125.
Ogata, Mayumi. "The Pilgrimage in Salinger's *Franny and Zooey*," *Kyushu Am Lit*,
    21 (1980), 62-65.

"Hapworth 16, 1924"
Lundquist, James. *J. D. Salinger*, 148-149.

"The Inverted Forest"
Lundquist, James. *J. D. Salinger*, 22-25.

"Just Before the War with the Eskimos"
Lundquist, James. *J. D. Salinger*, 90-92.

"The Last Day of the Last Furlough"
Lundquist, James. *J. D. Salinger*, 15-18.

"The Laughing Man"
Davison, Richard A. "Salinger Criticism and 'The Laughing Man': A Case of
    Arrested Development," *Stud Short Fiction*, 18 (1981), 1-15.
Lundquist, James. *J. D. Salinger*, 92-96.

"A Perfect Day for Bananafish"
Ahrends, Günter. ...*Kurzgeschichte*, 191-193.
Lundquist, James. *J. D. Salinger*, 79-87.

"Raise High the Roofbeam, Carpenters"
Alsen, Eberhard. "'Raise High the Roofbeam, Carpenters' and the Amateur
    Reader," *Stud Short Fiction*, 17 (1980), 39-47.
Galloway, David. *The Absurd Hero*..., 2nd rev. ed., 220-221.
Lundquist, James. *J. D. Salinger*, 137-142.
McSweeney, Kerry. "Salinger Revisited," *Critical Q*, 20 (Spring, 1978), 64-65.

"Seymour: An Introduction"
Lundquist, James. *J. D. Salinger*, 142-147.

"Teddy"
Lundquist, James. *J. D. Salinger*, 106-109.

"Uncle Wiggily in Connecticut"
Lundquist, James. *J. D. Salinger*, 87-90.

"Zooey"
*Galloway, David. *The Absurd Hero* . . ., 2nd rev. ed., 219–227.
Lundquist, James. *J. D. Salinger*, 125–134.
Ogata, Mayumi. "The Pilgrimage. . .," 62–65.

LUIS RAFAEL SÁNCHEZ

"Que sabe a paraíso"
Pilditch, Charles R. "'Like Heaven, Man!'" *R* (New York), 28 (January–April, 1981), 37–39.

MARI SANDOZ

"The Smart Man"
Oehlschlaeger, Fritz. "The Art of Mari Sandoz's 'The Smart Man,'" *So Dakota R*, 19, iv (1981), 65–75.

WILLIAM SANSOM

"Among the Dahlias"
Chalpin, Lila. *William Sansom*, 109–111.

"The Biter Bit"
Chalpin, Lila. *William Sansom*, 121–122.

"The Bonfire"
Chalpin, Lila. *William Sansom*, 126–129.

"A Contest of Ladies"
Chalpin, Lila. *William Sansom*, 106–107.

"The Dangerous Age"
Chalpin, Lila. *William Sansom*, 114–115.

"The Day the Life. . ."
Chalpin, Lila. *William Sansom*, 124–125.

"How Claeys Died"
Allen, Walter. *The Short Story* . . ., 286–287.

"The Last Ride"
Chalpin, Lila. *William Sansom*, 119–120.

"A Last Word"
Chalpin, Lila. *William Sansom*, 108.

"Love at First Sight"
Chalpin, Lila. *William Sansom*, 117–118.

"Mamma Mia"
Chalpin, Lila. *William Sansom*, 123-124.

"The Man with the Moon in Him"
Chalpin, Lila. *William Sansom*, 112.

"The Marmalade Bird"
Chalpin, Lila. *William Sansom*, 115-117.

"No Smoking in the Apron"
Chalpin, Lila. *William Sansom*, 131-134.

"Old Man Alone"
Allen, Walter. *The Short Story...*, 282-284.

"To the Rescue"
Chalpin, Lila. *William Sansom*, 111-112.

"Various Temptations"
Chalpin, Lila. *William Sansom*, 109-111.

"A Visit to the Dentist"
Chalpin, Lila. *William Sansom*, 120-121.

"A Waning Moon"
Chalpin, Lila. *William Sansom*, 113-114.

ELLEN C. SARGENT

"Wee Wi Ping"
Chu, Limin. *The Image of China...*, 187.

FRANK SARGESON

"A Man of Good Will"
Allen, Walter. *The Short Story...*, 331-332.

"The Old Man's Story"
Allen, Walter. *The Short Story...*, 333-335.

JEAN-PAUL SARTRE

"The Room"
Champigny, Robert. "La Perspective dans 'La Chambre' de Sartre," *Stanford French R*, 3 (1979), 91-96.
John, S. Beynon. "Insight and Madness in Sartre's 'La Chambre,'" *Mod Langs*, 62, i (1981), 7-12.
Rohrberger, Mary. *Instructor's Manual...*, 28.

ARTHUR SCHNITZLER

"Lieutenant Gustl"
Dethlefsen, Dirk. "Überlebenswille Zu Schnitzlers Monolognovelle 'Leutnant Gustl' in ihrem literarischen Umkreis," *Seminar*, 17 (1981), 50–75.

"Traumnovelle"
Jennings, Lee B. "Schnitzler's 'Traumnovelle': Meat or Poison?" *Seminar*, 17 (1981), 73–82.

FRANZ SCHUBERT

"My Dream"
Solomon, Maynard. "Franz Schubert's 'My Dream,'" *Am Imago*, 38 (1981), 137–154.

CHARLES SCOFIELD

"Fan Show's Thanksgiving"
Chu, Limin. *The Image of China...*, 184–185.

DUNCAN CAMPBELL SCOTT

"Charcoal"
Monkman, Leslie. *A Native Heritage...*, 72–73.

"The Desjardins"
Allen, Walter. *The Short Story...*, 202–203.

WALTER SCOTT

"My Aunt Margaret's Mirror"
Briggs, Julia. *Night Visitors...*, 35–36.

"The Tapestried Chamber"
Ziolkowski, Theodore. *Disenchanted Images...*, 96–97.

"The Two Drovers"
Allen, Walter. *The Short Story...*, 9–10.

"Wandering Willie's Tale"
Briggs, Julia. *Night Visitors...*, 36–38.
Doubleday, Neal F. *Variety of Attempt...*, 49–60.

ITZHAK SHAMI

"The Vengeance of the Fathers"
Shaked, Gershon. "Shami's 'The Vengeance of the Fathers': A Palestinian-Hebrew Novel [Novella]," *Edebiyat: J Middle Eastern Lit*, 3 (1978), 213–227.

IRWIN SHAW

"The Dry Rock"
Smith, Elliott L. and Wanda V. *Instructor's Manual.* . . , 14–15.
————, and Andrew W. Hart, Eds. *The Short Story.* . . , 57–59.

"The Eighty-Yard Run"
Higgs, Robert J. *Laurel & Thorn.* . . , 102–104.

SHENG CH'I-TENG

"I Love the Black Eyes"
Wang, C. H. "Fancy and Reality in Ch'i-teng Sheng's Fiction," in Faurot, Jeannette
L., Ed. *Chinese Fiction from Taiwan.* . . , 197–201.

"Impressions: Return to the Country Home"
Wang, C. H. "Fancy and Reality. . .," 201–203.

"Reflections in the Water"
Wang, C. H. "Fancy and Reality. . .," 195–196.

"Walking to the Black Bridge"
Wang, C. H. "Fancy and Reality. . .," 203–204.

SHIGA NAOYA

"Seibei's Gourds"
Petersen, Gwenn B. *The Moon.* . . , 19–20.

BENJAMIN PENHALLOW SHILLABER

"Christmas Hearths and Hearts"
Reed, John Q. *Benjamin Penhallow Shillaber*, 100.

"A Life's Fortune"
Reed, John Q. *Benjamin Penhallow Shillaber*, 97–98.

"Missing"
Reed, John Q. *Benjamin Penhallow Shillaber*, 98–99.

"A New Year's Revery"
Reed, John Q. *Benjamin Penhallow Shillaber*, 99–100.

SHIRSENDU MUKHOPADHYA

"Abelai"
Chakravarty, D. K. "Bengali Short Story Today," *Indian Lit*, 21, i (1978), 79.

SHYAMAL GANGOPADHYAYA

"The Fairy"
Chakravarty, D. K. "Bengali Short Story Today," *Indian Lit*, 21, i (1978), 78-79.

LESLIE SILKO

"Yellow Woman"
Madden, David. *Instructor's Manual*..., 5th ed., 113-114.

ALAN SILLITOE

"The Decline and Fall of Frankie Buller"
Allen, Walter. *The Short Story*..., 376-378.

"The Loneliness of the Long-Distance Runner"
Allen, Walter. *The Short Story*..., 378-380.
Gindin, James J. *Postwar British Fiction*..., 32-33.
Iserhagen, Hartwig. "The Thematic Unity of the 'Long-Distance Runner': The Short Story as a Semi-Qualified Medium of Social Criticism," *Literatur in Wissenschaft und Unterricht*, 12 (1979), 178-189.
_____. "Alan Sillitoes 'The Loneliness of the Long-Distance Runner': Versuch einer literatur- und genrehistorischen Einordnung," *Anglia*, 99 (1981), 134-161.
Quirk, Eugene F. "Social Class as Audience: Sillitoe's Story and Screen Play 'The Loneliness of the Long-Distance Runner,'" *Mid-Hudson Lang Stud*, 1 (1978), 157-171.

ROBERT SILVERBERG

"The Pain Peddler"
Clareson, Thomas D. "The Fictions of Robert Silverberg," in Clareson, Thomas D., Ed. *Voices for the Future*..., II, 7-9.

"To the Dark Star"
Nedelkovich, Alexander. "The Stellar Parallels: Robert Silverberg, Larry Niven, and Arthur C. Clarke," *Extrapolation*, 21 (1980), 348-360.

WILLIAM GILMORE SIMMS

"Caloya"
Scheick, William J. *The Half-Breed*..., 85-86.

"Major Rocket"
Wimsatt, Mary A. "Simms's Early Short Stories," *Lib Chronicle*, 41 (1977), 168-170.

"Oakatibbe"
Davis, Jack L. "W. Gilmore Simms' 'Oakatibbe' and the Failure of the Westering Imagination," in Lewis, Merrill, and L. L. Lee, Eds. *The Westering Experience*..., 112-121.

"The Plank"
Wimsatt, Mary A. "Simms's Early Short Stories," 166–168.

"Ponce de Leon"
Wimsatt, Mary A. "Simms's Early Short Stories," 171–173.

"Spirit Bridegroom"
Wimsatt, Mary A. "Simms's Early Short Stories," 170–171.

"Sweet William"
Wimsatt, Mary A. "Simms's Early Short Stories," 166.

ISAAC BASHEVIS SINGER

"Alone"
Kresh, Paul. *Isaac Bashevis Singer* . . . , 240–241.

"The Briefcase"
Kresh, Paul. *Isaac Bashevis Singer* . . . , 254–255.

"The Bus"
Kresh, Paul. *Isaac Bashevis Singer* . . . , 257–258.

"The Cafeteria"
Kresh, Paul. *Isaac Bashevis Singer* . . . , 271–272.

"The Colony"
Kresh, Paul. *Isaac Bashevis Singer* . . . , 249–250.

"A Day in Coney Island"
Kresh, Paul. *Isaac Bashevis Singer* . . . , 149–150.

"The Destruction of Kreshev"
Kresh, Paul. *Isaac Bashevis Singer* . . . , 231–232.

"Dreamers"
Kresh, Paul. *Isaac Bashevis Singer* . . . , 59–60.

"Esther Kreindel the Second"
Altenbernd, Lynn, and Leslie L. Lewis. *Instructor's Manual* . . . , 3rd ed., 51–52.

"Gimpel the Fool"
Kresh, Paul. *Isaac Bashevis Singer* . . . , 203–204.
Madden, David. *Instructor's Manual* . . . , 5th ed., 94.

"A Hannukah Eve in Warsaw"
Kresh, Paul. *Isaac Bashevis Singer* . . . , 49–50.

"Her Son"
Kresh, Paul. *Isaac Bashevis Singer* . . . , 280–281.

"The Last Demon"
Alexander, Edward. *The Resonance of Dust*. . ., 167.

"The Lecture"
Kresh, Paul. *Isaac Bashevis Singer*. . ., 252–254.

"The Letter Writer"
Kresh, Paul. *Isaac Bashevis Singer*. . ., 266–267.

"One Night in Brazil"
Kresh, Paul. *Isaac Bashevis Singer*. . ., 250–251.

"A Piece of Advice"
Kresh, Paul. *Isaac Bashevis Singer*. . ., 232–233.

"Power of Darkness"
Kresh, Paul. *Isaac Bashevis Singer*. . ., 291–292.

"The Psychic Journey"
Kresh, Paul. *Isaac Bashevis Singer*. . ., 256–257.

"Sabbath in Portugal"
Kresh, Paul. *Isaac Bashevis Singer*. . ., 251–252.

"Schloimele"
Kresh, Paul. *Isaac Bashevis Singer*. . ., 150–151.

"Two Weddings and One Divorce"
Kresh, Paul. *Isaac Bashevis Singer*. . ., 290–291.

"Yentl the Yeshiva Boy"
Kresh, Paul. *Isaac Bashevis Singer*. . ., 9–11.

CORDWAINER SMITH

"Game of Rat and Dragon"
Rose, Mark. *Alien Encounter*. . ., 188–189.

PAULINE SMITH

"The Father"
Allen, Walter. *The Short Story*. . ., 241–243.

"Ludovitje"
Allen, Walter. *The Short Story*. . ., 243–244.

WILLIAM JOSEPH SNELLING

"The Bois Brulé"
Scheick, William J. *The Half-Breed*. . ., 52–56.

Willy, Todd G. "Antipode to Cooper: Rhetoric and Reality in William Joseph Snelling's 'The Bois Brulé,'" *Stud Am Fiction*, 8 (1980), 69–79.

ALEXANDER SOLZHENITSYN

"An Incident at Krechetovka Station"
Ericson, Edward E. *Solzhenitsyn...*, 27–29.

"Matryona's House"
Ericson, Edward E. *Solzhenitsyn...*, 23–27.
Lottridge, Stephen S. "Solzhenitsyn and Leskov," *Russian Lit Tri-Q*, 6 (Spring, 1973), 482–484.

"Zahar-Kalita"
Lottridge, Stephen S. "Solzhenitsyn and Leskov," 481–482.

EDITH SOMERVILLE and MARTIN ROSS [VIOLET MARTIN]

"The Finger of Mrs. Knox"
Robinson, Hilary. *Somerville & Ross...*, 126–127.

"Great Uncle McCarthy"
Cronin, John. *Somerville and Ross...*, 54–57.

"The House of Fahy"
Robinson, Hilary. *Somerville & Ross...*, 129.

"Lisheen Races, Second-Hand"
Cronin, John. *Somerville and Ross*, 58.
O'Donnell, Donat. "The Novels and Stories of Somerville and Ross," *Irish Writing*, 30 (March, 1955), 8–10.

"Poisson D'Avril"
Cronin, John. *Somerville and Ross*, 63–65.

"The Pug-Nosed Fox"
Cronin, John. *Somerville and Ross*, 65–66.
Robinson, Hilary. *Somerville & Ross...*, 130–131.

"Sharper Than a Ferret's Tooth"
Robinson, Hilary. *Somerville & Ross...*, 134–135.

"Trinket's Colt"
Robinson, Hilary. *Somerville & Ross...*, 44–45.

"The Waters of Strife"
Cronin, John. *Somerville and Ross*, 59–60.

CASTRO SOROMENHO

"Calenga"
Moser, Gerald. "Castro Soromenho, An Angolan Realist," *Africa Today*, 15, vi
(December–January, 1968-1969), 22; rpt. Burness, Donald, Ed. *Critical
Perspectives . . .*, 69.

FERNANDO SORRENTINO

"The Fetid Tale of Antulin"
Meehan, Thomas C. "Scatological Humor in a Short Story by Fernando Sorren-
tino," in Minc, Rose S., Ed. *Latin American Fiction Today*, 119-130.
_____. "One-Upmanship in a Short Story by Fernando Sorrentino," *Perspectives
Contemp Lit*, 6 (1980), 125-134.

GILBERT SORRENTINO

"The Moon in Its Flight"
Emerson, Stephen. "Three Thoughts about 'The Moon in Its Flight,'" *R Contemp
Fiction*, 1 (1981), 81-82.
Friedman, Lawrence S. "Vision and Revision in Scorsese's *New York, New York*
and Sorrentino's 'The Moon in Its Flight,'" *Lit/Film Q*, 9 (1981), 103-109.

P. J. SOTO

"Garabatos"
Arellano Salgado, Olga. "El cuento y su influencia objectiva y subjetiva en niño,"
Novelle Revue Française, 13-14 (1979), 1-5.

MARGUERITE STABLER

"The Sale of Sooy Yet"
Chu, Limin. *The Image of China . . .*, 201.

JEAN STAFFORD

"Bad Characters"
Altenbernd, Lynn, and Leslie L. Lewis. *Instructor's Manual . . .*, 3rd ed., 52.

LAURENCE STALLINGS

"The Big Parade"
Brittain, Joan T. *Laurence Stallings*, 56-58.

"Gentleman in Blue"
Brittain, Joan T. *Laurence Stallings*, 65-68.

"Return to the Woods"
Brittain, Joan T. *Laurence Stallings*, 68–70.

"Turn out the Guard"
Brittain, Joan T. *Laurence Stallings*, 60–62.

"Vale of Tears"
Brittain, Joan T. *Laurence Stallings*, 60–62.

JAMES W. STEELE

"The Scout's Mistake"
Scheick, William J. *The Half-Breed...*, 22–24.

WILBUR DANIEL STEELE

"Never Anything That Fades.."
Walker, Warren S. "'Never Anything That Fades..': Steele's Eleusinian Mysteries,"
   Stud Short Fiction, 17 (1980), 127–132.

WALLACE STEGNER

"Carrion Spring"
Robertson, Jamie. "Henry Adams, Wallace Stegner, and the Search for a Sense
   of Place in the West," in Lewis, Merrill, and L. L. Lee, Eds. *The Westering
   Experience...*, 141–142.

"Maid in a Tower"
Ellis, James. "Wallace Stegner's Art of Literary Allusion: *The Marriage of Heaven
   and Hell* and *Faust* in 'Maid in a Tower,'" *Stud Short Fiction*, 17 (1980), 105–111.

JOHN STEINBECK

"The Chrysanthemums"
Kennedy, X. J. *Instructor's Manual...*, 2nd ed., 59–61.
Lisca, Peter. *...Nature and Myth*, 191–192.
McCarthy, Paul. *John Steinbeck*, 26–27.
Male, Roy R. *...Cloistral Fiction*, 66–68.
*Mitchell, Marilyn L. "Steinbeck's Strong Women: Feminine Identity in the Short
   Stories," in Hayashi, Tetsumaro, Ed. *Steinbeck's Women...*, 26–35.
Smith, Elliott L., and Andrew W. Hart, Eds. *The Short Story...*, 277–280.
Sullivan, Ernest. "The Cur in 'The Chrysanthemums,'" *Stud Short Fiction*, 16
   (1979), 215–217.

"Flight"
Lisca, Peter. *...Nature and Myth*, 194–195.
McCarthy, Paul. *John Steinbeck*, 28–29.

Piacentino, Edward J. "Patterns of Animal Imagery in Steinbeck's 'Flight,'" *Stud Short Fiction*, 17 (1980), 437–443.
Rohrberger, Mary. *Instructor's Manual*..., 26.

"The Gift"
Rao, B. Ramachandra. *The American Fictional Hero*..., 64–65.

"The Leader of the People"
Lisca, Peter. ...*Nature and Myth*, 199–200.

"The Raid"
Lisca, Peter. ...*Nature and Myth*, 193–194.

"The Snake"
Ahrends, Günter. ...*Kurzgeschichte*, 158–160.

"The White Quail"
McCarthy, Paul. *John Steinbeck*, 27–28.
*Mitchell, Marilyn L. "Steinbeck's Strong Women...," 26–35.

JACOB STEINBERG

"Among the Silver Poplars"
Komem, Aharon. "The Use of Setting in Jacob Steinberg's Short Stories," in Heinemann, Joseph, and Shmuel Werses, Eds. *Studies in Hebrew Narrative Art*..., 185–187.

"The Blind Woman"
Komem, Aharon. "The Use of Setting...," 183–184.

"In a Nobleman's Courtyard"
Komem, Aharon. "The Use of Setting...," 176–177.

"The Man of Wealth"
Komem, Aharon. "The Use of Setting...," 179–180.

"Melon Fields"
Komem, Aharon. "The Use of Setting...," 179.

"On the Ukraine Border"
Komem, Aharon. "The Use of Setting...," 180–181, 182–183.

"The Rabbi's Daughter"
Komem, Aharon. "The Use of Setting...," 175–176, 181–182, 184.

JAMES STERN

"The Broken Leg"
Allen, Walter. *The Short Story*..., 239–240.

CARL STERNHEIM

"Heidenstam"
Dietrick, Augustinus P. "Two Representative Expressionist Responses to the
    Challenge of the First World War: Carl Sternheim's *eigene Nuance* and Leonhard
    Frank's Utopia," in Genno, Charles N., and Heinz Wetzel, Eds. *First World
    War...*, 23-24.

"Meta"
Dietrick, Augustinus P. "Two Representative Expressionist Responses...," 20-21.

"Posinsky"
Dietrick, Augustinus P. "Two Representative Expressionist Responses...," 24-25.

"Ulrike"
Dietrick, Augustinus P. "Two Representative Expressionist Responses...," 21-22.

ROBERT LOUIS STEVENSON

"The Beach at Falesa"
Allen, Walter. *The Short Story...*, 16-18.

"The Force"
Allen, Walter. *The Short Story...*, 238-239.

"A Lodging for the Night"
Allen, Walter. *The Short Story...*, 14-15.

"The Man Who Was Loved"
Allen, Walter. *The Short Story...*, 236-238.

"Markheim"
Ziolkowski, Theodore. *Disenchanted Images...*, 187-190.

"Olalla"
Ziolkowski, Theodore. *Disenchanted Images...*, 108-109.

"The Strange Case of Dr. Jekyll and Mr. Hyde"
Hennelly, Mark M. "Stevenson's 'Silent Symbols' of 'Fatal Cross Roads' in 'Dr.
    Jekyll and Mr. Hyde,'" *Gothic*, 1 (1979), 10-16.
Jackson, Rosemary. *Fantasy...*, 114-116.
MacAndrew, Elizabeth. *The Gothic Tradition...*, 223-229.
Punter, David. *The Literature of Terror...*, 240-245.

"Thrawn Janet"
Briggs, Julia. *Night Visitors...*, 101-102.

THE STEVENSONS [no further identification]

"Chinatown: My Land of Dreams"
Chu, Limin. *The Image of China...*, 217.

ADALBERT STIFTER

"The Old Seal"
Gump, Margaret. "Alles um der Ehre willen: Stifters 'Das alte Siegel' und Fontanes *Effi Briest*," *Adalbert Stifter Institut*, 28 (1979), 49–50.
Watanbe-O'Kelley, Helen. "Stifters Schicksalstheorie in der Erzählung 'Das alte Siegel,'" *Adalbert Stifter Institut*, 30, i–ii (1981), 3–13.

"The Second-Hand Market"
Eisenmeier, Eduard. "Adalbert Stifter, 'Der Tandelmarkt': Ein unbekannter Vorabdruck," *Adalbert Stifter Institut*, 28 (1979), 3–17.

FRANK R. STOCKTON

"The Bee-Man of Orn"
Golemba, Henry L. *Frank R. Stockton*, 112–113.

"The Christmas Shadrach"
Golemba, Henry L. *Frank R. Stockton*, 96–97.

"Derelict, A Tale of the Wayward Sea"
Golemba, Henry L. *Frank R. Stockton*, 82–83.

"The Griffin and the Minor Canon"
Attebery, Brian. *The Fantasy Tradition . . .*, 70–72.

"The Knife That Killed Po Hancy"
Golemba, Henry L. *Frank R. Stockton*, 118–124.

"The Lady, or the Tiger?"
Golemba, Henry L. *Frank R. Stockton*, 144–146.

"My Translataphone"
Golemba, Henry L. *Frank R. Stockton*, 131–135.

"The Water-Devil"
Golemba, Henry L. *Frank R. Stockton*, 129–131.

THEODOR STORM

"Auf dem Staatshof"
Lohmeier, Dieter. "Erzählprobleme des Poetischen Realismus: Am Beispiel von Storms Novelle 'Auf dem Staatshof,'" *Schriften der Theodor-Storm-Gesellschaft*, 28 (1979), 109–122.

ALFONSINA STORNI

"Catalina"
Jones, Sonia. *Alfonsina Storni*, 129–130.

"A Crisis"
Jones, Sonia. *Alfonsina Storni*, 111–113.

"Cuca in Six Episodes"
Jones, Sonia. *Alfonsina Storni*, 127–128.

"An Elegant Soul"
Jones, Sonia. *Alfonsina Storni*, 113–117.

"A Letter"
Jones, Sonia. *Alfonsina Storni*, 124–125.

"Letter from a Bride-To-Be"
Jones, Sonia. *Alfonsina Storni*, 121–122.

"Letter to a Young Friend"
Jones, Sonia. *Alfonsina Storni*, 122–123.

"My School"
Jones, Sonia. *Alfonsina Storni*, 110.

"Refined Cruelty"
Jones, Sonia. *Alfonsina Storni*, 109–110.

"A Swallow"
Jones, Sonia. *Alfonsina Storni*, 117–121.

"Two Cents' Worth of Psychology"
Jones, Sonia. *Alfonsina Storni*, 123–124.

JESSE STUART

"Rain on Tanyard Hollow"
Patrick, Nancy. "Jesse Stuart's Water Symbolism in 'Rain on Tanyard Hollow' and 'The Storm,'" *Jack London Newsletter*, 13 (1980), 72–73.

"The Storm"
Patrick, Nancy. "Jesse Stuart's Water Symbolism...," 72–73.

WILLIAM STYRON

"The Long March"
*Galloway, David. *The Absurd Hero...*, 2nd rev. ed., 89–91.
Leon, Philip W. "Styron's Fiction: Narrative as Idea," in Morris, Robert K., and Irving Malin, Eds. *The Achievement...*, 2nd ed., 129–132.
*Malin, Irving. "The Symbolic March," in Morris, Robert K., and Irving Malin, Eds. *The Achievement...*, 2nd ed., 179–190.

"This Is My Daughter"
Firestone, Bruce M. "The Early Apprenticeship of William Styron," *Stud Short Fiction*, 18 (1981), 440–441.

RUTH SUCKOW

"A Start in Life"
Oehlschlaeger, Fritz. "The Art of Ruth Suckow's 'A Start in Life,'" *Western Am Lit*, 15 (1980), 177-186.

HERMANN SUDERMANN

"Die Reise nach Tilsit"
Motekat, Helmut. "Hermann Sudermanns 'Die Reise nach Tilsit,'" in Rix, Walter T., Ed. *Hermann Sudermann*..., 189-199.

SUI SIN FAR [EDITH EATON]

"A Chinese Ishmael"
Chu, Limin. *The Image of China*..., 200-201.

RONALD SUKENICK

"The Birds"
Rohrberger, Mary. *Instructor's Manual*..., 45-46.
Scott, Virgil, and David Madden. *Instructor's Manual*..., 4th ed., 65-68.

SUNIL GANGOPADHYAY

"Drought"
Chakravarty, D. K. "Bengali Short Story Today," *Indian Lit*, 21, i (1978), 76.

"The Man Who Wanted to Be Free"
Adkins, Joan F. "An Analysis of Three Short Stories," *Indian Lit*, 21, i (1978), 58-60.

"One Side of Revenge"
Chakravarty, D. K. "Bengali Short Story Today," 75-76.

JULES SUPERVIELLE

"The Adolescent"
Jones, Louisa E. *Poetic Fantasy*..., 24-25.

"Les Bonshommes du Cire"
Jones, Louisa E. *Poetic Fantasy*..., 57-60.

"A Child"
Jones, Louisa E. *Poetic Fantasy*..., 46-48.

"L'Enlèvement d'Europe"
Jones, Louisa E. *Poetic Fantasy*..., 38-40.

"Der Kuhreiher"
Bauer, Ruth. "'Der Kuhreiher,'" in Lehmann, Jakob, Ed. *Interpretationen*..., 62–67.

"The Minotaur"
Jones, Louisa E. *Poetic Fantasy*..., 31–32.

"Le Modèle des Epoux"
Jones, Louisa E. *Poetic Fantasy*..., 32–33.

"Noah's Ark"
Jones, Louisa E. *Poetic Fantasy*..., 20–22.

"Orpheus"
Jones, Louisa E. *Poetic Fantasy*..., 67–71.

"The Ox and the Ass of the Crèche"
Jones, Louisa E. *Poetic Fantasy*..., 42–44.

ITALO SVEVO [ETTORE SCHMITZ]

"The Hoax"
Moloney, Brian. *Italo Svevo*..., 96–97.
Robinson, Paula. "'Una Burla Riuseita': Irony as Hoax in Svevo," *Mod Fiction Stud*, 18 (1972), 65–80.

"The Murder on the Via Belpoggio"
Moloney, Brian. *Italo Svevo*..., 28–30.

"The Story of the Nice Old Man and the Pretty Girl"
Moloney, Brian. *Italo Svevo*..., 95–96.

TANIZAKI JUN'ICHIRŌ

"Aguri"
Petersen, Gwenn B. *The Moon*..., 89–90.

"Bridge of Dreams"
Petersen, Gwenn B. *The Moon*..., 71–76.

"Secrets of Lord Bushu"
Lippit, Noriko M. *Reality and Fiction*..., 90–91.

"Tattoo"
Lippit, Noriko M. *Reality and Fiction*..., 92.

TAYAMA KATAI

"One Cold Morning"
Henshall, Kenneth G., Ed. *"The Quilt" and Other Stories*..., 28–29.

PETER TAYLOR

"At the Drugstore"
Casey, James B. "A View of Peter Taylor's Stories," *Virginia Q R*, 54 (1978), 215–217.

"The Captain's Son"
Casey, James B. "...Peter Taylor's Stories," 218–220.

"Daphne's Lover"
Casey, James B. "...Peter Taylor's Stories," 220–222.

"The Hand of Emmagene"
Brooks, Cleanth, and Robert P. Warren. *Instructor's Manual...*, 3rd ed., 52–54.
———. *Understanding Fiction*, 3rd ed., 285–286.
Casey, James B. "...Peter Taylor's Stories," 214–215.

"In the Miro District"
Casey, James B. "...Peter Taylor's Stories," 223–230.

"A Lonely Fourth"
Casey, James B. "...Peter Taylor's Stories," 214–215.

"Miss Leonora When Last Seen"
Allen, Walter. *The Short Story...*, 321–322.

"What You Hear from 'Em?"
Allen, Walter. *The Short Story...*, 319–321.
*Mizener, Arthur. *A Handbook...*, 4th ed., 207–210.

VLADIMIR FĒDOROVICH TENDRIAKOV

"The Night after Graduation"
Shneidman, N. N. *Soviet Literature...*, 22.

"Potholes"
Brown, Deming. *...Literature Since Stalin*, 171–172.

"Twenty Years Late"
Trifonov, Yurii. "'Twenty Years Late,'" trans. Eve Manning, *Soviet Lit*, 8 (1981), 3–4.

"The Windfall"
Brown, Deming. *...Literature Since Stalin*, 169–170.

DYLAN THOMAS

"The Fight"
Allen, Walter. *The Short Story...*, 299–301.

JAMES THURBER

"The Catbird Seat"
Kennedy, X. J. *Instructor's Manual...*, 2nd ed., 14–15.

"A Couple of Hamburgers"
*Mizener, Arthur, Ed. *Modern Short Stories...*, 4th ed., 240–242.

"The Greatest Man in the World"
Rovit, Earl. "On James Thurber and 'The Greatest Man in the World,'" in Skaggs, Calvin, Ed. *The American Short Story*, II, 370–371.

"The Secret Life of Walter Mitty"
*Brooks, Cleanth, and Robert P. Warren. *Understanding Fiction*, 3rd ed., 17–19.
Smith, Elliott L., and Andrew W. Hart, Eds. *The Short Story...*, 47–48.

JOHANN LUDWIG TIECK

"The Elves"
Favier, Georges. "L'Age de raison: Note sur un conte de Tieck: 'Die Elfen,'" in Brunet, G., Ed. *Études allemandes...*, 47–91.

JAMES TIPTREE [ALICE HASTINGS SHELDON]

"Houston, Houston, Do You Read?"
Pei, Lowry. "Poor Singletons: Definition of Humanity in the Stories of James Tiptree, Jr.," *Sci-Fiction Stud*, 6 (1979), 276–277.

"Love Is the Plan the Plan Is Death"
Pei, Lowry. "Poor Singletons...," 272–273.

"Mama Comes Home"
Pei, Lowry. "Poor Singletons...," 274–275.

"The Screwfly Solution"
Pei, Lowry. "Poor Singletons...," 275–276.

J. R. R. TOLKIEN

"Leaf by Niggle"
Rogers, Deborah W. and Ivor A. *J. R. R. Tolkien*, 55–58.

LEO TOLSTOY

"The Death of Ivan Ilych"
Costa, Richard H. "Maugham's 'Partial Self': The 'Unexpected View' on the Way to 'The Death of Ivan Ilych,'" *Coll Engl Assoc Critic*, 43, iv (1981), 3–7.

Leitner, Andreas. "Leo Tolstois Novelle 'Der Tod des Iwan Iljitsch,'" *Sprachkunst*, 10 (1979), 79–86.
Matual, David. "*The Confession* as Subtext in 'The Death of Ivan Il'ich,'" *Int'l Fiction R*, 8, ii (1981), 124–128.
Russell, Robert. "From Individual to Universal: 'Smert Ivana Il'icha,'" *Mod Lang R*, 76 (1981), 629–642.
Schaarschmidt, Gunter. "Time and Discourse Structure in 'The Death of Ivan Il'ich,'" *Canadian Slavonic Papers*, 21 (1979), 356–366.

"Family Happiness"
Kisseleff, Natalia. "Idyll and Ideal: Aspects of Sentimentalism in Tolstoy's 'Family Happiness,'" *Canadian Slavonic Papers*, 21 (1979), 336–346.

"Hadji Murat"
Heier, Edmund. "'Hadji Murat' in the Light of Tolstoy's Moral and Aesthetic Theories," *Canadian Slavonic Papers*, 21 (1979), 324–335.

"Polikushka"
Parthe, Kathleen. "Masking the Fantastic and the Taboo in Tolstoj's 'Polikushka,'" *Slavic & East European J*, 25 (1981), 21–33.

"Three Deaths"
Pisarev, Dmitri. "'Three Deaths': A Story by Count L. N. Tolstoi," trans. Edmund Yarwood, *Russian Lit Tri-Q*, 11 (Winter, 1975), 186–195.

JEAN TOOMER

"Avey"
Benson, Brian J., and Mabel M. Dillard. *Jean Toomer*, 70–75.

"Blood-Burning Moon"
Benson, Brian J., and Mabel M. Dillard. *Jean Toomer*, 64–68.
Brannan, Tim. "Up from the Dusk: Interpretations of Jean Toomer's 'Blood-Burning Moon,'" *Pembroke Mag*, 8 (1977), 167–172.

"Bona and Paul"
Benson, Brian J., and Mabel M. Dillard. *Jean Toomer*, 82–86.

"Box Seat"
Benson, Brian J., and Mabel M. Dillard. *Jean Toomer*, 76–79.
Perry, Margaret. *Silence to the Drums . . .* , 37–38.
Schultz, Elizabeth. "Jean Toomer's 'Box Seat': The Possibilities for 'Constructive Crises,'" *Black Am Lit Forum*, 13 (Spring, 1979), 7–12.

"Esther"
Benson, Brian J., and Mabel M. Dillard. *Jean Toomer*, 60–64.
Perry, Margaret. *Silence to the Drums . . .* , 35–37.

"Fern"
Benson, Brian J., and Mabel M. Dillard. *Jean Toomer*, 58–60.

"Kabnis"
Benson, Brian J., and Mabel M. Dillard. *Jean Toomer*, 86-95.
MacKethan, Lucinda H. "Jean Toomer's *Cane*: A Pastoral Problem," *Mississippi Q*, 28 (1975), 433; rpt. in her *The Dream of Arcady*..., 122-124.
Payne, Ladell. *Black Novelists*..., 49-51.
Perry, Margaret. *Silence to the Drums*..., 38-42.

"Mr. Costyve Duditch"
Benson, Brian J., and Mabel M. Dillard. *Jean Toomer*, 119-125.
MacKethan, Lucinda H. *The Dream of Arcady*..., 211-215.

"Monrovia"
Rusch, Frederick L. "A Tale of the Country Round: Jean Toomer's Legend, 'Monrovia,'" *MELUS*, 7, i (1980), 37-46.

"Theater"
Benson, Brian J., and Mabel M. Dillard. *Jean Toomer*, 75-76.

"Winter on Earth"
Benson, Brian J., and Mabel M. Dillard. *Jean Toomer*, 112-119.

ESTELA PORTILLO TRAMBLEY [ESTELA PORTILLO]

"The Burning"
Salinas, Judy. "The Role of Women in Chicano Literature," in Jiménez, Francisco, Ed.... *Chicano Literature*, 207-210.

"If It Weren't for the Honeysuckles..."
Lattin, Patricia and Vernon. "Power and Freedom in the Stories of Estela Portillo Trambley," *Critique*, 21, i (1979), 97-99.

"The Paris Gown"
Lattin, Patricia and Vernon. "Power and Freedom...," 95-96.
Salinas, Judy. "The Role of Women...," 217-221.

"The Secret Room"
Lattin, Patricia and Vernon. "Power and Freedom...," 96-97.

"The Trees"
Lattin, Patricia and Vernon. "Power and Freedom...," 99-100.

BRUNO TRAVEN

"Assembly Line"
Gutierrez, Donald. "Maker Versus Profit-Maker: B. Traven's 'Assembly Line,'" *Stud Short Fiction*, 17 (1980), 9-14.

OWEN C. TRELEAVEN

"Poison Jim Chinaman"
Chu, Limin. *The Image of China*..., 218-219.

IURII TRIFONOV

"The House on the Embankment"
Shneidman, N. N. *Soviet Literature*..., 93-94.

"The Long Goodbye"
Shneidman, N. N. *Soviet Literature*..., 92.

"Preliminary Results"
Shneidman, N. N. *Soviet Literature*..., 91-92.

IVAN TURGENEV

"The Country Doctor" [same as "The District Doctor"]
Brooks, Cleanth, and Robert P. Warren. *Instructor's Manual*..., 3rd ed., 26-28.

"The Tryst"
Smith, Elliott L. and Wanda V. *Instructor's Manual*..., 16-17.

MARK TWAIN [SAMUEL L. CLEMENS]

"Captain Stormfield's Visit to Heaven"
Bellamy, Gladys. *Mark Twain*..., 368-370; rpt. McMahan, Elizabeth, Ed. ... *Twain's Short Stories*, 109-110.
Budd, Louis. *Mark Twain*..., 189-190; rpt. McMahan, Elizabeth, Ed. ... *Twain's Short Stories*, 111.
Cox, James M. ... *Fate of Humor*, 291-293; rpt. McMahan, Elizabeth, Ed. ... *Twain's Short Stories*, 112-113.
Gibson, William. *The Art*..., 83-89; rpt. McMahan, Elizabeth, Ed.... *Twain's Short Stories*, 113-117.

"The Celebrated Jumping Frog of Calaveras County"
Ahrends, Günter. ... *Kurzgeschichte*, 101-104.
Barker, Gerard A. *Instructor's Manual*..., 12-13.
*Bellamy, Gladys. "The Art of 'The Jumping Frog,'" in McMahan, Elizabeth, Ed. ... *Twain's Short Stories*, 16-18.
Cox, James M. ... *Fate of Humor*, 26-33; rpt. McMahan, Elizabeth, Ed. ... *Twain's Short Stories*, 32-36.
*Krause, Sydney J. "The Art and Satire of Twain's 'Jumping Frog' Story," in McMahan, Elizabeth, Ed. ... *Twain's Short Stories*, 21-31.
*Lynn, Kenneth S. "Upset Expectations in 'The Jumping Frog,'" in McMahan, Elizabeth, Ed. ... *Twain's Short Stories*, 18-20.
Smith, Henry N. *Mark Twain*..., 11; rpt. McMahan, Elizabeth, Ed. ... *Twain's Short Stories*, 20-21.
Smith, Lawrence R. "Mark Twain's 'Jumping Frog': Toward an American Heroic Ideal," *Mark Twain J*, 20, i (1979-80), 15-18.

"The Facts Concerning the Recent Carnival of Crime in Connecticut"
Geismar, Maxwell. *Mark Twain* . . . , 52–54; rpt. McMahan, Elizabeth, Ed. . . .
  Twain's Short Stories, 46–48.
Gibson, William. *The Art* . . . , 178–184; rpt. McMahan, Elizabeth, Ed. . . . *Twain's
  Short Stories*, 48–52.

"Grandfather's Ram"
Wadlington, Warwick. *The Confidence Game* . . . , 207–212.

"The Great Dark"
Kosinski, Mark. "Mark Twain's Absurd Universe and 'The Great Dark,'" *Stud
  Short Fiction*, 16 (1979), 335–340.

"The Man That Corrupted Hadleyburg"
*Bellamy, Gladys. "Moralism Versus Determinism in 'Hadleyburg,'" in McMahan,
  Elizabeth, Ed. . . . *Twain's Short Stories*, 65–66.
*Brodwin, Stanley. "Mark Twain's Mask of Satan: The Final Phase," in McMahan,
  Elizabeth, Ed. . . . *Twain's Short Stories*, 89–92.
*Burhans, Clinton S. "The Sober Affirmation of Mark Twain's 'Hadleyburg,'" in
  McMahan, Elizabeth, Ed. . . . *Twain's Short Stories*, 66–74.
*Geismar, Maxwell. "Twain's Ironic Parable on the Hypocrisy of Human Virtue,"
  in McMahan, Elizabeth, Ed. . . . *Twain's Short Stories*, 85–89.
Marshall, W. Gerald. "Mark Twain's 'The Man That Corrupted Hadleyburg' and
  the Myth of Baucis and Philemon," *Mark Twain J*, 20, ii (1980), 4–7.
*Rule, Henry B. "The Role of Satan in 'The Man That Corrupted Hadleyburg,'"
  in McMahan, Elizabeth, Ed. . . . *Twain's Short Stories*, 76–85.
Scharnhorst, Gary. "Paradise Revisited: Twain's 'The Man That Corrupted
  Hadleyburg,'" *Stud Short Fiction*, 18 (1981), 59–64.
Seelye, John. "On Mark Twain and 'The Man That Corrupted Hadleyburg,'"
  in Skaggs, Calvin, Ed. *The American Short Story*, II, 151–158.
Smith, Henry N. *Mark Twain* . . . , 183–184; rpt. McMahan, Elizabeth, Ed. . . .
  Twain's Short Stories, 74–75.

"The Mysterious Stranger"
Karnath, David. "'The Mysterious Stranger': Its Mode of Thought," *Mark Twain
  J*, 19, iv (1979), 4–8.
*May, John R. "The Gospel According to Philip Traum: Structural Unity of 'The
  Mysterious Stranger,'" in McMahan, Elizabeth, Ed. . . . *Twain's Short Stories*,
  124–134.
Varisco, Raymond. "Divine Foolishness: A Critical Evaluation of Mark Twain's
  'The Mysterious Stranger,'" *Revista/Review Interamericana*, 5 (1975), 741–749;
  rpt. in McMahan, Elizabeth, Ed. . . . *Twain's Short Stories*, 134–142.

"The £1,000,000 Bank Note"
Foner, Philip. . . . *Social Critic*, 160–161; rpt. McMahan, Elizabeth, Ed. . . . *Twain's
  Short Stories*, 54–55.
Morgan, Ricki. "Mark Twain's Money Imagery in 'The £1,000,000 Bank Note'
  and 'The $30,000 Bequest,'" *Mark Twain J*, 19 (Winter, 1977–1978), 6–10;
  rpt. McMahan, Elizabeth, Ed. . . . *Twain's Short Stories*, 56–63.

"The $30,000 Bequest"
Fenger, Gerald J. "The Complete Irony of 'The $30,000 Bequest,'" in McMahan,
  Elizabeth, Ed. . . . *Twain's Short Stories*, 98–104.

Geismar, Maxwell. *Mark Twain*..., 249–255; rpt. McMahan, Elizabeth, Ed.
...*Twain's Short Stories*, 94–98.
Morgan, Ricki. "Mark Twain's Money Imagery...," 6–10; rpt. McMahan,
Elizabeth, Ed. ...*Twain's Short Stories*, 56–63.

"A True Story, Repeated Word for Word as I Heard It"
Fenger, Gerald J. "Telling It Like It Was," in McMahan, Elizabeth, Ed. ...*Twain's
Short Stories*, 39–42.
Foner, Philip. ...*Social Critic*, 204; rpt. McMahan, Elizabeth, Ed. ...*Twain's
Short Stories*, 38.
Gibson, William. *The Art*..., 76–79; rpt. McMahan, Elizabeth, Ed. ...*Twain's
Short Stories*, 42–44.

MIGUEL DE UNAMUNO

"Abel Sánchez"
Campanella, Hebe N. "Unamuno: El motivo biblico de Caín en 'Abel Sánchez,'"
in *Mélanges à mémoire*..., 517–529.
Franz, Thomas R. "Nietzsche and the Theme of Self-Surpassing in 'Abel Sánchez,'"
in Ebersole, Alva V., Ed. *Perspectivas sobre la novela*..., 59–81.
Nicholas, Robert L. "El proceso de creación en 'Abel Sánchez,'" in Brancaforte,
Benito, Edward R. Mulvihill, Roberto G. Sánchez, and John Crispin, Eds.
Homenaje a Antonio Sánchez Barbudo..., 167–185.
Nieves Alonso, Maria. "'Abel Sánchez': Una historia de redencion," *Estudios
Filológicos*, 16 (1981), 109–125.
Turner, David G. *Unamuno's Webs*..., 63–77.
Wyers, Frances. ...*The Contrary Self*, 85–89.

"Aunt Tula"
Semprún Donahue, Moraima de. "El 'chauvinismo' femenino en 'La tía Tula,'"
Explicación de Textos Literarios, 8 (1979–1980), 219–223.
Turner, David G. *Unamuno's Webs*..., 92–106.
Wyers, Frances. ...*The Contrary Self*, 78–81.

"The Man Who Buried Himself"
Wyers, Frances. ...*The Contrary Self*, 82–85.

"Saint Manuel the Good, Martyr"
Blancos Aguinaga, Carlos. "Relectura de 'San Manuel Bueno, Mártir' para Sánchez
Barbudo," in Brancaforte, Benito, Edward R. Mulvihill, Roberto G. Sánchez,
and John Crispin, Eds. *Homenaje a Antonio Sánchez Barbudo*..., 109–115.
Brancaforte, Benito. "El objeto del deseo en 'San Manuel Bueno, Mártir,'" in
Brancaforte, Benito, Edward R. Mulvihill, Roberto G. Sánchez, and John
Crispin, Eds. *Homenaje a Antonio Sánchez Barbudo*..., 117–138.
Longhurst, C. A. "The Problem of Truth in 'San Manuel Bueno, Mártir,'" *Mod
Lang R*, 76 (1981), 581–597.
Turner, David G. *Unamuno's Webs*..., 122–129.
Wyers, Frances. ...*The Contrary Self*, 104–116.

JOHN UPDIKE

"A & P"
Allen, Walter. *The Short Story*. . ., 372-373.
Smith, Elliott L., and Andrew W. Hart, Eds. *The Short Story*. . ., 143-144.
Uphaus, Suzanne H. *John Updike*, 124-127.

"Ace in the Hole"
*Detweiler, Robert. "*The Same Door*: Unexpected Gifts," in Thorburn, David, and
Howard Eiland, Eds. *John Updike*. . ., 170-172.

"The Astronomer"
Hunt, George W. *John Updike*. . ., 21-30.

"The Bulgarian Poetess"
Hunt, George W. *John Updike*. . ., 161-162.
Samuels, Charles T. "*The Music School*: A Place of Resonance," *Nation*, 203 (October
3, 1966), 328; rpt. Thorburn, David, and Howard Eiland, Eds. *John Updike*. . .,
194-195.

"The Christian Roommates"
Samuels, Charles T. "*The Music School*. . .," 328; rpt. Thorburn, David, and Howard
Eiland, Eds. *John Updike*. . ., 193-194.

"The Day of the Dying Rabbit"
Culbertson, Diane. "Updike's 'The Day of the Dying Rabbit,'" *Stud Am Fiction*,
7, i (1979), 95-99.

"The Family Meadow"
Allen, Walter. *The Short Story*. . ., 371-372.

"Flight"
Mizener, Arthur. *The Sense of Life*. . ., 258-259; rpt. Thorburn, David, and
Howard Eiland, Eds. *John Updike*. . ., 180-181.

"Four Sides of One Story"
Blechner, Michael H. "Tristan in Letters: Malory, C. S. Lewis, Updike," *Tristania*,
6, i (1980), 30-37.

"The Happiest I've Been"
*Detweiler, Robert. "*The Same Door*. . .," 174-176.
Todd, Richard. "Updike and Barthelme: Disengagement," *Atlantic*, 126-128; rpt.
Thorburn, David, and Howard Eiland, Eds. *John Updike*. . ., 208-209.

"Here Come the Maples"
Uphaus, Suzanne H. *John Updike*, 129-130.

"Leaves"
Hunt, George W. "Reality, Imagination, and Art: The Significance of Updike's
'Best' Story," *Stud Short Fiction*, 16 (1979), 219-229.
———. *John Updike*. . ., 109-116.

"Museums and Women"
Todd, Richard. "Updike and Barthelme...," 128; rpt. Thorburn, David, and
Howard Eiland, Eds. *John Updike*..., 209–210.

"The Music School"
Sant'Anna, Norma. "Some Considerations on John Updike's 'Music School,'" *Estudos
Anglo-Americanos*, 3–4 (1979–1980), 200–205.

"Packed Dirt, Churchgoing, A Dying Cat, A Traded Car"
Mizener, Arthur. *The Sense of Life*..., 259–261; rpt. Thorburn, David, and Howard
Eiland, Eds. *John Updike*..., 181–182.
*Novak, Michael. "Updike's Quest for Liturgy," in Thorburn, David, and Howard
Eiland, Eds. *John Updike*..., 183–191.

"The Persistence of Desire"
Mizener, Arthur. *The Sense of Life*..., 258; rpt. Thorburn, David, and Howard
Eiland, Eds. *John Updike*..., 180.

"Pigeon Feathers"
Ahrends, Günter. ...*Kurzgeschichte*, 202–203.
Allen, Walter. *The Short Story*..., 373–375.
Uphaus, Suzanne H. *John Updike*, 122–124.

"A Sense of Shelter"
*Mizener, Arthur. *A Handbook*..., 4th ed., 43–46.

"Snowing in Greenwich Village"
*Detweiler, Robert. "*The Same Door*...," 172–174.

"Tomorrow and Tomorrow and So Forth"
Howard, Daniel F., and John Ribar. *Instructor's Manual*..., 4th ed., 81–82.

"Who Made Yellow Roses Yellow?"
Scott, Virgil, and David Madden. *Instructor's Manual*..., 4th ed., 94–97; Madden,
David. *Instructor's Manual*..., 5th ed., 99–101.

"Wife-Wooing"
Mizener, Arthur. *The Sense of Life*..., 257–258; rpt. Thorburn, David, and Howard
Eiland, Eds. *John Updike*..., 179.

GUADALUPE VALDÉS-FALLIS

"Recuerdo"
Rosinsky, Natalie M. "Mothers and Daughters: Another Minority Group," in
Davidson, Cathy N., and E. M. Broner, Eds. *The Lost Tradition*..., 281.

ELEODORO VARGAS VICUÑA

"Taita Cristo"
Suárez-Murias, Marguerite C. "Arquetipos místicos y existencialistas en 'Taita Cristo' de Eleodoro Vargas Vicuña," *Explicación de Textos Literarios*, 10, i (1981), 15-21.

NIRMAL VARMA

"The Burning Bush"
Adkins, Joan F. "An Analysis of Three Short Stories," *Indian Lit*, 21, i (1978), 62-65.

GIOVANNI VERGA

"Gramigna's Lover"
Brooks, Cleanth, and Robert P. Warren. *Instructor's Manual...*, 3rd ed., 2-4.
_____. *Understanding Fiction*, 3rd ed., 12-13.

"The She-Wolf"
Lucente, Gregory L. "The Ideology of Form in Verga's 'La Lupa': Realism, Myth, and the Passion of Control," *Mod Lang Notes*, 95 (1980), 104-138; rpt. in his *The Narrative of Realism...*, 54-94.
Ruderman, Judith G. "Lawrence's 'The Fox' and Verga's 'The She-Wolf': Variations on the Theme of the 'Devouring Mother,'" *Mod Lang Notes*, 94 (1979), 153-165.

JAVIER DE VIANA

"Leopoldo Almeida"
Barros-Lemez, Alvaro. "'Leopoldo Almeida': Un relato clave para la comprensión de la obra de Javier de Viana," *Hispamerica*, 10, xxix (1981), 63-69.

LUANDINGO VIEIRA

"Grandmother Xixi and Her Grandson Zeca Santos"
Jacinto, Tomás. "The Art of Luandingo Vieira," in Burness, Donald, Ed. *Critical Perspectives...*, 79-80.

"The Story of the Chicken and the Egg"
Jacinto, Tomás. "The Art of Luandingo Vieira," 81-83.

"The Thief and the Parrot"
Jacinto, Tomás. "The Art of Luandingo Vieira," 80-81.

[COUNT] VILLIERS DE L'ISLE-ADAM
[JEAN MARIE MATTHIAS PHILIPPE AUGUSTE]

"The Desire to Be a Man"
Ziolkowski, Theodore. *Disenchanted Images*..., 192–193.

"A Tale of Love"
Rose, Marilyn G. "Decadence in Villiers de l'Isle-Adam and His Followers," *Orbis Litterarum*, 36 (1981), 141–154.

"Véra"
Rashkin, Esther. "Truth's Turn: Rereading the Fantastic in Villiers' 'Véra,'" *Romanic R*, 72 (1981), 460–471.

ELIO VITTORINI

"Erica e i suoi fratelli"
Debenedetti, Giacomo. "Vittorini a Cracovia," *Paragone*, No. 206 (April, 1967), 111–118.
Potter, Joy H. "The Poetic and Symbolic Function of Fable in 'Erica,'" *Italica*, 48 (1971), 51–70; rpt. in part in her *Elio Vittorini*, 59–66.

"La Garibaldina" [originally titled "Il soldato e la garibaldina"]
Potter, Joy H. *Elio Vittorini*, 112–118.

"Giochi di ragazzi"
Panacali, Anna. "Un romanzo Vittoriniano interrotto: 'Giochi di ragazzi,'" *Letteratura*, Nos. 94–96 (July-December, 1968), 153–167.
Potter, Joy H. *Elio Vittorini*, 58–59.

"Portrait of King Giampiero"
Potter, Joy H. *Elio Vittorini*, 33–35.

VLADIMIR VOINOVICH

"Two Comrades"
Brown, Deming. ...*Literature Since Stalin*, 189–191.

"We Live Here"
Brown, Deming. ...*Literature Since Stalin*, 187–188.

KURT VONNEGUT

"Harrison Bergeron"
Madden, David. *Instructor's Manual*..., 5th ed., 50–51.

"Next Door"
Barker, Gerard A. *Instructor's Manual*..., 67–68.

JOHN WAIN

"Master Richard"
Salwak, Dale. *John Wain*, 110-111.

"Nuncle"
Gindin, James J. *Postwar British Fiction...*, 139-140.

ALICE WALKER

"The Child Who Favored Daughter"
Mickelson, Anna Z. *Reaching Out...*, 158-159.

"Everyday Use"
Mickelson, Anna Z. *Reaching Out...*, 159.
Rosinsky, Natalie M. "Mothers and Daughters: Another Minority Group," in
    Davidson, Cathy N., and E. M. Broner, Eds. *The Lost Tradition...*, 284.

"Her Sweet Jerome"
Mickelson, Anna Z. *Reaching Out...*, 156-157.

"Really, *Doesn't* Crime Pay?"
Mickelson, Anna Z. *Reaching Out...*, 155-156.

"Roselily"
Mickelson, Anna Z. *Reaching Out...*, 155.

"Strong Horse Tea"
Mickelson, Anna Z. *Reaching Out...*, 157-158.

"To Hell with Dying"
Mickelson, Anna Z. *Reaching Out...*, 159-160.

EDWARD LEWIS WALLANT

"The Days to Come"
Galloway, David. *Edward Lewis Wallant*, 26.

"Fathers"
Galloway, David. *Edward Lewis Wallant*, 24-26.

"Fight Night"
Galloway, David. *Edward Lewis Wallant*, 20-21.

"I Held Back My Hand"
Galloway, David. *Edward Lewis Wallant*, 26-27.

"Life Is a Fountain"
Galloway, David. *Edward Lewis Wallant*, 28-30.

"The Man Who Made a Nice Appearance"
Galloway, David. *Edward Lewis Wallant*, 21–23.
Mesher, David R. "Con Artist and Middleman: The Archetypes of Wallant's
    Published and Unpublished Fiction," *Yale Univ Lib Gazette*, 54 (1981), 43–44.

"Robert"
Galloway, David. *Edward Lewis Wallant*, 23–24.

JOHN H. WALSH

"Mr. Poudicherry and the Smugglers"
Chu, Limin. *The Image of China...*, 174.

WANG CHEN-HO

"Hsiao Lin in Taipei"
Yang, Robert Yi. "Form and Tone in Wang Chen-ho's Satires," in Faurot, Jeannette
    L., Ed. *Chinese Fiction from Taiwan...*, 140–141.

"An Oxcart for Dowry"
Birch, Cyril. "Images of Suffering in Taiwan Fiction," in Faurot, Jeannette L.,
    Ed. *Chinese Fiction from Taiwan...*, 79–82.

"A Story of Three Marriages"
Yang, Robert Yi. "Form and Tone...," 139–140.

"That Year, That Winter"
Yang, Robert Yi. "Form and Tone...," 141–143.

WANG TO

"Aunt Chin-shui"
Wang, Jing. "Taiwan *Hsiang-t'u* Literature: Perspectives in the Evolution of a
    Literary Movement," in Faurot, Jeannette L., Ed. *Chinese Fiction from
    Taiwan...*, 64–65.

EUNICE WARD

"Ah Gin"
Chu, Limin. *The Image of China...*, 213.

SYLVIA TOWNSEND WARNER

"But at the Stroke of Midnight"
Allen, Walter. *The Short Story...*, 252–256.

"A View of Exmoor"
Allen, Walter. *The Short Story*..., 251–252.

ROBERT PENN WARREN

"Blackberry Winter"
*Bohner, Charles. *Robert Penn Warren*, rev. ed., 80–82.
Ford, Thomas W. "Indian Summer and Blackberry Winter: Emily Dickinson
    and Robert Penn Warren," *Southern R*, 17 (1981), 542–550.
MacKethan, Lucinda H. *The Dream of Arcady*..., 154–155.
Rocks, James E. "Warren's 'Blackberry Winter': A Reading," *Univ Mississippi Stud
    Engl*, 1 (1980), 97–105.
Walker, Marshall. *Robert Penn Warren*..., 76–78.
Wilhelm, Albert E. "Images of Initiation in Robert Penn Warren's 'Blackberry
    Winter,'" *Stud Short Fiction*, 17 (1980), 343–345.

"Christmas Gift"
Walker, Marshall. *Robert Penn Warren*..., 79.

"The Circus in the Attic"
*Bohner, Charles. *Robert Penn Warren*, rev. ed., 82–83.
Walker, Marshall. *Robert Penn Warren*..., 73–76.

"Her Own People"
Walker, Marshall. *Robert Penn Warren*..., 82–83.

"The Patented Gate and the Mean Hamburger"
*Bohner, Charles. *Robert Penn Warren*, rev. ed., 82.
MacKethan, Lucinda H. *The Dream of Arcady*..., 208–209.
Scott, Virgil, and David Madden. *Instructor's Manual*..., 4th ed., 88–90; Madden,
    David. *Instructor's Manual*..., 5th ed., 90–93.
Walker, Marshall. *Robert Penn Warren*..., 80–81.

"Prime Leaf"
Walker, Marshall. *Robert Penn Warren*..., 83.

"Testament of Flood"
Walker, Marshall. *Robert Penn Warren*..., 81–82.

"When the Light Gets Green"
*Mizener, Arthur. *A Handbook*..., 4th ed., 187–192.
Walker, Marshall. *Robert Penn Warren*..., 78–79.

EVELYN WAUGH

"Scott-King's Modern Europe"
Lane, Calvin W. *Evelyn Waugh*, 32.

"Work Suspended"
Lane, Calvin W. *Evelyn Waugh*, 88–89.

H. G. WELLS

"Aepyornis Island"
Hammond, J. R. *An H. G. Wells Companion* . . . , 62.

"The Cone"
Punter, David. *The Literature of Terror* . . . , 327–328.

"The Country of the Blind"
Hammond, J. R. *An H. G. Wells Companion* . . . , 71–73.
McConnell, Frank. *The Science Fiction* . . . , 119–121.

"The Crystal Egg"
Hammond, J. R. *An H. G. Wells Companion* . . . , 67–68.
Huntington, John. "The Science Fiction of H. G. Wells," in Parrinder, Patrick,
   Ed. *Science Fiction* . . . , 35–36.

"A Deal in Ostriches"
Huntington, John. "Thinking by Opposition: The 'Two-World' Structure in H.
   G. Wells's Short Fiction," *Sci Fiction Stud*, 8 (1981), 244.

"The Diamond Maker
Hammond, J. R. *An H. G. Wells Companion* . . . , 171–173.
Huntington, John. "Thinking by Opposition . . . ," 244–245.

"The Door in the Wall"
Allen, Walter. *The Short Story* . . . , 79–80.
Haynes, Roslynn D. *H. G. Wells* . . . , 49–50.

"The Flowering of the Strange Orchid"
Huntington, John. "Thinking by Opposition . . . ," 246–248.

"The Flying Man"
Huntington, John. "The Science Fiction . . . ," 37–38.
————. "Thinking by Opposition . . . ," 251–253.

"The Lord of the Dynamos"
Haynes, Roslynn D. *H. G. Wells* . . . , 71–73.
Huntington, John. "Thinking by Opposition . . . ," 250–251.

"The Man Who Could Work Miracles"
Hammond, J. R. *An H. G. Wells Companion* . . . , 66–67.

"Miss Winchelsea's Heart"
Hammond, J. R. *An H. G. Wells Companion* . . . , 70–71.

"Mr. Skelmersdale in Fairyland"
Hammond, J. R. *An H. G. Wells Companion* . . . , 68–69.

"The New Accelerator"
Hammond, J. R. *An H. G. Wells Companion* . . . , 69–70.

"The Purple Pileus"
Hammond, J. R. *An H. G. Wells Companion* . . . , 64.
Lake, David J. "The White Sphinx and the Whitened Lemur: Images of Death
    in 'The Time Machine,'" *Sci-Fiction Stud*, 17, i (1979), 77–84.
_____. "Wells's Time Traveller: An Unreliable Narrator?" *Extrapolation*, 22
    (1981), 117–126.
McConnell, Frank. *The Science Fiction* . . . , 70–88.
Parrinder, Patrick. "Science Fiction as Truncated Epic," in Slusser, George E.,
    George R. Guffey, and Mark Rose, Eds. *Bridges* . . . , 91–106.
Philmus, Robert M. "Revisions of the Future: 'The Time Machine,'" *J Gen Ed*,
    28 (Spring, 1976), 23–30.
Rose, Mark. *Alien Encounter* . . . , 100–105.
Scafella, Frank. "The White Sphinx and 'The Time Machine,'" *Sci Fiction Stud*,
    8 (1981), 255–265.
Wasson, Richard. "Myth and the Ex-Nomination of Class in 'The Time Machine,'"
    Minnesota R, 15 (1980), 112–122.

"The Remarkable Case of Davidson's Eyes"
Huntington, John. "The Science Fiction . . .," 35.
_____. "Thinking by Opposition . . .," 240.

"The Star"
Hammond, J. R. *An H. G. Wells Companion* . . . , 66.
Ower, John. "Theme and Technique in H. G. Wells's 'The Star,'" *Extrapolation*,
    18 (1977), 167–175.
Rose, Mark. *Alien Encounter* . . . , 24–26.

"The Stolen Bacillus"
Huntington, John. "Thinking by Opposition . . .," 248–250.
McConnell, Frank. *The Science Fiction* . . . , 46–48.

"A Story of the Days to Come"
Huntington, John. "The Science Fiction . . .," 47–48.

"The Story of the Last Trump"
Hammond, J. R. *An H. G. Wells Companion* . . . , 179.

"The Time Machine"
Hammond, J. R. *An H. G. Wells Companion* . . . , 79–82.
Haynes, Roslynn D. *H. G. Wells* . . . , 56–58.
Hennelly, Mark M. "'The Time Machine': A Romance of 'The Human Heart,'"
    Extrapolation, 20 (1979), 154–167.
Huntington, John. "The Science Fiction . . .," 38–42.
Lake, David J. "The White Sphinx and the Whitened Lemur: Images of
    Death in 'The Time Machine,'" *Sci-Fiction Stud*, 17, i (1979), 77–84.
_____. "Wells's Time Traveller: An Unreliable Narrator?" *Extrapolation*, 22
    (1981), 117–126.
McConnell, Frank. *The Science Fiction* . . . , 70–88.
Parrinder, Patrick. "Science Fiction as Truncated Epic," in Slusser, George
    E., George R. Guffey, and Mark Rose, Eds. *Bridges* . . . , 91–106.
Philmus, Robert M. "Revisions of the Future: 'The Time Machine,'" *J Gen
    Ed*, 28 (Spring, 1976), 23–30.

Rose, Mark. *Alien Encounter...*, 100–105.
Scafella, Frank. "The White Sphinx and 'The Time Machine,' " *Sci Fiction Stud*, 8 (1981), 255–265.
Wasson, Richard. "Myth and the Ex-Nomination of Class in 'The Time Machine,' " *Minnesota R*, 15 (1980), 112–122.

"The Triumph of a Taxidermist"
Huntington, John. "Thinking by Opposition...," 245–246.

"The Wild Asses of the Devil"
Hammond, J. R. *An H. G. Wells Companion...*, 179.

EUDORA WELTY

"Asphodel"
Davenport, F. Garvin. "Renewal and Historical Consciousness in *The Wide Net*," in Prenshaw, Peggy W., Ed. *Eudora Welty...*, 195–196.
Evans, Elizabeth. *Eudora Welty*, 93–94.
Holder, Alan. *The Imagined Past...*, 130–133.
Kreyling, Michael. *...Achievement of Order*, 22–23.

"At the Landing"
Davenport, F. Garvin. "Renewal...," 199.
Kreyling, Michael. *...Achievement of Order*, 28–31.

"The Bride of Innisfallen"
Kreyling, Michael. *...Achievement of Order*, 134–139.
Polk, Noel. "Water, Wanderers, and Weddings: Love in Eudora Welty," in Dollarhide, Louis, and Ann J. Abadie, Eds. *Eudora Welty...*, 110–117.

"The Burning"
Holder, Alan. *The Imagined Past...*, 133–138.
Kreyling, Michael. *...Achievement of Order*, 124–125.

"Circe"
Kreyling, Michael. *...Achievement of Order*, 125–126.

"A Curtain of Green"
Arnold, St. George T. "The Raincloud and the Garden: Psychic Regression as Tragedy in Welty's 'A Curtain of Green,'" *So Atlantic Bull*, 44, i (1979), 53–60.
Kreyling, Michael. *...Achievement of Order*, 13–14.

"Death of a Traveling Salesman"
Ahrends, Günter. *...Kurzgeschichte*, 173–175.
Altenbernd, Lynn, and Leslie L. Lewis. *Instructor's Manual...*, 3rd ed., 53–54.
Devlin, Albert J. "Eudora Welty's Mississippi," in Prenshaw, Peggy W., Ed. *Eudora Welty...*, 162–163.
Kreyling, Michael. *...Achievement of Order*, 11–12.
McGinnis, Wayne D. "Welty's 'Death of a Traveling Salesman' and William Blake Once Again," *Notes Mississippi Writers*, 11 (1979), 52–54.

MacKethan, Lucinda H. *The Dream of Arcady...*, 207-208.
Romines, Ann. "The Powers of the Lamp: Domestic Ritual in Two Stories by Eudora Welty," *Notes Mississippi Writers*, 12 (1979), 1-8.

"The Delta Cousins"
Kreyling, Michael. *...Achievement of Order*, 55-60.

"The Demonstrators"
Romines, Ann. "The Powers of the Lamp...," 8-15.

"First Love"
Davenport, F. Garvin. "Renewal...," 192-193.
Evans, Elizabeth. *Eudora Welty*, 90-92.
Holder, Alan. *The Imagined Past...*, 138-142.
Kreyling, Michael. *...Achievement of Order*, 17-19.
Marrs, Suzanne. "The Conclusion of Eudora Welty's 'First Love': Historical Background," *Notes Mississippi Writers*, 13, ii (1981), 73-78.

"Flowers for Marjorie"
Evans, Elizabeth. *Eudora Welty*, 58-59.

"Going to Naples"
Kreyling, Michael. *...Achievement of Order*, 131-134.

"Hello and Goodbye"
Evans, Elizabeth. *Eudora Welty*, 44-45.

"June Recital"
Arnold, Marilyn. "When Gratitude Is No More: Eudora Welty's 'June Recital,'" *So Carolina R*, 13, ii (1981), 62-72.
Demmin, Julia, and Daniel Curley. "Golden Apples and Silver Apples," in Prenshaw, Peggy W., Ed. *Eudora Welty...*, 250.
Evans, Elizabeth. *Eudora Welty*, 69-74.
Kreyling, Michael. *...Achievement of Order*, 80-87.
Pitavy-Souques, Daniele. "Technique as Myth: The Structure of *The Golden Apples*," in Prenshaw, Peggy W., Ed. *Eudora Welty...*, 266-267.

"Keela, the Outcast Indian Maiden"
Rohrberger, Mary. *Instructor's Manual...*, 29.

"The Key"
McKenzie, Barbara. "The Eye of Time: The Photographs of Eudora Welty," in Prenshaw, Peggy W., Ed. *Eudora Welty...*, 392-394.

"Kin"
Evans, Elizabeth. *Eudora Welty*, 34-36.
Kreyling, Michael. *...Achievement of Order*, 128-131.

"Ladies in Spring"
Kreyling, Michael. *...Achievement of Order*, 126-128.

"Lily Daw and the Three Ladies"
Evans, Elizabeth. *Eudora Welty*, 36–37.
Kreyling, Michael. . . .*Achievement of Order*, 6–8.
McDonald, W. U. "Artistry and Irony: Welty's Revisions of 'Lily Daw and the
    Three Ladies,'" *Stud Am Fiction*, 9 (1981), 113–121.

"Livvie"
Davenport, F. Garvin. "Renewal. . .," 198.
Kreyling, Michael. . . .*Achievement of Order*, 24–25.
Prenshaw, Peggy W. "Persephone in Eudora Welty's 'Livvie,'" *Stud Short Fiction*,
    17 (1980), 149–155.

"The Lucky Stone"
Kreyling, Michael. . . .*Achievement of Order*, 81–83.

"A Memory"
Devlin, Albert J. "Eudora Welty's Mississippi," 174–176.

"Moon Lake"
Allen, John A. "The Other Way to Live: Demigods in Eudora Welty's Fiction,"
    in Prenshaw, Peggy W., Ed. *Eudora Welty*. . ., 32–35.
Demmin, Julia, and Daniel Curley. "Golden Apples. . .," 245–247.
Kreyling, Michael. . . .*Achievement of Order*, 87–91.
Pitavy-Souques, Daniele. "Technique as Myth. . .," 260–263.
Skaggs, Merrill M. "Morgana's Apples and Pears," in Prenshaw, Peggy W., Ed.
    Eudora Welty. . ., 225–228.

"Music from Spain"
Kreyling, Michael. . . .*Achievement of Order*, 94–100.

"No Place for You, My Love"
Evans, Elizabeth. *Eudora Welty*, 110–111.
Kreyling, Michael. . . .*Achievement of Order*, 120–124.
Polk, Noel. "Water, Wanderers, and Weddings. . .," 105–110.

"Petrified Man"
Brooks, Cleanth. "Eudora Welty and the Southern Idiom," in Dollarhide, Louis,
    and Ann J. Abadie, Eds. *Eudora Welty*. . ., 9–12.
Kennedy, X. J. *Instructor's Manual*. . ., 2nd ed., 63–64.
Kreyling, Michael. . . .*Achievement of Order*, 8–9.
Scott, Virgil, and David Madden. *Instructor's Manual*. . ., 4th ed., 78–81; Madden,
    David. *Instructor's Manual*. . ., 5th ed., 84–86.
Walker, Robert G. "Another Medusa Allusion in Welty's 'Petrified Man,'" *Notes
    Contemp Lit*, 9, ii (1979), 10.

"A Piece of News"
Evans, Elizabeth. *Eudora Welty*, 54–55.

"Powerhouse"
Evans, Elizabeth. *Eudora Welty*, 55–56.
Smith, Elliott L., and Wanda V. *Instructor's Manual*. . ., 8–9.

"The Purple Hat"
Davenport, F. Garvin. "Renewal...," 197-198.

"Shower of Gold"
Kreyling, Michael. ...Achievement of Order, 79-80.
Skaggs, Merrill M. "Morgana's Apples...," 231-232.

"Sir Rabbit"
Kreyling, Michael. ...Achievement of Order, 92-93.
Skaggs, Merrill M. "Morgana's Apples...," 232-236.

"A Still Moment"
Davenport, F. Garvin. "Renewal...," 193-195.
Evans, Elizabeth. Eudora Welty, 92-93.
Holder, Alan. The Imagined Past..., 142-145.
Kreyling, Michael. ...Achievement of Order, 21-22.

"The Wanderers"
Demmin, Julia, and Daniel Curley. "Golden Apples...," 254-257.
Griffith, Albert J. "Henny Penny, Eudora Welty, and the Aggregation of Friends,"
   in Prenshaw, Peggy W., Ed. Eudora Welty..., 90-92.
Kerr, Elizabeth M. "The World of Eudora Welty's Women," in Prenshaw, Peggy
   W., Ed. Eudora Welty..., 144-147.
Kreyling, Michael. ...Achievement of Order, 100-105.
Phillips, Robert L. "A Structural Approach to Myth in the Fiction of Eudora Welty,"
   in Prenshaw, Peggy W., Ed. Eudora Welty..., 66-67.
Skaggs, Merrill M. "Morgana's Apples...," 236-240.

"The Whole World Knows"
Kreyling, Michael. ...Achievement of Order, 91-94.

"The Wide Net"
Allen, John A. "The Other Way...," 46-47.
Allen, Walter. The Short Story..., 311-313.
Eisinger, Chester. "Traditionalism and Modernism in Eudora Welty," in Prenshaw,
   Peggy W., Ed. Eudora Welty..., 14-15.
Evans, Elizabeth. Eudora Welty, 95-96.
Griffith, Albert J. "Henny Penny...," 88-90.
Kreyling, Michael. ...Achievement of Order, 19-21.

"The Winds"
Davenport, F. Garvin. "Renewal...," 196-197.
Kreyling, Michael. ...Achievement of Order, 25-28.

"A Worn Path"
Dazey, Mary A. "Phoenix Jackson and the Nice Lady: A Note on Eudora Welty's
   'A Worn Path,'" Am Notes & Queries, 17 (1979), 92-93.
Keys, Marilynn. "'A Worn Path': The Way of Dispossession," Stud Short Fiction,
   16 (1979), 354-356.
*Mizener, Arthur. A Handbook..., 4th ed., 194-196.

DOROTHY WEST

"The Typewriter"
Perry, Margaret. *Silence to the Drums*..., 130–132.

"An Unimportant Man"
Perry, Margaret. *Silence to the Drums*..., 132–133.

NATHANAEL WEST

"A Cool Million"
Scharnhorst, Gary. "From Rags to Patches, or 'A Cool Million' as Alter-Alger,"
    Ball State Univ Forum, 21, iv (1980), 58–65.
Wadlington, Warwick. *The Confidence Game*..., 303–305.

"The Dream Life of Balso Snell"
Wadlington, Warwick. *The Confidence Game*..., 294–298.
Wyrick, Deborah. "Dadaist Collage Structure and Nathanael West's 'Dream Life
    of Balso Snell,'" *Stud Novel*, 11 (1979), 349–359.

"Miss Lonelyhearts"
Duncan, Jeffrey L. "The Problem of Language in 'Miss Lonelyhearts,'" *Iowa
    R*, 8 (Winter, 1977), 116–127.
Simons, John L. "A New Reading of the End of West's 'Miss Lonelyhearts,'" *Notes
    Mod Am Lit*, 5, iii (1981), Item 16.
Wadlington, Warwick. *The Confidence Game*..., 298–303.

A. B. WESTLAND

"A Chinese Misalliance"
Chu, Limin. *The Image of China*..., 212–213.

EDITH WHARTON

"Afterward"
Smith, Allan G. "Edith Wharton and the Ghost Story," *Women & Lit*, 1 (1980),
    154–155.

"All Souls"
Smith, Allan G. "...Ghost Story," 149–152.

"Beatrice Palmato"
Ammons, Elizabeth. ...*Argument with America*, 140–142.

"Bewitched"
Smith, Allan G. "...Ghost Story," 152.

"Bunner Sisters"
Ammons, Elizabeth. ...*Argument with America*, 13–15.

"Ethan Frome"
Ammons, Elizabeth. "Edith Wharton's 'Ethan Frome' and the Question of Meaning," *Stud Am Fiction*, 7 (1979), 127–140.
———. ...*Argument with America*, 62–67.

"The Eyes"
Barker, Gerard A. *Instructor's Manual...*, 77–79.
Smith, Allan G. "...Ghost Story," 157–158.

"Miss Mary Pask"
Smith, Allan G. "...Ghost Story," 152–153.

"The Mission of Jane"
Altenbernd, Lynn, and Leslie L. Lewis. *Instructor's Manual...*, 3rd ed., 54–55.

"Mr. Jones"
Smith, Allan G. "...Ghost Story," 156.

"The Moving Finger"
Ziolkowski, Theodore. *Disenchanted Images...*, 140–143.

"New Year's Day"
Saunders, Judith P. "A New Look at the Oldest Profession in Wharton's 'New Year's Day,'" *Stud Short Fiction*, 17 (1980), 121–126.

"Roman Fever"
Ahrends, Günter. ...*Kurzgeschichte*, 130–132.
*Mizener, Arthur. *A Handbook...*, 4th ed., 71–76.

"The Triumph of Night"
Smith, Allan G. "...Ghost Story," 154.

"The Valley of Childish Things"
Ammons, Elizabeth. ...*Argument with America*, 10–12.

J. C. WHITE

"The Miracle of the Thunder God"
Chu, Limin. *The Image of China...*, 220.

PATRICK WHITE

"Being Kind to Titina"
Myers, David. *The Peacocks...*, 54–61.

"A Cheery Soul"
Myers, David. *The Peacocks...*, 47–53.

"Clay"
Myers, David. *The Peacocks...*, 33–38.

"The Cockatoos"
Myers, David. *The Peacocks*..., 131–137.

"Dead Roses"
Myers, David. *The Peacocks*..., 17–23.

"Down at the Dump"
Allen, Walter. *The Short Story*..., 338–341.
Myers, David. *The Peacocks*..., 82–89.

"The Evening at Sissy Kamara's"
Myers, David. *The Peacocks*..., 39–46.

"Fête Galante"
Myers, David. *The Peacocks*..., 138–145.

"The Full Belly"
Myers, David. *The Peacocks*..., 105–107.

"A Glass of Tea"
Allen, Walter. *The Short Story*..., 336–338.
Myers, David. *The Peacocks*..., 28–32.
Ramaswamy, S. "Patrick White's 'A Glass of Tea,'" *Commonwealth Q*, 3, xii (1979),
  76–83.

"The Letters"
Myers, David. *The Peacocks*..., 66–72.

"Miss Slattery and Her Demon Lover"
Myers, David. *The Peacocks*..., 62–65.

"The Night Prowler"
Myers, David. *The Peacocks*..., 108–115.

"Sicilian Vespers"
Myers, David. *The Peacocks*..., 121–130.

"Willy-Wagtail by Moonlight"
Myers, David. *The Peacocks*..., 24–27.

"The Woman Who Wasn't Allowed to Keep Cats"
Myers, David. *The Peacocks*..., 73–81.

"A Woman's Hand"
Myers, David. *The Peacocks*..., 93–104.

WALT[ER] WHITMAN

"The Half-Breed" [originally titled "Arrow-Tip"]
Scheick, William J. "Whitman's Grotesque Half-Breed," *Walt Whitman R*, 23
  (1977), 133–136; rpt., with changes, in his *The Half-Breed*..., 36–38.

RUDY WIEBE

"Where Is the Voice Coming From?"
Monkman, Leslie. *A Native Heritage...*, 101–102.

ALLEN WIER

"Things About to Disappear"
Madden, David. *Instructor's Manual...*, 5th ed., 114–116.

L. WARREN WIGMORE

"The Revenge of Chin Chow"
Chu, Limin. *The Image of China...*, 179.

OSCAR WILDE

"The Happy Prince"
Martin, Robert K. "Oscar Wilde and the Fairy Tale: 'The Happy Prince' as Self-
Dramatization," *Stud Short Fiction*, 16 (1979), 74–77.

"The Selfish Giant"
Kotzin, Michael C. "'The Selfish Giant' as Literary Fairy Tale," *Stud Short Fiction*,
16 (1979), 301–309.

MICHAEL WILDING

"Hector and Freddie"
Ross, Bruce A. C. "Laszlo's Testament, or Structuring the Past and Sketching
the Present in Contemporary Short Fiction, Mainly Australian," *Kunapipi*,
1 (1979), 113–114.

KATE WILHELM

"The Funeral"
Berman, Jeffrey. "Where's All the Fiction in Science Fiction?" in Barr, Marleen
S., Ed. *Future Females...*, 164–176.

TENNESSEE WILLIAMS

"The Angel in the Alcove"
Richardson, Thomas J. "The City of Day and the City of Night: New Orleans
and the Exotic Unreality of Tennessee Williams," in Tharpe, Jac, Ed. *...A
Tribute*, 638–640.

"Desire and the Black Masseur"
Sklepowich, Edward A. "In Pursuit of the Lyric Quarry: The Image of the
    Homosexual in Tennessee Williams' Prose Fiction," in Tharpe, Jac, Ed. . . .
    A Tribute, 529–530.

"Hard Candy"
Sklepowich, Edward A. "In Pursuit. . .," 532–533.

"The Knight's Quest"
Sklepowich, Edward A. "In Pursuit. . .," 536–538.

"Mama's Old Stucco House"
Ramaswamy, S. "The Short Stories of Tennessee Williams," in Naik, M. K., et
    al., Eds. Indian Studies. . . , 280–281.

"The Mysteries of the Joy Rio"
Sklepowich, Edward A. "In Pursuit. . .," 531–533.

"Night of the Iguano"
Gunn, Drewey W. American and British Writers. . . , 212–213.

"One Arm"
Sklepowich, Edward A. "In Pursuit. . .," 527–529.

"The Resemblance Between a Violin Case and a Coffin"
Draya, Ren. "The Fiction of Tennessee Williams," in Tharpe, Jac, Ed. . . .A Tribute,
    651–652.

"The Roman Spring of Mrs. Stone"
Ramaswamy, S. "The Short Stories. . .," 264–266.

"Rubio y Morena"
Robinson, Cecil. Mexico. . . , 257–258.

"Two on a Party"
Sklepowich, Edward A. "In Pursuit. . .," 534–537.

"The Yellow Bird"
Richardson, Thomas J. "The City of Day. . .," 641–643.

WILLIAM CARLOS WILLIAMS

"The Accident"
Perloff, Marjorie. "The Man Who Loved Women: The Medical Fictions of William
    Carlos Williams," Georgia R, 34 (1980), 849–850.

"The Farmer's Daughter"
Perloff, Marjorie. "The Man Who Loved Women. . .," 850–853.

"The Girl with the Pimply Face"
Perloff, Marjorie. "The Man Who Loved Women. . .," 844–847.

"A Night in June"
Perloff, Marjorie. "The Man Who Loved Women...," 847-848.

"The Use of Force"
Madden, David. *Instructor's Manual...*, 5th ed., 1-2.

"The Venus"
Perloff, Marjorie. "The Man Who Loved Women...," 848-849.

JACK WILLIAMSON

"With Folded Hands"
Rose, Mark. *Alien Encounter...*, 165-166.
Warrick, Patricia S. *The Cybernetic Imagination...*, 151-152.

ANGUS WILSON

"A Bit of the Map"
Allen, Walter. *The Short Story...*, 290-293.

"Higher Standards"
Allen, Walter. *The Short Story...*, 289-290.

"A Little Companion"
Barker, Gerard A. *Instructor's Manual...*, 51-52.

"Ten Minutes to Twelve"
Allen, Walter. *The Short Story...*, 293-295.

YVOR WINTERS

"The Brink of Darkness"
Comito, Terry. "Winters' 'Brink,'" *Southern R*, 17 (1981), 851-872.

THOMAS WOLFE

"The Far and the Near"
Madden, David. *Instructor's Manual...*, 5th ed., 25-28.

"The Lost Boy"
Adams, Timothy D. "The Ebb and Flow of Time and Place in 'The Lost Boy,'"
    Southern Stud, 19 (1980), 400-408.

"A Portrait of Bascom Hawke"
Domnarski, William. "Thomas Wolfe's Success as Short Novelist: Structure and
    Theme in 'A Portrait of Bascom Hawke,'" *Southern Lit J*, 13 (1980), 32-41.

VIRGINIA WOOLF

"The Duchess and the Jeweller"
Fleishman, Avrom. "Forms of the Woolfian Short Story," in Freedman, Ralph,
    Ed. *Virginia Woolf*..., 59.

"The Haunted House"
Fleishman, Avrom. "...Woolfian Short Story," 62-63.

"The Introduction"
Fleishman, Avrom. "...Woolfian Short Story," 67-68.
Meyerowitz, Selma. "What Is to Console Us? The Politics of Deception in Woolf's
    Short Stories," in Marcus, Jane, Ed. *New Feminist Essays*..., 249-251.

"The Lady in the Looking-Glass"
DiBattista, Maria. ... *The Fables of Anon*, 237-238.
Fleishman, Avrom. "...Woolfian Short Story," 60.

"Lappin and Lappinova"
Meyerowitz, Selma. "What Is to Console Us?...," 241-244.

"The Legacy"
Fleishman, Avrom. "...Woolfian Short Story," 59-60.
Kiely, Robert. *Beyond Egotism*..., 90-91.
Meyerowitz, Selma. "What Is to Console Us?...," 244-247.

"The Man Who Loved His Kind"
Fleishman, Avrom. "...Woolfian Short Story," 58.

"The Mark on the Wall"
Mizener, Arthur. *A Handbook*..., 4th ed., 161-163.

"Moments of Being"
Fleishman, Avrom. "...Woolfian Short Story," 60-62.

"The New Dress"
Fleishman, Avrom. "...Woolfian Short Story," 55.
Meyerowitz, Selma. "What Is to Console Us?...," 247-249.

"The Searchlight"
Fleishman, Avrom. "...Woolfian Short Story," 66-67.

"The Shooting Party"
Fleishman, Avrom. "...Woolfian Short Story," 65-66.

"Solid Objects"
Watson, Robert A. "'Solid Objects' as Allegory," *Virginia Woolf Miscellany*, 16
    (Spring, 1981), 3-4.

"The String Quartet"
Fleishman, Avrom. "...Woolfian Short Story," 67.

"Together and Apart"
Fleishman, Avrom. ". . .Woolfian Short Story," 57-58.

RICHARD WRIGHT

"Big Black Good Man"
Felgar, Robert. *Richard Wright*, 160-164.

"Big Boy Leaves Home"
Avery, Evelyn G. *Rebels and Victims*. . ., 80-81.
Felgar, Robert. *Richard Wright*, 63-67.
Gayle, Addison. *Richard Wright*. . ., 108-110.

"Bright and Morning Star"
Felgar, Robert. *Richard Wright*, 75-76.
Gayle, Addison. *Richard Wright*. . ., 112-113.

"Down by the Riverside"
Gayle, Addison. *Richard Wright*. . ., 110-111.

"Fire and Cloud"
Agosta, Lucien L. "Millenial Embrace: The Artistry of Conclusion in Richard
    Wright's 'Fire and Cloud,'" *Stud Short Fiction*, 18 (1981), 121-129.
Felgar, Robert. *Richard Wright*, 71-75.

"Long Black Song"
Delmar, P. Jay. "Charles W. Chesnutt's 'The Web of Circumstance' and Richard
    Wright's 'Long Black Song': The Tragedy of Property," *Stud Short Fiction*, 17
    (1980), 178-179.
Felgar, Robert. *Richard Wright*, 69-71.
Gayle, Addison. *Richard Wright*. . ., 111-112.

"Man, God Ain't Like That"
Avery, Evelyn G. *Rebels and Victims*. . ., 33-34.
Felgar, Robert. *Richard Wright*, 168-171.

"The Man Who Killed a Shadow"
Felgar, Robert. *Richard Wright*, 164-166.
Rohrberger, Mary. *Instructor's Manual*. . ., 28-29.

"The Man Who Lived Underground"
Felgar, Robert. *Richard Wright*, 156-160.
Howard, Daniel F., and William Plummer. *Instructor's Manual*. . ., 3rd ed., 52-53;
    rpt. Howard, Daniel F., and John Ribar. *Instructor's Manual*. . ., 4th ed., 54.

"The Man Who Was Almost a Man"
Brooks, Cleanth, and Robert P. Warren. *Understanding Fiction*, 3rd ed., 220.
Madden, David. *Instructor's Manual*. . ., 5th ed., 87-88.

JOHN WYNDHAM [JOHN BEYNON HARRIS]

"The Lost Machine"
Warrick, Patricia S. *The Cybernetic Imagination*..., 103–104.

VELIMIR XLEBNIKOV

"Ka"
Baran, Jendryk. "On the Poetics of a Xlebnikov Tale: Problems and Patterns in 'Ka,'" in Kodjak, Andrej, Michael J. Connolly, and Krystyna Pomorska, Eds. ...*Narrative Texts*, 112–131.

YOKOMITSU RIICHI

"Machine"
Lippit, Noriko M. *Reality and Fiction*..., 108–113.

YUN T'ICH-CH'IAO

"The Story of a Laborer"
Link, E. Perry. *Mandarin Ducks*..., 188–189.

SAMUEL ARYEH ZAHLEN

"Salmah Mul 'Eder"
Werses, Shmuel. "Toward the History of the Hebrew Novella in the Early Nineteenth Century," in Heinemann, Joseph, and Shmuel Werses, Eds. *Studies in Hebrew Narrative Art*..., 107–124.

SERGEI ZALYGIN

"By the Irtysh"
Shneidman, N. N. *Soviet Literature*..., 64–66.

"Witnesses"
Shneidman, N. N. *Soviet Literature*..., 62–63.

ROGER ZELAZNY

"Divine Madness"
Monteleone, Thomas F. "Fire and Ice: On Roger Zelazny's Short FIction," *Algol*, 13, ii (1976), 11–12.

"The Doors of His Face, The Lamps of His Mouth"
Monteleone, Thomas F. "Fire and Ice...," 11.

"For a Breath I Tarry"
Monteleone, Thomas F. "Fire and Ice...," 12–13.
Sanders, Joe. "Zelazny: Unfinished Business," in Clareson, Thomas D., Ed. *Voices for the Future*..., II, 188–189.
Warrick, Patricia S. *The Cybernetic Imagination*..., 109–112.

"The Keys to December"
Monteleone, Thomas F. "Fire and Ice...," 12.

"Love Is an Imaginary Number"
Monteleone, Thomas F. "Fire and Ice...," 11.

"The Man Who Loved the Faioli"
Monteleone, Thomas F. "Fire and Ice...," 13–14.

"Passion Play"
Monteleone, Thomas F. "Fire and Ice...," 10.

"A Rose for Ecclesiastes"
Monteleone, Thomas F. "Fire and Ice...," 10–11.
Sanders, Joe. "Zelazny...," 185–187.

PAUL ZELEZA

"The Married Woman"
Little, Kenneth. ...*Urban Women's Image*..., 114–115.

ÉMILE ZOLA

"Adventures of Big Sidoine and of Little Mederic"
Austen-Smith, Jane. "A Zola Short Story: The Origins of a Political Mythology," *Nottingham French Stud*, 18, ii (1979), 46–60.

PAMELA ZOLINE

"The Heat Death of the Universe"
Rose, Mark. *Alien Encounter*..., 31.

CARL ZUCKMAYER

"The Walking Huts"
Mews, Siegfried. *Carl Zuckmayer*, 113–116.

A CHECKLIST OF BOOKS USED

Adams, Stephen. *The Homosexual as Hero in Contemporary Fiction*. New York: Barnes & Noble, 1980.

Adler, Ruth. *Women of the Shtetl —Through the Eyes of Y. L. Peretz*. Cranbury, N.J.: Associated Univ. Presses [for Fairleigh Dickinson Univ. Press], 1980.

Ahrends, Günter. *Die amerikanische Kurzgeschichte*. Stuttgart: Kohlhammer, 1980.

Aksenov, Varsily. *"The Steel Bird" and Other Stories*, trans. Rae Slonek *et al.*; introd. John J. Johnson. Ann Arbor: Ardis, 1979.

Alazraki, Jaime, and Ivar Ivask, Eds. *The Final Island: The Fiction of Julio Cortázar*. Norman: Univ. of Oklahoma Press, 1978.

Albright, Daniel. *Personality and Impersonality: Lawrence, Woolf, and Mann*. Chicago: Univ. of Chicago Press, 1978.

Aldiss, Brian W. *Billion Year Spree: The True History of Science Fiction*. New York: Doubleday, 1973.

Alexander, Edward. *The Resonance of Dust: Essays on Holocaust Literature and Jewish Fate*. Columbus: Ohio State Univ. Press, 1979.

Allen, Joan M. *Candles and Carnival Lights: The Catholic Sensibility of F. Scott Fitzgerald*. New York: New York Univ. Press, 1978.

Allen, Walter. *The Short Story in English*. Oxford: Clarendon, 1981; Am. ed. New York: Oxford Univ. Press, 1981.

Altenbernd, Lynn, and Leslie L. Lewis. *Instructor's Manual [for] "Introduction to Literature: Stories, Third Edition,"* 3rd ed. New York: Macmillan, 1980.

Ammons, Elizabeth. *Edith Wharton's Argument with America*. Athens: Univ. of Georgia Press, 1980.

Andersen, Richard. *Robert Coover*. Boston: Twayne, 1981.

Anderson, David D., Ed. *Critical Essays on Sherwood Anderson*. Boston: Hall, 1981.

Andrews, William L. *The Literary Career of Charles W. Chesnutt*. Baton Rouge: Louisiana State Univ. Press, 1980.

Anon., Ed. *Flaubert et le comble de l'art: Nouvelles recherches sur Bouvard et Pécuchet*. Paris: Société d'Édition d'Enseignement Supérieur, 1981.

Anthony, Geraldine. *John Coulter*. Boston: Twayne, 1976.

Apter, T. E. *Thomas Mann: The Devil's Advocate*. London: Macmillan, 1978.

Arroyo, Anita. *Narrativa hispanoamericana actual*. Barcelona: M. Pareja [for Univ. of Puerto Rico], 1980.

Attebery, Brian. *The Fantasy Tradition in American Literature from Irving to Le Guin*. Bloomington: Indiana Univ. Press, 1980.

Avery, Evelyn G. *Rebels and Victims: The Fiction of Richard Wright and Bernard Malamud*. Port Washington: Kennikat, 1979.

Bachem, Michael. *Heimito von Doderer*. Boston: Twayne, 1981.

Bailey, Jennifer. *Norman Mailer, Quick-Change Artist*. London: Macmillan, 1979.

Bair, Deirdre. *Samuel Beckett*. New York: Harcourt Brace Jovanovich, 1978.

Baker, Sheridan, and George Perkins. *Instructor's Manual to Accompany "The Practical Imagination."* New York: Harper & Row, 1980.

Bakker, J., and D. R. M. Wilkinson, Eds. *From Cooper to Philip Roth: Essays on American Literature*. Amsterdam: Rodopi, 1980.

Bargainnier, Earl F. *The Gentle Art of Murder: The Detective Fiction of Agatha Christie*. Bowling Green: Bowling Green Univ. Popular Press, 1980.

Bargen, Doris G. *The Fiction of Stanley Elkin*. Frankfurt: Peter D. Lang, 1980.

Barker, Gerard A. *Instructor's Manual [for]* "*Twice-Told Tales: An Anthology of Short Fiction.*" Boston: Houghton Mifflin, 1979.

Barksdale, E. C. *Daggers of the Mind: Structuralism and Neuropsychology in an Exploration of the Russian Literary Imagination.* Lawrence, Kans.: Coronado Press, 1979.

Barr, Marleen S., Ed. *Future Females: A Critical Anthology.* Bowling Green: Bowling Green State Univ. Popular Press, 1981.

Barthold, Bonnie J. *Black Time: Fiction of Africa, the Caribbean, and the United States.* New Haven: Yale Univ. Press, 1981.

Bartsch, Kurt, Gerhard Melzer, and Johann Strutz, Eds. *Über Franz Nabl: Aufsätze Reden.* Graz: Styria, 1980.

Becker, George J. *D. H. Lawrence.* New York: Ungar, 1980.

Bell, Michael D. *The Development of American Romance: The Sacrifice of Relation.* Chicago: Univ. of Chicago Press, 1980.

Bellamy, Gladys. *Mark Twain as a Literary Artist.* Norman: Univ. of Oklahoma Press, 1950.

Bellman, Samuel I. *Constance Rourke.* Boston: Twayne, 1981.

Bell-Villada, Gene H. *Borges and His Fiction: A Guide to His Mind and Art.* Chapel Hill: Univ. of North Carolina Press, 1981.

Benson, Brian J., and Mabel M. Dillard. *Jean Toomer.* Boston: Twayne, 1980.

Berland, Alwyn. *Culture and Conduct in the Novels of Henry James.* Cambridge: Cambridge Univ. Press, 1981.

Bernikow, Louise. *Among Women.* New York: Harmony Books, 1980.

Berthoud, Jacques. *Joseph Conrad: The Major Phase.* Cambridge: Cambridge Univ. Press, 1978.

Bickman, Martin. *The Unsounded Centre: Jungian Studies in American Romanticism.* Chapel Hill: Univ. of North Carolina Press, 1980.

Birnbaum, Henrik, and Thomas Eekman, Eds. *Fiction and Drama in Eastern and Southeastern Europe.* Columbus: Slavic Publishers, 1980.

Bohner, Charles. *Robert Penn Warren*, rev. ed. Boston: Twayne, 1981.

Bonney, William W. *Thorns & Arabesques.* Baltimore: Johns Hopkins Univ. Press, 1980.

Bowden, Mary W. *Washington Irving.* Boston: Twayne, 1981.

Bowman, Sylvia, *et al.*, Eds. *Studies in Honor of Gerald E. Wade.* Madrid: Turangas, 1979.

Bowring, Richard J. *Mori Ōgai and the Modernization of Japanese Culture.* Cambridge: Cambridge Univ. Press, 1979.

Bradbury, Nicola. *Henry James: The Later Novels.* Oxford: Clarendon Press, 1979.

Brancaforte, Benito, Edward R. Mulvihill, Roberto G. Sánchez, and John Crispin, Eds. *Homenaje a Antonio Sánchez Barbudo: Ensayos de literatura española moderna.* Madison: Department of Spanish & Portuguese, Univ. of Wisconsin, 1981.

Bretz, Mary L. *Concha Espina.* Boston: Twayne, 1980.

Briggs, Julia. *Night Visitors: The Rise and Fall of the English Ghost Story.* London: Faber, 1977.

Brittain, Joan T. *Laurence Stallings.* Boston: Twayne, 1975.

Brooke-Rose, Christine. *A Rhetoric of the Unreal.* Cambridge: Cambridge Univ. Press, 1981.

Brooks, Cleanth, and Robert Penn Warren. *Instructor's Manual [for]* "*Understanding Fiction, Third Edition.*" 3rd ed. Englewood Cliffs: Prentice-Hall, 1979.

———. *Understanding Fiction*, 3rd ed. Englewood Cliffs: Prentice-Hall, 1979.

Brown, Deming. *Soviet Russian Literature Since Stalin.* Cambridge: Cambridge Univ. Press, 1978.

Brown, John L. *Valery Larbaud.* Boston: Twayne, 1981.

Brown, Lloyd W. *Amiri Baraka*. Boston: Twayne, 1980.

_____. *Women Writers in Black Africa*. Westport, Conn.: Greenwood Press, 1981.

Bruccoli, Matthew J., and Richard Layman, Eds. *Fitzgerald/Hemingway Annual 1979*. Detroit: Gale, 1980.

Brunet, G., Ed. *Études allemandes: Recueil dédie à Jean-Jacques Anstett*. Lyon:PU de Lyon, 1979.

Bruss, Paul. *Conrad's Early Sea Fiction: The Novelist as Navigator*. Cranbury, N.J.: Associated Univ. Presses [for Bucknell Univ. Press], 1979.

Bucknall, Barbara J. *Ursula K. Le Guin*. New York: Ungar, 1981.

Budd, Louis.*Mark Twain: Social Philosopher*. Bloomington: Indiana Univ. Press, 1962.

Bufithis, Philip H. *Norman Mailer*. New York: Ungar, 1978.

Burness, Donald, Ed. *Critical Perspectives on Lusophone Literature from Africa*. Washington: Three Continents Press, 1981.

Caputo-Mayr, Maria L., Ed. *Franz Kafka: Eine Aufsatzsammlung nach einem Symposium in Philadelphia*. Berlin: Agora, 1978.

Carey, Glenn O., Ed. *Faulkner: The Unspeakable Imagination: A Collection of Critical Essays*. Troy, N.Y.: Whitson, 1980.

Carlisle, Janice. *The Sense of an Audience*. Athens: Univ. of Georgia Press, 1981.

Carroll, David. *Chinua Achebe*, 2nd ed. New York: St. Martin's Press, 1980.

Carter, Lin, Ed. *The Spawn of Cthulhu*. New York: Ballantine Books, 1971.

Casey, Daniel J. *Benedict Kiely*. Cranford, N.J.: Associated Univ. Presses [for Bucknell Univ. Press], 1974.

_____, and Robert E. Rhodes, Eds. *Irish-American Fiction: Essays in Criticism*. New York: AMS Press, 1979.

Cavaliero, Glen. *A Reading of E. M. Forster*. London: Macmillan, 1979.

Cecchetti, Giovanni. *Giovanni Verga*. Boston: Twayne, 1978.

Chalpin, Lila. *William Sansom*. Boston: Twayne, 1980.

Chambers, Robert D. *Sinclair Ross and Ernest Buckler*. Toronto: Copp Clark, 1975.

Chefdor, Monique. *Blaise Cendrars*. Boston: Twayne, 1980.

Chu, Limin. *The Image of China and the Chinese in the "Overland Monthly," 1868-1875, 1883-1935*. San Francisco: R. & E. Research Associates, 1974.

Clareson, Thomas D., Ed. *Voices for the Future: Essays on Major Science Fiction Writers*, II. Bowling Green: Bowling Green Univ. Popular Press, 1979.

Clark, L. D. *The Minoan Distance: The Symbolism of Travel in D. H. Lawrence*. Tucson: Univ. Arizona Press, 1980.

Clyne, Paul, William F. Hanks, and Carol L. Hofbauer, Eds. *The Elements: A Parasession on Linguistic Units and Levels, April 20-21, 1979*. Chicago: Chicago Linguistics Society, 1979.

Cohn, Dorrit. *Transparent Minds: Narrative Modes for Presenting Consciousness in Fiction*. Princeton: Princeton Univ. Press, 1978.

Cohn, Jan. *Improbable Fiction: The Life of Mary Roberts Rinehart*. Pittsburgh: Univ. of Pittsburgh Press, 1980.

Coles, Robert. *Flannery O'Connor's South*. Baton Rouge: Louisiana State Univ. Press, 1980.

Cope, Jackson I. *Joyce's Cities: Archaeologies of the Soul*. Baltimore: Johns Hopkins Univ. Press, 1981.

Cox, James M. *Mark Twain and the Fate of Humor*. Princeton: Princeton Univ. Press, 1966.

Creighton, Joanne V. *Joyce Carol Oates*. Boston: Twayne, 1979.

Cronin, John. *Somerville and Ross*. Cranbury, N.J.: Associated Univ. Presses [for Bucknell Univ. Press], 1972.

_____. *Gerald Griffin: A Critical Biography*. Cambridge: Cambridge Univ. Press, 1978.

Cross, Richard K. *Malcolm Lowry: A Preface to His Fiction*. Chicago: Univ. of Chicago Press, 1980.

Daemmrich, Horst S. *Wilhelm Raabe*. Boston: Twayne, 1981.

Dahiya, Bhim S. *The Hero in Hemingway: A Study in Development*. New Delhi: Bahri, 1978.

Dahlie, Hallvard. *Brian Moore*. Boston: Twayne, 1981.

Danly, Robert L. *In the Shade of Spring Leaves: The Life and Writings of Higuchi Ichiyo, A Woman of Letters in Meiji Japan*. New Haven: Yale Univ. Press, 1981.

David, Claude, Ed. *Franz Kafka: Themen und Probleme*. Göttingen: Vandenhoeck & Ruprecht, 1980.

Davidson, Arnold E. and Cathy N., Eds. *The Art of Margaret Atwood: Essays in Criticism*. Toronto: Anansi Press, 1981.

Davidson, Cathy N., and E. M. Broner, Eds. *The Lost Tradition: Mothers and Daughters in Literature*. New York: Ungar, 1980.

De Bolt, Joe, Ed. *Ursula K. Le Guin: Voyager to Inner Lands and to Outer Space*. Port Washington: Kennikat, 1979.

DeCoster, Cyrus. *Pedro Antonio de Alarcón*. Boston: Twayne, 1979.

Decottignies, Jean, Ed. *Les Sujets de l'écriture*. Lille: Univ. de Lille, 1981.

Desmond, John F. *A Still Moment: Essays on the Art of Eudora Welty*. Metuchen: Scarecrow Press, 1978.

DeVitis, A. A., and Albert E. Kalson. *J. B. Priestley*. Boston: Twayne, 1980.

DiBattista, Maria. *Virginia Woolf's Major Novels: The Fables of Anon*. New Haven: Yale Univ. Press, 1980.

Dietrich, Peter, Ed. *Sub Tua Platano: Festgabe für Alexander Beinlich*. Emsdetten: Lechte, 1981.

Diggins, John P., and Mark E. Kann, Eds. *The Problem of Authority in America*. Philadelphia: Temple Univ. Press, 1980.

Dillon, Millicent. *A Little Original Sin: The Work of Jane Bowles*. New York: Holt, Rinehart & Winston, 1981.

Dix, Carol. *D. H. Lawrence and Women*. London: Macmillan, 1980; Am. ed. Totowa, N.J.: Littlefield & Rowman, 1980.

Dollarhide, Louis, and Ann J. Abadie, Eds. *Eudora Welty: A Form of Thanks*. Jackson: Univ. Press of Mississippi, 1979.

Donald, Miles. *The American Novel in the Twentieth Century*. Newton Abbot: David & Charles, 1978; Am. ed. New York: Barnes & Noble, 1978.

Donovan, Josephine. *Sarah Orne Jewett*. New York: Ungar, 1980.

Doty, Mark A. *Tell Me Who I Am: James Agee's Search for Selfhood*. Baton Rouge: Louisiana State Univ. Press, 1981.

Doubleday, Neal Frank. *Variety of Attempt: British and American Fiction in the Early Nineteenth Century*. Lincoln: Univ. of Nebraska Press, 1976.

Doyle, John R. *William Charles Scully*. Boston: Twayne, 1978.

Drudy, P. J., Ed. *Irish Studies*, I. New York: Cambridge Univ. Press, 1980.

Dryden, Edgar A. *Melville's Thematics of Form: The Great Art of Telling the Truth*. Baltimore: Johns Hopkins Press, 1968.

Ducharme, Robert. *Art and Idea in the Novels of Bernard Malamud*. The Hague: Mouton, 1974.

Dunaway, John M. *The Metamorphosis of the Self: The Mystic, the Sensualist, and the Artist in the Works of Julien Green*. Lexington: Univ. Press of Kentucky, 1978.

Durán, Gloria B. *The Archetypes of Carlos Fuentes: From Witch to Androgyne*. Hamden, Conn.: Shoe String Press, 1980.

Duthie, Enid L. *The Themes of Elizabeth Gaskell*. Totowa, N.J.: Rowman & Littlefield, 1980.

Easson, Angus. *Elizabeth Gaskell*. London: Routledge & Kegan Paul, 1979.

Ebersole, Alva V., Ed. *Perspectivas sobre la novela española de los siglos XIX y XX, de distintos autores, con una nota in introductoria*. Valencia: Albatros, 1979.

Ericson, Edward E. *Solzhenitsyn: The Moral Vision*. Grand Rapids: Eerdmans, 1980.

Erlebach, Peter, Wolfgang G. Müller, and Klaus Reuter, Eds. *Geschichtlichkeit und Neuanfang im sprachlichen Kunstwerk: Studien zur englischen Philologie zu Ehren von Fritz W. Schulze*. Tübingen: Narr, 1981.

Evans, Elizabeth. *Ring Lardner*. New York: Ungar, 1979.

―――. *Eudora Welty*. New York: Ungar, 1981.

Fanger, Donald. *The Creation of Nikolai Gogol*. Cambridge: Harvard Univ. Press, 1979.

Farrow, Anthony. *George Moore*. Boston: Twayne, 1978.

Faurot, Jeannette L., Ed. *Chinese Fiction from Taiwan: Critical Perspectives*. Bloomington: Indiana Univ. Press, 1980.

Felgar, Robert. *Richard Wright*. Boston: Twayne, 1980.

Festa-McCormick, Diana. *Honoré de Balzac*. Boston: Twayne, 1979.

Fetterley, Judith. *The Resisting Reader: A Feminist Approach to American Fiction*. Bloomington: Indiana Univ. Press, 1978.

Fetzer, John F. *Clemens Brentano*. Boston: Twayne, 1981.

Fickert, Kurt J. *Hermann Hesse's Quest: The Evolution of the "Dichter" Figure in His Work*. Fredericton, New Brunswick: York Press, 1978.

―――. *Signs and Portents: Myth in the Works of Wolfgang Borchert*. Fredericton, New Brunswick: York Press, 1980.

Fiddian, Robin. *Ignacio Aldecoa*. Boston: Twayne, 1979.

Filler, Louis, Ed. *Seasoned Authors for a New Season: The Search for Standards in Popular Writing*. Bowling Green: Bowling Green Univ. Popular Press, 1980.

Finholt, Richard. *American Visionary Fiction: Mad Metaphysics as Salvation Psychology*. Port Washington: Kennikat, 1978.

Fogel, Daniel M. *Henry James and the Structure of Romantic Imagination*. Baton Rouge: Louisiana State Univ. Press, 1981.

Foner, Philip. *Mark Twain: Social Critic*. New York: International Publishers, 1958.

Foster, David W. *Augusto Roa Bastos*. Boston: Twayne, 1978.

―――. *Studies in the Contemporary Spanish-American Short Story*. Columbia: Univ. of Missouri Press, 1979.

Fowler, Doreen, and Ann J. Abadie, Eds. *Fifty Years of Yoknapatawpha*. Jackson: Univ. Press of Mississippi, 1980.

Franklin, Benjamin, and Duane Schneider. *Anaïs Nin: An Introduction*. Athens: Ohio Univ. Press, 1979.

Franklin, H. Bruce. *The Victim as Criminal and Artist: Literature from the American Prison*. New York: Oxford Univ. Press, 1978.

―――. *Robert A. Heinlein: America as Science Fiction*. New York: Oxford Univ. Press, 1980.

Fredrickson, Robert S. *Hjalmar Hjorth Boyesen*. Boston: Twayne, 1980.

Freedman, Ralph, Ed. *Virginia Woolf: Revaluation and Continuity*. Berkeley: Univ. of California Press, 1980.

Friedman, Ellen. *Joyce Carol Oates*. New York: Ungar, 1980.

Gale, Robert L. *John Hay*. Boston: Twayne, 1978.

Gallo, Rose A. *F. Scott Fitzgerald*. New York: Ungar, 1978.

Galloway, David. *Edward Lewis Wallant*. Boston: Twayne, 1979.

―――. *The Absurd Hero in American Fiction: Updike, Styron, Bellow, Salinger*, 2nd rev. ed. Austin: Univ. of Texas Press, 1981.

Ganz, Margaret. *Elizabeth Gaskell: The Artist in Conflict*. New York: Twayne, 1969.

Gardner, John. *On Moral Fiction*. New York: Basic Books, 1978.

Gardner, Philip. *Kingsley Amis*. Boston: Twayne, 1981.

Garson, Helen S. *Truman Capote*. New York: Ungar, 1980.

Gay-Crosier, Raymond, Ed. *Albert Camus 1980: Second International Conference, February 21–23, 1980*. Gainesville: Univ. of Florida Press, 1980.

Gayle, Addison. *Richard Wright: Ordeal of a Native Son*. Garden City, N.Y.: Doubleday, 1980.

Geismar, Maxwell. *Mark Twain: An American Prophet*. Boston: Houghton Mifflin, 1970.

Gekoski, R. A. *Conrad: The Moral World of the Novel*. London: Elek, 1978.

Genno, Charles N., and Heinz Wetzel, Eds. *The First World War in German Narrative Prose: Essays in Honor of George Wallis Field*. Toronto: Univ. of Toronto Press, 1980.

Gibson, William. *The Art of Mark Twain*. New York: Oxford Univ. Press, 1976.

Gilbert, Claire. *Nerval's Double: A Structural Study*. University: Univ. of Mississippi, 1979.

Gilbert, Sandra M., and Susan Gubar. *The Madwoman in the Attic: The Woman Writer and the Nineteenth-Century Literary Imagination*. New Haven: Yale Univ. Press, 1979.

Giles, James R. *James Jones*. Boston: Twayne, 1981.

Gindin, James J. *Postwar British Fiction: New Accents and Attitudes*. Berkeley: Univ. of California Press, 1962.

Gippius, V. V. *Gogol*, trans. Robert A. Maguire. Ann Arbor: Ardis, 1981.

Gittleman, Sol. *From Shtetl to Suburbia: The Family in Jewish Literary Imagination*. Boston: Beacon Press, 1978; Canadian ed. Toronto: Fitzhenry & Whiteside, 1978.

Glenn, Kathleen M. *Azorín [José Martínez Ruiz]*. Boston: Twayne, 1981.

Goeppert, Sebastian, Ed. *Perspektiven psychoanalytischer Literaturkritik*. Freiburg: Rombach, 1978.

Gohin, Yves, and Robert Ricatte, Eds. *Recherches en scientes des textes*. Grenoble: Univ. of Grenoble, 1977.

Golemba, Henry L. *Frank R. Stockton*. Boston: Twayne, 1981.

Gollin, Rita K. *Nathaniel Hawthorne and the Truth of Dreams*. Baton Rouge: Louisiana State Univ. Press, 1979.

González-del-Valle, Luis, and Bradley A. Shaw. *Luis Romero*. Boston: Twayne, 1979.

Gordon, Alan M., and Evelyn Rugg, Eds. *Actas del Sexto Congreso Internacional de Hispanistas celebrado en Toronto del 22 al 26 agostode 1977*. Toronto: Department of Spanish & Portuguese, Univ. of Toronto, 1980.

Gordon, Andrew. *An American Dreamer: A Psychoanalytic Study of the Fiction of Norman Mailer*. Cranbury, N.J.: Associated Univ. Presses [for Fairleigh Dickinson Univ. Press], 1979.

Gordon, John. *James Joyce's Metamorphoses*. Dublin: Gill & Macmillan, 1981; Am. ed. Totowa, N.J.: Barnes & Noble, 1981.

Gordon, Lois. *Donald Barthelme*. Boston: Twayne, 1981.

Grabo, Norman. *The Coincidental Art of Charles Brockden Brown*. Chapel Hill: Univ. of North Carolina Press, 1981.

Grant, Mary K. *The Tragic Vision of Joyce Carol Oates*. Durham: Duke Univ. Press, 1978.

Greenberg, Martin H., and Joseph D. Olander, Eds. *Ray Bradbury*. New York: Taplinger, 1980.

Grenander, M. E., Ed. *Helios: From Myth to Solar Energy — Images of the Sun in Myth and Legend*. Albany: State University of New York, 1978.

Gross, David. *The Writer and Society: Heinrich Mann and Literary Politics*. Atlantic Highlands, N.J.: Humanities Press, 1980.

Grossvogel, David I. *Mystery and Its Fiction: From Oedipus to Agatha Christie.* Baltimore: Johns Hopkins Univ. Press, 1979.

Guetti, James. *Word-Music: The Aesthetic Aspect of Narrative Fiction.* New Brunswick: Rutgers Univ. Press, 1980.

Gunn, Drewey W. *American and British Writers in Mexico, 1556–1973.* Austin: Univ. of Texas Press, 1974.

Gunn, Edward M. *Unwelcome Muse: Chinese Literature in Shanghai and Peking 1937–1945.* New York: Columbia Univ. Press, 1980.

Gutierrez, Donald. *Lapsing Out: Embodiments of Death and Rebirth in the Last Works of D. H. Lawrence.* East Brunswick, N.J.: Associated Univ. Presses [for Fairleigh Dickinson Univ. Press], 1980.

Gutiérrez de la Solana, Alberto, and Elio Alba-Buffill, Eds. *Festschrift José Cid Pérez.* New York: Senda Nueva, 1981.

Guttmann, Allen. *The Jewish Writer in America: Assimilation and the Crisis of Identity.* New York: Oxford Univ. Press, 1971.

Györgyey, Clara. *Ferenc Molnár.* Boston: Twayne, 1980.

Hague, John A., Ed. *American Character and Culture in a Changing World: Some Twentieth-Century Perspectives.* Westport, Conn.: Greenwood Press, 1979.

Hakutani, Yoshinobu. *Young Dreiser: A Critical Study.* Cranbury, N.J.: Associated Univ. Presses [for Fairleigh Dickinson Univ. Press], 1980.

Hall, Robert A. *Antonio Fogazzaro.* Boston: Twayne, 1978.

Hamilton, Alice and Kenneth. *Condemned to Life: The World of Samuel Beckett.* Grand Rapids: Eerdmans, 1976.

Hammond, J. R. *An H. G. Wells Companion: A Guide to the Novels, Romances and Short Stories.* London: Macmillan, 1979.

Hanson, Clare, and Andrew Gurr. *Katherine Mansfield.* New York: St. Martin's Press, 1981.

Harari, Josué V., Ed. *Textual Strategies: Perspectives in Post-Structuralist Criticism.* Ithaca: Cornell Univ. Press, 1979.

Harden, O. Elizabeth M. *Maria Edgeworth's Art of Prose Fiction.* The Hague: Mouton, 1971.

Hardy, Willene S. *Mary McCarthy.* New York: Ungar, 1981.

Hargreaves, Alec G. *The Colonial Experience in French Fiction: A Study of Pierre Loti, Ernest Psichari and Pierre Mille.* London: Macmillan, 1981.

Hart, John E. *Albert Halper.* Boston: Twayne, 1980.

Harter, Hugh A. *Gertrudis Gómez de Avellaneda.* Boston: Twayne, 1981.

Hawthorn, Jeremy. *Joseph Conrad: Language and Fictional Self-Consciousness.* Lincoln: Univ. of Nebraska Press, 1979.

Hawthorne, Mark D. *Doubt and Dogma in Maria Edgeworth.* Gainesville: Univ. of Florida Press, 1967.

Hayashi, Tetsumaro, Ed. *Steinbeck's Women: Essays in Criticism.* Muncie, Ind.: Steinbeck Society, 1979.

Haynes, Roslynn D. *H. G. Wells: Discovery of the Future.* New York: New York Univ. Press, 1980.

Heinemann, Joseph, and Shmuel Werses, Eds. *Studies in Hebrew Narrative Art Throughout the Ages.* Jerusalem: Hebrew Univ. Press, 1978.

Helwig, David, Ed. *The Human Elements: Critical Essays.* Ottawa: Oberon, 1978.

Henshall, Kenneth G., Ed. *"The Quilt" and Other Stories by Tayama Katai,* trans. Kenneth G. Henshall. Tokyo: Univ. of Tokyo Press, 1981.

Hershinow, Sheldon. *Bernard Malamud.* New York: Ungar, 1980.

Higgs, Robert J. *Laurel & Thorn: The Athlete in American Literature.* Lexington: Univ. Press of Kentucky, 1981.

Hingley, Ronald. *Dostoyevsky: His Life and Work.* New York: Scribner, 1978.

Hitchcock, Bert. *Richard Malcolm Johnston.* Boston: Twayne, 1978.

Hobsbaum, Philip. *A Reader's Guide to D. H. Lawrence.* London: Thames & Hudson, 1981.

Holder, Alan. *The Imagined Past: Portrayals of Our History in Modern American Literature.* Cranbury, N.J.: Associated Univ. Presses [for Bucknell Univ. Press], 1980.

Holman, C. Hugh. *Windows on the World: Essays on American Social Fiction.* Knoxville: Univ. of Tennessee Press, 1979.

Holt, Marion P. *José López Rubio.* Boston: Twayne, 1980.

Holtz, William, Ed. *Two Tales by Charlotte Brontë: "The Secret" and "Lily Hart."* Columbia: Univ. of Missouri Press, 1978.

Holzner, Johann, Michael Klein, and Wolfgang Wiesmüller, Eds. *Studien zur Literatur des 19. und 20. Jahrhunderts in Österreich: Festschrift für Alfred Doppler zum 60. Geburtstag.* Innsbruck: Kowatsch, 1981.

Homenaje a Humberto Piñera: Estudios de literatura, arte e historia. Madrid: Playor, 1979.

Howard, Daniel F., and William Plummer. *Instructor's Manual to Accompany "The Modern Tradition: Short Stories, Third Edition, ed. Daniel F. Howard,"* 3rd ed. Boston: Little, Brown, 1976.

———, and John Ribar. *Instructor's Manual to Accompany "The Modern Tradition: An Anthology of Short Stories, Fourth Edition, ed. Daniel F. Howard,"* 4th ed. Boston: Little, Brown, 1979.

Howard, Lillie P. *Zora Neale Hurston.* Boston: Twayne, 1980.

Huffaker, Robert. *John Fowles.* Boston: Twayne, 1980.

Hunt, George W. *John Updike and the Three Great Secret Things: Sex, Religion, and Art.* Grand Rapids: Eerdmans, 1980.

Illanes Adaro, Graciela. *La Novelística de Carmen Laforet.* Madrid: Editorial Gredos, 1971.

Inge, M. Thomas, Ed. *Bartleby the Inscrutable: A Collection of Commentary on Herman Melville's Tale "Bartleby the Scrivener."* Hamden: Archon Books, 1979.

Irwin, John T. *American Hieroglyphics: The Symbol of the Egyptian Hieroglyphics in the American Renaissance.* New Haven: Yale Univ. Press, 1980.

Jackson, Richard L. *Black Writers in Latin America.* Albuquerque: Univ. of New Mexico Press, 1979.

Jackson, Robert L. *The Art of Dostoevsky: Deliriums and Nocturnes.* Princeton: Princeton Univ. Press, 1981.

Jackson, Rosemary. *Fantasy: The Literature of Subversion.* London: Methuen, 1981.

Jameson, Frederic. *Fables of Aggression: Wyndham Lewis, The Modernist as Fascist.* Berkeley: Univ. of California Press, 1979.

Janes, Regina. *Gabriel García Márquez: Revolutions in Wonderland.* Columbia: Univ. of Missouri Press, 1981.

Jenkins, Lee. *Faulkner and Black-White Relations: A Psychoanalytic Approach.* New York: Columbia Univ. Press, 1981.

Jensen, Niels L. *Jens Peter Jacobsen.* Boston: Twayne, 1980.

Jiménez, Francisco, Ed. *The Identification and Analysis of Chicano Literature.* New York: Bilingual Press, 1979.

Johnson, Barbara. *The Critical Difference: Essays in the Contemporary Rhetoric of Reading.* Baltimore: Johns Hopkins Univ. Press, 1980.

Johnson, Claudia D. *The Productive Tension of Hawthorne's Art.* University: Univ. of Alabama Press, 1981.

Johnson, Lee A. *Mary Hallock Foote.* Boston: Twayne, 1980.

Johnson, Roberta. *Carmen Laforet.* Boston: Twayne, 1981.

Jones, Anne G. *Tomorrow Is Another Day: The Woman Writer in the South,, 1859-1936.* Baton Rouge: Louisiana State Univ. Press, 1981.

Jones, Judith P., and Guinevera A. Nance. *Philip Roth*. New York: Ungar, 1981.

Jones, Louisa E. *Poetic Fantasy and Fiction: The Short Stories of Jules Supervielle*. The Hague: Mouton, 1973.

Jones, Sonia. *Alfonsina Storni*. Boston: Twayne, 1979.

Joshi, S. T., Ed. *H. P. Lovecraft: Four Decades of Criticism*. Athens: Ohio Univ. Press, 1980.

Kappeler, Suzanne. *Writing and Reading in Henry James*. New York: Columbia Univ. Press, 1980.

Karcher, Carolyn L. *Shadow over the Promised Land: Slavery, Race, and Violence in Melville's America*. Baton Rouge: Louisiana State Univ. Press, 1980.

Keitner, Wendy. *Ralph Gustafson*. Boston: Twayne, 1979.

Kelly, A. A. *Mary Lavin, Quiet Rebel: A Study of Her Short Stories*. Dublin: Wolfhound Press, 1980; Am. ed. New York: Barnes & Noble, 1980.

Kennedy, X. J. *Instructor's Manual to Accompany "Literature: An Introduction to Fiction, Poetry, and Drama,"* 2nd ed. Boston: Little, Brown, 1979.

Kerr, Elizabeth. *William Faulkner's Gothic Domain*. Port Washington: Kennikat, 1979.

Kiell, Norman. *Varieties of Sexual Experience: Psychosexuality in Literature*. New York: International Univ. Press, 1976.

Kiely, Robert. *Beyond Egotism: The Fiction of James Joyce, Virginia Woolf, and D. H. Lawrence*. Cambridge: Harvard Univ. Press, 1980.

Kinney, Arthur F. *Dorothy Parker*. Boston: Twayne, 1978.

Kirby, David. *Grace King*. Boston: Twayne, 1980.

Kirchhoff, Frederick. *William Morris*. Boston: Twayne, 1979.

Kirk, Irina. *Anton Chekhov*. Boston: Twayne, 1981.

Klinkowitz, Jerome. *The Practice of Fiction in America: Writers from Hawthorne to the Present*. Ames: Iowa State Univ. Press, 1980.

Knapp, Bettina L. *Anaïs Nin*. New York: Ungar, 1978.

_____. *Gérard de Nerval: The Mystic's Dilemma*. University: Univ. of Alabama Press, 1980.

Knight, Stephen. *Form and Ideology in Crime Fiction*. Bloomington: Indiana Univ. Press, 1980.

Knopp, Josephine Z. *The Trial of Judaism in Contemporary Jewish Writing*. Urbana: Univ. of Illinois Press, 1975.

Kodjak, Andrej, Michael J. Connolly, and Krystyna Pomorska, Eds. *The Structural Analysis of Narrative Texts*. Columbus: Slavica, 1980.

_____, Krystyna Pomorska, and Kiril Taranovsky, Eds. *Alexander Puskin, Symposium II*. Columbus: Slavica, 1980.

Kramer, Leonie, Ed. *The Oxford History of Australian Literature*. Melbourne: Oxford Univ. Press, 1981.

Kresh, Paul. *Isaac Bashevis Singer: The Magician of West 86th Street*. New York: Dial Press, 1979.

Kreyling, Michael. *Eudora Welty's Achievement of Order*. Baton Rouge: Louisiana State Univ. Press, 1980.

Krumme, Peter. *Augenblicke — Erzählungen Edgar Allan Poes*. Stuttgart: Metzler, 1978.

Kryzytski, Serge, *The Works of Ivan Bunin*. The Hague: Mouton, 1971.

Krzyzanowski, Ludwik, Ed. *Joseph Conrad: Centennial Essays*. New York: Polish Institute of Arts and Sciences in America, 1976.

Kulshrestha, Chirantan. *Saul Bellow: The Problem of Affirmation*. New Delhi: Arnold-Heinemann, 1978.

Kurrik, Maire J. *Literature and Negation*. New York: Columbia Univ. Press, 1979.

Kurz, Paul K. *On Modern German Literature*, I, trans. Mary F. McCarthy. University: Univ. of Alabama Press, 1967.

La Bossière, Camille R. *Joseph Conrad and the Science of Unknowing*. Fredericton, New Brunswick: York Press, 1979.

Lacey, Henry C. *To Raise, Destroy, and Create: The Poetry, Drama, and Fiction of Imamu Amiri Baraka (Le Roi Jones)*. Troy, N.Y.: Whitston, 1981.

Lane, Calvin W. *Evelyn Waugh*. Boston: Twayne, 1981.

Langer, Lawrence L. *The Age of Atrocity: Death in Modern Literature*. Boston: Beacon, 1978.

Langguth, A. J. *Saki: A Life of Hector Hugh Munro*. New York: Simon & Schuster, 1981.

Lantz, K. A. *Nikolay Leskov*. Boston: Twayne, 1979.

Lazere, Donald. *The Unique Creation of Albert Camus*. New Haven: Yale Univ. Press, 1973.

Lease, Benjamin. *Anglo-American Encounters: England and the Rise of American Literature*. Cambridge: Cambridge Univ. Press, 1981.

Leatherbarrow, William J. *Fedor [sic] Dostoevsky*. Boston: Twayne, 1981.

Lee, Hermione. *Elizabeth Bowen: An Estimate*. London: Vision Press, 1981; Am. ed. Totowa, N.J.: Barnes & Noble, 1981.

Lee, Lynn. *Don Marquis*. Boston: Twayne, 1981.

Lehmann, Jakob, Ed. *Interpretationen moderner Kurzgeschichten*. Frankfurt am Main: Diesterweg, 1967.

Leiber, Fritz. *The Book of Fritz Leiber*. New York: DAW Books, 1974.

Léon, Pierre R., Henri Mitterand, Peter Nesselroth, and Pierre Robert, Eds. *Problèmes d'analyse textuelle / Problems of Textual Analysis*. Montreal: Didier, 1971.

Levy, Eric P. *Beckett and the Voice of Species: A Study of the Prose Fiction*. Dublin: Gill & Macmillan, 1980; Am. ed. Totowa, N.J.: Barnes & Noble, 1980.

Lévy, Isaac J., and Juan Loveluck, Eds. *Simposi Carlos Fuentes: Actas*. Columbia: Univ. of South Carolina, 1980.

Lewis, Merrill, and L. L. Lee, Eds. *The Westering Experience in American Literature: Bicentennial Essays*. Bellingham, Wash.: Western Washington Univ., 1977.

Ley, Ralph. *Brecht as Thinker*. Ann Arbor: Applied Literature Press, 1979.

Link, E. Perry. *Mandarin Ducks and Butterflies: Popular Fiction in Early Twentieth-Century Chinese Cities*. Berkeley: Univ. of California Press, 1981.

Lippit, Noriko M. *Reality and Fiction in Modern Japanese Literature*. White Plains, N.Y.: Sharpe, 1980.

Lisca, Peter. *John Steinbeck: Nature and Myth*. New York: Crowell, 1978.

Little, Kenneth. *The Sociology of Urban Women's Image in African Literature*. Totowa, N.J.: Rowman and Littlefield, 1980.

Lombardo, Agostino, Ed. *Studi inglesi: Raccolta di saggi e ricerche*. Bari: Adriatica, 1978.

Lord, Graham. *The Short Stories of Marcel Aymé*. Nedlands: Univ. of Western Australia Press, 1980.

Lottman, Herbert R. *Albert Camus: A Biography*. New York: Doubleday, 1979.

Lucente, Gregory L. *The Narrative of Realism and Myth: Verga, Lawrence, Faulkner, Pavese*. Baltimore: Johns Hopkins Univ. Press, 1981.

Luft, David. *Robert Musil and the Crisis of European Culture, 1880–1942*. Berkeley: Univ. of California Press, 1980.

Luker, Nicholas. *Alexander Kuprin*. Boston: Twayne, 1978.

Lundquist, James. *J. D. Salinger*. New York: Ungar, 1979.

MacAndrew, Elizabeth. *The Gothic Tradition in Fiction*. New York: Columbia Univ. Press, 1979.

McCarthy, Paul. *John Steinbeck*. New York: Ungar, 1980.

McClure, John A. *Kipling and Conrad: The Colonial Fiction*. Cambridge: Harvard Univ. Press, 1981.

McConnell, Frank. *The Science Fiction of H. G. Wells*. New York: Oxford Univ. Press, 1981.

McCormack, W. J. *Sheridan Le Fanu and Victorian Ireland*. Oxford: Clarendon Press, 1980.

McDowell, Margaret B. *Carson McCullers*. Boston: Twayne, 1980.

Mack, Maynard, *et al.*, Eds. *The Norton Anthology of World Masterpieces*, II, 4th ed. New York: Norton, 1979.

Mackenzie, Clara C. *Sarah Barnwell Elliott*. Boston: Twayne, 1980.

MacKethan, Lucinda H. *The Dream of Arcady: Place and Time in Southern Literature*. Baton Rouge: Louisiana State Univ., 1980.

Mackey, Douglas A. *The Rainbow Quest of Thomas Pynchon*. San Bernardino: Borgo Press, 1980.

McMahan, Elizabeth, Ed. *Critical Approaches to Mark Twain's Short Stories*. Port Washington: Kennikat, 1981.

MacMillan, Duane J., Ed. *The Stoic Strain in American Literature: Essays in Honor of Marston LaFrance*. Toronto: Univ. of Toronto Press, 1979.

McMullen, Lorraine. *Sinclair Ross*. Boston: Twayne, 1979.

McMurray, George R. *José Donoso*. Boston: Twayne, 1979.

———. *Jorge Luis Borges*. New York: Ungar, 1980.

Madden, David. *Instructor's Manual for "Studies in the Short Story, ed. Virgil Scott and David Madden, Fifth Edition,"* 5th ed. New York: Holt, Rinehart & Winston, 1980.

Male, Roy R. *Enter, Mysterious Stranger: American Cloistral Fiction*. Norman: Univ. of Oklahoma Press, 1979.

Manlove, C. N. *Modern Fantasy: Five Studies*. Cambridge: Cambridge Univ. Press, 1975.

March, Edward, Ed. *Essays by Diverse Hands: Transactions of the Royal Society of the United Kingdom*, N.S. Vol. 25. London: Oxford Univ. Press, 1950.

Marcus, Jane, Ed. *New Feminist Essays on Virginia Woolf*. Lincoln: Univ. of Nebraska Press, 1981.

Martin, Eleanor J. *René Marqués*. Boston: Twayne, 1979.

Mathews, Richard. *Worlds Beyond the World: The Fantastic Vision of William Morris*. San Bernardino: Borgo Press, 1978.

Maxwell, D[esmond] E. S. *Brian Friel*. Cranbury, N.J.: Associated Univ. Presses [for Bucknell Univ. Press], 1973.

Meagher, Robert E., Ed. *Albert Camus: The Essential Writings*. New York: Harper & Row, 1979.

Mélanges à la mémoire d'André Joucla-Ruau. Aix-en-Provence: Univ. of Provence, 1978.

Mellow, James R. *Nathaniel Hawthorne in His Time*. Boston: Houghton Mifflin, 1980.

Messenger, Christian K. *Sport and the Spirit of Play in American Fiction: Hawthorne to Faulkner*. New York: Columbia Univ. Press, 1981.

Mews, Siegfried. *Carl Zuckmayer*. Boston: Twayne, 1981.

Meyer, Priscilla, and Stephen Rudy, Eds. *Dostoevsky and Gogol: Texts and Criticism*. Ann Arbor: Ardis, 1979.

Meyers, Jeffrey, Ed. *Wyndham Lewis: A Revaluation*. Montreal: McGill-Queen's Univ. Press, 1980.

Mickelson, Anna Z. *Reaching Out: Sensitivity and Order in Recent American Fiction by Women*. Metuchen: Scarecrow Press, 1979.

Mileck, Joseph. *Hermann Hesse: Life and Art*. Berkeley: Univ. of California Press, 1978.

Miller, Gabriel. *Daniel Fuchs*. Boston: Twayne, 1979.

Millichap, Joseph R. *Hamilton Basso*. Boston: Twayne, 1979.

Milton, John R. *The Novel of the American West*. Lincoln: Univ. of Nebraska Press, 1980.

Minc, Rose S., Ed. *The Contemporary Latin American Short Story*. New York: Senda Nueva, 1979.

————. *Latin American Fiction Today*. Upper Montclair, N.J.: Montclair State College, 1980.

Mitchell, P. M. *Henrik Pontoppidan*. Boston: Twayne, 1979.

Mizener, Arthur. *The Sense of Life in the Modern Novel*. Boston: Houghton Mifflin, 1964.

————. *A Handbook [for] "Modern Short Stories: The Uses of Imagination, 4th Ed.,"* 4th ed. New York: Norton, 1979.

————, Ed. *Modern Short Stories: The Uses of Imagination*, 4th ed. New York: Norton, 1979.

Mohan, Ramesh, Ed. *Indian Writing in English*. Bombay: Orient Longman, 1978.

Mollinger, Robert N. *Psychoanalysis and Literature: An Introduction*. Chicago: Nelson-Hall, 1981.

Moloney, Brian. *Italo Svevo: A Critical Introduction*. Edinburgh: Edinburgh Univ. Press, 1974.

Monkman, Leslie. *A Native Heritage: Images of the Indian in English-Canadian Literature*. Toronto: Univ. of Toronto Press, 1981.

Montgomery, Marion. *Why Flannery O'Connor Stayed Home*. La Salle, Ill.: Sherwood Sugden, 1981.

Moore, Gerald. *Twelve African Writers*. Bloomington: Indiana Univ. Press, 1980.

Morgan, Ted. *Maugham*. New York: Simon & Schuster, 1980.

Morley, Patricia. *Margaret Laurence*. Boston: Twayne, 1981.

Morris, Robert K., and Irving Malin, Eds. *The Achievement of William Styron*, 2nd ed. Athens: Univ. of Georgia Press, 1981.

Morse, David. *Perspectives on Romanticism: A Transformational Analysis*. London: Macmillan, 1981; Am. ed. Totowa, N.J.: Barnes & Noble, 1981.

Muckle, James Y. *Nikolai Leskov and the "Spirit of Protestantism."* Birmingham: Dept. of Russian, Univ. of Birmingham, 1978.

Murdoch, Brian, and Malcolm Read. *Siegfried Lenz*. London: Oswald Wolff, 1978.

Murphy, James K. *Will N. Harben*. Boston: Twayne, 1979.

Mushabac, Jane. *Melville's Humor: A Critical Study*. Hamden: Shoe String Press, 1981.

Myers, David. *The Peacocks and the Bourgeoisie: Ironic Vision in Patrick White's Shorter Prose Fiction*. Adelaide: Adelaide Univ. Union Press, 1978.

Nagel, James. *Stephen Crane and Literary Impressionism*. University Park: Pennsylvania Univ. Press, 1980.

————, and Richard Astro, Eds. *American Literature: The New England Heritage*. New York: Garland, 1981.

Naik, M. K., S. K. Desai, and S. M. Mokashi-Punekar, Eds. *Indian Studies in American Fiction*. Dharwar: Karnatak Univ., 1974; Delhi: Macmillan India, 1974.

Nemo, John. *Patrick Kavanagh*. Boston: Twayne, 1979.

New, William, Ed. *Margaret Laurence*. Toronto: McGraw-Hill Ryerson, 1977.

Newcomer, James. *Maria Edgeworth*. Cranbury, N.J.: Associated Univ. Presses [for Bucknell Univ. Press], 1973.

Niven, Alistair. *D. H. Lawrence: The Writer and His Work*. New York: Scribner, 1980.

Ogungbesan, Kolawole. *The Writing of Peter Abrahams*. New York: African Publishing Co., 1979.

Olshen, Barry N. *John Fowles*. New York: Ungar, 1978.

O'Meally, Robert G. *The Craft of Ralph Ellison*. Cambridge: Harvard Univ. Press, 1980.

Osborne, Scott C., and Robert L. Phillips. *Richard Harding Davis*. Boston: Twayne, 1978.

Ownbey, Ray W., Ed. *Jack London: Essays in Criticism*. Santa Barbara: Peregrine Smith, 1978.

Pantzer, Eugene E. *Antun Gustav Matoš*. Boston: Twayne, 1981.

Parrinder, Patrick, Ed. *Science Fiction: A Critical Guide*. London: Longman, 1979.

Partlow, Robert B., and Harry T. Moore, Eds. *D. H. Lawrence: The Man Who Lived*. Carbondale: Southern Illinois Univ. Press, 1980.

Payne, Ladell. *Black Novelists and the Southern Literary Tradition*. Athens: Univ. of Georgia Press, 1981.

Peace, Richard. *The Enigma of Gogol*. Cambridge: Cambridge Univ. Press, 1981.

Pearson, Carol, and Katherine Pope. *The Female Hero in American and British Literature*. New York: Bowker, 1981.

Pettit, Arthur G. *Images of the Mexican American in Fiction and Film*. College Station: Texas A&M Univ. Press, 1980.

Phillips, Elizabeth. *Edgar Allan Poe: An American Imagination*. Port Washington: Kennikat, 1979.

Phillips, Robert. *William Goyen*. Boston: Twayne, 1979.

Pike, Burton. *The Image of the City in Modern Literature*. Princeton: Princeton Univ. Press, 1981.

Pilkington, John. *The Heart of Yoknapatawpha County*. Jackson: Univ. Press of Mississippi, 1981.

Pinion, F. B., Ed. *Budmouth Essays on Thomas Hardy: Papers Presented at the 1975 Summer School*. Dorchester, Dorset: Thomas Hardy Society, 1976.

Plater, William M. *The Grim Phoenix: Reconstructing Thomas Pynchon*. Bloomington: Indiana Univ. Press, 1978.

Pope, Randolph D., Ed. *The Analysis of Literary Texts: Current Trends in Methodology*. Ypsilanti: Bilingual Press, 1980.

Porter, Dennis. *The Pursuit of Crime: Art and Ideology in Detective Fiction*. New Haven: Yale Univ. Press, 1981.

Potter, Joy H. *Elio Vittorini*. Boston: Twayne, 1979.

Prang, Helmut, Ed. *E. T. A. Hoffmann*. Darmstadt: Wissenschaftliche Buchgesellschaft, 1976.

Prenshaw, Peggy W., Ed. *Eudora Welty: Critical Essays*. Jackson: Univ. Press of Mississippi, 1979.

Pryse, Marjorie. *The Mark and the Knowledge: Social Stigma in Classic American Fiction*. Columbus: Ohio State Univ. Press [for Miami Univ.], 1979.

Punter, David. *The Literature of Terror: A History of Gothic Fiction from 1765 to the Present Day*. London: Longman, 1980.

Rafroidi, Patrick, and Terence Brown, Eds. *The Irish Short Story*. Gerrards, Buckinghamshire: Colin Smythe, 1979; Am. ed. Atlantic Highlands, N.J.: Humanities Press, 1979.

Raimondi, Ezio, and Bruno Basile, Eds. *Dal "Novellino" a Moravia: Problemi della Narrativa*. Bologna: Mulino, 1979.

Rao, B. Ramachandra. *The American Fictional Hero: An Analysis of the Works of Fitzgerald, Wolfe, Farrell, Dos Passos and Steinbeck*. Chandigarth: Bahri, 1979.

Raper, Julius R. *From the Sunken Garden: The Fiction of Ellen Glasgow*. Baton Rouge: Louisiana State Univ. Press, 1980.

Reed, John Q. *Benjamin Penhallow Shillaber*. Boston: Twayne, 1972.

Reed, Kenneth T. *Truman Capote*. Boston: Twayne, 1981.

Remington, Thomas J., Ed. *Selected Proceedings of the 1978 Science Fiction Research Association National Conference*. Cedar Falls: Univ. of Northern Iowa, 1979.

Revell, Peter. *Paul Laurence Dunbar*. Boston: Twayne, 1979.

Richardson, Robert D. *Myth and Literature in the American Renaissance*. Bloomington: Indiana Univ. Press, 1978.

Ridgely, J. V. *Nineteenth-Century Southern Literature*. Lexington: Univ. Press of Kentucky, 1980.

Riggan, William. *Picaros, Madmen, Naifs, and Clowns: The Unreliable First-Person Narrator*. Norman: Univ. of Oklahoma Press, 1981.

Rimer, J. Thomas. *Modern Japanese Fiction and Tradition: An Introduction*. Princeton: Princeton Univ. Press, 1978.

Rix, Walter T., Ed. *Hermann Sudermann: Werk und Wirkung*. Würzburg: Könighausen & Neumann, 1980.

Rizzuto, Anthony. *Camus' Imperial Vision*. Carbondale: Southern Illinois Univ. Press, 1981.

Robinson, Cecil. *Mexico and the Hispanic Southwest in American Literature*. Tucson: Univ. of Arizona Press, 1977.

Robinson, Hilary. *Somerville & Ross: A Critical Appreciation*. Dublin: Gill & Macmillan, 1980; Am. ed. New York: St. Martin's Press, 1980.

Rodgers, Bernard F. *Philip Roth*. Boston: Twayne, 1978.

Rogers, Deborah W. and Ivor A. *J. R. R. Tolkien*. Boston: Twayne, 1980.

Rohrberger, Mary H. *The Art of Katherine Mansfield*. Ann Arbor: Univ. Microfilms International, 1977.

_____. *Instructor's Manual [for] "Story to Anti-Story."* Boston: Houghton Mifflin, 1979.

Rolf, Robert. *Masamune Hakuchō*. Boston: Twayne, 1979.

Rorabacher, Louise E. *Frank Dalby Davidson*. Boston: Twayne, 1979.

Rose, Mark. *Alien Encounter: Anatomy of Science Fiction*. Cambridge: Harvard Univ. Press, 1981.

Rosenberry, Edward H. *Melville*. London: Routledge & Kegan Paul, 1979.

Rzhevsky, Leonid. *Solzhenitsyn: Creator and Heroic Deed*, trans. Sonja Miller. University: Univ. of Alabama Press, 1978.

Salgado, María A. *Rafael Arévalo Martínez*. Boston: Twayne, 1979.

Salwak, Dale. *John Wain*. Boston: Twayne, 1981.

Salzman, Jack. *Albert Maltz*. Boston: Twayne, 1978.

Schaub, Thomas H. *Pynchon: The Voice of Ambiguity*. Urbana: Univ. of Illinois Press, 1981.

Scheick, William J. *The Half-Breed: A Cultural Symbol in 19th-Century American Fiction*. Lexington: Univ. Press of Kentucky, 1979.

Schlueter, Paul. *Shirley Ann Grau*. Boston: Twayne, 1981.

Schneider, Daniel J. *The Crystal Cage: Adventures of the Imagination in the Fiction of Henry James*. Lawrence: Regents Press of Kansas, 1978.

Scholes, Robert. *Elements of Fiction*. New York: Oxford Univ. Press, 1969; 2nd ed., 1981.

_____. *Fabulation and Metafiction*. Urbana: Univ. of Illinois Press, 1979.

Schraepen, Edmond, Ed. *Saul Bellow and His Work*. Brussels: Free Univ. of Brussels, 1978.

Schultze, Hans H., and Gerald Chapple, Eds. *Thomas Mann: Ein Kolloquium*. Bonn: Bouvier, 1978.

Schwarz, Daniel R. *Conrad —"Almayer's Folly" to "Under Western Eyes."* Ithaca: Cornell Univ. Press, 1980.

Schweitzer, Darrell. *The Dream Quest of H. P. Lovecraft*. San Bernardino: Borgo Press, 1978.

Scorza, Thomas J. *In the Time Before Steamboats: "Billy Budd," The Limits of Politics, and Modernity*. DeKalb: Northern Illinois Univ. Press, 1979.

Scott, Virgil, and David Madden. *Instructor's Manual to Accompany "Studies in Short Fiction, Fourth Edition,"* 4th ed. New York: Holt, Rinehart & Winston, 1976.

Sears, Donald A. *John Neal.* Boston: Twayne, 1978.

Senn, Werner. *Conrad's Narrative Voice.* Bern: Francke Verlag, 1980.

Sharma, Govind Narain. *Munshi Prem Chand.* Boston: Twayne, 1978.

Sherrill, Rowland A. *The Prophetic Melville: Experience, Transcendence, and Tragedy.* Athens: Univ. of Georgia Press, 1978.

Shloss, Carol. *Flannery O'Connor's Dark Comedies: The Limits of Inference.* Baton Rouge: Louisiana State Univ. Press, 1980.

Shneidman, N. N. *Soviet Literature in the 1970s: Artistic Diversity and Ideological Conformity.* Toronto: Univ. of Toronto Press, 1979.

Sicker, Philip. *Love and the Quest for Identity in the Fiction of Henry James.* Princeton: Princeton Univ. Press, 1980.

Simpson, Lewis P. *The Brazen Face of History.* Baton Rouge: Louisiana State Univ. Press, 1980.

Skaggs, Calvin, Ed. *The American Short Story*, I. New York: Dell, 1977.

_____. *The American Short Story*, II. New York: Dell, 1980.

Skulsky, Harold. *Metamorphosis: The Mind in Exile.* Cambridge: Harvard Univ. Press, 1981.

Slavick, William H. *DuBose Heyward.* Boston: Twayne, 1981.

Slusser, George E., George R. Guffey, and Mark Rose, Eds. *Bridges to Science Fiction.* Carbondale: Southern Illinois Univ. Press, 1980.

Smith, Anne, Ed. *The Art of Malcolm Lowry.* London: Vision Press, 1978.

Smith, Elliott L. and Wanda V. *Instructor's Manual to Accompany "Access to Literature: Understanding Fiction, Drama, and Poetry."* New York: St. Martin's Press, 1981.

_____, and Andrew W. Hart, Eds. *The Short Story: A Contemporary Looking Glass.* New York: Random House, 1981.

Smith, Henry N. *Mark Twain: The Development of a Writer.* Cambridge: Harvard Univ. Press, 1962.

Smith, Larry R. *Kenneth Patchen.* Boston: Twayne, 1978.

Sollors, Werner. *Amiri Baraka / Le Roi Jones: The Quest for a "Populist Modernism."* New York: Columbia Univ. Press, 1978.

Souza, Raymond D. *Lino Novás Calvo.* Boston: Twayne, 1981.

Staley, Thomas F. *Jean Rhys: A Critical Study.* Austin: Univ. of Texas Press, 1979.

Stark, John O. *Pynchon's Fiction: Thomas Pynchon and the Literature of Information.* Athens: Ohio Univ. Press, 1980.

Stavola, Thomas J. *Scott Fitzgerald: Crisis in an American Identity.* London: Vision Press, 1979.

Stock, Irvin. *Fiction as Wisdom from Goethe to Bellow.* University Park: Pennsylvania State Univ. Press, 1980.

Stone, Donald D. *The Romantic Impulse in Victorian Fiction.* Cambridge: Harvard Univ. Press, 1980.

Stowell, H. Peter. *Literary Impressionism, James and Chekhov.* Athens: Univ. of Georgia Press, 1980.

Strelka, Joseph P., Robert F. Bell, and Eugene Dobson, Eds. *Protest — Form — Tradition: Essays on German Exile Literature.* University: Univ. of Alabama Press, 1979.

Suleiman, Susan R., and Inge Crossman, Eds. *The Reader in the Text: Essays on Audience and Interpretation.* Princeton: Princeton Univ. Press, 1980.

Sullivan, Jack. *Elegant Nightmares: The English Ghost Story from Le Fanu to Blackwood.* Athens: Ohio Univ. Press, 1978.

Sumner, Rosemary. *Thomas Hardy: Psychological Novelist.* New York: St. Martin's Press, 1981.

Suther, Judith D., Ed. *Essays on Camus's "Exile and the Kingdom."* University, Miss.: Romance Monographs, 1980.

Swales, Martin. *Thomas Mann: A Study*. London: Heinemann, 1980; Am. ed. Totowa, N.J.: Rowman and Littlefield, 1980.

Sylvander, Carolyn W. *James Baldwin*. New York: Ungar, 1980.

———. *Jesse Redmon Fauset, Black American Writer*. Troy, N.Y.: Whitston, 1981.

Tatar, Maria M. *Spellbound: Studies on Mesmerism and Literature*. Princeton: Princeton Univ. Press, 1978.

Taylor, Anne R. *Male Novelists and Their Female Voices: Literary Masquerades*. Troy, N.Y.: Whitston, 1981.

Tharpe, Jac, Ed. *Tennessee Williams: A Tribute*. Jackson: Univ. Press of Mississippi, 1977.

Thomas, Clara. *The Manawaka World of Margaret Laurence*. Toronto: McClellan and Stewart, 1975.

Thompson, Bruce. *Franz Grillparzer*. Boston: Twayne, 1981.

Thompson, G. R., and Virgil L. Lokke, Eds. *Ruined Eden of the Present: Hawthorne, Melville, and Poe*. West Lafayette: Purdue Univ. Press, 1981.

Thorburn, David, and Howard Eiland, Eds. *John Updike: A Collection of Critical Essays*. Englewood Cliffs: Prentice-Hall, 1979.

Thorson, James L., Ed. *Yugoslav Perspectives on American Literature: An Anthology*. Ann Arbor: Ardis, 1980.

Thunecke, Jörg, Ed. *Formen Realistischer Erzählkunst: Festschrift for Charlotte Jolles*. Nottingham: Sherwood, 1979.

Timko, Michael, Ed. *38 Short Stories*, 2nd ed. New York: Knopf, 1979.

Tomory, William M. *Frank O'Connor*. Boston: Twayne, 1980.

Torrance, Robert. *The Comic Hero*. Cambridge: Harvard Univ. Press, 1978.

Tschirky, René. *Heimito von Doderers "Posaunen von Jericho": Versuch einer Interpretation*. Berlin: Erich Schmidt, 1971.

Tulloch, John. *Chekhov: A Structuralist Study*. London: Macmillan, 1980; Am. ed. New York: Barnes & Noble, 1980.

Turner, David G. *Unamuno's Webs of Fatality*. London: Tamesis, 1974.

Twitchell, James B. *The Living Dead: A Study of the Vampire in Romantic Literature*. Durham: Duke Univ. Press, 1980.

Ugrinsky, Alexej, Frederick J. Churchill, Frank S. Lambasa, and Robert F. von Berg, Eds. *Heinrich von Kleist Studies*. New York: AMS Press, 1980; Germ. ed. Berlin: Schmidt, 1980.

Underhill, Lonnie E., and Daniel F. Littlefield, Eds. *Hamlin Garland's Observations on the American Indian, 1895–1905*. Tucson: Univ. of Arizona Press, 1976.

Uphaus, Suzanne H. *John Updike*. New York: Ungar, 1980.

Van Dusen, Gerald C. *William Starbuck Mayo*. New York: Twayne, 1979.

Várvaro, Alberto, Ed. *XIV Congresso internazionale di linguistica e filologia romanza: Atti, V*. Naples: Macchiaroli, 1981; Amsterdam: Benjamins, 1981.

Vera, Catherine, and George R. McMurray, Eds. *In Honor of Boyd G. Carter: A Collection of Essays*. Laramie: Univ. of Wyoming, 1981.

Wadlington, Warwick. *The Confidence Game in American Literature*. Princeton: Princeton Univ. Press, 1975.

Waelti-Walters, Jennifer R. *J. M. G. Le Clézio*. Boston: Twayne, 1977.

Wagenknecht, Edward. *Eve and Henry James: Portraits of Women and Girls in His Fiction*. Norman: Univ. of Oklahoma Press, 1978.

Wagner, Linda W., Ed. *Critical Essays on Joyce Carol Oates*. Boston: Hall, 1979.

Waldeck, Peter B. *The Split Self from Goethe to Broch*. Cranbury, N.J.: Associated Univ. Presses [for Bucknell Univ. Press], 1979.

Waldeland, Lynne. *John Cheever*. Boston: Twayne, 1979.

Waldmeir, Joseph J., Ed. *Critical Essays on John Barth*. Boston: Hall, 1980.

Walker, Marshall. *Robert Penn Warren: A Vision Earned*. Edinburgh: Paul Harris, 1979; Am. ed. New York: Barnes & Noble, 1979.

Warren, Robert P., Ed. *Katherine Anne Porter: A Collection of Critical Essays*. Englewood Cliffs: Prentice-Hall, 1979.

Warrick, Patricia S. *The Cybernetic Imagination in Science Fiction*. Cambridge: Massachusetts Institute of Technology Press, 1980.

Way, Brian. *F. Scott Fitzgerald and the Art of Social Fiction*. New York: St. Martin's Press, 1980.

Welsh, Alexander. *Reflections on the Hero as Quixote*. Princeton: Princeton Univ. Press, 1981.

West, Rebecca J. *Eugene Montale: Poet on the Edge*. Cambridge: Harvard Univ. Press, 1981.

White, Allon. *The Uses of Obscurity: The Fiction of Early Modernism*. London: Routledge and Kegan Paul, 1981.

White, Sidney H. *Sidney Howard*. Boston: Twayne, 1977.

Williams, Blanche C. *Our Short Story Writers*. New York: Moffat, Yard, 1920.

Williams, Wirt. *The Tragic Art of Ernest Hemingway*. Baton Rouge: Louisiana State Univ. Press, 1981.

Wilt, Judith. *Ghosts of the Gothic: Austin, Eliot, and Lawrence*. Princeton: Princeton Univ. Press, 1980.

Winner, Anthony. *Characters in the Twilight: Hardy, Zola, and Chekhov*. Charlottesville: Univ. Press of Virginia, 1981.

Winston, Richard. *Thomas Mann: The Making of an Artist, 1875-1911*. New York: Knopf, 1981.

Wittenberg, Judith B. *Faulkner: The Transfiguration of Biography*. Lincoln: Univ. of Nebraska Press, 1979.

Wolfe, Peter. *Jean Rhys*. Boston: Twayne, 1980.

Wolff, Robert L. *William Carleton, Irish Peasant Novelist: A Preface to His Fiction*. New York: Garland, 1980.

Woodward, James B. *Ivan Bunin: A Study of His Fiction*. Chapel Hill: Univ. of North Carolina Press, 1980.

Wren, Robert M. *Achebe's World: The Historical and Cultural Context of the Novels*. Washington: Three Continents Press, 1980.

Wright, Robert C. *Frederick Manfred*. Boston: Twayne, 1979.

Wyers, Frances. *Miguel de Unamuno: The Contrary Self*. London: Tamesis, 1976.

Yamanouchi, Hisaaki. *The Search for Authenticity in Modern Japanese Literature*. Cambridge: Cambridge Univ. Press, 1978.

Yarwood, Edmund. *Vsevolod Garshin*. Boston: Twayne, 1981.

Young, Thomas D. *The Past in the Present: A Thematic Study of Modern Southern Fiction*. Baton Rouge: Louisiana State Univ. Press, 1981.

Zaller, Robert, Ed. *A Casebook on Anaïs Nin*. New York: New American Library, 1974.

Ziolkowski, Theodore. *Disenchanted Images: A Literary Iconology*. Princeton: Princeton Univ. Press, 1977.

A CHECKLIST OF JOURNALS USED

Adalbert Stifter Institut	*Adalbert Stifter Institut des Landes Oberösterreich: Vierteljahrsschrift*
	Africa Today
	Algol
Aligarh J Engl Stud	*The Aligarh Journal of English Studies*
Am Hispanist	*The American Hispanist*
Am Imago	*American Imago: A Psychoanalytic Journal for Culture, Science, and the Arts*
Am Lit	*American Literature: A Journal of Literary History, Criticism, and Bibliography*
Am Lit Realism	*American Literary Realism, 1870–1910*
Am Notes & Queries	*American Notes and Queries*
Am Stud (Kansas)	*American Studies* (Kansas)
Am Stud	*Amerikastudien/American Studies*
Am Transcendental Q	*American Transcendental Quarterly: A Journal of New England Writers*
	Anales Ştiinţifice ale Universităţii Iaşi
Anglia	*Anglia: Zeitschrift für Englische Philolgie*
	Anglistik & Englischunterricht
Anglo-Welsh R	*The Anglo-Welsh Review*
Annali Sezione Slava (Naples)	*Annali Istituto Universitario Orientale. Sezione Slava* (Napoli)
	L'Année Balzacienne
Anuario del Departamento de Inglés	*Anuario del Departamento de Inglés* (Barcelona, Spain)
	Arbeiten aus Anglistik und Amerikanistik
Arizona Q	*Arizona Quarterly*
	Arquipélago

Asian Folklore Stud	*Asian Folklore Studies*
Atlantic	*The Atlantic Monthly*
Australian J French Stud	*Australian Journal of French Studies*
Australian Lit Stud	*Australian Literary Studies*
Baker Street J	*The Baker Street Journal: An Irregular Quarterly of Sherlockiana*
Ball State Univ Forum	*Ball State University Forum*
Black Am Lit Forum	*Black American Literature Forum* [formerly *Negro American Literature Forum*]
Boletín de la Academia Norteamericana	*Boletín de la Academia Norteamericana de la Lengua Española*
Bucknell R	*Bucknell Review: A Scholarly Journal of Letters, Arts and Sciences*
Bull Hispanic Stud	*Bulletin of Hispanic Studies*
Bull West Virginia Assoc Coll Engl Teachers	*Bulletin of the West Virginia Association of College English Teachers*
	Cahiers Algériens de Littérature Comparée
Cahiers de l'Association Internationale	*Cahiers de l'Association Internationale des Études Françaises*
	Cahiers Universitaires Catholiques
Cahiers Victoriens et Edouardiens	*Cahiers Victoriens et Edouardiens: Revue du Centre d'Etudes et de Recherches Victoriennes et Edouardiennes de l'Université Paul Valéry, Montpellier*
Canadian J Irish Stud	*Canadian Journal of Irish Studies*
Canadian-Am Slavic Stud	*Canadian-American Slavic Studies*
Canadian Slavonic Papers	*Canadian Slavonic Papers: An Inter-Disciplinary Quarterly Devoted to the Soviet Union and Eastern Europe*
	Catholic World
Centennial R	*Centennial Review*
Centerpoint	*Centerpoint: A Journal of Interdisciplinary Studies*

Chicago R	*Chicago Review*
Chimères	*Chimères: A Journal of French and Italian Literature*
Chinese Lit	*Chinese Literature*
Christianity & Lit	*Christianity and Literature*
Chu-Shikoku Stud Am Lit	*Chu-Shikoku Studies in American Literature*
Cithara	*Cithara: Essays in the Judaeo-Christian Tradition*
Claflin Coll R	*Claflin College Review*
Colby Lib Q	*Colby Library Quarterly*
Coll Engl Assoc Critic	*CEA Critic: An Official Journal of the College English Association*
Coll Lang Assoc J	*College Language Association Journal*
Coll Lit	*College Literature*
Colloquia Germanica	*Colloquia Germanica, Internationale Zeitschrift für Germanische Sprach- und Literatur-wissenschaft*
Commonwealth Q	*Commonwealth Quarterly*
Comparatist	*The Comparatist: Journal of the Southern Comparative Literature Association*
Comp Lit	*Comparative Literature*
Comp Lit Stud	*Comparative Literature Studies*
	Confluents
Conradiana	*Conradiana: A Journal of Joseph Conrad*
Contemp Lit	*Contemporary Literature*
	Critica Hispánica
	Critical Inquiry
Critical Q	*Critical Quarterly*
Criticism	*Criticism: A Quarterly for Literature and the Arts*
Critique	*Critique: Revue Générale des Publications Françaises et Étrangres*
Critique	*Critique: Studies in Modern Fiction*

Cuadernos Americanos

Cuadernos Hispano-   *Cuadernos Hispanoamericanos: Revista Mensual de*
americanos   *Cultura Hispanica*

D. H. Lawrence R   *The D. H. Lawrence Review*

Delta   *Delta: Revue du Centre d'Études et de Recherche sur les*
                              Écrivains du Sud aux États-Unis

Deutshce Vierteljahrsschrift   *Deutsche Vierteljahrsschrift für Literaturwissenschaft und*
                              Geistesgeschichte

Der Deutschunterricht   *Der Deutschunterricht: Beiträge zu seiner Praxis und*
                              wissenschaftlichen Grundlegung

                              Deutschunterricht in Südafrika

Diacritics   *Diacritics: A Review of Contemporary Criticism*

Dispositio   *Dispositio: Revista Hispánica de Semiótica Literaria*

                              Doris Lessing Newsletter

Dostoevksy Stud   *Dostoevsky Studies: Journal of the International*
                              Dostoevsky Society [formerly *International*
                              Dostoevsky Society Bulletin]

                              Drab

Dutch Q R   *Dutch Quarterly Review of Anglo-American*
                              Letters

                              Eco

                              Edda: Nordisk Tidsskrift for Litteraturforskning

Edebiyat: J Middle   *Edebiyat: A Journal of Middle Eastern Literatures*
Eastern Lit

Éire   *Éire-Ireland: A Journal of Irish Studies*

                              enclitic

Engl Lang Notes   *English Language Notes*

Engl Lit Hist   *English Literary History* [formerly *Journal of English*
                              Literary History]

Engl Lit Transition   *English Literature in Transition*

Engl Stud Africa   *English Studies in Africa: A Journal of the Humanities*

Engl Stud Canada   *English Studies in Canada*

L'Epoque Conradienne	*L'Epoque Conradienne: Bulletin annuel de la Société Conradienne*
Escritura	*Escritura: Teoría y Crítica Literarias*
ESQ: J Am Renaissance	*ESQ: Journal of the American Renaissance*
Essays Arts & Sciences	*Essays in Arts and Sciences*
Essays Crit	*Essays in Criticism: A Quarterly Journal of Literary Criticism*
Essays French Lit	*Essays in French Literature*
Essays Lit	*Essays in Literature* (Western Illinois)
	Estudos Anglo-Americanos
	Estudios Filológicos
Études Anglaises	*Études Anglaises: Grande Bretagne, États-Unis*
Études de Lettres	*Études de Lettres* (Lausanne)
	Études Germaniques
Euphorion	*Euphorion: Zeitschrift für Literaturgeschichte*
	Explicación de Textos Literarios
	Explicator
	Extrapolation
Faulkner Stud	*Faulkner Studies: An Annual of Research, Criticism, and Reviews*
Fiction Int'l	*Fiction International*
	Fitzgerald/Hemingway Annual 1974
	Fitzgerald/Hemingway Annual 1975
	Fitzgerald/Hemingway Annual 1979
Folio	*Folio: Papers on Foreign Languages and Literature*
	Folklore
Forum Mod Lang Stud	*Forum for Modern Language Studies*
	French Forum
French R	*French Review: Journal of the American Association of Teachers of French*

Frontier	*Frontier: A Journal of Women Studies*
Fu Jen Stud	*Fu Jen Studies: Literature & Linguistics* (Taipei)
	Genre
Geographical R	*The Geographical Review*
Georgia R	*Georgia Review*
Germ Life & Letters	*German Life and Letters*
Germ Notes	*Germanic Notes*
Germ Q	*German Quarterly*
Germ R	*Germanic Review*
Germanisch-Romanische Monatsschrift	*Germanisch-Romanische Monatsschrift,* Neue Folge
Glyph	*Glyph: Johns Hopkins Textual Studies*
	Gothic
Gypsy Scholar	*Gypsy Scholar: A Graduate Forum for Literary Criticism*
Hartford Stud Lit	*University of Hartford Studies in Literature: A Journal of Interdisciplinary Criticism*
	Haunted
Hebrew Univ Stud Lit	*Hebrew University Studies in Literature*
Heine J	*Heine Jahrbuch*
Hemingway R	*Hemingway Review* [formerly *Hemingway Notes*]
Henry James R	*Henry James Review*
Hispamerica	*Hispamerica: Revista de Literatura*
Hispania	*Hispania: A Journal Devoted to the Interests of the Teaching of Spanish and Portuguese*
Hispanic J	*Hispanic Journal*
Hitotsubashi	*Hitotsubashi Journal of Arts & Sciences*
	Hollins Critic
Horizontes	*Horizontes: Revista de la Universidad Católica de Puerto Rico*

Hudson R	*Hudson Review*
Humanities	*Humanities: Christianity & Culture*
	Ibero-Amerikanisches Archiv
	Imprévue
Indian Lit	*Indian Literature*
Int'l Dostoevsky Soc Bull	*International Dostoevsky Society Bulletin*
Int'l Fiction R	*International Fiction Review*
Int'l Folklore R	*International Folklore Review*
Int'l J Middle East Stud	*International Journal of Middle East Studies*
Int'l R Psycho-Analysis	*International Review of Psycho-Analysis*
Iowa R	*Iowa Review*
	Irish Writing
	Italica
	Jack London Newsletter
	Jahrbuch für Internationale Germanistik
James Joyce Q	*James Joyce Quarterly*
John O'Hara J	*John O'Hara Journal*
	Joseph Conrad Today
J Am Oriental Soc	*Journal of the American Oriental Society*
J Commonwealth Lit	*The Journal of Commonwealth Literature*
J Engl	*Journal of English* (Sana'a Univ.)
J Gen Ed	*Journal of General Education*
J Illinois State Hist Soc	*Journal of the Illinois State Historical Society*
J Joseph Conrad Soc	*Journal of the Joseph Conrad Society*
J Karnatak Univ	*Journal of the Karnatak University — Humanities*
J Mod Lit	*Journal of Modern Literature*
J Narrative Technique	*Journal of Narrative Technique*

J Pop Culture	*Journal of Popular Culture*
J School Lang	*Journal of the School of Languages*
J Semitic Stud	*Journal of Semitic Studies*
J So Asian Lit	*Journal of South Asian Literature*
J Ukrainian Stud	*Journal of Ukrainian Studies*
	Kate Chopin Newsletter
Kentucky Folklore Record	*Kentucky Folklore Record: A Regional Journal of Folklore and Folklife*
Kentucky Romance Q	*Kentucky Romance Quarterly*
Kipling J	*The Kipling Journal*
Kunapipi	
Kyushu Am Lit	*Kyushu American Literature*
Lagos R Engl Stud	*Lagos Review of English Studies*
Lang & Style	*Language and Style: An International Journal*
Lang Q	*The University of Southern Florida Language Quarterly*
	Les Langues Modernes
Latin Am Lit R	*Latin American Literary Review*
	Letteratura
	Les Lettres Romanes
Lib Chronicle	*Library Chronicle*
Liberal & Fine Arts R	*Liberal & Fine Arts Review*
Linguistics in Lit	*Linguistics in Literature*
Lit & Hist	*Literature and History: A New Journal for the Humanities*
Lit & Psych	*Literature and Psychology*
Lit Criterion	*Literary Criterion*
Lit East & West	*Literature East and West*
Lit/Film Q	*Literature/Film Quarterly*

Lit North Queensland	*Literature in North Queensland*
Lit Onomastics Stud	*Literary Onomastics Studies*
	Literatur in Wissenschaft und Unterricht
	Literatur und Kritik
Littérature	*Littérature* (Paris)
Lost Generation J	*Lost Generation Journal*
Mark Twain J	*Mark Twain Journal*
Markham R	*Markham Review*
Massachusetts R	*Massachusetts Review: A Quarterly of Literature, the Arts and Public Affairs*
MELUS	*MELUS: Multi-Ethnic Literature in the United States*
Michigan Academician	*Michigan Academician: Papers of the Michigan Academy of Science, Arts, and Letters*
Midamerica	*Midamerica: The Yearbook of the Society for the Study of Midwestern Literature*
Mid-Hudson Lang Stud	*Mid-Hudson Language Studies* (Bulletin of the Mid-Hudson Modern Language Association)
Minnesota R	*Minnesota Review*
Mississippi Q	*Mississippi Quarterly: The Journal of Southern Culture*
	Mitteilungen der E. T. A. Hoffmann-Gesellschaft-Bamberg
Mod Austrian Lit	*Modern Austrian Literature: Journal of the International Arthur Schnitzler Research Association*
Mod Fiction Stud	*Modern Fiction Studies*
Mod Lang Notes	*Modern Language Notes* [retitled *MLN*]
Mod Lang Q	*Modern Language Quarterly*
Mod Lang R	*Modern Language Review*
Mod Lang Stud	*Modern Language Studies*
Mod Langs	*Modern Languages: Journal of the Modern Language Association* (London)

Mod Philol	*Modern Philology: A Journal Devoted to Research in Medieval and Modern Literature*
	Moderna Sprak
Monatshefte	*Monatshefte: Für Deutschen Unterricht, Deutsche Sprache und Literatur*
Mosaic	*Mosaic: A Journal for the Comparative Study of Literature and Ideas for the Interdisciplinary Study of Literature*
Names	*Names: Journal of the American Names Society*
Nassau R	*The Nassau Review: The Journal of Nassau Community College Devoted to Arts, Letters, and Sciences*
Nathaniel Hawthorne J	*Nathaniel Hawthorne Journal*
	Nation
Neohelicon	*Neohelicon: Acta Comparationis Litterarum Universatum*
	Neophilologus
Neue Sammlung	*Neue Sammlung: Zeitschrift für Erziehung und Gesellschaft*
	Die Neueren Sprachen
Neuphilologische Mitteilungen	*Neuphilologische Mitteilungen: Bulletin de la Société Néophilologique / Bulletin of the Modern Language Society*
Neusprachliche Mitteilungen	*Neusprachliche Mitteilungen aus Wissenschaft und Praxis*
New Germ Stud	*New German Studies*
New Orleans R	*New Orleans Review*
	New Republic
New York R Books	*The New York Review of Books*
	Nineteenth-Century Fiction
Nineteenth-Century French Stud	*Nineteenth-Century French Studies*
Notes & Queries	*Notes and Queries*
Notes Contemp Lit	*Notes on Contemporary Literature*

Notes Mississippi Writers	*Notes on Mississippi Writers*
Notes Mod Am Lit	*NMAL: Notes on Modern American Literature*
Nottingham French Stud	*Nottingham French Studies*
	Nouvelle Revue Française
	Nueva Dimensión
	Nueva Revista del Pacifico
Nuova Corrente	*Nuova Corrente: Rivista di Letteratura*
	Nyctalops
Obsidian	*Obsidian: Black Literature in Review*
Odyssey	*Odyssey: A Journal of the Humanities*
Orbis Litterarum	*Orbis Litterarum: International Review of Literary Studies*
Österreich in Geschichte und Literatur	*Österreich in Geschichte und Literatur (mit Geographie)*
Oxford Germ Stud	*Oxford German Studies*
Paideia	*Paideia: Journal of Foundational Studies in Education*
	Papers in Romance
Papers Lang & Lit	*Papers on Language and Literature: A Journal for Scholars and Critics of Language and Literature*
Paragone	***Paragone: Rivista Mensile di Arte Figurativa e Letteratura***
Partisan R	*Partisan Review*
Pembroke Mag	*The Pembroke Magazine*
Pennsylvania Engl	*Pennsylvania English*
Perspectives Contemp Lit	*Perspectives on Contemporary Literature*
Philol Q	*Philological Quarterly*
Philosophy & Lit	*Philosophy and Literature*
	Phoenix (Korea)
Phylon	***Phylon: The Atlanta University Review of Race and Culture***

Platte Valley R	*Platte Valley Review*
PMLA	*PMLA: Publications of the Modern Language Association of America*
Poe Stud	*Poe Studies*
Poetics Today	*Poetics Today: Theory and Analysis of Literature and Communication* (Tel Aviv, Israel)
	Prairie Schooner
Présence Africaine	*Présence Africaine: Revue Culturelle du Monde Noir/Cultural Review of the Negro World*
Présence Francophone	*Présence Francophone: Revue Littéraire*
Proceedings Pacific Northwest Conference Foreign Langs	***Proceedings of the Pacific Northwest Conference on Foreign Languages***
Prospects	*Prospects: An Annual Journal of American Cultural Studies*
Psychocultural R	*Psychocultural Review: Interpretations in the Psychology of Art, Literature and Society*
PTL: J Descriptive Poetics and Theory Lit	*PTL: A Journal for Descriptive Poetics and Theory of Literature*
Pubs Missouri Philol Assoc	*Publications of the Missouri Philological Association*
	Quarber Merkur
R (New York)	*Review* (New York)
R Contemp Fiction	*Review of Contemporary Fiction*
R Engl Lit	*Review of English Literature*
	RE: Artes Liberales
	Il Re in Giallo
Recherches et Études	*Recherches et Études Comparatistes Ibéro-Françaises de la Sorbonne*
Renascence	*Renascence: Essays on Value in Literature*
Rendezvous	*Rendezvous: Journal of Arts and Letters*
Research Stud	*Washington State University Research Studies*

	Revista Canadiense de Estudios Hispánicos
Revista de Critica	*Revista de Critica Literaria Latinoamericana*
	Revista de Estudios Hispánicos
	Revista de Estudios Hispánicos (Puerto Rico)
	Revista Letras
	Revista Nacional de Cultura
	Revista / Review Interamericana
Revue Belge	*Revue Belge de Philologie et d'Histoire*
	Revue de Littérature Comparée
	La Revue des Lettres Modernes
	Revue Française d'Études Américaines
	Revue Romane
	Revue Roumaine de Linguistique
Rivista di Letterature	*Rivista di Letterature Moderne e Comparate* (Florence)
Rocky Mt R	*Rocky Mountain Review* [formerly *Bulletin of the Rocky Mountain Modern Language Association*]
	Romance Notes
Romanic R	*Romanic Review*
Romantisme	*Romantisme: Revue du Dix-Neuvième Siècle*
Russian Lang J	*Russian Language Journal*
Russian Lit Tri-Q	*Russian Literature Triquarterly*
Russian R	*Russian Review: An American Quarterly Devoted to Russia Past and Present*
Saul Bellow J	*Saul Bellow Journal* [formerly *Saul Bellow Newsletter*]
	Schriften der Theodor-Storm-Gesellschaft
Sci-Fiction Stud	*Science-Fiction Studies*
Selecta	*Selecta: Journal of the Pacific Northwest Council on Foreign Languages* [formerly *Proceedings of the Pacific Northwest Conference on Foreign Languages*]

Seminar	*Seminar: A Journal of Germanic Studies*
Semiosis	*Semiosis: Cuadernos del Seminario de Semiótica Literaria*
	Sin Nombre
Slavic & East European J	*Slavic and East European Journal*
Slavic R	*Slavic Review: American Quarterly of Soviet and East European Studies*
So Asian R	*South Asian Review*
So Atlantic Bull	*South Atlantic Bulletin: A Quarterly Journal Devoted to Research and Teaching in the Modern Languages and Literatures*
So Atlantic Q	*South Atlantic Quarterly*
So Carolina Bull	*South Carolina Bulletin*
So Carolina R	*South Carolina Review*
So Central Bull	*South Central Bulletin*
So Dakota R	*South Dakota Review*
Southern Hum R	*Southern Humanities Review*
Southern Lit J	*Southern Literary Journal*
Southern Q	*The Southern Quarterly: A Journal of the Arts in the South*
Southern R	*Southern Review* (Baton Rouge)
Southern Stud	*Southern Studies: An Interdisciplinary Journal of the South*
Soviet Lit	*Soviet Literature*
Soviet Stud Lit	*Soviet Studies in Literature*
Sphinx	*The Sphinx: A Magazine of Literature and Society*
Sprachkunst	*Sprachkunst: Beiträge zur Literaturwissenschaft*
Stanford French R	*Stanford French Review*
Stud Am Fiction	*Studies in American Fiction*
Stud Am Humor	*Studies in American Humor*

Stud Am Jewish Lit	*Studies in American Jewish Literature*
Stud Black Lit	*Studies in Black Literature*
Stud Hum	*Studies in the Humanities*
Stud Novel	*Studies in the Novel*
Stud Romanticism	*Studies in Romanticism*
Stud Short Fiction	*Studies in Short Fiction*
Stud Twentieth Century Lit	*Studies in Twentieth Century Literature*
	Studi Francesi
	Studia Romanica et Anglica Zagrabiensia
	Studii şi Cercetări Lingvistice
Sub-Stance	*Sub-Stance: A Review of Theory and Literary Criticism*
Sur	*Revista Sur*
Swiss-French Stud	*Swiss-French Studies / Études Romandes* (Wolfville, Canada)
	Symposium
Tennessee Folklore Soc Bull	*Tennessee Folklore Society Bulletin*
Texas Stud Lit & Lang	*Texas Studies in Literature and Language: A Journal of the Humanities*
	Texto Critico
Thalia	*Thalia: Studies in Literary Humor*
Thesaurus	*Thesaurus: Boletín del Instituto Caro y Cuevo*
Travaux de Linguistique et de Littérature	*Travaux de Linguistique et de Littérature Publiés par le Centre de Philologie et de Littératures Romanes de l'Université de Strasbourg*
Tristania	*Tristania: A Journal Devoted to Tristan Studies*
Turkish Stud Assoc Bull	*Turkish Studies Association Bulletin*
Twentieth Century Lit	*Twentieth Century Literature: A Scholarly and Critical Journal*
Ukrainian Q	*Ukrainian Quarterly: Journal of East European and Asian Affairs*

Ulbandus R	Ulbandus Review: A Journal of Slavic Languages and Literatures
Unisa Engl Stud	Unisa English Studies: Journal of the Department of English, University of South Africa
Univ Dayton R	University of Dayton Review
Univ Mississippi Stud Engl	University of Mississippi Studies in English
Universidad	Universidad de la Habana
	Vermont History
Virginia Q R	Virginia Quarterly Review: A National Journal of Literature and Discussion
	Virginia Woolf Miscellany
Virginia Woolf Q	Virginia Woolf Quarterly
Walt Whitman R	Walt Whitman Review
Wascana R	Wascana Review
West Virginia Univ Philol Papers	West Virginia University Philological Papers
Western Am Lit	Western American Literature
Western Hum R	Western Humanities Review
	Whisper
Wirkendes Wort	Wirkendes Wort: Deutsche Sprache in Forschung und Lehre
Women & Lit	Women & Literature
Women's Stud	Women's Studies: An Interdisciplinary Journal
World Lit Today	World Literature Today: A Literary Quarterly of the University of Oklahoma
World Lit Written Engl	World Literature Written in English
Xavier R	Xavier Review [formerly Xavier University Studies]
Yale French Stud	Yale French Studies
Yale R	The Yale Review: A National Quarterly

Yale Univ Lib Gazette   *Yale University Library Gazette*

Zeitschrift für französuche Sprache und Literatur

INDEX OF SHORT STORY WRITERS

RECEIVED
MAY 1986
Mission College
Learning Resource
Services